Springer Series
on Family Violence

Albert R. Roberts, PhD, Series Editor

1998 Battered Women and Their Families
Intervention Strategies and Treatment Programs, second
edition
  Albert R. Roberts, PhD, editor

Forthcoming volumes

1998 Preventing Teenage Violence
An Empirical Paradigm for Schools and Families
  John S. Wodarski, PhD, and
  Lois A. Wodarski, PhD

1998 The Heart of Intimate Abuse
Empowering Strategies for Working with Battered Women and
Their Children
  Linda G. Mills, PhD, LCSW, JD

Albert R. Roberts, PhD, is a Professor of Social Work at the School of Social Work, Rutgers University, New Brunswick, NJ. Dr. Roberts conducts seminars and teaches courses on research methods, crisis intervention and brief treatment, program evaluation, family violence intervention, adolescence, victimology, social policy, and juvenile justice. He previously taught at the Indiana University School of Social Work in Indianapolis. He received his doctorate in social work from the University of Maryland School of Social Work in 1978.

Dr. Roberts is the founding Editor of the new Springer Series on Family Violence Through the Life Span. He is also the founder and current Editor of the Springer Publishing Company's 28-volume Series on Social Work. Dr. Roberts is the founding Editor-in-Chief of the journal *Crisis Intervention and Time-Limited Treatment.* He has authored, edited, or coedited 20 books. Dr. Roberts serves on the Editorial Boards of *The Justice Professional* and the *Journal of Human Behavior in the Social Environment.* For many years, he served as a reviewer for the *Hospital and Community Psychiatry* journal and *The Journal of Social Service Research.* He has over 130 published articles, chapters, and books to his credit.

Dr. Roberts is a Fellow of the American Orthopsychiatric Association, a lifetime member of the Academy of Criminal Justice Sciences, and an active member of the National Association of Social Workers (NASW), and the Council on Social Work Education (CSWE). He is a member of the New Jersey Supreme Court's Probation Advisory Board and the Advisory Board of the National Victim Assistance Training Academy of the U.S. Department of Justice.

During the past 2 decades, he has served as Project Director or consultant on several research and evaluation projects including: the National Institute of Justice-funded study on the Effectiveness of Crisis Intervention with Crime Victims at the Victim Services Agency in New York City, and the American Correctional Association's National Study on the Utilization of Instructional Technology in Corrections.

Battered Women and Their Families

2nd Edition

Intervention Strategies and Treatment Programs

Albert R. Roberts, PhD
Editor

Ann N. Burgess, RN, CS, DNSc, FAAN
Foreword

Springer Publishing Company

Springer Publishing Company, Inc.
536 Broadway
New York, NY 10012-3955

Cover design by Margaret Dunin
Acquisitions Editor: Bill Tucker
Production Editor: Pamela Lankas
Cover photo by: David Antebi, M.S.W., Associate Professor Emeritus, Rutgers University School of Social Work

98 99 00 01 02/5 4 3 2 1

Library of Congress Cataloging-in-Publication Data

Battered women and their families : intervention strategies and
    treatment programs / Albert R. Roberts, editor. — 2nd ed.
        p.   cm. — (Springer series on family violence)
    Includes bibliographical references and indexes.
    ISBN 0-8261-4591-4
    1. Abused wives—Services for—United States. 2. Family
violence—United States. 3. Social work with women—
United States. I. Roberts, Albert R. II. Series.
HV699.B37   1998
362.82'925'0973–dc21   97-40907
                                                           CIP

Printed in the United States of America

This book is dedicated in loving memory to my parents, Harry and Evelyn, whose love, faith, unconditional acceptance, and family values instilled in me the fervent belief that all women and children should be cherished and treated with compassion. Since my adolescence I have been *inspired* by my mother's quiet fighting spirit, resilience, and altruistic nature as she survived 17 years after having been diagnosed with breast cancer. This is my 20th book; it could not have been completed without the compassion and perseverance my parents instilled in me.

To Beverly, my wife of 26 years, whose love, altruism, and intellectual stimulation provide me with balance and focus.

This book is also dedicated to the many nurses, social workers, and counselors who provide essential health care, social services, and clinical intervention to battered women and their vulnerable children. The lives of thousands of chronically battered women in life-threatening situations are saved each year, because of the commitment of these nurses and social workers.

Contents

Foreword

The significance of violence against women as an American problem was underscored by the U.S. Congress in 1994 when it passed the Violence Against Women Act as part of the Violent Crime Control and Law Enforcement Act. President Clinton moved quickly to establish an Office on Violence Against Women in the U.S. Department of Justice. By 1996, in order to fill a congressional request, my interdisciplinary panel recommended research priorities and an agenda focusing on increased understanding of the phenomenon of violence against women. By the year 2001, important research findings should be available to guide our therapeutic interventions for the 21st century.

As the former Chair of the National Research Council's Panel on Research on Violence Against Women, I applaud this second edition because of the need for comprehensive research and practical guidelines for clinicians working with battered women. The second edition of *Battered Women and Their Families* has been thoroughly revised, and it is more like a new book than most of the revisions of other books that I have seen. It has doubled in size from the first edition; only one of the 19 chapters is reprinted from the original book. All of the other chapters are brand new and reflect the latest scholarship and clinical practice innovations.

Many of the chapters are prescriptive and provide concrete and straightforward step-by-step guidelines on effective methods for treating battered women. This comprehensive volume is ideal for all health care, mental health, and domestic violence professionals. It includes valuable adult abuse protocols, treatment models, and techniques on how to intervene effectively with women and children in violent homes. Most of the 28 chapter authors have demonstrated an important ability to transmit personal knowledge, clinical experience, practice wisdom, and patient observations in a reader-friendly and realistic style. The case study applications demonstrate how battered women in crisis can first become stabilized and then gain mastery over previously overwhelming fear, trauma, anxiety, depression, and/or suicidal gestures and ideation.

In 1984, when I first met Dr. Albert Roberts, he had completed two groundbreaking books: *Battered Women and Their Families* (first edition) and *Sheltering Battered Women: A National Study and Service Guide*. In the second edition Dr. Roberts and his 27 collaborators have produced an internationally significant work. Dr. Roberts is one of the first scholars to document the growing number of middle-class and ethnically diverse battered women.

I am particularly impressed with the breadth and depth of the topics covered here, which range from emergency department triage teams to primary care settings, to group therapy, to shelters for abused women and their at-risk children. Each chapter includes case studies that bring the life-threatening and acute battering incidents to life. The scope of this volume is most commendable as it includes chapters on subgroups of women victims who have not typically received special attention: the elderly, welfare mothers, Japanese women, Chinese Americans, Puerto Ricans, Jewish women, lesbians, battered mothers dealing with the intersection of domestic-violence and child-protective services, as well as vulnerable women with developmental disabilities and cognitive impairments.

This book is highly recommended for all clinical nurse specialists, psychiatric nurses, nurse practitioners, emergency room physicians and nurses, clinical psychologists, clinical social workers, primary care practitioners, victim advocates, family court judges, and presiding judges. In conclusion, this volume is extremely well-written, insightful, and thoroughly up-to-date—it is a *must read* for all clinicians. *This is the first book of major importance that emphasizes the mutually rewarding and growing alliance between clinical nurse specialists and clinical social workers.* Although this significant book is important for helping nurses and social workers understand the complexities of domestic violence intervention, it is equally important that all health care and community mental health center administrators read it to gain an understanding about what the *new* nurse specialist and social worker have to offer and the vital role they play in both inpatient and outpatient settings.

ANN W. BURGESS, RN, CS, DNSc, FAAN
van Ameringen Professor of Psychiatric–
Mental Health Nursing
University of Pennsylvania
School of Nursing
Philadelphia, PA

Preface

Woman battering, couple violence, and abusive family patterns are all too pervasive in American society. Recent developments in the family violence field have resulted in improved screening and detection of woman battering and child maltreatment. New and improved adult abuse protocols, treatment continua, clinical pathways, treatment plans, and practice models have resulted in improved detection and some reduction in the prevalence of domestic violence. This volume includes the newest interdisciplinary methods of detection, assessment, and intervention on behalf of battered women and their families.

During the 15 years since the first edition of this book was written, significant changes have taken place. The most important changes at both the federal and state levels have been the enactment of specific legislation responsive to the legal, social service, and mental health needs of battered women. Legislation without a major appropriation of funds attached to it is usually doomed to fail. In sharp contrast, the federal Violence Against Women Act of 1994 included a $1.3-billion appropriation and state domestic violence acts usually include an appropriation tied to a marriage license, a divorce decree surcharge, or a percentage of all gun license fees.

During the past decade, about one dozen clinical studies have documented the prevalence of bipolar disorder, depression, anxiety attacks, post-traumatic stress disorder (PTSD), panic disorder, phobias, acute stress disorders, substance abuse, and/or suicidal ideation among battered women. Three national surveys of clinicians, psychologists, social workers, marital and family therapists, and counselors have documented a very serious problem. The majority of the hundreds of clinicians in these studies do not know how to assess lethality among battered women, or how to effectively intervene with an appropriate practice model and treatment plan. This book was written in order to fill the domestic violence knowledge base and skill gap among clinicians.

This is a handbook about family violence from the perspective of intergenerational linkages—it includes traumatized and often abused children of battered women, adolescent abuse, woman battering, the intersection of child abuse and spouse abuse, and elder abuse. It also focuses on cross-cultural issues, patterns, and intervention programs with domestic violence. The primary emphasis of this book is on the nuclear family, and the violence found within that unit. Unlike most books on family violence, which limit their discussion solely to battered women, this volume addresses the impact of the violence on the women, the children, and the adolescents in the home. Also different from other recent books, this volume provides step-by-step guidelines and practical applications of crisis intervention and short-term treatment approaches with battered women and their children. As we prepare for the 21st century with major health insurance restrictions and managed care looming over our clients and patients, the time-limited clinical strategies in this book become of paramount importance.

As mentioned in the first edition of this book, most other books on family violence examine the plight of the battered woman as an entity separate from her family. The overriding purpose of this book is to focus on the need for therapeutic intervention for all members of the violent family. The wide range of service delivery issues, treatment techniques, and research findings discussed in this book go beyond monolithic approaches to understanding woman battering. Throughout this book, case illustrations, programmatic issues, and effective intervention strategies are presented.

Chronic and severe partner violence can be a living hell that lasts for a few years, 8–15 years, or over 20 years.

- Why would anyone stay in a battering relationship for 2 years, 208 Saturdays and Sundays, or 731 consecutive days?

- How could a battered woman survive 15, 20, or 25 years of chronic battering?
- Why do thousands of abused women believe the false promises of the batterer that he will never hit her again?
- Do battered women stay with the batterer because of their own low self-esteem, their martyr-like endurance of frustration, their poor sexual self-image, and/or traumatic bonding?
- What is the new role of clinical social workers and nurse specialists in effectively treating battered women and their children?
- How does a clinician apply an assessment protocol and develop a treatment plan with a chronically battered woman?
- Which clinical techniques work best with battered women?
- What are the steps to implementing crisis intervention with traumatized children of battered women?

The answers to these questions are provided in this book.

ACKNOWLEDGMENTS

First and foremost I am grateful to all the members of my author team, leaders in the field of domestic violence, for writing original chapters and meeting all deadlines in a timely fashion. Four contributing authors went beyond the "call of duty," and added an important dimension to the book: Dr. Patricia Brownell wrote three chapters; Dr. Bonnie Carlson is the senior author of two chapters; Dr. Mieko Yoshihama updated her well-written and comprehensive chapter several times immediately on returning from research visits to Japan; and Dr. Linda Mills wrote one chapter, and thoroughly edited and rewrote a second chapter. The clarity of many of the chapters greatly benefited from the discussions I had with my intellectually gifted colleagues—Professors Ann Burgess, Pat Brownell, Bonnie Carlson, Mo-Yee Lee, Linda Mills, Pam Valentine, Diane Valle, Katherine van Wormer, and Mieko Yoshihama.

Special thanks go to Dr. Ursula Springer for her long-time commitment—over four decades—of publishing cutting-edge books by nurses and social workers. Her responsiveness, encouragement, and support of the new Family Violence Series is most appreciated. I am grateful to Bill Tucker, Managing Editor, for his generous and sage advice, guidance, and editorial suggestions on conflict resolution. Special thanks go to Pamela Lankas, Senior Production Editor, for her diligence and care for detail. My heartfelt appreciation goes to Beverly Jean Roberts for preparing the subject and author indexes with me. Finally, I am forever indebted to Imogene, a former battered woman and social work student from Brooklyn, NY, who openly shared her painful battering history with me in 1979. Her experiences with police and social service staff inspired my early research on shelters for battered women and the effectiveness of crisis intervention. During the 1990s, several former students and professionals assisted me in data collection on 1,500 battered women: Dr. Gloria Bonilla-Santiago, Sgt. James Brady, Lisa Cassa, Patricia Cassidy, Shara Corrigan, Sgt. Vincent Henry, Prof. Gina Pisano-Robertello, and Lt. Ronald Schmalz. I express my sincere gratitude to the above-mentioned individuals.

Contributors

Irvin Abelman, MSW
Consultant
Retired Director, Adult
   Protective Services
New York State Department
   of Social Services
New York, NY

Joseph J. Alessi, MSW, ACSW
Psychiatric Social Worker
Adult, Child, and Family Clinic
Department of Psychiatry and
   County Medical Center
Buffalo, NY

Patrick Au, DiP, PSW, CQW
Executive Director
Family Services
Toronto, Canada

Mary E. Boes, DSW
Assistant Professor of Social
   Work
University of Northern Iowa
Sabin 30
Cedar Falls, IA 50614

Patricia Brownell, PhD
Assistant Professor
Graduate School of Social
   Services
Fordham University at Lincoln
   Center
New York, NY

Ann W. Burgess, RN, CS,
   DNSc, FAAN
van Ameringen Professor
   of Psychiatric–Mental Health
   Nursing
University of Pennsylvania
Philadelphia, PA

Sunny Burman, PhD
Assistant Professor
School of Social Work
Rutgers University
New Brunswick, NJ 08903

Lynda Marie Carson, BA
Advocate
New Jersey Coalition for
    Battered Women
Hamilton, NJ

Bonnie E. Carlson, PhD, ACSW
Professor
School of Social Welfare
University at Albany
State University of New York
Albany, NJ 12222

Sandra Clark
Assistant Director
New Jersey Coalition for
    Battered Women
Hamilton, NJ

Elaine P. Congress, PhD, ACSW
Associate Professor and
    Associate Dean
Graduate School of Social
    Services
Fordham University at Lincoln
    Center
New York, NY

Diana Valle Ferrer, PhD
Associate Professor
Graduate School of Social
    Work
University of Puerto Rico
San Juan, PR 00902

Janet A. Geller, EdD, ACSW
Clinical Social Worker
    in Private Practice
New York, NY

Eileen Grogan, MSW, ACSW
Clinical Social Worker
    in Private Practice
Bunker Hill Counseling Center
Princeton, NJ 08520

Kristin Hearn, EdD
Child Care Coordinator
Erie County Coalition
    for Victims of Domestic
    Violence
Buffalo, NY

Christine Heer, MSW, ACSW
Former Clinical Director
Somerset County Battered
    Women's Shelter
Currently Clinical Social
    Worker in Private Practice
Warren, NJ

Shirley Lebovics, LCSW
Lecturer
University of California School
    of Social Work and
    Private Practice
Beverly Hills, CA 90212

Mo-Yee Lee, PhD, ACSW
Assistant Professor
College of Social Work
Ohio State University
Columbus, OH 43210

Peter Lehmann, PhD
Assistant Professor of Social
    Work
University of Texas at Arlington
Arlington, TX 76019

Louise-Anne McNutt, PhD
Assistant Professor
School of Public Health
University at Albany
State University of New York
Albany, NY 12222

Linda G. Mills, PhD, JD, ACSW
UCLA School of Public Policy
  and Social Research
Los Angeles, CA 90095-1656

Leone Murphy, RN, MS
Nurse Practitioner
Ambulatory Care Center
ARC of Monmouth County
Tinton Falls, NJ

Maura O'Keefe, PhD, ACSW
Associate Professor
University of California School
  of Social Work
Los Angeles, CA 91039

Nancy J. Razza, PhD
Clinical Psychologist
Ambulatory Care Center
ARC of Monmouth County
Tinton Falls, NJ

Pamela Valentine, PhD, ACSW
Assistant Professor
Department of Social Work
University of Alabama
Birmingham, AL

Katherine S. van Wormer, PhD
Professor of Social Work
University of Northern Iowa
Sabin 30
Cedar Falls, IA 50614

Mieko Yoshihama, PhD
Assistant Professor
School of Social Work
University of Michigan
Ann Arbor, MI 48109

Overview, Crisis Intervention, and Short-Term Treatment

Crisis Intervention and Cognitive Problem-Solving Therapy with Battered Women: A National Survey and Practice Model

Albert R. Roberts and Sunny Burman

Battering of women is one of the most pervasive and dangerous social problems in American society. Recent estimates indicate that 8.7 million women are victimized by partner abuse in their homes each year. Some of the women are assaulted by smacking or punching once or twice; others are repeatedly battered with increasing frequency and intensity for several months or years. As a result of being chronically abused, many battered women suffer from bipolar disorder, anxiety, post-traumatic stress disorder (PTSD), panic disorder, and/or suicide ideation (Petretic-Jackson & Jackson, 1996;

Walker, 1985). Three clinical studies of abused women, living in shelters or attending support groups, have found PTSD rates ranging from 45% to 84% (Astin, Lawrence, Pincus, & Foy, 1990; Housekamp & Foy, 1991; Roberts, 1996). Descriptive and clinical studies have consistently found a high incidence of somatic problems and depressive symptomatology among battered women (Cascardi & O'Leary, 1992; Gelles & Harrop, 1989).

Crisis intervention units and emergency shelters for battered women have made great strides in the past 20 years. In 1975, for example, there were only a handful of such shelters, but by 1995 there were over 1,250 shelters for battered women and their children in the United States (Roberts & Roberts, 1990; Roberts, 1995). Respondents to Roche's (1996) national survey of 622 shelters indicated that the shelters' major function is to advocate for social change and the empowerment of battered women. The average shelter was approximately 9 years old, with an annual operating budget ranging from $135,000 to $160,000, employing 6 full-time and 4 part-time paid staff and 25 volunteers.

A scarcity of research documenting the types of counseling and treatment modalities or intervention approaches used at shelters for battered women was also evident. In addition, studies on the short and long-term adjustment of battered women receiving crisis intervention and cognitive therapy were minimal. Only four descriptive reports at local shelters have examined the types and components of shelter-based treatment. Dziegielewski, Resnick, and Krause (1996) illustrated the importance of crisis theory and crisis intervention in their work at a battered women's organization in Tennessee. The A-B-C model of crisis intervention was used at the shelter in Fort Myers, Florida (Roberts & Roberts, 1990). Webb (1992) examined the ways in which cognitive behavior techniques can be utilized to reeducate and change distorted belief systems among battered women at a North Carolina shelter. Geller and Wasserstrom (1984) conducted long-term psychotherapy and conjoint therapy with battered women and their partners at V.I.B.'s, a community outreach and residential program for battered women in Long Island, New York.

This chapter presents the findings of a national research study that was conducted to fill the knowledge gap in areas pertaining to clinical practice with battered women. A case study is presented, utilizing an innovative approach to treatment—the sequence of a dual, congruent practice model consisting of crisis intervention and cognitively oriented problem solving. Because of battered women's propensity to return to the abusive partner, it is being proposed that a longer, more intensive therapeutic experience is necessary than those now conducted by shelters and other agencies. This will reinforce ego strengths and empower battered women to make wise and appropriate decisions concerning their own welfare and that of their children.

A NATIONAL STUDY OF SHELTERS FOR BATTERED WOMEN

Until this national survey (Roberts, 1997) was conducted, there was very little information on the availability of clinical staff who provide crisis intervention, cognitive treatment, or other types of therapeutic interventions for traumatized and abused women. In this study with 176 respondents, 223 (24.4%) of the 907 staff members had an M.S.W. or M.A. degree; 11 had Ph.D.s. However, the overwhelming majority of the shelter staff had no graduate degree or clinical training. The data collected examines staffing patterns and the organizational structure of these battered women's shelters and units. Data were also collected concerning funding sources and different types of services provided by the shelters.

Due to the dearth of research on the nature and types of clinical practice models used by shelter staff, the aim of this study was also to learn the diversity of current models in use and how they are incorporated in interventions with battered women. The findings reported in this article will indicate the nature of three intervention formats utilized by shelters throughout the United States: intake assessments, practice models, and empowerment strategies. An illustration of these fundamental activities, the application of the proposed crisis intervention and cognitively oriented problem solving practice model will be demonstrated through a case study of a battered woman. This will serve to illustrate the utility of this model in providing the battered woman with the tools to not only cope with current situations and resulting acute problems, but also to prevent more chronic dysfunction by learning strategies that will reenforce stabilization, healing, and growth. A wide variation of types of interventions that are likely to be used by shelter staff will be examined, for example, peer counseling, support groups, advocacy, empowerment, generalist practice, crisis intervention, cognitive therapy, and the problem-solving method.

Methodology

The current study reported is part of a larger research project of 176 shelter directors. The sample is comprised of 87 subjects, or 49% of the respondents from the original study.

A mailing list was developed of 20% or 250 of the 1,250 battered women's shelters from the National Organization for Victim Assistance (NOVA) directory and the Office for Victims of the U.S. Department of Justice. Using a random digits table, a 20% sample was obtained. A four-page questionnaire was devised, pretested (with three administrators of shelters), revised, and mailed with a cover letter to 250 programs in early January 1994. One month after the initial mailing, a follow-up letter and another copy of the questionnaire were sent to the nonrespondents. By April 1994, 176 completed questionnaires were returned—a 70% response rate.

The study examined program objectives, staffing patterns, funding sources, types of services offered, approximate number of clients served by each program in 1993, self-reported strengths and weaknesses of the programs, and significant changes made in the past 2 years. This study was designed to be relevant to administrators and program development specialists. Unfortunately, hardly any information was provided on the nature and extent of clinical interventions by shelter staff. Therefore, a follow-up letter with a one-page questionnaire was sent to the 176 respondents in the first study. This questionnaire starts with a case scenario of a battered woman with medical injuries coming to a shelter in acute crisis, with her three children, in the middle of the night. Eighty-seven of the 176 shelters (almost 50%) responded to this survey.

The clinical survey collected data in three areas:

1. Intake forms and assessment protocols.
2. Types and components of crisis intervention and other clinical practice models.
3. Methods of empowering battered women.

Findings

There were 87 responses to the mailing of 176 clinical question-naires—a 49% response rate. From the type and use of intake forms and assessment-protocols category, it was found that all of the respon-dents conduct a basic intake, ranging from a few questions to a 7-page form. The content of the intake forms includes medical injuries, safety needs, demographics, listings of the presenting problem, alco-hol and drug use, current abusive incident, prior abusive incidents, prior use of services, and any abuse of children. The respondents indicated that an intake assessment can be delayed as long as 24 hours, until the battered woman in acute crisis is stabilized. Surpris-ingly, only two of the clinical directors used standardized assessment scales to assess and measure suicide risk, depression, intrusive thoughts and fears, post-traumatic stress disorder, or other psychiat-ric disorders.

The second part of the survey examined the type and extent to which shelter staff are likely to use a clinical practice model to intervene with a severely battered woman. There were eight different patterns which emerged in terms of the treatment strategy or practice model used by respondents:

For the most part, the overwhelming majority of respondents did not answer the question that was asked. They do not seem to understand what constitutes a practice theory, practice model, or clinical/treatment strategy (Table 1.1). We firmly believe it is im-

TABLE 1.1 Practice Models and Techniques at Abused Women's Shelters

Technique	n
1. Provide support by reviewing options and choices and referring to a support group	28
2. Explore and validate feelings	19
3. Assess immediate needs of clients	15
4. Work with client to plan and formulate goals	14
5. Short-term crisis intervention	12
6. Active listening	9
7. Problem-solving method	8
8. Referral to community resources and private practitioner	8

portant for clinicians to assure safety and stabilize the client, explore and validate feelings, listen actively and reflectively, examine coping skills, empower by exploring options together, and help the client to formulate an action plan. However, it is too simplistic and potentially harmful to assume that ventilation, active listening, and referral are solutions to severe and intense battering.

For the majority of battered women, permanently leaving the batterer, regaining their self-esteem, finding a safe place to live, and obtaining a steady, well-paying job are all needed. The ego-bolstering accomplished when a survivor returns to school or obtains a steady job is critical to recovery. However, in view of the large group of battered women with major depressive disorders, post-traumatic stress disorder, and generalized anxiety disorder, crisis intervention and cognitive and trauma therapy are necessary to prevent relapse. Battered women suffering from post-traumatic stress disorder often find themselves in a state of high arousal and avoidance behaviors that cut off their attempts at establishing constructive interpersonal relationships. These survivors often have flashbacks, nightmares, and intrusive recollections of the traumatic battering events. The result of not resolving the trauma is a continued sense of danger and intense fears. Moderate to severe depression, accompanied by continued periods of loneliness, sadness, and crying, keeps them isolated and stuck. Through therapy, depressive and PTSD symptoms can be markedly reduced. Therapists need to help battered women identify their strengths and explore options, alternatives, and decision making (Walker, 1994).

To elicit a response to the methods of empowering-battered-women category, a question was asked in reference to the case of Sandra (described subsequently): "As a victim/survivor advocate, what suggestions would you have to help empower this client?" The responses can be grouped into seven categories (see Table 1.2).

Empowerment is critically important in order for battered women to recover, heal, and lead productive lives in nonviolent relationships. But many severely battered and traumatized women need both empowerment and therapy to survive and thrive. There are no quick fixes or easy solutions. Commitment to change and permanent escape from the battering relationship requires a trusting and empathic therapeutic relationship that bolsters ego strengths and reempowers

TABLE 1.2   Types of Empowerment Methods Used to Help Battered Women

Empowerment methods	n
1. Examine options or choices, and refer to self-help/support group	38
2. Explore legal options and encourage client to file criminal charges	32
3. Educate about cycle of violence and power/control issues	24
4. Provide information about community resources, numerous referrals, and make first appointment for victim	24
5. Reassure client that abuse is not her fault, and correct victim-blaming	10
6. Initiate advocacy for welfare or housing	9
7. Accompany to court appearances and provide advocacy with judge	8

the survivor through positive reinforcement of small changes as well as large ones.

The application of the dual practice model (crisis intervention and cognitively oriented problem solving) will coordinate each step of the process in the case study of Sandra. This case study portrays the tribulations of a battered woman as she struggles with her life of pain and fears that keep her trapped and unable to make constructive decisions that will alter the status quo. Through treatment, she began to realize that change was not only possible, but within her reach. A higher level of functioning and self-fulfillment was achieved through her perseverance and courage.

PRELIMINARY CASE REPORT

Sandra, a 28-year-old waitress with three children between the ages of 2 and 6 years, had just had an argument with her intoxicated husband, Luke. Although the argument started out small, it progressed and ended with Luke shoving Sandra and giving her a broken nose.

After Luke was asleep, Sandra decided she could not take the abuse any longer. She left the house with her three children. At 3:00 a.m., Sandra arrived at the center with a bruised face, no money, and fearful that she will be hurt again. She also revealed that this was not the first time Luke had abused her.

Initial Assessment

The information, taken by an intake worker, provided important data suggesting the physical harm and emotional turmoil Sandra had experienced in her relationship with Luke. A more detailed history was necessary to ascertain the most appropriate individualized treatment plan for her and her children. Nevertheless, from this brief report, it was hypothesized that Sandra had reached a turning point that was the catalyst for mobilizing her strengths and resources to not only seek safety and protection, but also some measure of positive change. This could provide a vital opportunity to help her gain the supports, knowledge, and skills that would prevent future occurrences of domestic violence.

THE PERSONAL IMPACT OF DOMESTIC VIOLENCE

As Sandra mentioned in the intake, this was not the first time she was abused in her marriage. A more in-depth, structured interview determined the extent and duration of the battering and the deleterious effects on her and the children. Over a 5-year period, she was intermittently brutalized and held captive by fear and the inability to control the inevitable recurrence of her husband's violent episodes.

Sandra was aware of Luke's dysfunctional upbringing as the only child of alcoholic parents. During the short courtship and early years of their marriage, Luke never displayed the kind of rage and bitterness that typified his parents' relationship. Sandra knew that he was never physically harmed at home, but the emotional impact of watching his father physically abuse his mother left wounds that he still felt.

Before the children were born, Sandra and Luke spent "good times" together, often socializing with friends at parties. She drank very little, compared to Luke, yet was always amazed (and somewhat pleased) at "how many he could put away" without showing signs of losing control and becoming "sloppy" drunk. She recalled, with sharp disapproval, how her own father would drink too much at times and become verbally abusive. With pride, she would point out that Luke could "hold his liquor," often becoming more amusing and affectionate. That this could change was not foreseen, and early years together were described as "happy and without problems."

With the pressures of raising a family and increasing financial debts, conflicts arose in the marriage. Luke held a steady job as a construction worker, and with Sandra's income and tips as a waitress, they were able to pay their bills and even save a small amount each month. But this was short-lived, as Luke began to gamble heavily. He feared that his job was in jeopardy, as his drinking began to interfere with his performance. The escalating stresses particularly affected his relationship with Sandra, often climaxing in loud arguments that catapulted to torturous beatings.

Although he never physically hurt the children, Sandra often feared that he would someday. She also anticipated that witnessing their father severely injuring her could leave indelible emotional scars. The altercation and resultant bruises that actually triggered her leaving with the children was not as severe as past injuries in which a concussion and multiple fractures and bruises were inflicted. At those times, she fleetingly thought of escaping the pain of living, and occasionally considered taking the children and moving far away. But these fantasies vanished quickly, as she thought, "Where would I go?" "How can I support the children and myself?" "Will I be safe anywhere?" So she remained in a fearful, helpless, and untenable position, feeling more and more isolated within herself and incapacitated by the escalating depressive symptoms. She was unable to tell anyone about her fragile marriage and the battering. This was perceived as a failure on her part—one that provoked guilt and shame.

Yet there was a struggling part of Sandra that wished to deny the reality of her existence, hoping that Luke would change and become the man she once knew and loved. At times, there were signs that he cared, displaying regret that he hurt her and promising he would never do it again. However, this latest episode of violence, with no provocation, was the final straw—her perseverance was tested to the limit. She felt she had to do something before it was too late—for herself, for her children, and even for her husband. This led to the first stage of interventive guidance and support to help bring an end to the traumas she had been living through.

ROBERTS' CRISIS INTERVENTION MODEL

Facing her fears and taking control was a self-empowering act that began the journey through and beyond the crisis Sandra was experiencing. An existence of pain and discomfort was being challenged by a shift toward hope and renewal. Assistance in this endeavor was forthcoming once the decision was made to seek help.

Utilizing Roberts' 7-stage model (for further details see pp. 224–227), the goal is to assure immediate safety and stabilization, followed by problem solving and the exploration of alternative options that would culminate in a meaningful action plan. Implicit in this model is a cognitive restructuring of perceptions, attitudes, and beliefs that will confront irrational distortions, misconceptions, and contradictions. The identification of erroneous thought patterns ("I can't make it alone without him") and a redirection to empowering affirmations and beliefs ("If other women have made it, so can I") can enhance self-worth and self-reliance, while reinforcing constructive coping mechanisms. With support, guidance, and acceptance, meaningful solutions that were once unrecognized can become objectives to attain.

The use of standardized test measurements is highly recommended in making a comprehensive assessment. Several scales and checklists will provide pertinent information to add to the data collected. Among these are the Expanded Conflict Tactics Scales of Aggression—both verbal aggression and physical violence scales (Straus, 1990). Severe violence is defined as the occurrence of any of the following: beat up, choked, or strangled; threatened with a knife or gun; or use of a knife or gun. All clinical directors at shelters should use the Beck Depression Inventory (BDI) (Beck, 1967), the Derogatis Symptom Checklist-90-Revised (SCL-90-R) (Derogatis, 1977), and the Trauma Symptom Checklist-40 (Briere & Runtz, 1988, 1989; Elliott & Briere, 1992). These scales have been widely used in clinical practice with battered women, and they give the clinician a normative standard of comparison. Since many battered women have multiple trauma histories, using all three scales seems most appropriate. The overlap of items will permit the multiple assessment of depression, anxiety, sexual problems, dissociation, sleep disturbances, and post-sexual abuse trauma.

Sandra's test results displayed low verbal aggression and physical violence scores (which concurred with her inability to defend herself against the abuse); a chronically depressed and anxious state, with intermittent suicidal ideations; and sleep disturbances. Her level of stabilization and immediate danger determination were also assessed through the use of the STAGE 1 Crisis Assessment (Table 1.3). She appeared to be rational, but anxiety and agitation were high. Her safety needs posed a threat in returning to Luke, as the potential of physical violence remained. Other assessment items on this list were not evident, but the possibility existed that some of these might occur in the future.

After safety needs were established, rapport and trust were developed in an effort to assist Sandra in identifying and prioritizing major problems. The worker encouraged her to express feelings and concerns about the events that prompted her to leave her husband and seek help. An assessment of her coping skills was prompted by the question, "How did you handle those traumatic situations?" It was important to listen empathically and attentively and to acknowledge the intensity of her pain. The barriers and obstacles that undermined the ability to alter her life (e.g., lack of funds, perceived supports, or knowledge of available resources) were identified. From this data, possible solutions and their consequences were formulated.

TABLE 1.3   Stage I: Crisis Assessment (Including Lethality Measures)

1. First and foremost, patient/client needs to be stabilized.
   * Assess level of consciousness and orientation
     * rationality
     * anxiety
     * agitation
2. Determine if client is in immediate danger.
   * Any guns or rifles in the home; threatened to use it on client
   * Any weapons used in prior battering incidents
   * Any threats with weapons
   * Any threats to kill client
   * Any criminal history of batterer
   * Client needed emergency medical attention
   * Threats or actually killing a pet
   * Threats of suicide by abuser
   * Batterer's fantasies about suicide or homicide
   * Marital rape or forced sex among cohabitants
   * Increased battering during pregnancy
   * Medical problems as result of pregnancy
   * Medical problems as result of rape (e.g., infections, STDs, HIV infection, unwanted pregnancy, risk to fetus in a pregnant woman)
   * Psychological torture (e.g., degradation, forced drug use, isolation of victim, sleep or food deprivation, threats to family of victim)

Arriving at an action plan required the development of alternate options and solutions to resolve the crisis (e.g., a legal separation; a court-ordered restraining order). Sandra's progress through this intervention phase was supported and monitored closely. With her resolve and determination, she was able to reduce the distressful symptoms of the acute crisis and begin to act on the second stage—a plan to acquire the tools to move on with her life.

COGNITIVELY ORIENTED PROBLEM SOLVING

After insuring the safety and survival issues of the battered woman, additional aid is often needed to continue stabilization while helping her resolve major issues and formulate important decisions that will affect her present and future functioning. The Roberts' (1991, 1995) Seven-Stage Crisis Intervention Model has provided the guidelines for the crucial stage of early crisis resolution, using an integrated problem-solving approach. This critical phase is designed to assist the client in establishing adaptive and constructive coping skills that will reestablish the equilibrium necessary to pursue actions that can overcome obstacles to personal well-being.

Building on Roberts' crisis intervention model, which has developed the foundation for problem solving, positive change, and empowerment, the client is ready to move towards another stage in the healing and growth-producing process. This sequence can be likened to a progression from the resolution of an acute, debilitating crisis state to working with clients on sustaining previous advances made, while attending to new modes of learning that will reinforce the prolonged acquisition and internalization of survival and actualization skills. Towards this aim, a cognitively oriented, problem-solving approach will encompass the groundwork of cognitive therapy and problem solving that has been influential in behavioral and emotional change, as well as the needed alterations in environmental systems that block desired objectives.

We know that a battered woman's fears and problems are not completely allayed once the immediate crisis has dissipated. If she returns to her partner, the violence will probably reoccur (particularly if the perpetrator has not received help). If she leaves, the probability of battering and harassment, even death, becomes a constant risk. Proceeding successfully through the critical phase of crisis resolution can reestablish a sense of balance, rebuild self-esteem and a strong sense of self, and increase the determination to pattern a life free of turmoil and suffering. But the awareness of vulnerability, dependency, and helplessness may still remain within the realm of consciousness, provoking an unsettling indecisiveness as to the direction that should be taken. This is often magnified by any disconcerting emotional attachments that still linger. In the case of battered women, a traumatic bonding effect (Dutton, 1988) may be developed through the intermittent abusive behaviors and reinforcement of pleasant conditions. This process sustains the dependency cycle, characterized by a power imbalance between the perpetrator and the subjugated female. Even after leaving the relationship, the unrecognized attachment and needs fulfilled by the partner can manifest itself, causing the woman to impulsively return.

Given the enormity and depth of the problems encountered, battered women need a continuity of supportive networks and helping services to transcend the horrifying situations they experienced (and may continue to face, if no dramatic changes are made). Crisis intervention is often the critical starting point of a longer journey that will not be culminated until safety is no longer threatened and emancipation and stability are finally achieved. Once the acute problems are addressed, the more chronic difficulties and dilemmas that persist must be assessed. Besides recurrent fears, dysfunctional symptoms of post-traumatic stress disorder and emotional difficulties may intrude into daily routines. These problems must be dealt with in order for the battered woman to regain a sense of adequacy and normalcy.

A cognitively oriented, problem-solving approach is a natural supplement to Roberts' crisis intervention model. It adheres to the basic format, concentrating on behavioral, emotional, and environmental change through the incorporation of cognitive and problem-solving strategies. The integrated principles will be identified, followed by their application to the assessment and treatment phases of the case previously cited.

Cognitive Therapy

Cognitive therapeutic methods have been developed from various theories of learning, primarily operant conditioning (Skinner, 1938) and social learning (Bandura, 1977). These theories espouse that behavior is a learned process that occurs through transactions between individuals and their social environments. Through operant conditioning, a response that is reinforcing (rewarded) will reoccur; and according to social learning theory, learning takes place by modeling (observing and imitating others), as well as through self-reinforcement and self-evaluations (Longres, 1995).

These theoretical frameworks have set the stage for the adoption of many strategies, such as systematic desensitization to treat anxiety and phobias; aversion therapy to eliminate an undesirable behavior; shaping behaviors by rewarding successive approximations of the desired result; positive and negative reinforcement to increase or reduce targeted behaviors; and role modeling of adaptive behaviors (Longres, 1995). Cognitive restructuring, identifying dysfunctional core beliefs, role plays and rehearsals, relaxation and stress management training, self-monitored homework assignments, and problem solving are now widely in use to reinforce the goals of positive learning and change (Beck, Wright, Newman, & Liese, 1993).

Problem Solving

This approach has been a strategic mainstay of many professional disciplines. According to Hepworth and Larsen (1993), "[Problem solving skills are taught] not only to remedy immediate problems but also to enhance clients' future coping capacities . . . the principles can be readily transferred from one situation to another" (pp. 434–435). Through effective problem solving, a range of options can be generated that will enhance decision making, self-reliance, self-esteem, confidence, and self-efficacy; and tensions, anxiety, and depressive symptoms can be allayed.

The problem-solving model provides a step-by-step framework to intervention planning and implementation. An integral part of any therapeutic process is the initial engaging of the client in a relationship built on trust and rapport. Based on this foundation, the following tasks can be actuated by the mutual team effort of both practitioner and client:

1. Assessment developed from the data collected;
2. Problem identification and implications;

3. Goal-setting and contracting;
4. Implementation of interventions;
5. Termination and referrals; and
6. Evaluation of effectiveness of interventions.

THE THERAPEUTIC EXPERIENCE

As the client progresses from the acute crisis resolution phase to a continuing stage of healing and growth, several alterations in functioning have developed. From a fearful, defenseless, and disempowered woman, resulting from numerous battering experiences, emerges a stronger, more self-assured individual who is ready to accept new challenges. This has not been an easy process, but one that has often been fraught with indecision and trepidations of great magnitude. If she does not succumb to old, familiar patterns that entice her to return to an unchanged partner (or a similar substitute), with persistent support and monitoring from practitioners and paraprofessionals, a major hurdle has been overcome. Her self-esteem has improved; her attitude toward life is fortified; and the obstacles that once seemed insurmountable now appear less formidable.

Yet the precarious journey ahead remains potentially unsteady, with sharp turns and sudden upheavals. The motivation to move forward and not fall back must constantly be reinforced. Relating to the case previously presented, the therapeutic means (a cognitively oriented problem solving model) of achieving this goal will be explored.

The Assessment

Sandra's anguished experience mirrors many commonalities with other battered women. Avni's (1991) questionnaire findings of abused women expressed a lengthy range of battering, from 2 to 30 years, with the earliest reported during the first month of marriage. Of Sandra's 7 years with Luke, 5 of these were characterized as abusive. Hamberger and Holtzworth-Munroe (1994) state that victims of battering live in constant terror and stress, resulting in depression, anxiety, and somatic complaints. Yet there is a period in which concern, apologies, and assurances of ending the violence are offered which tend to restabilize the emotional bonds (Walker, 1994). This dubious and precarious reality typified Sandra's and Luke's relationship.

A variety of stresses can increase the potential for violence (Stith & Rosen, 1990). The birth of children (Watkins & Bradbard, 1982), losing a job (or fear of job loss), and the concomitant financial instability that has a negative impact on an individual's self-esteem (Stith & Rosen, 1990) can all exacerbate the risk of abuse. Add to this the excessive use of alcohol or other drugs, and the frequency and severity of battering (and possible death) are heightened (Walker, 1989). Reviewing Sandra's experience, we can readily identify these factors that might have created the perilous exposure to physical and emotional harm.

This reign of terror can be endured indefinitely. What actually motivates women to escape these abusive relationships has been the subject of Davis and Srinivasan's (1995) research. Conducting focus groups as a means of learning their subjects' personal experiences, they found several rationales for leaving and seeking help (pp. 57–58):

1. overcoming fear (by finding a way out, that is, a change in attitudes/policies that are more supportive of battered women);
2. children as major catalysts (to protect their children from psychological harm); and
3. getting older and wiser through time (and the experience and wisdom that follows).

In Sandra's situation, the children definitely influenced her decision; and, perhaps, with no evidence of concrete changes in Luke's behavior, we can also attribute her subsequent move to the passage of time. These significant operative forces, coupled with Sandra's vulnerable position, the continued threat of severe violence and possible death, and the recognition of her own potential for retaliation substantiated the necessity for taking action.

Nevertheless, it took many years before Sandra could fortify herself and make the decision to leave. She had become more and more isolated and depressed, unable to reach out for help. As Fiene (1995) points out, "[B]attered women are reluctant to disclose their victimization even to close family members. . . . This reticence increases their isolation, and thus they forgo the potential social support available" (p. 179). Sandra's "secret" was kept well hidden, as the failing marriage was perceived as a personal failure. With her diminishing self-confidence and pervading emotional attachments to Luke, she began to accept much of the blame for the occurrences that followed. Many battered women feel impotent for their lack of control and influence over these events, thereby viewing themselves negatively. A belief of helplessness often expresses itself in passivity and submission that is continually being reinforced by their victimization (Walker, 1979). This learned helplessness reflected Sandra's growing image of herself—one that was so different from her earlier persona and relationship with Luke.

Additionally, Sandra's fear of being unable to manage on her own and take care of the children, and of Luke's finding her and the possible consequences this could entail, kept her immobilized. Her job training was in waitressing, an occupation that usually provides limited salaries and benefits. Without therapy and anger management skills, Luke may very well have bent his frustrations on Sandra for leaving. So this was certainly a realistic outlook on her part. Similar factors have affected many battered women's resistance to searching for safety through constructive channels (Walker, 1994).

The role that alcohol abuse played in the battering must also be taken into account. According to Bennett (1995), violence may be aggravated by substance use in some men, but it cannot be concluded that eliminating substances will stop the violence. The power-aggression relationship may be more applicable: "[A]ny quantity of alcohol for problem drinkers increases their sense of personal power over others. A man concerned with personal power and control is also more likely to drink heavily and more likely to be aggressive" (Bennett, 1995, p. 761). Violence as a learned behavior can be demonstrated by the high probability of reenactments in later years, when children observe spousal abuse in the home (Burman & Allen-Meares, 1994). These concepts afford a likely explanation for Luke's assaultive behaviors. His father was overtly abusive to his mother, and Luke internalized these unsettling memories. But Luke's assaultive acts toward Sandra could most likely be expressed as a consequence of feeling a lack of control in other areas of his life (e.g., increasing financial pressures; possible loss of employment due to heavy drinking). The power and control he desired was transferred to his perceived domination of Sandra by the continuous acts of physical and emotional abuse.

When viewing learning theories (operant conditioning; social learning), it can be surmised that in her early years at home with her parents, although she was disturbed by her father's verbal abuse after heavy drinking, she observed her mother being targeted with no active recourse displayed. Sandra commented, "My mother almost expected it and geared herself for the torment." Sandra's marriage was somewhat reminiscent of her mother's. Her role as victim recreated her mother's role. With her low self-esteem and feelings of powerlessness and helplessness, Sandra's submissiveness increased, and Luke learned that he could control her through the use of verbal and physical assaults. When Sandra finally left, her help-seeking actions were rewarded by the immediate attention to her safety and emotional needs—a sharp contrast from her experience with Luke. Although still vulnerable and uncertain as to which direction to take, she became more amenable to partaking of the guidance offered by its reinforcing elements.

Problem Identification and Implications

The primary problem, identified by Sandra in the first stage of crisis resolution, was the continuous battering experiences she had endured over a 5-year period with no assurance of its stopping. She also realized that her children could be severely damaged by witnessing the battering. Associated with this were fears of continued violence and harassment if she would leave Luke and not being able to provide for the children and herself, without his assistance. Despite the traumas, there existed an underlying attachment to him, which made her ambivalent about ending the relationship. Her lack of self-confidence and low self-esteem and self-worth were also prominent. Through the initial therapeutic process, the immediate crisis was allayed, but lingering trepidations and ambivalence remained that could diminish the gains already made. Without additional treatment, anticipatory problems were expected to arise, especially if she were to return to Luke and the violence that would invariably continue.

Goal-Setting and Contracting

Preliminary goals were aimed to fortify some of the previous goals made during the crisis resolution phase: (1) continuing to strengthen Sandra's emotional stability, self-esteem, and resolve; and (2) empowering her to make desirable, self-assured decisions based on what would promote optimal safety and a better quality of life for her and the children. This would entail helping her to challenge self-defeating thoughts and beliefs that restrain rational decisions; to explore the options and alternatives available; and to recognize and tap into her strengths that would facilitate problem solving. As therapy continued with Sandra, the assessment and goals were expected to expand, depending on the circumstances experienced. Contracting comprised a verbal agreement to work together on the proposed goals for a period of 20 sessions, after which progress would be evaluated. The need for additional meetings would be assessed at that time.

Implementation of Interventions

After a brief, but intensive, crisis-intervention foundation, Sandra was stabilized and acquired the tools to improve her coping and decision-making abilities. Nevertheless, self-doubts and fears still existed that needed qualifying and assuaging. Without sustaining, cognitive explorations of these elements and a dramatic change in emotional and belief manifestations, the depressive and anxiety reactions that were previously noted could result in more debilitating symptoms similar to a post-traumatic stress disorder. These imagery disturbances are evidenced by incapacitating flashbacks, intrusive thoughts, and nightmares that created profound emotional and cognitive upsets (McCann & Pearlman, 1990). To allay the possibility of regression and additional problems, the second stage of rehabilitation immediately followed. This allowed Sandra needed time to recover from past traumas and to develop new coping strategies to empower her to problem-solve effectively.

Instrumental in working with Sandra was the development of a relationship, based on rapport, trust, and empathy. When a woman experiences the extent and duration of violations against her (as is the case in battering), efforts must be taken to relay indelible support and guidance. Trust, hopes, and dreams have been previously shattered; vulnerability has been exploited. In order to rebuild a maligned ego and a self-concept weakened from years of abuse, feelings should be explored and validated, and options and solutions should be forthrightly presented that are personally meaningful and recognizably workable. In addition, the belief system should be modified to alter distressing and self-defeating thoughts that undermine progress towards positive change. Teaching Sandra to monitor and correct these thoughts proved to be an important step towards self-preservation and fulfillment of her goals.

Sandra began to realize that returning to Luke would be an error in judgment that she would forever regret—the promises to end the battering would continue, but the injuries and subjugation would not cease. Yet her ambivalence about leaving him was influenced by the fears of being autonomous and independent, coupled with an uneasy emotional attachment that lingered. Nevertheless, she did agree on the action plan to try a separation, moving with her children into an apartment that she could afford and obtaining a restraining order for added protection. In the interim, therapy continued to help her adjust to her new status and setting. This experience served to fortify her decision to make a fresh start, based on rational considerations of past events and present and future possibilities, options, and alternatives. An important part of the plan was to bolster her ego strengths and coping skills in order to overcome any difficulties that might occur, while providing supportive structures and resources as needed.

An essential element in the process was the initial turning point that initiated the help-seeking. This was seen as self-empowerment that had to be reinforced and supported continuously. Her depression and anxiety were treated with medication until they were markedly reduced. Acknowledging that maladaptive emotional reactions and subsequent behaviors are manifested through distorted thoughts and beliefs, cognitive strategies (Beck et al., 1993) were implemented to help her challenge and interrupt these perceptions through reality testing and logic.

It was important for Sandra to recognize how her belief system had been keeping her trapped and immobilized, unable to seek help until years after the abuse had begun. And even more specifically, those intrusive thoughts could reappear to undermine the progress she had already made. Through reflective listening and feedback, she was taught to monitor and modify thought patterns that created unsettling emotions. By reciting these beliefs aloud (e.g., "I'll never be able to make it on my own") and confronting the message ("I haven't tried, so how can I know?"), a more positive attitude emerged. Finding meaning in her actions ("I stayed so long, not because of love for Luke, but because I was afraid of being independent") also helped to strengthen her commitment to change the status quo.

A cost-benefit analysis, citing the advantages and disadvantages of living with Luke, was heavily tipped in favor of a permanent separation. To desensitize her fears of being alone, an imagery technique was conducted, encouraging her to visualize this situation after being in a relaxed state. She was able to imagine the possibilities and alternatives open to her, such as the increased freedom of making her own decisions and returning to school and advancing her employment potential. She admitted that her waitress job was too limiting, and that in the past, she had wanted to improve her potential, but Luke had dissuaded her from advancing. His demeaning comments had discouraged her and shattered her self-confidence. The fear that Luke would retaliate when left without her was still credible, but Sandra knew that staying could be just as emotionally and physically injurious as leaving, and she was developing supports to call on for protection.

To reinforce her capabilities and talents, she was taught the "as if" strategy. In fearsome or problematic situations, she acted as if she could handle it (even visualizing it beforehand by approximating each step closer to the goal). This reinforced her confidence and prompted her to attempt difficult tasks. Role plays of stressful events provided practice in overcoming ineffective responses to adverse conditions. And each day, she incorporated positive affirmations into her routine, thereby counteracting trepidations and negative thoughts.

Early fond memories of Luke kept disrupting the horror of what their relationship had become. These held together a weakened, yet enduring, attachment to him. By emphatically reframing the positive recollections to the disillusionment she felt and recognized in succeeding years, Sandra was able to displace the fragile bonds to other supports and to take pride in her own ability to decipher latent emotional dependency from the reality that her needs and expectations were not being met. Her former persona of normalcy, stability, and security had been essentially destroyed in the marriage. When this awareness solidified, she became angry and began opening up to new experiences. She had blamed herself for the failing marriage; now she realized that Luke's abusive behaviors and controlling nature were inexcusable and caused most of the friction between them. He had placed her in a defenseless and precarious position— one that provoked fears, isolation, shame, and guilt.

She was prompted to participate in a therapy group of abused women who gained strength from one another in their quest to break the destructive bonds they endured. She also joined a self-help support group that included women who left their abusive partners and were managing their lives quite satisfactorily. Many of these women formed special relationships that sustained them in moments of apprehension and indecisiveness.

Termination and Referrals

Primary treatment was completed when Sandra stabilized enough to pursue her own goals of independent living with appropriate supports and resources. Referrals were made for legal and financial assistance, and educational guidance was provided by a local academic institution. Follow-up was agreed to, with monthly contacts to determine her current functioning and needs. In addition, it was stressed that any problems and safety concerns would be addressed immediately. It was imperative to clarify this policy so that she would understand that provisions would be available promptly, when necessary.

Evaluation of Effectiveness of Interventions

It should be emphasized that the evaluation of interventions conducted should be an ongoing process. As work with the client continues, issues might arise that were unforeseen previously, and the action plan must be flexible enough to adjust accordingly. In summarizing Sandra's progress in treatment, problem solving entailed all the knowledge and skills she had learned from crisis intervention and cognitive therapy. She was able to critically ponder each problem, while weighing the consequences of her actions. Without the extended therapeutic experience, she might not have been ready to combat detrimental, impulsive responses that would have prevented necessary changes. She was amazed at her own strengths, which were unrecognized before, to make decisions that could finally end a disastrous relationship and save herself and her children from future turmoil.

DISCUSSION

This chapter integrates the findings of a research study and a practice model, demonstrating the strategies used by shelters for battered women and a more comprehensive strategic model that is designed to address the many inherent problems of domestic violence. It is suggested that limitations are placed on the helping process by not affording a more intensive, intervention-action plan, utilizing both crisis intervention and cognitively oriented problem solving. The dangers involved in battering can be so emotionally and physically devastating that extreme measures must be taken to ensure safety and increase the awareness of the dangers involved in remaining in an abusive relationship, while teaching and developing coping skills to resist any repetition of assaults in the future. The critical analysis and consequences of a battered woman's decisions should not be treated lightly. If she decides to return to the perpetrator, death or severe and prolonged injuries can occur. Therefore, every effort should be made to help her make an informed decision based on logic, not emotion.

The proposed model can be effectively utilized by generalist practitioners, specialists, and professionals in agencies and shelters. A multidisciplinary team can assume various responsibilities and tasks in carrying out the rehabilitative stages, from the acute crisis to the more chronic condition with related problems. The goal is to follow the client through the healing and growth phases, empowering her to protect herself and look after her best interests, while tapping and building ego strengths to prevent recurrent psychological and behavioral incapacitation. It is a present and future-oriented approach to security, healthy functioning, and self-sufficiency. With continual support and reality-oriented feedback, a battered woman who previously had lost hope can once again perceive life with optimism and a renewed sense of determination and the capability to strive towards independence and self-fulfillment.

REFERENCES

Astin, M. C., Lawrence, K., Pincus, G., & Foy, D. (1990, October). *Moderator variables for PTSD among battered women.* Paper presented at the convention of the International Society for Traumatic Stress Studies, New Orleans, LA.

Avni, N. (1991). Battered wives: The home as a total institution. *Violence and Victims, 2,* 137–149.

Bandura, A. (1977). *Social learning theory.* Englewood Cliffs, NJ: Prentice-Hall.

Beck, A. (1967). *Depression: Clinical, experimental and theoretical aspects.* New York: Harper & Row.

Beck, A. T., Wright, F. D., Newman, C. F., & Liese, B. S. (1993). *Cognitive therapy of substance abuse.* New York: Guilford.

Bennett, L. W. (1995). Substance abuse and the domestic assault of women. *Social Work, 40,* 760–771.

Briere, J., & Runtz, M. (1988). Multivariate correlates of childhood and physical maltreatment among university women. *Child Abuse and Neglect, 12,* 331–341.

Briere, J., & Runtz, M. (1989). The Trauma Symptom Checklist (TSC-33): Early data on a new scale. *Journal of Interpersonal Violence, 4,* 151–163.

Burman, S., & Allen-Meares, P. (1994). Neglected victims of murder: Children's witness to parental homicide. *Social Work, 39,* 28–34.

Cascardi, M., & O'Leary, K. D. (1992). Depressive symptomatology, self-esteem, and self-blame in battered women. *Journal of Family Violence, 7,* 249–259.

Davis, L. V., & Srinivasan, M. (1995). Listening to the voices of battered women: What helps them escape violence. *Affilia, 10,* 49–69.

Derogatis, L. (1977). *SCL-90R Manual-L.* Towson, MD: Clinical Psychometric Research.

Dutton, D. G. (1988). *The domestic assault of women: Psychological and criminal justice perspectives.* Boston: Allyn & Bacon.

Dziegielewski, S., Resnick, C., & Krause, N. (1996). Shelter-based crisis intervention with battered women. In A. R. Roberts (Ed.), *Helping battered women: New perspectives and remedies* (pp. 159–171). New York: Oxford University Press.

Elliot, D. M., & Briere, J. (1992). Sexual abuse trauma among professional women: Validating the Trauma Symptom Checklist–40 (TSC–40). *Child Abuse and Neglect, 16,* 391–398.

Fiene, J. I. (1995). Battered women: Keeping the secret. *Affilia, 10,* 179–193.

Geller, J., & Wasserstrom, J. (1984). Conjoint therapy for the treatment of domestic violence. In A. R. Roberts (Ed.), *Battered women and their families: Intervention strategies and treatment programs* (pp. 33–48). New York: Springer.

Gelles, R. J., & Harrop, J. W. (1989). Violence, battering, and psychological distress among women. *Journal of Interpersonal Violence, 4,* 400–411.

Hamberger, L. K., & Holtzworth-Munroe, A. (1994). Partner violence. In F. M. Dattilio & A. Freeman (Eds.), *Cognitive-behavioral strategies in crisis intervention* (pp. 302–324). New York: Guilford.

Hepworth, D. H., & Larsen, J. A. (1993). *Direct social work practice: Theory and skills* (4th ed.). Pacific Grove, CA: Brooks/Cole.

Housekamp, B. M., & Foy, D. W. (1991). The assessment of posttraumatic stress disorder in battered women. *Journal of Interpersonal Violence, 6,* 367–375.

Longres, J. F. (1995). *Human behavior in the social environment* (2nd ed.). Itasca, IL: F. E. Peacock.

McCann, L., & Pearlman, L. A. (1990). Constructivist self-development theory as a framework for assessing and treating victims of family violence. In S. M. Smith, M. B. Williams, & K. Rosen (Eds.), *Violence hits home: Comprehensive treatment approaches to domestic violence* (pp. 305–329). New York: Springer Publishing.

Petretic-Jackson, P., & Jackson, T. (1996). Mental health interventions with battered women. In A. R. Roberts (Ed.), *Helping battered women: New perspectives and remedies* (pp. 188–221). New York: Oxford University Press.

Roberts, A. R. (Ed.). (1991). *Contemporary perspectives on crisis intervention and prevention.* Englewood Cliffs, NJ: Prentice-Hall.

Roberts, A. R. (Ed.). (1995). *Crisis intervention and time-limited cognitive treatment.* Thousand Oaks, CA: Sage.

Roberts, A. R. (Ed.). (1996). *Crisis management and brief treatment: Theory, technique, and applications.* Chicago: Nelson-Hall.

Roberts, A. R. (Ed.). (1997). The organizational structure and functions of 177 shelters for battered women. *American Journal of Community Psychology, 32,* 400–418.

Roberts, A. R., & Roberts, B. J. (1990). A comprehensive model for crisis intervention with battered women and their children. In A. R. Roberts

(Ed.), *Crisis intervention handbook: Assessment, treatment, and research* (pp. 105–123). Belmont, CA: Wadsworth.

Roche, S. E. (1996). Social action for battered women. In A. R. Roberts (Ed.), *Helping battered women: New perspectives and remedies* (pp. 13–30). New York: Oxford University Press.

Skinner, B. F. (1938). *The behavior of organisms: An experimental analysis.* New York: Appleton-Century-Crofts.

Stith, S. M., & Rosen, K. H. (1990). Overview of domestic violence. In S. M. Stith, M. B. Williams, & K. Rosen (Eds.), *Violence hits home: Comprehensive treatment approaches to domestic violence* (pp. 1–21). New York: Springer Publishing.

Straus, M. A. (1990). The Conflict Tactics Scales and its critics: An evaluation and new data on validity and reliability. In M. A. Straus & R. J. Gelles (Eds.), *Physical violence in American families: Risk factors and adaptations to violence in 8,145 families* (pp. 49–71). New Brunswick, NJ: Transaction.

Walker, L. E. (1979). *The battered woman.* New York: Harper & Row.

Walker, L. E. (1985). Psychological impact of the criminalization of domestic violence on victims. *Victimology: An International Journal, 10,* 281–300.

Walker, L. E. (1989). *Terrifying love: Why battered women kill and how society responds.* New York: Harper & Row.

Walker, L. E. A. (1994). *Abused women and survivor therapy: A practical guide for the psychotherapist.* Washington, DC: American Psychological Association.

Watkins, H., & Bradbard, M. (1982). Child maltreatment: An overview with suggestions for intervention and research. *Family Relations, 31,* 323–333.

Webb, W. (1992). Treatment issues and cognitive behavior techniques with battered women. *Journal of Family Violence, 7,* 205–217.

CHAPTER 2

The Stress-Crisis Continuum: Its Application to Domestic Violence

Pamela V. Valentine, Albert R. Roberts, and Ann W. Burgess

Women-battering, occurring in 25%–30% of families, is a pervasive, severe problem in society today (Roberts & Roberts, 1990). The depth of the problem in America is illustrated by the frequency of domestic violence incidents as well as the severity and cost of physical injuries related to domestic violence. Each year, over 8 million American women are victims of domestic violence (Roberts, 1996). Domestic violence causes more injuries to women victims than accidents, muggings, and cancer deaths combined (Nurius, Hilfrink, & Rifino, 1996). Almost 35% of emergency room visits are made by women seeking help for injuries related to abuse by a partner. The health-care cost per year for medical services to battered women and children is $1,633 per person, or an annual total of $857.3 million (Lewin, 1997).

Not only does women-battering cost society in terms of medical bills, but women-battering strains society by the disruption of families with which it is associated. Children who witness marital violence are found to be affected in at least three areas of functioning: internalizing behavior, such as depression and anxiety; externalizing behavior, such as aggression and uncooperativeness; and impaired social competence (Carlson, 1996; Malmquist, 1986). A report from the American Bar Association (1994) found that 75% of boys who were present when their mothers were beaten had behavior problems. Living in a home where their mothers were beaten was a factor in 20%–40% of chronically violent teens. Additionally, 63% of males in the 11–20-year-old age category were incarcerated for having killed the man who battered their mothers (Roberts, 1996a). Not only does women-battering affect children who witness it, but its effects are exacerbated when children are themselves victims of child-battering (Carlson, 1996). Also, please see chapters 5 through 8.

Women-battering is a traumatic and multifaceted phenomenon. Often, women-battering presents itself as emotional, economic, and/ or sexual abuse. Trauma disrupts cognitive functioning, resulting in feelings of worthlessness, helplessness, traumatic bonding, and phobic responses (Dziegielewski, Resnick, & Krause, 1996). Furthermore, the cognitive distortions often lead to intergenerational abuse. Finally, "one-fourth of all suicide attempts are directly related to abuse" (Dziegielewski et al., 1996, p. 164).

While domestic violence has existed for centuries, America's focus on the problem has waxed and waned over time. Two manifestations of America's shifting responses to battered women are the degree of help offered to battered women and the frequency of articles published concerning domestic violence. In 1885, Chicago established the Chicago Protective Agency for Women and Children. This led to a widespread movement to establish protective agencies for women (Roberts, 1996b). Between 1885 and 1949, many women victims of domestic violence received shelter, personal assistance, legal aid, court advocacy, equitable property settlements, and protection through divorce or separation from their husbands. However, in the late 1940s, protective agencies for women were replaced by crime prevention bureaus, and female police social workers were replaced by male police administrators. Help for battered women became rare until the rise of the feminist movement in the 1970s.

In addition to the degree of help offered to battered women, society's attitude about women-battering is reflected in its journals. From 1939 until 1969, the literature on domestic violence replicated the pattern found in the protective agencies. During this period, no reference to domestic violence was made in the *Journal of Marriage and Family Therapy* (Schecter, 1982). Thereafter, 30 articles were published, 21 of which came after 1986.

Since the rise of the feminist movement in the 1970s, society began responding once more to women-battering. In 1990, more than 1,250 battered women's shelters had been opened in the United States and Canada. Trauma centers, hotlines, welfare and court advocacy, housing, employment, peer counseling, and parenting education are some of the services that are provided to victims of women-battering (Roberts, 1996a).

More recently, battering has been defined in a broader sense than acts of physical violence. Experts have begun to realize the psychological consequences of battering, noting that physical violence seldom happens in isolation (Petretic-Jackson & Jackson, 1996). Often emotional, economic, and sexual abuse accompany physical abuse. Therefore, communities have begun to offer psychological counseling to battered women in addition to traditional services.

Psychological counseling has been impacted by the 1990s' managed health care movement wherein American health insurance companies began to demand cost-efficient psychological interventions. Consequently, treatment providers started trying to demonstrate the veracity of the interventions given patients. Traditional scientific tools are the means for demonstrating effectiveness. These tools (theory, operationalization, replication and prediction) serve to explain, specify, and predict. Scientific tools: (1) explain which treatments work and why; (2) help specify the treatment procedures and the anticipated treatment results; and (3) help make predictions or prognoses about the length of treatment. As a result of applying scientific tools to psychotherapeutic interventions, brief (generally one to six sessions), goal-oriented, crisis-intervention, cognitive-behavioral, and/or group and family therapy has largely replaced longer, less defined, individual psychoanalytic therapy.

Specified, focused interventions can benefit clients as well as managed care. Brief treatment often allows clients to participate in (1) prioritizing the most important problem to solve, (2) visualizing the desired, behavioral results, and (3) recognizing the alleviation of the presenting problem(s) as it occurs.

Psychological interventions must start with therapists' recognition of woman-battering. Two national studies have documented a serious problem in terms of therapists' ability to identify domestic violence. Drs. Michelle Harway and Marsali Hansen (1993, 1994) conducted two studies on therapists' perceptions of family violence. These studies found that, when presented a case vignette and asked to "describe what was happening in the family, what interventions they would make and what outcomes they would expect from their intervention" (Harway & Hansen, 1994, pp. 6–7), many therapists lacked the needed skills and knowledge to both identify domestic violence and to assess its lethality. In the first study, the clinical researchers sent a questionnaire which included a case vignette of a violent family to a random sample of members of the American Association of Marriage and Family Therapy (AAMFT) ($n = 362$). Only 60% of the respondents recognized the issue of violence within the relationship. Yet even these respondents clearly minimized the extent of the problem, as evidenced by the finding that 91% considered the violence mild or moderate when, in reality, there was a good possibility of there being deadly consequences. Only 2.2% both recognized that the battering could become lethal and called for immediate intervention.

Because the researchers were so alarmed by the latter findings, they completed a second study. The case vignette was modified so that it clearly stated that domestic violence was involved and that it had a lethal outcome. Of 405 members of the American Psychological Association (APA), 71% of whom were men, 27% said that they lacked sufficient evidence to judge the seriousness of the case; they said that they would ask the client to return for another assessment appointment. We firmly believe that it is the therapist's ethical and legal responsibility to be able to recognize women-battering and to provide immediate intervention.

The tools required for effective intervention in the domain of women-battering are multiple. The tools, while similar to those required of mental health practitioners, are more complex, considering that victims of women-battering most often present in crises and that the stakes are high. In other words, there may be no second chance for the clinician or the client.

The tools for intervening with the victim of women-battering are the following: First, a clinician needs to be able to recognize the presenting circumstances as being those of women-battering. Next, the clinician must move in a determined way to secure safety for the client. Another essential step is the collection of accurate data. A thorough picture of the client's present and past life circumstances informs the clinician about appropriate treatment modalities. Furthermore, a clinician either needs proficiency in various treatment modalities or an awareness of the need to link the client with a suitable treatment specialist who can address one or more of the various components in the client's profile. Because domestic violence is a crisis situation in which effective, timely intervention can make a life-and-death difference, it is important that a clinician have access to an assessment tool that will guide them along the steps as outlined above.

With the movement toward brief, empirical, psychotherapeutic interventions, *and* given the critical nature of women-battering, the Stress-Crisis Continuum (Burgess & Roberts, 1995) emerges as a timely instrument. It can aid the clinician in recognizing the severity of the crisis, linking appropriate treatment modalities with the level of crises, and grouping clients of similar internal conflicts and levels of chronicity. Based on an expansion and adaptation of Baldwin's (1978) crisis classification, the stress-crisis continuum delineates seven levels of stress-crisis: (1) somatic; (2) transitional distress; (3) traumatic stress-crisis; (4) family crisis; (5) severe mental illness; (6) psychiatric emergencies; and (7) catastrophic and/or cumulative crises. The levels progress as the nature and intensity of internal conflicts become more severe.

This chapter contains domestic violence case scenarios of each level of stress in the continuum. Following each given case scenario are the research and interventions associated with that level.

LEVEL 1: SOMATIC DISTRESS

Case Example

Ms. Abel, a 27-year-old occupational therapist, was a victim of emotional abuse. She sought counseling at a local mental health agency for relational problems associated with her live-in lesbian partner. Ms. Abel reported that she had not been struck by her partner, but viewed her partner as intimidating, controlling, and threatening. She said that her partner would stare at her for long periods of time, never saying a word. Her partner would also call her degrading names. Finally, her partner would periodically throw objects in the house and take a baseball bat to an outdoor tree to show her displeasure with Ms. Abel. Ms. Abel presented with depressive symptoms such as binge eating, crying, a lack of enthusiasm for work, and periodic absences from work due to migraine headaches. Ms. Abel took prescription medications for the headaches. She was also a victim of childhood sexual and emotional abuse.

Having addressed issues of safety, the therapist and Ms. Abel agreed that treatment should address Ms. Abel's passivity in her relationship with her lover. Believing that there was an association between Ms. Abel's childhood sexual abuse and her current passivity, the therapist engaged Ms. Able in an intense, brief, trauma treatment called Traumatic Incident Reduction (TIR) (Gerbode, 1989). The intervention called for the repeated visualization of that particularly painful scene in which she had been sexually abused by her parents. After approximately 30 minutes of visualization, Ms. Abel reported that she had a migraine headache. Her counselor asked Ms. Abel if she wished to continue the treatment, and Ms. Abel said, "Yes." However, with another viewing of the childhood incident, Ms. Abel asked the counselor to stop the session, dim the lights, place a trash can before her in case of vomiting, and call her primary physician requesting her prescription medication. The counselor did as Ms. Abel requested, and another staff member drove her to the emergency room to pick up the medication.

The following day Ms. Abel, sounding strong and chipper, called the counselor and requested an appointment. The counselor was surprised that Ms. Abel could be doing so well so quickly. That afternoon, the counselor met with Ms. Abel who reported that she had never been so surprised in her life . . . that the following had never before occurred to her. Ms. Abel said that by the time she arrived at the emergency room, her headache symptoms were completely gone. She deducted that her body was cooperating in a convincing way to keep her from addressing the memory of the childhood sexual abuse. With this conviction, Ms. Abel completed the aborted session and found relief from the presenting symptoms. Additionally, Ms. Abel learned to seek intervention at the first sign of physical distress rather than waiting for either a headache or a crisis to develop.

Research

The word "somatic" refers to the body or to the physical. Distress is "(1) pain or suffering of mind or body; (2) severe psychological strain; or (3) the condition of being in need of immediate assistance" (*American Heritage Concise Dictionary*, 1994, p. 249). Somatic stress is a physical manifestation of a biomedical or psychiatric difficulty. Somatic stresses come from stress which is either biomedical or psychological in origin. It is not always clear whether the stressor is biomedical or psychological in nature. For example, one who has cancer, lupus, diabetes or other diseases that suppress the immune system experiences somatic stress. Depending on one's response to one of the abovementioned diseases, one may also experience minor psychiatric symptoms, such as anxiety or depressive symptoms. Breast cancer patients, for example, who express more distress about their illness, have lower levels of a natural killer (NK) cell activity than other patients (Burgess & Roberts, 1995).

On the other hand, an underlying psychosocial difficulty might manifest itself in the physical. Barsky (1981) reports that between 40% and 60% of all visits to primary health providers such as physicians and nurses involve symptoms for which no biomedical disease can be detected. Mechanic (1994) postulates a close connection between the physical and mental domains and argues that physical and mental health care need to be integrated to address the coexistence of physical and mental disorders.

Somatic distress taxes the general medical sector, which provides approximately half of all mental health care (Burgess & Roberts, 1995). Studies show that the need for medical care increases when physical problems are accompanied by underlying psychosocial issues. Somatizers who are under stress overuse ambulatory medical services (Burgess & Roberts, 1995). Depressive symptoms, which occur in between 3 and 5% in the general population, are higher yet with disadvantaged populations.

Intervention

Patients with defined medical illnesses should be treated with appropriate medical protocols (Burgess & Roberts, 1995). For those patients with somatic symptoms but without a clear medical diagnosis, clinicians should conduct a thorough psychosocial history. In the interest of safety, the social history should include an assessment of the patient's current living conditions. The clinician should also inquire about prior occurrences of traumatic events to assess for residual effects of such events. Finally, the counselor needs to determine whether the symptomatology meets the criteria for the *Diagnostic and Statistical Manual of Mental Disorders* (4th ed.) (DSM-IV; American Psychiatric Association, 1994) since early intervention has been shown to reduce symptoms and interrupt the progression toward major psychiatric disorders (Burgess & Roberts, 1995).

Engaging patients in the therapeutic process is the next intervention. It is an important part of treatment, for it facilitates the patient's feelings of ownership about his or her recovery. Engaging the patient also implies that recovery is the primary responsibility of the patient.

Several steps are involved for the patient to become involved in his or her recovery. First, the clinician should meet with the patient to share his or her clinical impressions of the patient's condition. If more than one presenting problem is identified (which is often the case), the therapist should then ask the patient to prioritize the problems to see which problem resolution matters most to the patient. Often, patients feel overwhelmed and are reluctant to try to prioritize their problems. Assisting the patient in prioritizing his or her problems can take the form of having him or her rank the level of distress he or she feels regarding each presenting problem. The therapist can list the problems, note the ranking assigned to each problem, and show the list to the patient. Another technique for promoting a patient to become engaged with problem resolution is to ask a question such as: "If you could only solve *one* problem, what would it be?" After prioritizing the problems, the clinician should ask the client to articulate what the solution to that problem would "look like." Here, one is aiming for an operationalized definition of the problem. It is important that the patient name the goal in terms of behavior acquisition rather than behavior disappearance. For example, rather than stating, "I'll know when the problem has gone away when I am no longer depressed," it is preferable that the patient visualizes something like the following: "I'll know that I am better when I have the energy to get out of bed and take a shower." Once the problems and goal have been prioritized and operationalized, the therapist engages the client by having both the client and the therapist sign a therapy contract, which lists the problem(s), the behaviors associated with problem resolution, the level of participation required of the patient, and the anticipated number of sessions required for treatment completion.

Reflecting respect for the patient and his or her perspectives is an integral part of the therapeutic process (Valentine, 1995). Valentine (1995) interviewed clients who had been a recipient of a brief therapeutic intervention. She found that clients experienced respect by having therapists honor rather than dispute their accounts of incidents.

Intervention with Level 1 patients may take the form of education. Teaching patients about their illness(es) and available forms of treatment is a classical intervention. It is also safe and nonintrusive. However, if patients have been under medical care for some time, they may have already received the educational component. Proceeding to cognitive-behavioral therapy and/or trauma-related techniques, where appropriate, is in order.

LEVEL 2: TRANSITIONAL STRESS

Case Example

Ms. Stewart, age 49, said, "I'm sleeping these last few weeks, but it feels like I haven't. My mind is always racing because I think of the worst. I can hardly go to work cause I cry so much, and I don't want my co-workers to see me like this."

Ms. Stewart, a secretary, was married to a man who spent money wildly, denied her money for necessities, called her to verify that she was at work, yelled at her when she arrived home 1 minute later than what he believed the drive home required, and choked her on repeated occasions.

In therapy, Ms. Stewart minimized the domestic violence that occurred in her home by calling her husband's aggressive acts "idiosyncrasies." In fact, Ms. Stewart reported that she was accustomed to living with her husband's "idiosyncrasies," and felt no need to address the domestic abuse in therapy. Rather, she focused on her aged, widowed mother.

Ms. Stewart was recently tearful due to her mother's imprisonment. Ms. Stewart's mother, who was lonely after the death of her husband, had rented her two spare bedrooms to two young men. Having grown fond of the men, Ms. Stewart's mother was eager to please them, and she was arrested for transporting the men's drugs across the state line. Attorney costs were such that Ms. Stewart's mother needed to sell her home to pay legal fees. Ms. Stewart felt helpless and depressed over her mother's condition.

Research

The combination of an unanticipated event and a developmental challenge is called a transitional stress (Burgess & Roberts, 1995). A developmental challenge entails a life task common to many people at a given phase of development. Learning to crawl, toilet training, going to school, graduating from high school, attaining a job, marrying, parenting, launching children into adulthood, retiring, and caring for aged parents are examples of developmental events. An unanticipated event might interrupt a developmental challenge, making it a transitional stress. Birth injuries, a child's untimely separation from his or her primary care giver(s), learning disabilities, accidents that mar one's appearance, disabilities, illnesses, adolescent pregnancies, infertility, imprisonment, and chronic illness are examples of unanticipated events that have the potential of interrupting or delaying the completion of a developmental task. One who experiences a transitional stress is likely to feel out of control and rigid (Burgess & Roberts, 1995). One frequently repeats acts that are counterproductive in an effort to regain control.

The case example of Ms. Stewart describes an unfortunate event in her mother's life. The event also represents an interruption in the developmental task of caring for aged parents. Ms. Stewart's wakefulness and tearfulness were due, in part, to her frustration at having had the developmental task interrupted. A psychosocial interview revealed that the symptoms were associated with the disruption of a strong intention or promise that Ms. Stewart had made as a child. Beginning at age 5, Ms. Stewart repeatedly witnessed her father battering her mother. When the abuse began, Ms. Stewart would run to her bed, close the door to muffle her mother's screams, pull the covers over her head, and promise herself that when she grew bigger, she would protect her mother from harm. Her mother's imprisonment impeded Ms. Stewart's ability to protect her mother, thus thwarting a developmental task and a lifelong promise. This was her transitional stress.

Intervention

Interventions for transitional stress are several, consisting primarily of three approaches: (1) focused, individual educational sessions; (2) group sessions that both educate and offer support; and (3) when appropriate, brief trauma techniques that address prior incidents. Group sessions are particularly appropriate. Because a transitional stressor has a developmental challenge that is common to many people, clients may feel strengthened to hear other group members say that they are experiencing similar challenges and responses. The group setting normalizes the event, taking away a sense of isolation. A group setting can also aid in freeing clients of introspective concerns such as "What's wrong with me?" Clients are now able to absorb the educational component of the intervention. Some clients, however, do not appear receptive to nor capable of applying the education presented in group *or* individual sessions. This may cue the therapist that a prior traumatic event is having a strong influence on current behavior, and prompt the therapist to introduce a brief trauma technique for altering cognitive distortions.

LEVEL 3: TRAUMATIC STRESS CRISES

Mrs. Baker, a victim of women-battering, arrived at the shelter with her two children, Danny (3) and Missy (9). Mrs. Baker had left her husband for battering her, sexually violating her daughter, and torturing the baby by placing a fork up the child's rectum to extract fecal material. Shortly after arriving at the shelter, Mrs. Baker enrolled her children in school, found a job, and began trying to rebuild her life.

One day, Mrs. Baker received a call from the sheriff's department, asking that she come to the station to make a deposition on her husband. The sheriff informed her that her husband had been charged with the murder of two men with whom Mr. Baker had suspected her of having an affair. A staff member drove Mrs. Baker to the sheriff's office, but had to stop the car various times to allow her to vomit. With her husband's incarceration, Mrs. Baker was now safe from his threats. However, instead of feeling relieved, she felt guilty. Rather than feeling as if she had been given back her life, she felt as if it had been taken away. Mrs. Baker experienced nightmares, despondency, and long crying spells.

Mrs. Baker's traumatic crisis was precipitated by a strong, externally imposed stressor. Trauma is distinguished from stress by severity and duration (Valentine, 1997). A traumatic event must be serious enough to challenge basic assumptions such as justice, fairness, safety, and predictability (Janoff-Bulman, 1992). One main effect of trauma is disorganization (Waites, 1993). One's cognitive schema is threatened, rules about how life works are shattered, and solace and hope evade the trauma victim. Trauma also elicits physiological responses to emergency situations. The victim's sense of "flight or fight" is increased. Responses are mediated by the autonomic nervous system (van der Kolk, 1987). Most alterations in microstructural neurochemistry will be temporary, but it is possible to have a traumatic event permanently alter structure.

Research

Post-traumatic stress disorder (PTSD), a phenomenon that was first associated with veterans of war, is a condition that some victims of traumatic events develop (Figley, 1989). Currently, PTSD is associated with precipitating events such as "abortion, burns, broken bones, surgery, overwhelming loss, animal attacks, drug overdoses, near drownings, bullying and intimidation," as well as criminal victimization (Moore, 1993, p. 116). The DSM-IV (APA, 1994) states that PTSD may occur to those who either experience or witness an event that involves "death, injury, serious harm, or threat to the physical integrity of another person" (p. 424).

The three headings under which symptoms for PTSD fall are (1) intrusion, (2) avoidance, and (3) increased arousal (DSM-IV) (APA, 1994). Intrusive symptoms mean that a person with PTSD will reexperience the event in the form of distressing dreams, memories, flashbacks, and/or a strong reaction to something that comes to symbolize the event. Avoidance manifests itself in one of the following ways: a strong tendency to avoid thinking or speaking about the event; a tendency to avoid activities that arouse recollection of the event; memory loss; a feeling of detachment; a restricted range of emotions (numbing); and/or a foreboding feeling about the future. The DSM-IV (APA, 1994) specifies that increased arousal refers to a level of arousal that the person did *not* experience before the traumatic event. Increased arousal could be manifested by difficulty falling or staying asleep, hypervigilance, difficulty concentrating, outbursts of anger, exaggerated startle response, or a physiologic reactivity to something that symbolizes or resembles the traumatic event. In short, PTSD begins with an "exaggerated reaction to the trauma and a subsequent preoccupation with it" (Waldinger, 1990, p. 217). The diagnosis of PTSD is made if a number of symptoms from each category continue beyond 4 weeks (Waldinger, 1990).

In addition to the three categories of PTSD symptoms found in the DSM-IV (APA, 1994), Moscarello (1991) speaks of four phases through which a victim of interpersonal violence passes: anticipatory, impact, recoil, and resolution. He links the three categories of PTSD symptoms with the impact phase and the recoil phase. The impact phase includes "rapid oscillation of intrusive and avoidance symptoms" (p. 240), while recoil is characterized by numbing. During the impact phase, one loses control, resulting in regression of the ego (Moscarello, 1991). During the recoil phase, one might have the outward appearance of adjustment, or alternatively fear, phobias, and depression. Other symptoms of PTSD include anxieties, insecurities, panic disorder, anger, rage, guilt complexes, mood anomalies, self-esteem problems, and compulsions (Dansky, Roth, & Kronenberger, 1990). PTSD can become worse as a person ages (Moscarello, 1991).

The notion that all survivors of traumatic incidents are dysfunctional is false (Everstine & Everstine, 1993). One's coping ability depends on several factors. Variables that exacerbate the immobilizing effects of a traumatic event include the following: if the traumatic event was at the hands of another person; if the action was intentional; if the perpetrator was known and trusted; the length of time since the incident (Everstine & Everstine, 1993); and a weak social support system. Additionally, how one's social support network explains the traumatic event (i.e., whether they blame the victim) has a large impact on the victim's psychological state and his/her self-esteem. Being blamed for the occurrence of the traumatic event increases one's subjective distress. Girelli, Resick, Mashoefer-Dvorak, and Hutter (1986) found that subjective distress is a better predictor of anxiety and fear than is observable violence. These multiple variables raise very complicated social-psychological issues.

Intervention

As for any victim of battering, the traumatized victim should first be assessed for safety issues. Once a safety net is in place, treatment can begin to address the emotional and cognitive processing of the event.

Effective assessment and treatment for the effects of traumatization is complex. Many theorists concur that the emotions, memory, and cognition are affected by the traumatic experience and that treatment, therefore, must address those three components. Foa, Rothbaum, and Steketee (1993) speculate that PTSD occurs because victims fail to *emotionally* process the traumatic event. They propose that therapy should be aimed at reducing symptoms associated with failed emotional processing. Symptoms associated with failed emotional processing are obsessions, nightmares, phobias, or inappropriate emotional processing. Other theorists posit that traumatic *memories* are central to manifestation of PTSD (Shapiro, 1989). These theories share the belief that reliving the painful memory allows the aborted emotional process to be completed, thus reducing PTSD symptoms. Roth and Newman (1991) argue that re-experiencing the painful memories allows the victim to understand the meaning of the event and to integrate the traumatic experience. This integration leads to a reduction of symptoms. Both Raimy (1975) and Gerbode and Moore (1994) emphasize the importance of *cognitive* restructuring along with emotional expression, since a physiological, cognitive, and affective component is involved in one's response to trauma.

Cathartic theory (Straton, 1990) incorporates emotions, memory, and cognition. The theory explains that the threatening incident strongly stirred the victim's emotions. Additionally, the mind was opened to new input by the heightened physiological response the victim experienced at the time of the incident. Typically, the victim finds it "impossible" to silence the survival messages received during the event. Messages given him or her when he or she is *not* experiencing a heightened physiological state do not impact the victim to the same extent as the message received during the crisis. Therefore, cathartic theory posits that it is necessary to "reexperience" the stressful event in order to change the victim's conditioned response(s). Reexperiencing the event via repeated visual imaging engages the client's memory, emotions, and finally cognition. The patient "tunes into" (recreates) the "frequency" (the heightened physiological state) that was present at the time of the incident to access the emotions, thinking, and decisions that occurred in crisis. When the patient understands the incident in a different light, after having reexperienced the incident, the insight is called a "redecision" (Straton, 1990).

Several promising brief trauma techniques are based on a similar understanding of the etiology of traumatic responses. Among them are Eye Movement Desensitization (EMDR) (Shapiro, 1989), Calahan's Thought Field Therapy (TFT) (1987), and Gerbode's (1989) Traumatic Incident Reduction (TIR).

LEVEL 4: FAMILY CRISIS

Case Example

Monica, a mother of a 4-year-old boy, was introduced to Jose at a singles' club. Over the course of the evening, she grew to like him. The feeling was mutual. Soon Jose began sending Monica flowers and surprising her with romantic gifts; a sexual relationship developed. In the first few months of their relationship, Monica learned that Jose had previously been incarcerated in a federal corrections institute. She pondered why she was neither alarmed nor fearful about the safety of her son, toward whom she felt very protective.

Some months later, Monica lost interest in Jose and told him that she desired to "be just friends." Jose pleaded with Monica to change her mind, but to no avail. In the next weeks, his repeated phone calls, stalking, and veiled threats caused Monica much anxiety.

One night, after picking up her son from day care on her way home from work, Monica found that Jose had broken into her home and was waiting for her. Monica put her son to bed and asked Jose to leave the house. He refused. All night, Jose held her captive. He tore her clothes off her, raped her, threatened to kill her, and threatened to kill himself. Believing that he had succeeded in subduing her, Jose asked her to handcuff him to the bed and perform oral sex on him. She handcuffed him to the bed and fled the house with her child. At 2 o'clock in the morning, Monica and her son arrived at the shelter. Over the weeks, the shelter staff observed that Monica demonstrated watchfulness, hypervigilance, an exaggerated startle response, and depressive symptoms such as sobbing inconsolably.

The family crisis presented above dealt primarily with an interpersonal situation that developed within the family network. Other family crises might be "child abuse, the use of children in pornography, parental abductions, adolescent runaways, battering and rape, homelessness and domestic homicide" (Burgess & Roberts, 1995, p. 40).

Emotional crises involve an interaction of external stressors, internal stressors, and an unresolved developmental issue. An external stressor is an unanticipated forceful event. An internal stressor is a vulnerability due to an unresolved developmental task. Frequently a developmental issue will involve "dependency, value conflict, sexual identity, emotional intimacy, power issues or attaining self-discipline" (Burgess & Roberts, 1995, p. 40). For Monica, the external stressors were Jose's stalking, invading her home, raping her, threatening, and endangering her child. The internal stressor was related to an unresolved issue with her father. The internal stressor manifested itself in that she was not alarmed upon learning of Jose's incarceration.

Research

Burgess and Roberts (1995) write that a shift occurs in Level 4. While each level of stress in the Stress–Crisis Continuum (Burgess &

Roberts, 1995) involves an interaction of an external stressor and a vulnerability of the individual, Level 4 transfers the weight of the balance toward preexisting psychopathology (Baldwin, 1978). Monica's unresolved issue with her father left her vulnerable to be raped; the sexual violence Monica experienced with Jose manifested her vulnerability.

Rape victims often fit the criteria of PTSD. In fact, Resnick and associates found that 57% of rape victims met the lifetime diagnostic criteria for PTSD. The lifetime diagnostic criteria for PTSD are defined as having the symptoms 4 weeks after the event. Saunders, Arata, and Kilpatrick (1987) report that 16.5% of women who experienced PTSD at the time of their study had had it for an average duration of 17 years.

One distinguishing feature between the reaction to rape (often called the rape trauma syndrome) and PTSD is the traumatic event itself. That rape is the result of humans willfully acting to hurt another exacerbates the victim's reaction to the traumatic incident. The majority of rape victims are assaulted by acquaintances (Koss & Burkhart, 1989). When rape occurs with a known and trusted perpetrator such as a family member or a friend, it is called confidence rape. Confidence rape destroys trust and instills shame, making the reaction more severe and longer lasting than other traumatic events (APA, 1994).

When raped, a woman is treated as if she has no "rights, needs, or physical boundaries" (Koss & Burkhart, 1989). Physical injury is usually present (Everstine & Everstine, 1993). Rape often is concomitant with shame, self-blame, a sense of being powerless, fear of AIDS in stranger rape, hatred, paradoxical gratitude, defilement, sexual inhibition manifesting itself in loss of libido and a reduced capacity for intimacy, fear of being alone, broken will, revictimization through the criminal justice system, and a downward shift in status. Women feel shame intensified when their autonomic nervous system loses control, resulting in vomiting, urination, defecation, or physiological sexual arousal (Moscarello, 1991).

Rape trauma syndrome is a common, persistent, and far-reaching problem among rape victims: "Only 25% of rape victims were free of significant symptoms on standard psychological test one year after the assault" (Koss & Burkhart, 1989, p. 28). Burgess and Holmstrom (1974) report that 4 to 6 years later, 26% of victims still did not feel recovered. One to 16 years post-assault, 31% to 48% of the victims sought psychotherapy (Koss & Burkhart, 1989). Rape produces a wider range of PTSD symptoms than do other traumatic events (Waites, 1993). Such symptoms are distorted patterns of attachment, pervasive problems of identity integration, and belief systems that rationalize the rape.

The rape trauma syndrome resembles the post-abuse reaction characteristic of sexually victimized children (Burgess & Holmstrom, 1974). The victim is likely to become socially isolated and is more prone to drop out of counseling due to feeling unworthy. The victim is less sure that confidence rape *is* rape (Bowie, Silverman, Kalich, & Edbril, 1990; Koss & Burkhart, 1989). Kilpatrick, Veronen, and Best (1988) found that, of the women who met the legal definition of rape (force or threat of force, nonconsent, and involving the act of penetration), only 50% responded in the affirmative when asked if they had ever been victims of rape (Bowie et al., 1990).

Intervention

The treatment of a rape victim entails addressing safety issues, assessing for physical and psychological damage, creating a safe therapeutic environment, and allowing the client to tell her story repeatedly. Often, because traumatic events shatter assumptions of safety (Janoff-Bulman, 1992) and/or alter physiological chemistry in the brain (van der Kolk, 1987), traditional talk therapy fails to assuage fears or restore a client to her prior level of functioning.

Brief trauma-related interventions differ from talk therapy in several ways: (1) the sessions are focused on one particular troubling event; (2) the client is more active than the therapist; (3) the sessions often last longer than an hour; and (4) frequently, imaginal flooding is a component of brief therapies. Repeated visualization facilitates the client's becoming desensitized to the event. Open-ended sessions allow the client to become emotionally reengaged with the event, reach a heightened physiological state, grow desensitized to the event, and gain new insight about the event. TFT (Calahan, 1987) addresses anxiety and PTSD via stimulating particular meridians of the body to produce chemicals that help restore the body and brain to their pre-trauma levels of functioning. While research is inconclusive on EMDR and TIR, it appears that each of these brief interventions are appropriate for rape victims. Caution should be used, however, in that EMDR (Shapiro, 1989) and TIR (Gerbode, 1989) be used only on verbal adults who are stable enough to focus on a troubling event for a sustained period of time.

LEVEL 5: SERIOUS MENTAL ILLNESS

Case Example

Nona (age 43) was an artist from a "well-to-do" family. She and her husband Rick had two little girls, ages 10 and 12. Never having found a career that suited him, Rick repeatedly borrowed money from Nona's father. Over the years, Rick grew ashamed and more frantic about his failure to support his family. His alcohol consumption increased.

One night when the children were at their grandparents' home, Nona came home to find Rick intoxicated, depressed, and acting out. Rick took a pistol from the drawer, placed it to Nona's head, and then to his own. In his rage, he stormed around the house making threats. At one point, he placed the gun in his mouth, walked toward Nona, and tripped on the coffee table. The gun fired, killing Rick.

Shortly after Rick's death, Nona entered therapy and was given an antidepressant. She felt depressed, lethargic, afraid to leave the home, unable to continue painting, and was nauseated at the thought of food. Nona began losing weight. Nona also began hallucinating, sure that she had a penis and that others could see it. Nona avoided going to the bathroom and undressing. An initial psychosocial history revealed no childhood incidents of abuse.

After 2 months of psychotherapy, Nona began to see "visions." The visions pertained to hands grabbing her as she urinated. Intense visualization techniques elicited more details. In time (without the therapist making reference to abuse), Nona realized that she was the victim of severe childhood sexual abuse. One memory revealed that her father had had coitus with the family dog, and then turned to Nona, demanding that she perform oral sex on him.

This crisis reflects serious mental illness as evidenced by Nona's depression and hallucinations. Her husband's violent death precipitated the crisis, but the preexisting abuse by her father was instrumental in her presenting symptoms. Her state was such that she was significantly impaired. Her usual coping mechanism had failed her.

Other examples of serious mental illness are psychosis, dementia, bipolar disorder, and schizophrenia. Seriously mentally ill patients experience disorganized thinking and behavior. The etiology of their symptoms is neurobiological in nature (Burgess & Roberts, 1995).

Research

The example of Nona is more complicated than the case scenarios that preceded it. Contained herein is a victim of domestic violence, a witness of an accidental suicide, and a victim of grotesque sexual abuse by her father. That Nona had suppressed the memory is not unusual. As a child, Nona had been the victim of "inescapable stress," that which results from being overpowered, helpless, and out of control (Waites, 1993). Memory loss is one form of symptom resulting from inescapable stress, and unfortunately can lead to accusations of being a malingerer. Identity confusion and lower self-esteem are concomitant with memory loss.

The symptoms of inescapable shock can present themselves in somatization, physical illness, substance abuse, and/or revictimization (Waites, 1993). The specific effects of inescapable shock affect the following domains: learning and memory; addiction, immunity, and stress tolerance; identity formation and personality integration; and fantasy.

Intervention

Severe mental illness usually require long-term treatment. One traditional intervention is pharmaceutical medications. Empirical research is insufficient to prove that any particular psychotherapeutic, nonpharmacological intervention is more effective in the treatment of hallucinations and depression than pharmacology alone. However, many believe that psychotherapy enhances treatment progress. Since pharmacology is beyond the scope of this chapter, the research referenced will pertain to psychotherapeutic interventions that address severe abuse, memory work, and self-concepts.

As in other case examples, the author presumes a treatment foundation of safety. Of central concern in Nona's case is her weight loss. Monitoring the weight loss and conferring with a nutritionist as well as an anorexia specialist is appropriate. A thorough history should be taken to see the multifaceted dimensions of the client's life. Family members should be brought in for collaboration and triangulation of data. Consents should be obtained to release information from other treatment providers. And, when possible, the case should be reviewed in the context of a treatment team. Once data is gathered, support systems are in place, specialists have been apprised of the case, and the threat of imminent danger is gone, one may proceed to address root causes of distress.

Treatment will have to accommodate individual coping responses (Lazarus & Folkman,1984). Coping responses of victims of severe trauma vary. Variables identified by Everstine and Everstine (1993) that mediate the coping response are: whether the event altered one's vocation or role in life; whether the event occurred in what was considered a safe and nurturing place; whether surviving the incident was a source of pride or humiliation; and, whether the victim had a previous trauma or psychological condition that heightened the effect of the current trauma. Resick (1988) noted that a history of incest, substance abuse, and personality disorders also complicate one's response to rape.

Since memory enhances one's sense of personal control (Waites, 1993), memory work may be called for in Nona's case. Recovery comes more slowly for incest victims who lose their memory (Maltz, 1987; Waites, 1993). The interventions that aid in memory restoration are similar to and encompass the brief trauma techniques mentioned in Level 5.

LEVEL 6: PSYCHIATRIC EMERGENCIES

Case Example

Mrs. Richards, age 32, had been blind since birth. She married a partially blind man. Within 2 years of their marriage, Mr. Richards began choking Mrs. Richards until she turned blue. Feeling depressed, Mrs. Richards sought counseling. She told the counselor that she felt desperate to leave Mr. Richards, but was also afraid to leave him, knowing that she depended on him for assistance in daily life skills.

One day, Mrs. Richards frantically phoned the counselor. She reported that she wanted to kill herself . . . that she had just learned that Mr. Richards was having an "e-mail affair." Her counselor immediately arranged to see Mrs. Richards. The counselor assessed the lethality of the suicide threat and determined that Mrs. Richards was not in imminent danger of harming herself. The counselor then arranged for both Mr. and Mrs. Richards to come to conjoint therapy.

Before the scheduled appointment, the counselor received a phone call informing her that Mrs. Richards had thrown herself from a moving automobile. The driver of the car stopped and called the police, who then transported Mrs. Richards to the hospital.

Research

Psychiatric emergencies involve situations in which the patient is a danger to herself or to others. Clearly Mrs. Richards was a danger to herself. Her judgment was impaired, and she was unable to exert control over feelings of betrayal and helplessness. Other examples of psychiatric emergencies include rape, homicide, drug overdose, and personal assault. Irrationality, rage, anxiety, and disorientation are symptoms that indicate the need for immediate intervention. Burgess and Roberts (1995) write that drug overdoses and suicide attempts reveal self-abusive behavior, while acts of aggression manifest a need for dominance and control. The case of Mrs. Richards involved self-abusive behavior. Therefore, the research presented here pertains to self-injurious behavior.

Self-injurious behavior has been explained by two variables: learned helplessness, and escapable and inescapable shock (Waites, 1993). Mice who were previously defeated, for example, take a posture of defeat even before being attacked again. It is speculated that people who injure themselves have previously been abused by another human being; the experience of abuse was out of their control. Being in control raises one's self-appraisal; being out of control lessens the same. Therefore, victims of abuse may choose to injure themselves to exert a level of control.

Waites (1993) postulated that the desirability of escapable shock (e.g., slashing one's arms with a razor blade) over inescapable shock (e.g., incestuous molestation) could explain why traumatized individuals exhibit self-injurious behaviors. Those who harm themselves are replacing inescapable pain with escapable, controllable pain. In animals as well as humans, whether the traumatic event was escapable is a major predictor of the ultimate effect of the trauma on the victim (Waites, 1993).

Intervention

Psychiatric emergencies vary in nature, but each emergency has an element of out-of-control behavior. The first intervening step of the clinician is that of inquiry. The clinician should find out the location of the patient, what the patient has done, and who else is present. In the case of a suicide attempt, the clinician has to assess the lethality of the act. Published lethality scales can serve as an aid (Burgess & Roberts, 1995). Where medical or biological danger exists *or* where there is insufficient data for that determination, emergency medical attention is mandated. Naturally, police and rescue squads should handle immediately dangerous situations, providing rapid transportation to the hospital.

Confounding factors in psychiatric emergencies are multiple. The clinician may not be able to accurately assess the patient's condition due to incomplete or conflicting information. Disruptive behavior by the patient also makes psychiatric emergencies perhaps the most difficult of the crises to manage. Combatting these obstacles requires effective communication between therapists and other crisis care providers, as well as the ability to work calmly and effectively in a highly charged situation. After the patient is stabilized, the clinician should be careful to arrange for follow-up services to insure continuity of treatment (Burgess & Roberts, 1995).

LEVEL 7: CATASTROPHIC AND/OR CUMULATIVE CRISIS

Case Example

Susie (24), the fifth child in a family of 10, was reared on a farm. She was raped by her older brother (19) and his friends when she was

12. At age 15, her father committed suicide by hanging himself from a rafter in the barn. When Susie was 16, her widowed mother arranged for her to marry a 35-year-old man who beat Susie whenever he was intoxicated. The beatings grew more severe once her husband learned that Susie was infertile. Susie, too, felt distraught over the news, for she had hoped that a child would distract her from her dismal life and decrease the severity of the beatings. Susie became depressed; she ceased performing her ritual house-cleaning and cooking, and she rarely left the house.

Concerned about not having seen Susie for a protracted period of time, Susie's neighbor came to the house to see if there was a problem. Finding the door ajar, the neighbor entered and discovered Susie sitting in a corner, disheveled and stuporous. Susie was covered in lacerations. The neighbor drove Susie to the hospital where the staff learned that Susie was a victim of woman-battering. The staff found safe temporary housing for Susie, treated her depression with medications, and discharged her.

Three months later, the hospital received a phone call from the resident manager at the temporary shelter. The manager reported that Susie had slashed her wrists and was catatonic. Immediately, Susie was hospitalized. After some time, Susie told a staff member why she had slashed her wrists: Susie had attended a Thanksgiving family reunion where Uncle Rob, Susie's father's brother, approached her and told her that she was the cause of her own father's suicide.

Level 7 is a complicated level of crisis. It "can occur in the aftermath of multiple traumatic crises and/or cumulative crises that were not resolved" (Burgess & Roberts, 1995, p. 45). Level 7 crises involve crises from levels 4, 5, and 6. For example, in Susie's family, there were multiple family crises (Level 4) (her rape, her father's suicide, her arranged marriage, and her uncle's accusation). Furthermore, Susie's prolonged depression hints of serious mental illness, a Level 5 crisis. Finally, Susie's attempted suicide constituted a psychiatric emergency, a Level 6 crisis. The preceding summary does not take into account the incompleted developmental tasks that must have happened in a family wrought with traumatic events such as Susie's. In other words, a Level 7 patient experiences trauma upon trauma. Treatment of Level 7 patients will require experienced practitioners who are familiar with crisis intervention, assessment, team work, and trauma work.

Interventions will vary according the level of the crisis. Sometimes a crisis will resolve itself in a relatively short period of time. Other times, there is eminent danger associated with the crisis, and treatment is complex and lengthy (Burgess & Roberts, 1996).

Applying the Stress-Crisis Continuum (Burgess & Roberts, 1995) to victims of women-battering and classifying the victim into one of the levels of the continuum requires knowledge of the following: domestic violence; the continuum; the victim's past; and the victim's perceptions about her life events. Victims are grouped into levels according to the nature, duration, and intensity of the stressful event(s), as well as their perception of the life events (Burgess & Roberts, 1995). It is, therefore, crucial that practitioners access accurate information and respectfully listen to the victim.

To assure that the appropriate treatment is administered, it is important that practitioners continue making careful notes of client histories, previous treatments, and their results. Specificity and replication will call forth the most efficient treatments that will serve both battering victims and managed care.

REFERENCES

American Bar Association. (1994). *The impact of domestic violence on children.* Chicago: Author.

American Heritage Concise Dictionary (3rd ed.). (1994). Boston: Houghton Mifflin Company.

American Psychiatric Association. (1994). *Diagnostic and statistical manual of mental disorders* (4th ed.). Washington, DC: Author.

Baldwin, B. A. (1978). A paradigm for the classification of emotional crises: Implications for crisis intervention. *American Journal of Orthopsychiatry, 48,* 538–551.

Barsky, A. (1981). Hidden reasons some patients visit doctors. *Annals of Internal Medicine, 94,* 492.

Bowie, S. I., Silverman, D. C., Kalick, S. M., & Edbril, S. D. (1990). Blitz rape and confidence rape: Implications for clinical intervention. *American Journal of Psychotherapy, 44,* 180–188.

Burgess, A. W., & Holmstrom, L. L. (1974). *Rape: Victims of crisis.* Bowie, MD: Robert J. Bradley.

Burgess, A. W., & Roberts, A. R. (1995). Levels of stress and crisis precipitants: The stress-crisis continuum. *Crisis Intervention and Time-Limited Treatment, 2*(1), 31–47.

Calahan, R. (1987). *Successful treatment of phobia and anxiety by telephone and radio.* Unpublished manuscript.

Carlson, B. E. (1996). Children of battered women: Research, programs, and services. In A. Roberts (Ed.), *Helping battered women: New perspectives and remedies* (pp. 172–187). New York: Oxford University Press.

Corsilles, A. (1994). Note: No-drop policies in the prosecution of domestic violence cases: Guaranteed to action or dangerous solution. *Fordham Law Review, 63,* 853–881.

Council on Scientific Affairs, American Medical Association. (1992). Editorial. *Journal of the American Medical Association, 267,* 3184–89.

Dansky, B. S., Roth, S., & Kronenberger, A. G. (1990). The trauma constellation identification scale: A measure of the psychological impact of a stress life event. *Journal of Traumatic Stress, 3,* 557–572.

Dziegielewski, S. F., Resnick, C., & Krause, N. B. (1996). Shelter-based crisis intervention with battered women. In A. Roberts (Ed.), *Helping battered women: New perspectives and remedies* (pp. 159–171). New York: Oxford University Press.

Everstine, D., & Everstine, L. (1993). *The trauma response: Treatment for emotional injury.* New York: W. W. Norton.

Figley, C. (1989). *Treating stress in families.* New York: Brunner/Mazel.

Foa, E., Rothbaum, B., Riggs, D., & Murdock, T. (1991). Treatment of posttraumatic stress disorder in rape victims: A comparison between cognitive-behavioral procedures and counseling. *Journal of Consulting and Clinical Psychology, 59,* 715–723.

Foa, E., Rothbaum, B., & Steketee, G. (1993). Treatment of rape victims. *Journal of Interpersonal Violence, 8,* 256–276.

French, G. D., & Gerbode, F. A. (1993). *The Traumatic Incident Reduction Workshop* (2nd ed.). Menlo Park, CA: IRM.

Gerbode, F. (1989). *Beyond psychology: An introduction to metapsychology.* Palo Alto, CA: IRM.

Gerbode, F., & Moore, R. (1994). Beliefs and intentions in RET. *Journal of Ration-Emotive & Cognitive-Behavior Therapy, 12,* 27–45.

Girelli, A. A., Resick, P. A., Mashoefer-Dvorak, S., & Hutter, K. (1986). Subjective distress and violence during rape: Their effects on long-term fear. *Victim Violence, 1,* 35–46.

Hansen, M., & Harway, M. (Eds.). (1993). *Battering and family therapy.* Newbury Park, CA: Sage.

Harway, M., & Hansen, M. (1994). *Spouse abuse: Assessing and treating battered women, batterers and their children.* Sarasota, FL: Professional Resource Exchange Monographs.

Janoff-Bulman, B. (1992). *Shattered assumptions.* New York: Free Press.

Kilpatrick, G., Veronen, A., & Best, G. (1988). *The psychological impact of crime: A study of randomly surveyed crime victims.* Charleston, SC: Crime Victims Research and Treatment Center, University of South Carolina.

Koss, M. P. (1987). *The rape victim: Clinical and community approaches to treatment.* Lexington, MA: Greene.

Koss, M., & Burkhart, B. (1989). A conceptual analysis of rape victimization: Long-term effects and implications for treatment. *Psychology of Women Quarterly, 13,* 27–40.

Lazarus, R. S., & Folkman, S. (1984). *Stress, appraisal, and coping.* New York: Springer Publishing Company.

Lewin, T. (June 22, 1997). Seeking a public health solution for a problem that starts at home. *New York Times,* Section 14, p. 19.

Malmquist, C. (1986). Children who witness parental murder: Posttraumatic aspects. *Journal of the American Academy of Child Psychiatry, 25,* 320–325.

Maltz, W. (1987). *Incest and sexuality: A guide to understanding and healing.* Lexington, MA: Lexington Books.

Mechanic, D. (1994). Integrating mental health into a general health care system. *Hospital and Community Psychiatry, 45,* 893–897.

(Miranda & Munoz, 1994 in Roberts, 1996, p. 35)

Moore, R. H. (1993). Cognitive-emotive treatment of the posttraumatic stress disorder. In W. Dryden & L. Hill (Eds.), *Innovations in rational-emotive therapy* (pp. 176–195). Newbury Park, CA: Sage.

Moscarello, R. (1991). Posttraumatic stress disorder after sexual assault: Its psychodynamics and treatment. *Journal of the American Academy of Psychoanalysis, 19,* 235–253.

National Crime Survey. (1981). *National Sample, 1973–1979.* Ann Arbor, MI: Inter-University Consortium on Political and Social Research, University of Michigan.

Nurius, P., Hilfrink, M., & Rifino, R. (1996). The single greatest health threat to women: Their partners. In P. Raffoul & C. A. McNeece (Eds.), *Future issues in social work practice.* Boston: Allyn & Bacon.

Petretic-Jackson, P. A., & Jackson, T. (1996). Mental health interventions with battered women. In A. Roberts (Ed.), *Helping battered women: New perspectives and remedies* (pp. 188–221). New York: Oxford University Press.

Raimy, V. (1975). *Misunderstandings of the self.* San Francisco: Jossey-Bass.

Resick, P. (1983). The rape reaction: Research findings and implications for intervention. *The Behavior Therapist, 6,* 129–132.

Resick, P., Jordan, C., Girelli, S., Hutter, C., & Marhoefer-Divorak, S. (1988). A comparative outcome study of behavioral group therapy for sexual assault victims. *Behavior Therapy, 19,* 385–401.

Resick, P., & Schnicke, M. (1992). Cognitive processing therapy for sexual assault victims. *Journal of Clinical Psychology, 60,* 748–756.

Resnick, H. S., Kilpatrick, D. G., & Lipovsky, J. A. (1991). Assessment of rape-related posttraumatic stress disorder: Stressor and symptom dimensions. *Psychological Assessment: A Journal of Consulting and Clinical Psychology, 3,* 561–572.

Roberts, A. (1996a). *Helping battered women: New perspectives and remedies.* New York: Oxford University Press.

Roberts, A. (1996b). Introduction: Myths and realities regarding battered women. In A. Roberts (Ed.), *Helping battered women: New perspectives and remedies* (pp. 3–30). New York: Oxford University Press.

Roberts, A., & Roberts, B. (1990). A comprehensive model for crisis intervention with battered women and their children. In A. Roberts (Ed.), *Crisis intervention handbook: Assessment* (pp. 105–123). Belmont, CA: Wadsworth.

Roth, S., Dye, E., & Lebowitz, L. (1988). Group therapy for sexual-assault victims. *Psychotherapy, 25,* 82–95.

Roth, S., & Newman, E. (1991). The process of coping with sexual trauma. *Journal of Traumatic Stress, 4,* 279–297.

Rothbaum, B. O., Dancu, C., Riggs, D. S., & Foa, E. (1990, September). *The PTSD Symptom Scale.* Paper presented at the European Association of Behavior Therapy Annual Conference, Paris, France.

Rothbaum, B., Foa, E., Riggs, D., Murdock, T., & Walsh, W. (1992). A prospective examination of post-traumatic stress disorder in rape victims. *Journal of Traumatic Stress, 5,* 455–475.

Schecter, S. (1982). *Women and male violence: The visions and struggles of the battered women's movement.* Boston: South End Press.

Shapiro, F. (1989). Efficacy of the eye movement desensitization procedure in the treatment of traumatic memories. *Journal of Traumatic Stress, 2,* 199–223.

Straton, D. (1990). Catharsis reconsidered. *Australian and New Zealand Journal of Psychiatry, 24,* 543–551.

Valentine, P. (1995). Traumatic incident reduction: A review of a new intervention. *Journal of Family Psychotherapy, 6*(2), 73–78.

Valentine, P. (1997). Traumatic incident reduction: Brief treatment of trauma-related symptoms in incarcerated females. *Dissertation Abstracts International, 54*(01), 534B, University Microfilms No. AAD93-15947.

Valentine, P. V., & Smith, T. E. (in press). A qualitative study of client perceptions of Traumatic Incident Reduction (TIR): A brief trauma treatment. *Crisis Intervention and Time-limited Treatment, 4*(1).

van der Kolk, B. (1987). *Psychological trauma.* Washington, DC: American Psychiatric Press.

van der Kolk, B., Blitz, R., Burr, W., Sherry, S., & Hartmann, E. (1984). Nightmares and trauma: A comparison of nightmares after combat with lifelong nightmares in veterans. *American Journal of Psychiatry, 141,* 187–190.

Waites, E. A. (1993). *Trauma and survival: Post-traumatic and dissociative disorders in women.* New York: W. W. Norton.

Waldinger, R. J. (1990). *Psychiatry for medical students* (2nd ed.). Washington, DC: American Psychiatric Press.

Wodarski, J. (1987). An examination of spouse abuse: Practice issues for the profession. *Clinical Social Work Journal, 15,* 172–179.

CHAPTER 3

The Organizational Structure and Function of Shelters for Battered Women and Their Children: A National Survey

Albert R. Roberts

SCOPE OF THE PROBLEM

The battering of women is one of the most prevalent and dangerous social problems in the United States today. Recent estimates indicate that between 4 and 8.7 million women are victimized by partner abuse in their own homes annually (Roberts, 1996a). Some of these women are assaulted by being smacked or punched once or twice, whereas others are attacked with increasing frequency and escalating intensity over months and years. Every week, in different parts of the United States, there are several shocking reports of a woman murdered by her husband, ex-husband, or ex-boyfriend. Unfortunately, these homicides are not rare. Every year, approximately 2,000 women are killed by spouses, ex-spouses or boyfriends. Approximately 750 chronically battered women have killed their partners as a result of posttraumatic stress disorder (PTSD), explicit death threats, and/or recurring nightmares or intrusive thoughts of their own death at the hands of the batterer (Roberts, 1996b). In addition, their children are often the targets of the batterer. If the children are not victims themselves, they are traumatized by witnessing the battering of their mothers.

As a result of being chronically abused, many battered women suffer from bipolar disorder, depression, anxiety, PTSD, panic disorder, and/or suicidal ideation (Cascardi & O'Leary, 1992; Kemp, Rawlings, & Green, 1991; Walker, 1985). Four separate studies of women living in shelters or attending support groups, yielded PTSD rates ranging from a low of 45% to a high of 84% (Astin, Lawrence, Pincus, & Foy, 1990; Houskamp & Foy, 1991; Roberts, 1996a; Saunders, 1994). Other studies have consistently found a high incidence of somatic problems and depressive symptomatology among battered women (Cascardi & O'Leary, 1992).

In response to the pressing needs of abused women, the first crisis intervention units and emergency shelters were established in the 1970s. There has also been a major effort to train police officers, usually the first "crisis workers" to address the problem, in the strategies necessary to reduce both immediate and long-term costs to the women and their children while simultaneously securing the crime scene (Roberts, 1996a).

As a consequence of the increased awareness of the chronic nature of battering relationships, short-term shelters for women who have been the target of violence and their children have grown in numbers and the scope of services in the past 20 years. For example, in 1975, there were only a half dozen emergency shelters, but by 1995, there were 1,250 such facilities throughout the United States. During the late 1970s, the primary services available for battered women were 24-hour telephone hotlines and emergency housing and food lasting from 1 to 8 weeks. Once a woman was ready to leave the shelter, she was usually given referrals to welfare and/or legal advocacy depending on her individual needs but little else (Roberts, 1981 and 1995). By the 1990s, many shelters had begun to provide counseling, vocational training, and job placement for the women and counseling for the children. Transitional second-stage housing is also offered on a limited basis at some shelters. Shelter staffing has changed from the original grassroots movement of paraprofessionals and former battered women to the utilization of trained professionals, many of whom have bachelor's and/or master's degrees (Roche & Sadoski, 1996).

In the State of New Jersey, the services for survivors of sexual assault and battering have maintained the 24-hour hotlines, crisis intervention centers and shelters, while adding group and individual counseling for survivors and "prosurvivors" (adults and adolescents), and companionship at the hospital, in court, and with the police. Statewide coalitions and task forces such as the New Jersey Coalition on Battered Women lobby for new legislation to protect the rights of battered women, distribute booklets and brochures and conduct community education programs at middle schools, high schools, and colleges. They also offer in-service education and training for police officers and other professionals. These services are frequently available in Spanish. All these programs, however, may be threatened by severe governmental budget cuts and decreasing levels of charitable support. Many of the women who once would have been able to volunteer their time may now be working, thus increasing the financial constraints on services.

CONTROVERSIAL ISSUE: SECRECY OF SHELTER LOCATIONS VS. PUBLIC DISCLOSURE OF THEIR LOCATIONS

A newly emerging and controversial issue relates to the decision of a small but growing number of shelters to publicize their location. From the inception of the shelter movement in the mid-1970s, the shelter locations were always kept secret from the public because of the fear that an enraged batterer who knew where his wife was staying would storm the facility, injuring his family and any bystanders who happened to get in his way. The first national survey of shelters for battered women found that secrecy of the shelter's location was of paramount importance (Roberts, 1981). For the first 20 years in the shelter movement, the wisdom of this approach was unquestioned.

The shelter directors who have recently decided to go public with their location have done so for a variety of reasons, including the following: (a) to help the local battered women know where to go for assistance, (b) to help the community-at-large become more aware of the extent of the problem of domestic violence, (c) to increase their fund-raising capability and to develop improved inter-actions with the police and other public officials through increased public awareness of the extent of domestic violence, and (d) to promote the message to the entire community that the abused women should not have to seek services in a hidden location because they have done nothing wrong (Belluck, 1997).

In July 1997 a horrific act of violence was committed against a female employee of the St. Jude House shelter in Crown Point, Indiana. The shelter employee was brutalized and raped by a batterer whose wife was seeking refuge at St. Jude House. The shelter had decided to publicize its location, going so far as to install a bright-green sign that identified it as a shelter for battered women. The local police chief informed reporters that the perpetrator had told the victim, "If I can't get to my wife, you'll do" (Belluck, 1997, p. 1).

Those shelters that have chosen to publicize their whereabouts do insist that careful precautions need to be taken, because they are fully cognizant of the potential for retaliation from the batterer when the location is known. The most important feature is installation of a state-of-the art security system. However, even the most sophisticated security system cannot guarantee the safety of everyone who is con-nected to the shelter. For example, the St. Jude shelter in Indiana, mentioned previously, which was the site of a brutal attack on a staff person, had been outfitted with a system that cost $50,000, consisting of "bullet-proof glass, security cameras, a 'safe room' where women can be hidden in case of emergency and several fire-proofed walls to keep women and children safe from firebombs" (Belluck, 1997, p. 20).

It appears that the majority of shelters adhere to the original philosophy that the best method of providing for the battered wom-en's safety is by insisting that the shelter's location remain a secret. Shelter directors who insist on maintaining the secrecy of their loca-tion view the publicizing of shelter addresses as a naive and foolish attempt to strive for a philosophical goal while putting the victimized women and children at risk of additional violent attacks. Some shelters view the secrecy of their location as so essential to the women's safety that they move periodically, as soon as the staff determine that too many people know the address, because of the fear that a batterer will be able to track down and harm his wife.

In view of the dangers posed by violent batterers, the author recommends that all shelters remain secretive about their location, unless they are next to or attached to the local police department building. The life-threatening risks and intense fears of battered women entering or leaving a shelter are very real, particularly when the batterer has access to handguns or rifles. Roberts (1996b) in his New Jersey study of 210 battered women provides vivid case illustrations of the types of terroristic and explicit death threats battered women experienced, which led to repeated nightmares, flashbacks, hyperarousal, intrusive thoughts about the violent battering incidents, PTSD, and homicide. For the most part, battered women going to shelters go there as a last resort. They have tried hiding out at friends or relatives homes, and the batterer has found them. Some batterers are habitually abusive toward their partners, and have a borderline or antisocial personality disorder. These types of batterers, suffering from Axis I or Axis II psychiatric disorders (American Psychiatric Association, 1994), frequently are obsessed with finding their female partner and teaching her a lesson (e.g., more severe abuse and injuries, and/or murder).

BRIEF HISTORY OF THE FUNDING OF SHELTERS

During the past 15 years the sources and amounts of grant funds received by shelters for battered women has improved dramatically. In the late 1970s, many of the 89 shelters included in Roberts' (1981) first national survey reported that they were trying to survive on shoestring budgets. Today, in the mid-1990s, millions of dollars are being allocated to fund large shelters, particularly in Florida, Maryland, Missouri, Minnesota, New York, Pennsylvania, and Texas. The early shelters were usually staffed by volunteers, student interns, and CETA (Federal Comprehensive Employment and Training Act) workers. Sixty-five percent of the early shelters were staffed by CETA workers—economically disadvantaged, unemployed, or underemployed citizens. Slightly less than one third or 29 of the shelters had a full-time professional social worker on staff. The shelters of the past relied heavily on paraprofessionals, volunteers, and formerly battered women.

By the mid-1990s the funding and professional staffing of shelters has made significant progress. During the decade of the 1980s many states passed statewide domestic violence legislation with appropriations of several million dollars to go to shelters earmarked from penalty assessments, marriage license or divorce surcharges, and fines on criminal offenders.

The fervent advocacy and lobbying efforts of statewide victim rights coalitions and women's groups led to important legislative reforms. State and county funding was bolstered considerably by the federal VOCA (the Victims of Crime Act) funds, which gave priority state block grant funding to states that were responsive to both domestic violence and sexual assault victims. By November 1995 payments to the Federal Crime Victims Fund by criminal offenders had passed the $1 billion mark. Half of these funds—$557 million had been given to the states for battered women's shelters, rape crisis programs, and child abuse treatment programs.

As a result of the increased funding for shelters, the predominant staffing pattern for shelters in the 1990s is 6–10 full-time professional staff, several part-time staff, and volunteers. Sixty-six or 37.5% of the shelter directors have master's degrees. In sharp contrast only three directors have 2-year associate degrees, and six have no degrees. Therefore, 167 or 94.8% of the shelter directors have at least a bachelor's degree.

METHODOLOGY

A nationwide organizational study of 176 shelters for battered women was conducted to determine the staffing patterns, funding sources, caseloads, functions and services provided, and self-reported strengths and weaknesses of the shelters. The study sample was derived from a 20% (250) sample of the 1,250 battered women's shelters listed in the National Organization for Victim Assistance (NOVA) directory and the Office for Victims of the U.S. Department of Justice mailing list. A four-page questionnaire was developed, pretested (with three administrators of shelters), revised, and mailed with a cover letter to 250 programs in early January 1994. One month after the initial mailing, a follow-up letter and another copy of the questionnaire were sent to the nonrespondents. By April 1994, the author had received 176 completed questionnaires from 37 different states—a 70% response rate.

The respondents represent a cross-section of shelters in urban, suburban, and rural areas throughout the United States. This chapter summarizes the quantitative and qualitative data on program objectives, types of services offered, staffing patterns, funding sources, approximate number of clients served by each program in 1993, underserved victim groups, self-reported strengths and weaknesses of the program, and significant changes made in the past 2 years.

A four-page questionnaire was distributed by mail to 250 shelters. The questions focused on organizational structure, services delivered, sources of funding, and the self-reported perceptions of strengths and weaknesses of each program. Staffing patterns (e.g., educational level and numbers of full-time employees) were also tapped.

Findings

The respondents were from all parts of the United States and represented a wide geographic distribution. There were respondents from 37 states, representing all major regions of the United States. Those states with the largest number of responding programs were Minnesota (12), Texas (11), North Carolina (11), Missouri (8), Pennsylvania (9), California (8), Washington (8), and Montana (8). The following states were underrepresented, having no respondents— Arkansas, Connecticut, Colorado, Delaware, District of Columbia, Georgia, Hawaii, Kentucky, Illinois, Indiana, Louisiana, Michigan, and South Carolina. The most representative regions were Region V—the Great Lakes states, with 26 shelters responding; Region VII— the wheatbelt, with 22 respondents; and Region III, the mid-Atlantic states, with 22 shelters responding (see Table 3.1).

With regard to demographics, the battered women shelters were distributed across jurisdictions that varied considerably in total popu-

TABLE 3.1 Regional Representation of Battered Women Shelters[a]

Region I		Region II	
Connecticut	0	New Jersey	5
Maine	2	New York	5
Massachusetts	3	Total	10
New Hampshire	2		
Rhode Island	1		
Vermont	4		
Total	12		
Region III		Region IV	
Delaware	0	Alabama	1
District of Columbia	0	Florida	1
Maryland	7	Georgia	0
Pennsylvania	9	Kentucky	0
Virginia	5	Mississippi	2
West Virginia	1	North Carolina	11
Total	22	South Carolina	0
		Tennessee	3
		Total	18
Region V		Region VI	
Illinois	0	Arkansas	0
Indiana	0	Louisiana	0
Michigan	0	New Mexico	1
Minnesota	12	Oklahoma	4
Ohio	5	Texas	11
Wisconsin	9	Total	16
Total	26		
Region VII		Region VIII	
Iowa	7	Colorado	0
Kansas	1	Montana	8
Missouri	8	North Dakota	3
Nebraska	6	South Dakota	7
Total	22	Utah	1
		Wyoming	1
		Total	20
Region IX		Region X	
Arizona	4	Alaska	1
California	8	Idaho	2
Hawaii	0	Oregon	5
Nevada	2	Washington	8
Total	14	Total	16

[a]Total respondents = 176.

lation. The six largest areas in terms of population were New York City (7.4 million residents); Dallas, TX (1,008,000); Phoenix, AZ (983,000 residents); Baltimore, MD (736,000); Memphis, TN (610,000) and Seattle, WA (516,000). The six smallest areas in terms of population were as follows:

Clarksville, OH (485 residents)
Eagle Butte, SD (489 residents)
Upper Marlboro, MD (745 residents)
Harlem, MT (882 residents)
Rocky Mountain, VA (1,051 residents)
Grand Marais, MN (1,107 residents)

Budget Totals

The size of the 1993 annual budgets for battered women's shelters varied considerably from a low of under $50,000 for 14 shelters to a high of $1 million plus reported by 5 shelters. When comparing the different states as a whole, Maine had the lowest annual budget of $163,000. Missouri had the highest annual budget of $8.56 million. The state with the second highest total annual budget for 11 responding programs was Texas at $4.32 million. The state with the lowest average annual budget was Montana, with an average budget of $45,187. The state with the highest average annual budget was Missouri, with an average annual budget of $1.07 million.

Funding

Of the responding shelters, 92.6% (163) gave specific information on their funding sources and the approximate percentage of their annual budget covered by each source. Many of the shelters had more than one source of funding. The overwhelming majority of the shelters (147 or 90.1%) received state and/or county general-revenue funding. These two funding sources combined accounted for 70%–100% of many of the shelter's budgets in 1993.

Local United Way agencies provided funding to 53 or 32.5% of the shelters. In fact, 25 of the shelters received their primary funding from United Way. Federal funding through VOCA was provided to 44 shelters, Title XX grants were given to 10 shelters, and 9 other shelters received other federal grants (e.g., Housing and Urban Development funding). Finally, a small number of shelters reported that they received small amounts of funding from foundation grants, corporate grants, and fund-raising events.

Utilization of the Shelters' 24-Hour Hotlines

In 1992, there were 213,877 reported calls to the hotlines with an average of 1,495 per shelter. In contrast, 72,789 women were counseled in person for an average of 627 per shelter. In 1993, the number of hotline calls increased to 244,468 (an average of 1,630 per shelter), whereas the number of women counseled in-person rose to 109,362 (average 875). Recent estimates of the number of both hotline and in-person contacts in the years following Nicole Brown Simpson's murder indicate that the number of hotline callers tripled in a number of jurisdictions in 1995.

Self-Reported Strengths

Eighty-nine shelters responded to this query. Most of the shelters emphasized the comprehensiveness of the services provided to the survivors, especially counseling (about 20%). Other assets included children's programs, educational services, crisis intervention, and support groups. Over 14% suggested that their "empowerment" philosophy was one of their major strengths. Additional strengths that might be considered by other agencies included bilingual and bicultural services, the availability of transportation, case management techniques, and both outreach and follow-up services. Over 57% of the shelters who answered this question reported that dedicated and professional counselors were a major strength, whereas over a third (34.2%) considered their equally dedicated and well-trained volunteers to be an asset. Teamwork was also mentioned.

Twenty-eight shelters answered the question on advocacy. Seven (25%) had advocacy programs with six having legal advocacy, four having court advocacy, three having personal support, three using networking, and two having medical advocacy.

Fifteen of the 25 shelters that responded to the question on community involvement reported strong community support; others emphasized their good relations with the community. Only a few emphasized their physical shelter facilities as an advantage. It is possible to infer that some programs could benefit from new or renovated buildings. Some need better locations (see the section on weaknesses that follows).

Among the other strengths infrequently mentioned were "secure funding" (only three facilities), "free services from clinicians" (one) and "long-term work with severely dissociated clients" (one). In sum, most shelters that responded to this question were proud of their comprehensive services, staff, and volunteers.

Underserved Groups

In terms of the underserved victims identified by the respondents, 36 or 20.3% indicated that they provide services to all violent crime victims and that no groups are underserved. An additional 36 or 20.3% reported that they provide hardly any services to the children of battered women. Twelve respondents indicated that they underserve victims from rural areas, 11 respondents do not provide services to elderly battered women, 10 respondents indicated that they do not have the resources and network to provide transitional housing to women leaving their shelter.

Self-Reported Weaknesses

It should come as no surprise, in these times of economic exigency, that underfunding (reportedly 64%), limited resources, and inadequate salaries and benefits were sore points with most agencies. Some of the respondents were also concerned about the strength of their children's programs, their outreach efforts, public awareness, legal/ court advocacy, and the actual treatment program.

Other concerns included understaffing, lack of training and/or formal education, high staff turnover, lack of volunteers, the need for bilingual/bicultural staff, and staff conflict. The respondents were also worried about the inadequate facilities, lack of transitional housing, and the poor location of the shelter. There were complaints about lack of community involvement, poor relations with law-enforcement officers, and problems with the court systems and hospitals. Many of the respondents were very concerned that their geographic areas were underserved and they did not meet the clients' needs or that the area was simply too large to serve.

The overwhelming majority of shelters reported that they received state or county general revenue grants in addition to funding from state penalty assessment funds or marriage license surcharges. The well-established and comprehensive shelters also receive funding from United Way and corporate and private foundations.

If we examine one center in the Midwest with an annual budget of $1,143,842, we can see how complicated the fund-raising process must be. The agency receives $436,678 from the United Way, $323,000 from its state, $157,348 from private sources, $136,310 from fund-raising events, $65,490 from third-party insurance payments, $50,000 from Title XX funds, and $28,000 from VOCA. There are city funds, funds from a child abuse prevention organization, money from The Department of Corrections, and $20,000 from two separate foundations. Bookkeeping must be a nightmare.

Grants from private foundations generally come from community foundations or banks. These foundations are frequently named for the cities, counties, or states where their interests lie. Others are named for well-known public figures or celebrities who have committed themselves to combating domestic violence. For example, the Nancy Reagan Foundation donated $10,000 in 1993 to a shelter for the promotion of a program created to enhance the self-esteem of children who had been exposed to domestic violence. In studying the annual reports of shelters, it is not always easy to identify whether or not the grants were targeted for specific purposes.

Many shelters receive donations of modest amounts from a variety of sources. Although individually each donation may not be considered substantial, the totals can mean the difference among remaining open, severely curtailing services, or, perhaps, closing altogether. The effort to raise some funds can become a full-time occupation.

Budget Allocations

The budgets ranged from lows of under 30,000 to a very few programs with allocations of $1.25 million to $1.5 million. The total budget for all of the programs ($N = 141$) that provided budget information in 1992 was $39,759,424. The total budget for 1993 based on 165 programs was 61.54 million. The mean for 1992 was 281,981, whereas the mean for 1993 was 373,029. The mode was about $250,000.

Changes in Budget Allocations

With 141 shelters responding, 9% of the shelters received a decrease in funding, 65.6% actually received an increase, whereas 5.6% indicated no change at all. Unfortunately, many of the increases were insufficient to cover rising costs.

Self-Reported Staffing Patterns

One hundred seventy-three shelters of the total sample responded to the question concerning the number of full-time employees. The range was from a low of no full-time employees to as few as 5 to a high of over 40. Fifty two percent of the sample (92 shelters) have five or fewer full-time staff. Many, however, supplement the full-time staff with part-timers and volunteers. Twenty-three percent of the sample employ 6–10 full-time workers. Unfortunately, only 18.1% of the shelters had large full-time staffs of 11–20 employees.

The Board of Directors: Structural Components

The importance of boards of directors for domestic violence programs should not be underestimated. Similar to all agency boards, they are charged with the vital function of providing general direction to and control of their organizations, while taking basic responsibility for the operation. More specifically, boards engage in policy and program development, personnel issues, finance, public relations, and accountability for operations (Gelman, 1995).

Legally speaking, these boards are held to the same standards of conduct as those that are applied to the directors of "for-profit" organizations (Collin, 1987; Pasley, 1966; Streett, 1985). Among the basic areas in which charges of negligence may be brought against board members are the following: Failure to manage and supervise the activities of the agency, neglect or waste of agency assets, conflicts of interest or self-benefit, improper delegation of authority, and harm done to third parties through tort or breach of contract actions (Gelman, 1995). Boards of nonprofit agencies have recently faced increasing scrutiny as revelations about organization excess and board misconduct have surfaced. It is clear that members need to exercise high levels of care, skill, diligence, and loyalty, while always acting in the agency's best interest, which means not forgetting the "bottom line." Individuals volunteer to serve on agency boards for a variety of reasons. Motivations vary from a vested personal interest in domestic violence (i.e., being a relative or friend of a victim of domestic violence), to expressions of religious or moral obligation, to quests for prestige and power within their chosen occupations (i.e., a businessman who wants to increase his chances for advancement to vice president in a socially responsible corporation). Former clients of shelters are frequently found on these boards as they provide the greatest awareness and understanding of clients' needs and concerns (Gelman, 1995). No matter what their motivations, board members are required to have strong interpersonal skills and a strong sense of responsibility, as well as the time, the interest, and the willingness to be of service to the agency. In addition, board members are generally expected to help raise money for the agency.

It is difficult to specify an optimum size for the board. Size varies from agency to agency, although each board should ultimately be proportionate to the size of the agency itself. Boards that are too large may impede progress and may even result in a decreased sense of commitment and obligation. There must, however, be a sufficient number of members regularly present at meetings to ensure a fairly equitable division of labor. There must also be the requisite expertise to monitor and evaluate the various elements of the agency operations. Thus, because these boards are entrusted with such vast and diverse responsibilities (for which they are legally liable), it follows that a board with a sufficient number of members who have expertise in a variety of fields is necessary to carry out the shelter's functions effectively. In most cases, the respondents to this survey reported that their boards were primarily composed of a combination of health care and mental health professionals, with some members of the corporate and retail business communities.

To illustrate the typical board composition of domestic violence programs, an analysis of occupations of board members and average board size of 129 such programs is presented in Table 3.2.

The largest representation on shelter boards came from a combination of health care and mental health professionals (252). One-hundred-and-forty-one mental health counselors, social workers and psychologists served on agency boards, whereas 111 physicians, nurses, and other health professionals also served on those boards.

The second largest representation on domestic violence agency boards came from the corporate and retail business community. The most frequent occupation of board members reported by program directors were retirees and concerned community members (160); business men and women (130); attorneys (112); teachers, college professors, and education administrators (107); corporate executives and owners of small business (77); and social workers (61); as well as clergy—ministers, priests, or rabbis (61).

The smallest representation came from former victims (30), journalists and entertainment-industry executives (18), substance-abuse counselors (7), sales personnel (6), and artists (2).

CONCLUSIONS

Although many of the respondents were proud of the comprehensive programs that they offer, it is clear that along with many other important organizations, shelters are suffering from underfunding. The consequences of budgeting shortfalls are staff cuts, decreased training opportunities, elimination of services, and whole geographic areas without adequate coverage. Given the serious nature of domestic violence and its impact not only on the survivors but also on the children who are themselves targets or who witness battering, the limited support of shelters in many states needs to be bolstered. At the same time, the prevention/antivictimization programs offered by many shelters in schools and colleges should be increased. By

TABLE 3.2 Board Composition of Battered Women's Shelters

Profession	Total number	Mean number
Mental health professionals		
Medical doctors	22	.16
Registered nurses	29	.22
Unspecified/others	60	.45
Psychologists	26	.19
Social workers	61	.46
Counselors		
Substance abuse counselors	7	.05
Unspecified/other counselors	47	.35
Education professionals		
College/graduate professors	26	.19
Teachers	55	.41
Administrators	26	.19
Unspecified/other	36	.27
Police/Law-enforcement officers	47	.35
Law		
Attorneys	112	.84
Other law related jobs	29	.22
Corporate		
CEOs/presidents/vice presidents	35	.26
Business unspecified	130	.97
Sales personnel	6	.04
Small business owners	42	.31
CPA/accountants	42	.31
Religious/clergy	61	.45
Media	18	.13
Retired/concerned citizens	160	1.19
Former victims	30	.22
Other[a]	242	1.8
Mean board size	10.45	

[a]Note: "Other" includes artists, blue-collar workers, craftsmen, bank tellers, retail salespersons, etc.

the time a woman reaches a shelter her situation is serious, probably chronic, and difficult to treat. This troubling fact should make prevention efforts and education in the schools and the media a high priority for government and foundation funding.

REFERENCES

American Psychiatric Association. (1994). *Diagnostic and statistical manual of mental disorders* (4th ed.). Washington, DC: American Psychiatric Association Press.

Astin, M. C., Lawrence, K., Pincus, G., & Foy, D. (1990, October). *Moderator variables for PTSD among battered women.* Paper presented at the Convention of the International Society for Traumatic Stress Studies, New Orleans, LA.

Belluck, P. (1997). Shelters for women disclose their locations, in Spite of Risk. *New York Times,* August 10, 1997, pp. 1, 20.

Bureau of Justice Statistics (BJS). (1994). *Criminal victimization in the United States, 1992.* Washington, DC: U.S. Department of Justice, Bureau of Justice Statistics.

Cascardi, M., & O'Leary, K. D. (1992). Depressive symptomatology. Self-esteem, and self-blame in battered women. *Journal of Family Violence, 7,* 249–259.

Collin, R. W. (1987). Toward a new theory of nonprofit liability. *Administration in Social Work, 11,* 15–24.

Gelman, S. R. (1995). Boards of directors. In R. L. Edwards (Ed.), *Encyclopedia of social work* (19th ed., pp. 305–312). Washington, DC: National Association of Social Workers.

Houskamp, B. M., & Foy, D. W. (1991). The assessment of posttraumatic stress disorder in battered women. *Journal of Interpersonal Violence, 6,* 367–375.

Kemp, A., Rawlings, E. I., & Green, B. L. (1991). Post-traumatic stress disorder (PTSD) in battered women: A shelter sample. *Journal of Traumatic Stress, 4,* 137–148.

Pasley, R. S. (1966). Non-profit corporations—accountability of directors and officers. *Business Lawyers, 21,* 621–642.

Pence, E., & Paymar, M. (1993). *Education groups for men who batter: The Duluth model.* New York: Springer Publishing Co.

Pleck, E. (1987). *Domestic tyranny.* New York: Oxford University Press.

Reiss, A. J., Jr., & Roth, J. A. (Eds.). (1993). *Understanding and preventing violence* (Vol. 3, Social influences). Washington, DC: National Academy Press.

Resick, P. A., & Reese, D. (1986). Perception of family social climate and physical aggression in the home. *Journal of Family Violence, 1,* 71–83.

Roberts, A. R. (1981). *Sheltering battered women.* New York: Springer Publishing Co.

Roberts, A. R. (1984). *Battered women and their families: Intervention strategies and treatment programs.* New York: Springer Publishing Co.

Roberts, A. R. (1995). *Crisis intervention and time-limited cognitive treatment.* Thousand Oaks, CA: Sage.

Roberts, A. R. (1996a). Introduction: Myths and realities regarding battered women. In A. R. Roberts (Ed.), *Helping battered women: New perspectives and remedies* (pp. 3–12). New York: Oxford University Press.

Roberts, A. R. (1996b). A comparative analysis of incarcerated battered women and a community sample of battered women. In A. R. Roberts (Ed.), *Helping battered women: New perspectives and remedies* (pp. 31–43). New York: Oxford University Press.

Roche, S. E., & Sadoski, P. J. (1996). Social action for battered women. In A. R. Roberts (Ed.), *Helping battered women: New perspectives and remedies* (pp. 13–30). New York: Oxford University Press.

Saunders, D. G. (1994). Posttraumatic stress symptom profiles of battered women: A comparison of survivors in two settings. *Violence and Victims, 9,* 31–44.

Sherman, L. W. (1992). *Policing domestic violence: Experiments and dilemmas.* New York: Free Press.

Stark, E., & Flitcraft, A. (1982). Medical therapy as repression: The case of the battered woman. *Health and Medicine, 1,* 29–32.

Stark, E., & Flitcraft, A. (1991). Spouse abuse. In M. Rosenberg & M. A. Fenley (Eds.), *Violence in America: A public health approach* (pp. 123–154). New York: Oxford University Press.

Straus, M., & Gelles, R. (1990). *Physical violence in American families.* New Brunswick, NJ: Transaction Books.

Streett, S. C. (1985). Board powers, responsibilities and liabilities. In E. Anthes, I. Cronin, & M. Jackson (Eds.), *The nonprofit board book: Strategies for organizational success* (pp. 9–22). West Memphis, AR: Independent Community Consultants.

Walker, L. A. (1985). Psychological impact of the criminalization of domestic violence on victims. *Victimology: An International Journal, 10*(1–4), 281–300.

Walker, L. A. (1989). *Terrifying love.* New York: Harper & Row.

CHAPTER 4

Conjoint Therapy for the Treatment of Partner Abuse: Indications and Contraindications

Janet A. Geller

Th his chapter is an updated version of a chapter that first appeared in 1984 in the first edition of this volume (Geller & Wasserstrom, 1984). Although the concept of the efficacy of conjoint treatment for partner abuse is much more widely chosen by practitioners than when I first pioneered it in 1977 (Geller & Walsh, 1977–1978), and often is the treatment of choice, there have been changes in my approach, reflecting 13 more years of professional experience with this modality. In this updated chapter I will discuss the changes that have come about through critical application over the years, numerous discussions with my colleagues, teaching, training, and review of the literature. I believe these changes have resulted in a more refined approach to conjoint treatment for helping battered women.

I would like to add that conjoint treatment represents but one method. The treatment model that I have developed, and have written about elsewhere, includes individual treatment with both battered women as well as batterers, group treatment for battered women, group treatment for batterers, and multiple couples groups (Geller, 1992). Although all battered women have battering in common, not all of their needs are the same (Geller, 1992, p. 14). A multimodality approach offers practitioners the opportunity to apply a cadre of techniques and modalities to service a broader range of the needs that battered women present. (For a fuller description of this treatment model, see chapters 1 and 2.) For the purposes of this writing, however, I will focus on the modality of conjoint therapy, with its many caveats. The original chapter first appearing in 1984 will be treated similar to a critiqued process recording, indicating how my thinking has been altered from the time that this chapter was first written. I hope that this approach will prove to be both interesting and informative.

When I first began working with battered women in 1976, the women I saw held traditional values, aspiring to be primary caretakers, with family as the cornerstone of their lives, which was their "gender pride and self-respect" (Goldner, Penn, Steinberg, & Walker, 1990, p. 357). These were not women who needed or wanted to go to shelters for battered women, use legal options against their husbands, or separate and divorce. Simply put, they wanted abuse to cease, but their marriages to remain. There are many women today who still hope for the same dream; as Virginia Satir (1967, p. 1) later stated, the couple "is the axis around which all other family relationships are formed." Often, the most common method for achieving the cessation of abuse has been to see each member of the couple separately: for the woman, either individually or in groups and for the batterer, generally, in group treatment. Although I subscribe to this approach and have both employed and described it myself, another method could be conjoint treatment, which I have successfully used for over 20 years, both alone and with staff whom I have trained.

Researchers have now documented the effectiveness of conjoint treatment (O'Leary, 1996). There are, however, contraindications to using conjoint therapy, as well as certain caveats of which to be aware. Using the case study from the chapter in the first edition, the caveats and contraindications to conjoint therapy will be explicated, as well as the changes I have made in the treatment approach. Following is the story of Tom and Terry, who represented the prototypic case in which this model proved effective.

INTRODUCTION

Teresa called the agency saying she had heard that we work with women whose husbands hit them. She stated that she was really in need of such help. "You see, this is the second time I married a guy like that." Terry's first husband used to hit her when drunk. She had married young and had two small girls. She didn't know what to do. She finally left the marriage and thought she would never marry again. Then along came Tom. She had been single for about 10 years. As things were going well, when he proposed to her, she accepted. She was devastated when he turned out to be a "wife-beater" too. The worker asked Terry what she had done about this the first time and she replied, "Nothing." Terry said, "I didn't know there was anything I could do other than calling the cops." Terry said she never heard of us before, but now that she knows of our existence, she wants help. The worker asked Terry if she thought about her plans with this husband. Did she want a divorce from him too? Terry stated that what she had to say might sound "crazy" but she loves Tom and when he doesn't hit her, he's a very good husband. The worker assured her that this didn't sound crazy to her and that a lot of wives felt as she did. Terry was surprised to hear that and said, "Well, that's a relief. I thought there was something wrong with me." When Terry asked when she could come in, the worker suggested that she bring her husband. Since Terry wanted to stay married, the worker thought it would be better to see him too. Terry told her that Tom would never come. The worker explained that a lot of wives think that, but husbands do come in. Terry told the worker that her husband was Italian and they were very "close-mouthed" about their problems. The worker said that other Italians had come here, and that unless he came for help, the battering would never stop. The worker correlated how our seeing her would stop Tom from hitting her. The worker directly stated that unless she got him to come in, nothing in the marriage would change. The worker asked Terry if she would like him to come for help, to which she replied, "Of course." Then the worker suggested that she find a way to get him in. She asked the worker what she could do. The worker turned the question back to her, stating that she knew her husband better and that Terry could find a way to get him in. When Terry hesitated, the worker suggested they go through all of her options. Together they figured out that her choices were as follows: she could end the marriage; she could come in alone but the violence wouldn't stop; she could get an Order of Protection; or she could convince him to get help for himself. Terry stated that she didn't want to end the marriage, that an Order of Protection was ineffective as she had gotten one before. She did not think Tom would come in with her, and he surely wouldn't go for help himself. Of the options available, she could see that the best one was to come in with him. She stated she thought she did know a way to get him in. The worker could hear the determination in her voice when she said, "I'll threaten him with an Order of Protection. That will get him to come in! After all, what do I have to lose? If things continue as they are, I'll either be dead or divorced." The worker reinforced her statements. She asked Terry to call her back the next day to tell her what happened, to which Terry agreed.

The next day Terry called to tell the worker that it had worked. She said, "I told him either he comes to you people or I go to court." We made an appointment. Just before we hung up Terry said that she didn't really know if this was going to work. She asked the worker, "Do you think he'll change?" The worker suggested that Tom and she come in and they would all find out.

DISCUSSION

At the time that the first edition appeared, there was an insistence on my part on seeing the dyad together for conjoint to be successful. This has since been amended in the following ways.

An assessment must occur regarding: (a) the severity of abuse; (b) whether conjoint is the woman's choice;* and (c) individual

---

*Note. Although in this chapter I will refer to the dyad as husband/wife or man/woman, the population includes all adult partner relationships, heterosexual or same-sex, married or not.

contacts between the worker and clients should be mixed with conjoint. There should also be regular phone calls. Allow me to discuss each of these points below.

Assessing Severity of Abuse

Initially, during the first phone contact, the severity of abuse should be briefly assessed. This can be achieved by asking the woman to describe the worst incidence of abuse, which does not have to be the most recent. Questions expanding and clarifying this incident are asked by the worker. These are critical questions for two reasons. First, conjoint should only be offered when the abuse is mild and possibly moderate which can be determined as defined by the Criminal Justice System (see criminal codes), or by scales measuring levels of abuse, such as Hudson's (1994). If abuse is severe, the element of danger can be great to the woman who makes statements in the conjoint sessions that anger her abuser; therefore, this becomes an essential assessment criterion. Secondly, and in some ways more importantly, there may be a need for immediate intervention if abuse is severe.

Was Conjoint the Woman's Choice?

Women may be coerced into conjoint by their partners. It may not be possible to determine this over the phone; therefore, if conjoint is initially assessed as possible based on the abuse being mild or possibly moderate, the next step is for a more in-depth assessment through an individual session for each partner before conjoint treatment has begun. The couple can be interviewed separately back-to-back or on different days, depending on the needs of the case. In the individual session, each partner is asked to describe the worst incidence of abuse in detail and a standardized test to measure level of abuse is administered, such as the Conflict Tactic Scale (CTS), Hudson's Partner Abuse Scale: Physical (1994), and so on. The remainder of the time can be used as needed, but in addition, the woman is questioned concerning her desire for conjoint.

This is the time to discover whether she genuinely is comfortable and desirous of being seen in this modality. "What if's" are discussed;

for example: "What if he gets angry at something that you say?" "Could that lead to abuse after the session?" It is also determined whether there are certain topics to stay away from. I have even developed code words with women that signal me to withdraw from certain issues because she knows they are not safe. Some women wish to pursue conjoint even with some prohibitions, as just described, but others may not. Under no circumstances should conjoint be offered or advised if the woman does not wish it. Issues of resistance or homeostatis do not apply, as she knows her batterer best, and that is to be honored and respected. While it is true that the batterer most likely will not stop battering unless he receives help, and she is advised of this, there are other options for helping her as delineated in the multimodal model described earlier in chapters 1 & 2. Further, even if the woman is in favor of conjoint, if the worker assesses it as too dangerous, then it is contraindicated. A compromise position is to treat the couple individually until it is safe for conjoint.

The Use of Individual and Conjoint Therapy

Because of the potential for violence in partner-abuse cases, even once conjoint has been assessed as suitable and safe, individual sessions are regularly held to insure that conjoint continues to be indicated, as conditions can rapidly shift with partner-abuse cases. This is also the purpose of the phone calls. Individual sessions mixed with conjoint and phone calls between the worker and woman deviate from traditional systems couples therapy theory, where the worker avoids the potential for coalitions to develop between worker and client and endeavors to remain neutral. Because of the element of violence, it becomes a necessary and an essential safeguard against abuse to deviate in this way. If antitherapeutic coalitions do develop, they are worked through in the sessions.

FIRST SESSION

Terry and Tom arrived on time. They both appeared very nervous. The Abdellas were a very attractive couple. Tom was a broadly built, six-foot tall, dark-haired, bearded man. Terry was small in contrast, about five feet four inches tall, and a Cheryl Tiegs look-a-like. Tom had never been married before. The Abdella household consisted of Tom, Terry, and her two daughters, ages 14 and 16. Tom was a construction worker and Terry a housewife.

Most of the session was spent with Tom and Terry ventilating. Terry talked about how upset she was with Tom's violence, while Tom attempted to defend himself by blaming her for his hitting her; this resulted in her blaming him. When Tom was not defending himself, he was questioning his reasons for being here, saying, "I don't know what I'm doing here. I never thought I'd be in a shrink's office." At one point Tom turned to the worker and said, "This is no use. You're probably on her side anyway."

Before the worker could respond, Tom went on to say that he didn't want to hit her. "I know it's wrong, but she makes me." The worker asked him how. Tom replied, "She just nags and nags." He turned to Terry and said, "if you would just quit your nagging, I wouldn't have to hit you."

Terry's response was to defend herself and then blame him. The only role the worker was able to play in this session was to remain neutral, assuring both parties that she was not on anyone's side. The worker said, "I'm not going to take sides here. This is not a court of law and I'm not interested in finding someone to blame. Anyway, the two of you do that quite well. What I am interested in is finding a way to help the two of you, as I can see that both of you are in pain. Both of you are not happy with things as they are. Maybe we can find a way to make things better for the two of you." The session ended as it began. Another appointment was set for the following week.

DISCUSSION

Treatment begins long before the client enters the office (Haley, 1976). In the waiting room, the worker could sense Tom and Terry's self-consciousness and discomfort. One can guess that were it not for their pressing need, this couple would never think of going for help. For many people, seeking help is alien to their subcultural values and beliefs (Minuchin, 1974). Therefore, care must be taken to facilitate the helping process.

The initial point of entry for the clients is the initial phone call to the agency and then the waiting room. In this agency, the person chosen to greet people as they came in the door was friendly, respectful of others, and warm. Clients were offered tea or coffee to indicate hospitality. The waiting room was attractive, with comfortable chairs and a couch. All of this was deliberately designed to create a therapeutic atmosphere with the intention of relaxing troubled people.

The first session was expected to be used for ventilation with little else occurring. Couples who are violent have little opportunity for arguing in a violence-free atmosphere. At home, the same issues could escalate to violence. Arguing in the therapist's office offers the couple an opportunity to get things off their chests in an environment with safeguards; the therapist can stop them or help modify the atmosphere. Workers who are uncomfortable working with violent couples might tend to suppress anger or prematurely cut off angry expressions. In addition to the safety-valve feature, it is important to permit a free expression of anger so that the worker can first, monitor patterns of arguing in the couple and second, convey to the couple that the worker is accepting and tolerant of their arguing. Contrasted to family therapy practice, the couple are encouraged to talk to the worker, not to each other. This allows the worker to monitor both the batterer's anger level and the woman's discomfort level, and keeps control primarily in the worker's hands.

Beginning sessions are also a time for establishment of a therapeutic environment and rapport. By assuring Tom and Terry that the worker was interested in helping to ease their pain, the worker helped to create the necessary atmosphere in which help could take place. The worker's conscious neutrality was a critical factor in helping both members of the dyad. It is unusual today for men to be ignorant that battering is against the law. Were they assaulting anyone but their wives, they could be charged with assault and battery (New York State Law, 1977). Men not cognizant of the law know that they are causing physical harm. As a result, they are sensitive to blame and often expect to be blamed. Further, the couple's pattern focuses on the issue of blame. If the worker were to continue that pattern, he or she would be joining the system rather than offering something different. If the worker did think the husband was to blame, which is different from being solely responsible for abuse, she or he would not be able to help him. One of the basic tenets of therapeutic practice is freedom from judgments (Minuchin, 1974). Without it, a therapeutic alliance between worker and client is not possible. It is no different with partner abuse.

At the end of the session, the worker points out commonalities between Tom and Terry. Couples who live with violence are in enemy camps. Life is war. They do not cooperate, they are not a team, and there is no mutuality. Whatever opportunity presents itself to pull them together must be capitalized upon. In order for change to take place, there must be healthy bonding. The presentation of mutual goals, feelings, and needs will help create a bond between them which will begin to bridge the gulf that divides them.

THIRD SESSION

By the third session the couple was doing much better. For the first time they could openly express mutual love, caring, and commitment. Tom expressed to both his wife and the worker that if Terry continued to act like this he would never have to hit her again. The worker allowed and encouraged the positive expression of feelings. As far as Tom's statements about the batterings were concerned, she addressed Tom concerning his responsibility for his actions. When he protested, saying his wife nags him so much that it "drives him crazy," the worker asked whether Tom thought that other wives were nagging too. Tom stated that his friends also complained about their nagging wives. The worker wondered if those women got beaten because they nagged. When Tom said he didn't know, he did agree that they may not. The worker then wondered, if some women were hit for nagging and others weren't—was the only response to nagging, hitting? Tom could see the logic in this and had to agree that it was his choice to respond by hitting. The worker also asked whether Tom knew what the law stated concerning assault and battery. Tom did. The worker wondered if the law said that assaulting a person was wrong, did that apply to a wife, too. Tom became very defensive and said that he knew everyone thought he was to blame. The worker reiterated that that was not an important issue for her, but rather, it was important to know how he felt about hitting his wife. Tom stated that he already said he didn't want to hit her. Before he could once again blame Terry, the worker stated that she thought he needed to change this for himself because it clearly wasn't making him feel good.

The worker focused on change for him, not for Terry. Finally Tom said that he would like to stop hitting her and it was true that he felt terrible about this. The worker said that she would be available to help him and asked Terry if she would help too. Terry agreed. The worker attempted to move to a plan for doing this, but Tom said he needed to think things over first. They agreed that this would be the focus of the next session.

DISCUSSION

It is not unusual for people in treatment to experience a flight into health (Framo, 1965). Tom and Terry went into what is commonly called "a honeymoon period." While the worker knew that this was temporary, she capitalized on the positive, as it would lay groundwork for change when a regression occurred. In other words, when things turned for the worse, the worker could remind them of the positive feelings they had experienced as an example of how things could be between them. Further, most therapy time is devoted to the negative. It can be therapeutic to focus on the positive when it occurs. Violent couples are at such extreme odds with one another that emphasis on the positive is healing and continues the bonding response.

The worker used this session to discuss the responsibility for the violence. As things were calm between them and the tone had been set by the worker in previous sessions concerning the purpose of their meetings, it appeared that this controversial issue could now be discussed. It is difficult to discuss emotionally charged issues when people are already feeling emotionally upset, as during crisis. It must be noted and underscored that an unequivocal stance about who is responsible for the violent behavior must be taken. With couples who live with abuse, the wife is often targeted as causing the battering. In actuality, however, the husband externalizes blame, and the most convenient person to blame is, of course, his wife. In his eyes, he does believe that she is at fault. Because of her "learned helplessness" (Walter, 1989, p. 42) and gender development, she accepts the blame.

If there is to be any change in this system, the worker must be clear and consistent about the batterer's responsibility for violence. This statement alone is an attempt at changing the homeostasis. This approach is consistent with therapeutic practice in which people are helped to assume responsibility for their functioning. A focus on responsibility for violence must be established early in the therapeutic process before the patterns that are entrenched at home become embedded in the therapy sessions as well.

Once Tom and Terry acknowledged that he was responsible for the violence, a therapeutic contract was established. The couple agreed to focus on how the battering could stop. Without a therapeutic contract, no help is possible. Asking Terry to be of assistance to Tom was again an attempt at bringing the couple together with both working cooperatively. It also changes Terry's role from that of victim to that of partner. Although Tom was not ready to focus on the "how" of change, he did admit to the need to change.

DISCUSSION

It was previously my theory that battering was related to an impulse disorder. I now believe that this reasoning is too linear, as is any one explanation of causality, such as the power-and-control theory relating to patriarchy. It may be true, and I believe that it is, that some men batter because of an impulse disorder such as intermittent explosive disorder (American Psychiatric Association, 1994). Some men may batter because they can, as those who favor a power-and-control theory believe (Brownmiller, 1975). However, it is now my belief that men batter for numerous reasons, some of which are amenable to a counseling approach while others are not. I have stated in my book that assessing men for counseling requires taking into account psychobiological disorders, psychiatric disorders, environmental and subcultural issues, and altered states (Geller, 1992). A case-by-case assessment may be an accurate method for determining causality.

Some men batter because of other issues; for example, narcissistic vulnerability with accompanying feelings of vulnerability and betrayal (Siegel, 1992), or gender development and societal acceptance of violence (Straus & Hotaling, 1980). Why battering occurs, in other words, is complex and multicausal, taking into account psychological, psychiatric, biological, sociopolitical, and behavioral and learning theories.

FOURTH SESSION

The day before the fourth session there was a phone call from a crying Terry who said that she and Tom had had a terrible fight, that she had gotten hit, and he was not coming to the session. While the worker expressed sympathy, she cut off a flow of feelings, saying that this was too important to talk about over the phone, and that she would like to hear more about it from both of them in the session. When Terry doubted that Tom would come, the worker reiterated her expectation that they would both be there.

Terry came alone saying that Tom refused to come. Terry began to vent and question whether Tom would ever change. The worker discussed this a little further in the office, but stated that there could not be a couple session without a couple. She suggested that they call for a new appointment. Terry wanted to be seen alone, but the worker insisted, saying that they had contracted for couple sessions. If there was to be a change in the contract, they would have to come in and discuss it. Since Tom didn't keep the appointment with her, the worker said that she would call him at home.

DISCUSSION

Originally, the couples therapy theory that couples be seen conjointly prevailed in my treatment. I now believe that this should not automatically apply in cases of abuse. The main consideration is for the woman's safety.

When Terry called to say she had been hit again, the focus first needed to be on her injuries, the care they required, and on her safety. Questions concerning both are addressed, as well as suggestions for her care; whether this be a safety plan, discussion of legal options, or fleeing to a safe haven. This may be an appropriate time for an individual session. In Terry's case, her request for an individual session would be honored, with a new assessment made concerning conjoint treatment.

Another abusive episode does not necessarily rule out conjoint treatment, but the batterer must be held fully accountable and responsible for his abusive behavior. In addition to a focus on injuries and safety, there is always an emphasis on batterer responsibility.

Determining if conjoint treatment is continued or not is based on repeating the initial assessment, which, once again, focuses on the woman's willingness and level of abuse. Any form of abuse is unequivocally unacceptable, but as clinicians, we must have an understanding of symptom regression. Because abuse arouses such concern, and rightly so, it appears to be the only time treatment resorts to a "cut-it-out" school of therapy, with regression not tolerated. The danger is that a case that may be salvageable could be lost to the therapeutic process altogether. I am reminded of certain colleagues' work wherein a contract is made: if there is a resumption of abuse while conjoint is used, the therapy terminates, or "You're not going to do it and she's not going to take it." This is a trap for the worker, putting the worker in a self-made bind as described by Michelle Bograd (1986). I believe that a more therapeutic approach would be to focus the session on the batterer, holding him accountable for his regressive behavior, reinforcing the contract representing alternatives to violence and subsequently described (see page 91), and imposing a stiff consequence for his abusive behavior that is meaningful to him. For example, one consequence may be to fine the batterer an amount of money significant to him and given to her; or excluding him from the home for a certain length of time. Each decided consequence needs to be case-specific.

In the event that a member of the couple absents himself from the session, conveying that message through the other party, as did Tom, it would be important for the worker to call. If the batterer did this, as Tom did, the message to him is for him to cancel directly, with the worker, and not through his wife. In Tom's case, it was difficult for him to continue to avoid coming in the face of a direct confrontation from the worker. Her call caused him to focus on individual responsibility for actions, which was consistent with the discussion in the previous session.

This phone call was one of several outreach calls. Often, men who batter will refuse to come in after a regression. The worker must be prepared to reach out and reestablish the therapeutic contract, as men need reminding of long-range goals (a cessation of violence) when they are disappointed in their ability to be nonviolent. If the woman cancels, sending the message through her partner, calling her directly also provides the opportunity to check on her safety and continued willingness for conjoint.

FIFTH SESSION

Most of this session was a recapitulation of the first session. The couple had regressed and said change was futile. The worker focused on Tom, reminding him of his desire to change for himself. She got him to focus on how unhappy he was feeling, and she confirmed that he looked miserable. Feebly, he said that Terry wanted to get hit. The worker didn't think that was so, but felt it was beside the point. She again focused on his own motivation for change, regardless of what it would do for his wife. He needed to feel better, to which Tom agreed. Tom then reiterated his desire to improve the marriage. Dialogue around this issue occurred with both partners. The worker stated that she was glad to hear this and thought that maybe they were ready to figure out how to accomplish this. When Tom and Terry agreed, the worker asked Tom how he thought he could accomplish this; he didn't know. The worker asked for a description of what happens when he becomes violent. He talked about his inability to stop his anger once it starts, and the only way it stops is as a result of an explosion. He could not think of what he could do to control this, which was to be the following week's discussion.

DISCUSSION

It was natural for the couple to regress. However, this time, the worker did not encourage a venting session. She already knew the couple's arguing pattern, and she had already demonstrated her acceptance of their anger. Since the regression was a direct result of their attempt to change, staying with the arguing would have been counterproductive in that it would have fed into their unconscious resistance to change, and would have been an avoidance of the pain that they were both experiencing as a result of the violence.

It was clear to the worker that with the couple so divided, attempting to have Tom change for the sake of the relationship probably would have failed. At that moment neither of them felt positive about the other, nor hopeful that the marriage would succeed. Each partner was preoccupied with his or her own sense of disappointment and hurt. Therefore, the only possible leverage the worker had was in appealing to Tom's sense of internal discomfort surrounding his disappointment in himself for resorting to violence. Batterers often feel victimized by their wives, as evidenced by Tom's consistent statements that Terry "made him hit her." While some of the literature indicates that externalizing blame is a defensive maneuver, others feel that batterers do feel victimized (S. Shapiro, personal communications, 1980–1982). Telling Tom that he needs to change for himself serves more than one purpose; it makes clear that change is up to him, and that no one can absolve him of responsibility or make him behave in any particular way. Tom also restated his hopelessness by saying he didn't see any use in coming for help. Workers at times need to shore up clients' strengths and remotivate them. Outreach and expectation for change is a way of doing this.

The worker moved quickly here in establishing a change-oriented treatment plan; first, because they left off at this point in the last session, before the regression occurred. Had the worker not moved for change (that is, upset the homeostatis), there could be a resumption of battering for the purpose of maintenance of the homeostatis. When Tom said that he didn't know what he could do to change, the worker acted to facilitate and clarify so that all three of them might understand the pattern of violence. The suggestions for how to change had to come from Tom. It would reinforce his responsibility for change; but also, only he would know what would be helpful for him. Although certain personality types can be classified as violence-prone (Fromm, 1973), and a batterer's profile can be developed, the ingredients needed to change must be tailored to the individual and to his unique circumstances. Further, when a batterer develops his own ideas for change, he can claim it as his own plan, and the chances for internalization are greater.

The contract for change is developed as early as possible, preferably no later than the second session. Since it is a tangible tool, couples find comfort in having a specific plan to use. More important, this is a method for dealing with the violence, which is employed as early as possible for obvious reasons.

While Tom was able to develop a treatment plan himself for rechanneling his violence, I usually develop such a plan in the session with the abuser, formalizing and ritualizing it as "the contract," and drawing upon cognitive/behavioral techniques for alternatives to abusive behavior. For a fuller explanation of how to develop a contract, as well as a sample contract, see Geller (1992). It should be noted that no discussion concerning the details of the violence ensued; this would have been counterproductive. It was clear that the couple felt badly about the fight. To recount the details might have reactivated angry feelings, preventing a positive movement (development of a change plan). There are occasions in which dwelling on the details of the fight might be necessary. One such occasion would be the need to gain greater clarity of the dynamics. There are times that dwelling on the details helps to convey the seriousness of the situation. Sometimes one or another of the dyad has not internalized this, and the worker can dramatize the destructiveness of violence through recapitulation.

In the following session, Tom did come in with a treatment plan for rechanneling his violence. The couple began to feel more comfortable with one another. Due to the noncritical nature of the subsequent sessions, the worker was able to gather background information on the couple and to focus on improving communication and enhancing interaction.

With couples who are desperate—as partner-abusing couples are—it is better to attempt the gathering of background information after the crisis subsides. When these couples come for help, they are bursting with feelings. Psychosocial material gathering at that time impedes their ability to unburden their troubles, and can be a source of frustration to them. After the crisis subsides, there is time for information-gathering, and it may even be helpful in making the transition from crisis orientation to conjoint therapy.

A word about ethnicity seems appropriate here. Tom would regularly declare that people in his family did not go for help but kept their problems to themselves. He would question his coming for help. However, he continued to attend sessions, and put to use in his life what was discussed. In Tom's close-knit Italian-American community, it was not common to seek help. The same was true among his co-workers and friends. References to psychology were made only at someone's expense or if someone was crazy. The worker interpreted Tom's objections not as resistance to treatment, but as an ethnic consideration which was supported and deserving of respect.

> *After about ten sessions of conjoint therapy another crisis occurred. Once again Tom refused to attend the session, and Terry was left to convey this information to the worker. She stated that they had had a very bad fight the previous night. The worker reiterated the importance of both parties coming in.* She gave Terry the choice of convincing Tom herself, or of enlisting the aid of the worker. Terry chose the latter. When the worker called Tom, after his initial declaration that he did not take his problems "outside," he said to the worker, "Well, I guess I just better come in because you're going to try and convince me of that anyway, right?" Tom and Terry came in, once again depressed and dejected. The major difference, however, was that there had been no violence. Tom said that Terry tried to defend herself with a chair which stopped him "dead in his tracks." He turned to the worker and said that there was "no way" she could have stopped him had he wanted to "get her." He went on to say, when he saw Terry "so defenseless with only that chair to protect her," he just couldn't hit her. He looked at Terry and then at the worker and said that he didn't want to hurt Terry; he loved her. The couple seemed set to focus on the hopelessness of their situation. The worker thought that the argument was a success as there was no violence. The worker told the couple that fighting between couples was normal. Up until that time they had been having abnormal fights, but this time they had just had a fight like all other couples.*

This session marked a turning point in the Abdellas' relationship. For the first time, Tom was able to see beyond his own feelings and empathize with Terry's position. Once that occurred, the desire to hit her dissipated. Stephen Shapiro of Volunteer Counseling Service of Rockland County, in a personal communication, stated that one characteristic of the batterer is lack of empathy. He has noted that one way to help batterers control their violence is to teach the abuser to develop such empathy.

Note: How this approach has been amended has been explained in full on page 87.

In the same light, observations made while working with acting-out adolescents showed how their anger could escalate without direct provocation (Geller & Walsh, 1977–1978). During what they perceived as confrontation, these young people appeared to go into a daze; their eyes became glassy; they weren't able to focus on any one in particular and they thythmically stated over and over again their intention to harm (Fadely & Hasler, 1979). Such behavior can be likened to a sports coach giving his team a pep talk. Perhaps something similar occurs to people (like batterers) who inflict violence without premeditation.

After this breakthrough session, the violence did not recur. The Abdellas were seen for another year and a half. Other family problems were uncovered. For that reason, and to ensure that the gains made in treating battering were sustained, there was a continuation of weekly sessions, but with a change to family therapy. Terry's two daughters were brought into the sessions because of the emotional difficulty they had suffered from witnessing the violence, as well as the upheaval they underwent in their adjustment to having a father. Communication between Tom and Terry's daughters were poor, and they were not getting along as a family. Tom became the strongest advocate for family sessions. The daughters were resistant and rebellious, making the sessions very difficult. However, Tom and Terry joined together in ensuring their continuation, and eventually they began to prove successful.

CONCLUSION

Eliminating the patterns of abuse among couples choosing to stay together is a laborious process. There are many pressures on the couple that may impede the process, as was shown in this case, not the least of which are the roots of violence which remain deep within the fabric of our society (Straus, 1976). Cultural background, ethnic identity, and certain personality features may keep the couple from seeking treatment. Nonetheless, the model presented here has been successful in reversing the cycle of violence. The case presentation format was attempted in order to shed light on the mechanics of adopting this model. It is hoped that it could be useful to practitioners interested in using these techniques with partner-abuse cases.

Working with the dyad, as opposed to the entire family, is preferred initially because it is a method of isolating the behavior and not diluting it with the many other relevant family issues. In addition, there is an awareness that other family members are affected by the violence that occurs between the partners, and that they too need an opportunity for working through being in a violent household. A basic premise of family therapy relates to the way in which the entire system is affected by a problem in one of its members (Haley, 1976). Family therapists would then choose to treat the entire family constellation, rather than only certain of its members.

In the case of Tom and Terry, the children were brought in at a certain point, and this proved helpful. Many of the children of other couples in treatment participated in peer-group therapy. The question arises as to whether it would have been more expeditious to start with the whole family, rather than with just the couple. In this model, the choice was to work solely with the couple. This arose from a consideration for the family therapy theory, that proposes that if patterns are changed between partners, thereby changing the homeostasis, benefits will filter down to the entire family (Satir, 1967), and also because of the focus on the need to ameliorate the violence.

This model has been successfully used with well over 250 couples. However, model design can be studied further. Conjoint treatment for couples with the presenting problem of partner abuse, when delivered responsibly, has proven to be one viable and therapeutic option; but the use of family therapy, a combination of couple and family therapy, or couple and children's groups combined with violence-eliminating techniques is open to further exploration.

There has been a prohibition in certain circles against any treatment where the couple is seen together. This is informed more by a sociopolitical context than a clinical context. Dogmatically dictating how treatment should be conducted parallels what it is that we are addressing in the first place with partner abuse: control exerted over one party by another. We should not repeat what it is that we are opposed to, but more importantly, to close ourselves to any modality that is useful for some is a disservice to ourselves and to those battered women whom we are dedicated to helping.

REFERENCES

American Psychiatric Association. (1994). *Diagnostic and statistical manual of mental disorders* (4th edition). Washington, DC: American Psychiatric Press.

Bograd, J. (1986, May–June). Holding the line: Confronting the abusive partner. *Family Therapy Networker,* pp. 44–47.

Brownmiller, S. (1975). *Against our will.* New York: Simon and Schuster.

Fadley, J. T., & Hasler, V. (1979). *Confrontation in adolescence.* St. Louis: C. V. Mosby Co.

Framo, J. L. (1965). Rationale and techniques of intensive family therapy. In I. Boazormeny-Nagy & J. Framo (Eds.), *Internal family therapy* (pp. 177–182). New York: Harper & Row.

Fromm, E. (1973). *The anatomy of human destructiveness.* New York: Holt, Rinehart & Winston.

Geller, J. (1992). *Breaking destructive patterns: Multiple strategies for treating partner abuse.* New York: Free Press.

Geller, J., & Walsh, J. C. (1977–1978). A treatment model for the abused spouse. *Victimology, 1*(1), 627–632.

Geller, J., & Wasserstrom, J. (1984). Conjoint therapy for the treatment of domestic violence. In A. Roberts (Ed.), *Battered women and their families.* New York: Springer.

Goldner, V., Penn, L., Steinberg, M., & Walker, G. (1990). Love and violence: Gender paradoxes in volatile attachments. *Family Process, 29*(4), 357.

Haley, J. (1976). *Problem-solving therapy.* San Francisco: Jossey-Bass.

Hudson, W. (1994). Partner Abuse Scale: Physical (PASPH). In J. Fischer & K. Corcoran (Eds.), *Measures for clinical practice* (pp. 461–462). New York: Free Press.

Minuchin, S. (1974). *Families and family therapy.* Cambridge, MA: Harvard University Press.

New York State Law S.6617-A.8842, 1977.

O'Leary, K. D. (1996, September). Physical aggression in intimate relationships can be treated within a marital context under certain circumstances. *Journal of Interpersonal Violence,* pp. 450–455.

Satir, V. (1967). *Conjoint family therapy.* Palo Alto, CA: Science & Behavior Books.

Siegel, J. (1992). *Repairing intimacy.* Northvale, NJ: Aronson.

Straus, M. (1976). Social perspective on the causes of family violence. In M. R. Greene (Ed.), *Violence in the family* (pp. 7–31). Boulder, CO: Westview Press.

Straus, M., & Hotaling, G. (1980). *The social causes of husband/wife violence.* Duluth, MN: University of Minnesota Press.

Walker, L. (1989). *Terrifying love: Why battered women kill and how society responds.* New York: Harper & Row.

Children and Adolescents from Violent Homes

Crisis Intervention with Traumatized Child Witnesses in Shelters for Battered Women

Peter Lehmann and Bonnie E. Carlson

T he large numbers of shelters for battered women and their children illustrate the seriousness and prevalence with which families experience violence. With more than 1200 shelters and 800 children's programs in the United States (National Coalition Against Domestic Violence, 1991) and 433 shelters in Canada, 31% of which have a children's program (National Clearinghouse on Family Violence, 1995), shelters often represent the first haven of safety for children and their mothers. This safety net provides a source of protection for those who must cope with the stressful experience of having been threatened or violently assaulted by their husbands or partners. Shelters also offer family members the opportunity to address the crises that accompany serious abuse. A growing literature demonstrates how the use of crisis intervention approaches can be helpful with battered women (Andrews, 1990; Dziegielewski & Resnick, 1996; Dziegielewski, Resnick, & Krause, 1996; A. R. Roberts, 1984; A. R. Roberts & B. Roberts, 1990).

However, little has been written about how crisis intervention might be applicable to children who have witnessed interparental violence and temporarily reside in shelters with their abused mothers. This is surprising, given the frequency with which children regularly witness violence. One possible reason for the limited information on crisis intervention is that children may have been overlooked as shelters focused their efforts on the crises of their mothers (A. R. Roberts & B. Roberts, 1990). Early models of intervention for children developed group approaches aimed at crisis intervention. For example, Rhodes and Zelman (1986) emphasized the crisis intervention principles of relieving feelings of isolation and alienation and strengthening the relationship between mothers and children, whereas Alessi and Hearn (1984) focused on identifying feelings, problem solving, love, and termination. Current group modalities tend to be less oriented towards crisis management, instead focusing on psychoeducational, emotional, and attitudinal changes (for comprehensive reviews, see Peled & Davis, 1995; Peled & Edleson, 1995).

Recently, witnessing mother assault has been recognized as potentially traumatic for children, and the need for crisis intervention has been considered. Jaffe, Wolfe, and Wilson (1990) suggested that children residing in shelters may be in a posttraumatic state, and Rossman (1994) has argued that children who exhibit trauma symptoms should be allowed to work through traumatic issues in a safe setting. Likewise, Hughes and Marshall (1995) have recommended that crisis work with children be one of the first steps a child advocate takes when a family enters a shelter. In addition to being faced with the traumatic effects of witnessing the interparental abuse, children need to address issues of safety, temporary separation from one or both parents, and ongoing changes in their lives.

The purpose of this chapter is to present a model of crisis intervention with children who are residing in shelters for battered women, some of whom are traumatized as a result of witnessing the abuse of their mothers. The underlying assumption of this model is that witnessing mother-assault is a frightening experience, placing children under such extreme stress that a crisis is created. The chapter begins with a definition of trauma and a rationale for use of the trauma perspective. Next, a model of crisis intervention with child witnesses is presented. Finally, two cases are presented to illustrate how a crisis management approach can be used with children in shelter settings.

RATIONALE FOR THE TRAUMA PERSPECTIVE

A growing body of research has documented the impact on children of witnessing abuse toward a parent. Carlson (1996) has summarized this literature, concluding that child witnesses manifest complex outcomes, most commonly externalizing behavior problems, internalizing behavior problems, and impaired social competence. Some studies have found variation by age and gender, whereas others have not. Affected children tend not to manifest problems in all areas of functioning, although many studies have found that most children exposed to interparental abuse demonstrate problems in some area of development. Adolescent boys who have witnessed abuse of their mothers have been found to be at risk for hitting their mothers, running away, and suicidal thoughts (Carlson, 1990). Thus, in general, observing violence between parents has been found to be associated with diminished well-being in children and adolescents (Carlson, 1991).

A subgroup of children who witness violence toward a parent is traumatized by this experience and merits a diagnosis of posttraumatic stress disorder (PTSD). To warrant a diagnosis of PTSD, three diagnostic criteria must be met (American Psychiatric Association [APA], 1994). First, there must be exposure to a traumatic stressor that results in a response of fear, helplessness, horror, or, in the case of children, agitated or disorganized behavior. A trauma or traumatic stressor is an experience that involves the threat or perceived threat of death or serious injury. In addition, to receive a PTSD diagnosis, three clusters of symptoms must be experienced for at least 1 month:

1. reexperiencing of the traumatic event (e.g., repetitive play, upsetting dreams, or psychological and physiological distress in response to reminders of the traumatic event);

2. avoidance of stimuli associated with the trauma and emotional numbing (e.g., avoiding thoughts or feelings connected with the event, a sense of foreshortened future, or restricted affect); and
3. symptoms of arousal (e.g., angry outbursts, irritability, or trouble sleeping).

Acute Stress Disorder can be diagnosed if these responses occur within 1 month of the event (APA, 1994).

There have been suggestions to broaden the PTSD conceptualization, because current criteria may not constitute an exhaustive list (Udwin, 1993; Wolfe & Birt, 1995). For example, some authors have reported other negative coping behaviors such as guilt, shame, fear of recurrence of the event, worry about another person, intervention fantasies, and grief reactions as commonly occurring in the aftermath of exposure to traumatic events (Monahon, 1993; Mowbray, 1988; Nader & Pynoos, 1990). In addition, type II trauma responses of depression, anger, and dissociation (Terr, 1990, 1991) are said to be common in children exposed to violent events. Likewise, in a study of traumatized infants, new fears and aggressive behaviors not present before the trauma were found (Scheeringa & Zeanah, 1994). Although these behaviors may represent a clinical subtype of trauma responses, they are relevant to the child witness, and need to be taken into account when assessing in situations of crisis.

The inclusion of a trauma conceptualization in a model of crisis intervention with child witnesses to domestic violence is important for a number of reasons. First, anecdotal and empirical evidence from shelter and nonshelter settings shows that child witnesses are at risk for exhibiting PTSD symptoms (e.g., Arroyo & Eth, 1995; Jaffe, Sudermann, & Reitzel, 1992, 1993; Jaffe et al., 1990; Lehmann, in press; Lehmann, Rabenstein, Duff, & Van Meyel, 1994; Pynoos & Eth, 1986; Pynoos & Nader, 1990; Rosenberg & Rossman, 1990; Rossman, 1994; Silvern, Karyl, & Landis, 1995; Wolfe & Jaffe, 1991). These studies have found that witnessing violence constituted a traumatic stressor and that substantial numbers of children showed trauma-specific symptoms in most domains as defined by the DSM-IV (APA, 1994).

A second reason relates to the nature of witnessing domestic violence as a traumatic event, which is elaborated below. Third, crisis intervention models have been used effectively with children and adolescents who have experienced traumatic stressors such as community violence (Pynoos & Nader, 1988), natural disasters (Haizlip & Corder, 1996; Terr, 1992), homicide and rape (Eth & Pynoos, 1994; Pynoos & Eth, 1986; Pynoos & Nader, 1990, 1993), and school suicide (Wenckstern & Leenaars, 1993). In each case, addressing trauma symptoms was considered essential to reducing the stress of those involved. Finally, the trauma perspective informs us that the optimal time for prevention and intervention is during the acute period following exposure to the traumatic event, when intrusive reminders are most identifiable and associated affect is most available (Pynoos & Nader, 1993).

Advocacy services for child witnesses and their families are provided primarily in shelter settings (Peled & Edleson, 1994), and most battered women who seek shelter services are accompanied by children. For example, MacLeod (1987) found that at least 70% of all women coming to shelters had children, with 17% bringing three or more children. Thus, shelter-based child advocates are in a unique position to observe and respond to the immediate crisis needs of child witnesses. Advocates should be familiar with the trauma perspective so that they can be alert to the possibility that children entering shelters may be in crisis and/or exhibiting trauma-related symptoms.

A CONCEPTUAL MODEL OF CRISIS INTERVENTION WITH CHILD WITNESSES

The proposed model is an adaptation and integration Roberts' Crisis Intervention Model (A. R. Roberts, 1991, 1996) and the developmental model of child traumatic response of Pynoos and associates (e.g., Pynoos & Nader, 1988, 1990, 1993). In an early paper, A. R. Roberts and B. Roberts (1990) noted that knowledge of crisis theory and intervention approaches is essential to workers in shelter settings. Furthermore, A. R. Roberts and B. Roberts (1990) supported the crisis-based theoretical perspectives of Caplan (1964), Aguilera and Messick (1984), and Janosik (1984) who suggested that four events can precipitate a crisis state for survivors of violence. First, the survivor experiences a dangerous event that is perceived as threatening to herself and her children. Tension and distress intensify, but customary attempts at problem solving do not ameliorate the problem. As a result, the event creates unbearable discomfort, creating a sense of imbalance or disequilibrium and a subsequent state of crisis.

A. R. Roberts' (1991, 1996) model describes seven stages of working through crises. These stages include:

1. assessing lethality and safety needs;
2. establishing rapport;
3. identifying major problems;
4. dealing with feelings and providing support;
5. exploring alternatives;
6. formulating an action plan; and
7. follow-up.

Dziegielewski et al. (1996) have characterized this approach as "clearly applicable in the case of intervention with those involved with domestic violence" (p. 129). As currently formulated, the model is intended for adults, although Jobes and Berman (1996) have applied it to suicidal adolescents.

The Roberts' model takes the position that crisis intervention can be a positive experience, bringing about balance as well as change. At the heart of the model is the worker-client relationship, through which support is offered and expression of feelings and alternative problem solving are facilitated, thereby providing the context for the client to return to the state of functioning that existed prior to the crisis (A. R. Roberts, 1990, 1996; A. R. Roberts & B. Roberts, 1990).

Crisis intervention with child witnesses requires a special focus on trauma symptoms as well as consideration of the child's stage of development. The developmental model of child trauma responses of Pynoos and associates (Pynoos, 1996; Pynoos & Eth, 1984, 1985, 1986; Pynoos & Nader, 1988, 1990, 1993) recognizes the fundamental interrelationship of traumatic events, traumatic symptoms, and stage of development. Traumatic experiences can interfere with critical developmental transitions and lead to dysfunction, which has been labeled proximal stress-related psychopathology (Pynoos, 1996; Pynoos, Steinberg, & Goenjian, 1996). The authors have found that developmental milestones such as attachment, autonomy, self-efficacy, impulse control, and cognitive and moral development are key areas at risk for delay when children are exposed to traumatic events such as violence.

The developmentally sensitive assessment schema of Pynoos and associates recognizes that "distress derives not only from the nature of the experience itself, but also from the subsequent traumatic reminders and secondary stresses" (Pynoos, 1996, p. 184). Thus, child responses are a function of three interrelated sets of variables: objective features of the event, subjective perceptions of the event and associated reminders, and concurrent secondary stressors.

First, the traumatic stress a child experiences is related to the characteristics or objective features of the traumatic event. Pynoos (1996) and Pynoos et al. (1996) review literature indicating that numerous aspects of an event are predictive of posttraumatic stress symptoms. Several are commonly present in situations where children witness domestic violence. These include being physically close to the violent event; experiencing recurrent violent incidents; having a close relationship with the assailant or victim; being exposed to the threat of death or personal injury; hearing cries for assistance or distress; witnessing injuries; weapon use; and the presence of physical coercion, brutality, or malevolent intent.

Child witnesses have been exposed to violent events by being immediately present or nearby and in some cases have actually attempted to intervene. Children may also be exposed to physical injuries resulting from the abuse, such as bleeding, bruising, broken bones, and so forth. In addition to observing abuse, children may also have witnessed police intervention in their homes, as well as the distress and anxiety of their mothers. Children needing comfort or reassurance may find their mothers unable to respond due to preoccupation with their own stress, guilt, depression, health concerns, and fears about safety, thereby rendering them unable to cope effectively with the demands of parenting (Holden & Ritchie, 1991; Wolfe, Jaffe, Wilson, & Zak, 1985; Wolfe, Jaffe, Wilson, & Zak, 1988; Wolfe, Zak, Wilson, & Jaffe, 1988). Children may have left their homes hurriedly, leaving behind toys, clothing, pets, and perhaps the abusive parent. In addition, many children may not have been told where they were going, or will have been misinformed about the reasons they have left their homes (Hughes & Marshall, 1995).

Second, internal threats are associated with the child's subjective perceptions of the danger and physical and affective responses to it, such as a sense of helplessness, being overwhelmed, or fears of abandonment (Pynoos & Nader, 1993). Developmental factors strongly influence both perceptions of external threats and internal responses. The most recent violent episode and its aftermath are likely to be foremost in the child's mind, leading to a variety of behavioral responses. These responses may range from extreme fearfulness, terror, and crying to being confused, withdrawn, or angry.

Finally, the impact of secondary stressors will influence child coping efforts. For example, if abuse of one's mother creates the need to leave the family home for a shelter, parental divorce, or changing schools, these situations can create stress and become additional challenges with which the child must cope. Having to appear in court as a witness for one parent against another can also create significant stress. Pynoos' assessment typology recognizes that traumatic experiences are multilayered and that all three factors are strongly related to both the onset and persistence of PTSD symptoms in children. For all of these reasons, the experience of witnessing domestic violence and its sequelae may precipitate symptoms of posttraumatic stress and constitute a crisis for children.

The crisis intervention perspective and the developmental perspective on trauma share a number of commonalities that may have implications for child advocates:

1. the management of trauma symptoms is time-limited and present-oriented;
2. interventions are intended to relieve the child of traumatic stress reactions and increase self-competence and positive coping efforts;
3. expression of feelings is facilitated; and
4. the person who intervenes must be actively involved and directive.

CRISIS INTERVENTION WITH TRAUMATIZED CHILD WITNESSES

The following section presents a model of crisis intervention specific to child witnesses for use by child advocates. Roberts' seven-stage crisis intervention approach (A. R. Roberts, 1991, 1996) has been modified and collapsed into five stages. The model is flexible in that symptoms and problems may appear at different stages, and tasks or activities from earlier stages may be employed in subsequent stages. For example, although safety should be assessed in the initial stage, child advocates must be mindful of the need to assess safety during the entire intervention process.

Stage I: Establishing Rapport and Assessing Danger

Establishing rapport forms the basis for developing a relationship between the child witness and child advocate. Rapport-building generally begins shortly after families enter the shelter and the advocate is introduced to the child. Children may be upset, appear passive, inhibited or agitated, demonstrating the initial signs of posttraumatic stress. Providing information, smiles, positive gestures, or touring the shelter can convey a sense of respect, nonintrusiveness, and safety to the child.

Additional methods of establishing rapport can occur via the intake process or use of introduction booklets which provide the advocate with an opportunity to interview the child about who they are, what has occurred, what the child may have seen, how the child feels about the violence, and whether the child has been assaulted. This process can create a "window of opportunity" to help establish initial trust, a sense of safety, and a working relationship with the child. Introduction booklets encourage the child to describe personal strengths, talents, and special interests. Examples of such resources may be found in Peled and Davis (1995), Jaffe et al. (1990), and Carlson (1996).

The safety of all family members must be the first priority. Because the risk to family members for further harm by the abuser may continue during the shelter stay, it is important to assess lethality during the initial stage of crisis intervention. Consequently, advocates need to ask mothers about the extent of risk for current and/or future harm to children as early as possible. Information on factors such as the severity and frequency of injury, availability of weapons, isolating behaviors, substance abuse, sexual assault, criminal or stalking behavior, and potential triggers provides the child advocate with information regarding the level of danger. An informal assessment

tool such as the Severity of Violence Matrix (Domestic Abuse Intervention Project [DAP], 1996) that lists a number of variables on a
serious to severe risk continuum can be useful for the purpose.
Additional factors to screen for include proximity of children to the
violence, relationship with the perpetrator, parental psychopathology, chronicity of the violence, previous trauma, family response,
and child worry about the safety of significant others (Pynoos &
Nader, 1988, 1990, 1993).

The preceding variables are important because the impact of the
abuse on mothers will affect their caretaking abilities with children.
There is accumulating evidence that children's trauma symptoms
are mediated by their mothers' own traumatic experiences, as well
as her responses (Osofsky & Fenichel, 1994, 1996; Pynoos, 1996).
When mothers are in distress and frightened, their ability to nurture
their children and maintain routines and predictability is likely to
be compromised as they attempt to cope with the abuse and its
aftermath. Mothers may need assistance to understand the link between exposure to chronic violence and their children's trauma
symptoms, such as posttraumatic play, regressive behavior, nightmares, or being easily startled.

Children who witness the violent assaults of their mothers are also
at risk for maltreatment themselves, including physical and/or sexual
abuse or neglect. Peled (1996) has noted that there is often an
overlap in families between violence towards mothers and violence
towards children, with 40% to 60% of families experiencing multiple
forms of abuse. Furthermore, studies have found that children who
experience multiple forms of maltreatment exhibit more behavioral
problems than nonabused children (e.g., Carlson, 1991; Davis &
Carlson, 1987; Fantuzzo et al., 1991; Hughes, 1988; Hughes, Parkinson, & Vargo, 1989; Jaffe, Wolfe, Wilson, & Zak, 1986). Interviews
with children and mothers can be used to determine if other forms
of maltreatment are present and, if so, who the perpetrator is. Because the perpetrator is typically the child's father, stepfather, or
mother's partner, serious attention must be paid to potential for
lethality when children have contact with the abuser during their
shelter stay. At the same time, child advocates must also be aware
of the possibility of abusive behaviors by mothers. There may be
circumstances where physical abuse, such as neglect or spanking
with an object, is observed and must be reported to child protective

authorities. Being an advocate for children means holding both parents accountable for their behavior with children.

Stage II: Identifying Problems and Symptoms

Some children who enter a shelter may react immediately to the violence, whereas others may seem to show no initial reaction. Regardless of a child's early response, there is a tendency for traumatic memories to resurface, sometimes in response to internal or external triggers that are reminiscent of the trauma and at other times seemingly unpredictably. Because children need to make sense of what has happened, their minds remain active in processing the traumatic event, both in the immediate aftermath and more long-term (Pynoos & Nader, 1993). Over time the witnessed events will be processed and reprocessed and meaning will be attached to what was witnessed.

During Stage II, child advocates need to assess for the presence of symptoms in four domains.

Re-experiencing Symptomatology.   A hallmark of this domain is experiencing intrusive memories, coupled with intense physiological reactions. Most children will not have flashbacks (Pynoos & Nader, 1988), but instead, their recall will be organized around anchor points. "Anchor points" refer to certain features of the traumatic event that become central and serve as cues for recall (Pynoos, 1996). Children may have many anchor points (e.g., remembering a mother's scream, injury or blood, the fear of being hurt and feeling unsafe, the angry look of the perpetrator) that will influence their disclosures and the emotional intensity of responses. Upsetting nightmares are another common form of reexperiencing where children may incorporate direct reenactment of the violence and/or experience fears of a recurrence of violence (Pynoos & Nader, 1988). Such dreams can be particularly troublesome due to the fears and anxiety they engender. Traumatic play is yet another reexperiencing symptom. Examples include the redramatization of episodes of the event or the repetition during play of traumatic themes (Pynoos, 1996; Pynoos & Nader, 1990, 1993). Observing and responding to traumatic play in shelter children may be critical, particularly in the case of toddlers who may not have the verbal maturity to express themselves. The outcome of traumatic play will be dependent on whether it provides relief for the child or instead only creates more anxiety (Nader & Pynoos, 1990).

Avoidance Symptoms.   This is the second domain of traumatic responses. These responses have been found inconsistently in children during the aftermath of trauma (Pynoos & Nader, 1988). Avoidance symptoms may appear as a general distancing or withdrawal from the external world. Following the witnessing of a mother's assault, children may exhibit a number of specific avoidance behaviors, including: "(1) lessened interest in play or usually other enjoyable activities, (2) feeling more distant from their parents or friends and/ or more alone with their feelings, and (3) not wishing to be aware of feelings" (Pynoos & Nader, 1988, pp. 448–449). Other avoidance reactions include regression and a sense of a foreshortened future (Arroyo & Eth, 1995).

Arousal.   In their work with children exposed to violent death, Pynoos and Nader (1990) described behaviors typical of this third domain, including prolonged hypervigilance and exaggerated startle reactions, concentration problems at school, and irritability in response to reminders of the traumatic event. For example, child advocates may see children in extended states of physical and mental readiness, as if the violent event could reoccur at any moment. Impaired learning is thought to be associated with sleep disturbance and intrusive reminders.

Intervention Fantasies.   One final area that remains active in the child's mind and which child advocates should assess concerns intervention fantasies (Pynoos & Nader, 1993). Such conscious or unconscious fantasies are essential to the processing of traumatic events and involve real or imagined actions related to the child's cognitive development about what might have been done to counteract the traumatic event. Intervention fantasies can include modifying or interrupting the event, reversing the outcome, retaliating or gaining revenge. Child advocates can access these fantasies and assist child witnesses to come to terms with traumatic events by asking questions such as "What did you want to do even though you couldn't help Mom?" "How would Superman have stopped Dad from hitting

Mom?" or "How angry are you at Dad and what would you like to see happen to him?"

Children may also exhibit a wide range of symptoms that are not part of the PTSD diagnostic criteria, yet that may be characteristic of children's posttraumatic responses. These include guilt, shame, rage and difficulties controlling aggression, fear that the event will recur, loss and grief reactions, worries about others, or dissociative reactions. Each will be exhibited according to the child's stage of development (Pynoos, 1996; Pynoos & Nader, 1988).

The technology for assessing PTSD in children is growing rapidly, and child advocates have a number of options from which to choose. For very young children, assessment should include direct observation of behaviors and asking mothers about possible problems or symptoms (Osofsky & Fenichel, 1994, 1996; Zeanah & Scheeringa, 1994). Nader and Pynoos (1991), Pynoos and Eth (1986), and Arroyo and Eth (1995) have also identified play and drawing techniques that may be useful with older children and adolescents. The play and drawing (draw-a-picture, tell-a-story) exercises allow for "reexamination and giving new meaning to aspects of the event or for reexperiencing and reworking of the memory and the emotions" (Nader & Pynoos, 1991, p. 378).

Arroyo and Eth (1995) recommend a three-stage evaluation interview that is appropriate for crisis intervention work. The opening, trauma, and closure phases of the interviews facilitate exploration of the child's subjective experience and provide an opportunity to discuss the early emotional and traumatic impact of the witnessed violence. In the opening phase, the child is provided with reassurance that the adult is experienced and knows something about what the child has gone through. The child is then invited to partake in a drawing or clay-modeling exercise of their own choosing. After it is completed, the child is asked to talk about the drawing or figures.

During the trauma phase of the evaluation, the child is asked about references to the trauma that are evident in the drawing or figure. It is essential to proceed slowly, offering support and reassurance throughout. When appropriate, the child is encouraged to describe exactly what happened, as well as his or her feelings and fantasies about what occurred. Wishes for revenge are common.

During the closure phase, the focus is on ending the interview and separating from the interviewer. The content of the session should be summarized and reviewed.

"By emphasizing how understandable, realistic, and universal their responses have been, children come to feel less stigmatized and isolated and are more willing to accept support from others" (Arroyo & Eth, 1995, p. 38). These exercises not only identify the intrusive events, but also assist the child in finding the words to talk about their experiences. Because traumatic responses change with development, cognitive distortions regarding rescue, intervention, and/or revenge can be clarified through play or drawings.

Child advocates can also use paper-and-pencil questionnaires to assess PTSD symptoms. As a supplement to information from parents or teachers, the benefit of such questionnaires lies in their ability to evaluate specific symptoms and to differentiate trauma-specific symptoms from general stress symptoms. Comprehensive summaries of PTSD questionnaires may be found in the reviews of Hudnall (1996) and Nader (1997). For some of these measures, specialized training may be necessary.

Stage III: Providing Support and Addressing Feelings

Two important components of providing support and facilitating expression of feelings in times of crisis are personal qualities of the child advocate and their relationship-building skills. Myer and Hanna (1996) have listed some worker qualities which may be helpful in shelter settings. Child advocates must be quick-thinking; they must be able to assess the severity of the situation and a child's responses in a brief time period. The ability to maintain a sense of calm in the face of a child's upset is very important and should allow rapport to develop. Appropriate humor is also an important attribute, and patience is essential in working with these families. In addition, child advocates must be creative and flexible in responding to stressful situations, and able to provide nonjudgmental support and validation to children and mothers (Hughes & Marshall, 1995). Finally, knowledge of normal child development is critically important.

The ability to be supportive in the face of crisis calls for relationship-building skills, and Hughes and Marshall (1995) offer useful guidelines for those who wish to work with child witnesses. Empathy, patience, and flexibility are crucial characteristics. Power struggles should be avoided. Children must be allowed to talk at their own pace, taking into account their age and stage of development. Advocates must also be mindful of the fear, anxiety, and sense of displacement children will experience. They must also be sensitive to the burden of secrecy that children experience about what they have witnessed (Peled, 1996). When they talk to others about what has happened in their family, children may fear retribution from parental figures for violating family rules. Unraveling such secrecy must be done in a noncoercive manner. Children need to know they have permission to talk about such secrets, and mothers can prove helpful by giving children explicit permission to talk about what has happened. At the same time, advocates must carefully and respectfully explain the limits of confidentiality, noting that if children share information that suggests they are being harmed by someone, the advocate may need to speak to other adults. Children must feel empowered to discuss issues freely, but also have the right to withdraw at any stage of the interview.

Similarly, the writings of Pynoos and Nader (1988) offer some specific skills for dealing with support and feelings. They suggest that support should convey acceptance and a willingness to hear everything, regardless of how terrible some events may have been. The integrity of the child can begin to be restored when he or she has permission to speak of the most terrifying experiences. An opportunity is created in a safe and comfortable setting to begin the process of making sense of these frightening events. Being able to discuss the traumatic experience in detail can give the child a sense of mastery and sets them on the road to healthy coping. Dealing with feelings also helps link some of the cognitive understandings to the event as well as to the feelings of helplessness. For example, clarification of revenge fantasies helps to normalize these feelings and prevent a preoccupation with them. The child may also experience a sense of relief from carrying painful secrets. Support and talking about feelings may also assist the child in putting some continuity in their life experiences. Some children may show a marked change in life attitudes or disclose coexisting stresses, and discussion of events and feelings can provide a vehicle for linking events and stressors. Child advocates will find numerous aids to assist in this process in the form of feeling workbooks, story books, and videos in the reviews of Peled and Davis (1995) and Carlson (1996).

One final issue of this stage concerns the personal costs to child advocates who are repeatedly exposed to hearing the stories of chronic violence from children. Listening to the threats to the child and hearing the child's distress at witnessing injury is likely to exacerbate empathic strain (Nader, 1994) and can lead to vicarious traumatization (Saakvitne & Pearlman, 1996), whereby the child advocate is rendered unable to directly discuss the child's pain, becomes overprotective, or becomes secondarily traumatized. Child advocates need their own sources of support among supervisors and colleagues. They must have ample opportunity to "de-brief" and engage in self-care away from their work (Hughes & Marshall, 1995).

Stage IV: Exploring Alternatives and Formulating an Action Plan

The traumatic experience of witnessing the violent assault of one's mother and entrance into a shelter can lead to a wide range of changes in the child's life situation (Pynoos & Nader, 1993). Often there is a period of uncertainty as the mother decides whether she will return to the abusive partner or start her life anew. There may be changes in life circumstances and distress related to traumatic symptoms, disrupted peer relations, anger control difficulties, poor school performance, and feelings of incompetence. The child advocate must remain attentive to all these issues, taking an active stance with mothers and school personnel, and be prepared to assist the child with practical and helpful responses.

At this stage, two alternatives face child witnesses. Some children will be returning to the home where the abuse took place and thus to the abusive parent, whom they may have missed while staying at the shelter. They may have intensely ambivalent feelings about going home and are at continued risk of posttraumatic symptoms due to fears of recurrence. On the other hand, some mothers will be relocating, starting a new life apart from the abusive partner, in a new home. Their children are likely to have mixed reactions, especially if the new home is also in a different neighborhood or community. This may mean the need to adjust to a new set of circumstances with accompanying stressors, such as a new school, having to make new friends, reduced economic circumstances, and so forth. Children will need assistance in preparing for and adjusting to these changes.

Stage V: Follow-Up

After children have left the shelter, there may be opportunities for follow-up activities to monitor their post-shelter adjustment. If aftercare services are available, providing an ongoing group experience for children can be helpful.

Because traumatic experiences require time to process, traumatized child witnesses are likely to continue to be working on these issues after leaving the shelter. They may continue to encounter reminders of the violent incident, for instance, when their father gets angry and yells loudly. They are also at risk for developing longer-term reactions to the abuse they have witnessed, including mental disorders, such as phobias or conduct disorder. As a result, they may need to be referred to a mental health center or family agency for evaluation by a mental health professional specializing in child mental health. Such reactions are more likely when children have experienced exposure to severe and/or chronic traumatic events, especially if other stressors are also present (Pynoos, 1996). Referral for a physical examination or evaluation of school-related difficulties may also be appropriate.

Tables 5.1, 5.2, and 5.3 offer some practical suggestions for addressing trauma-related symptoms in preschoolers, school-age children, and adolescents in shelters for abused women, according to the five stages of the crisis intervention model. Each table gives examples of problems and symptoms likely to be exhibited by children in each age range, as well as child advocate roles and activities and tools to support these activities. These suggestions are not meant to be comprehensive or exhaustive and should be adapted based on the individual case and circumstances. Two case examples illustrate how the suggestions in the tables might be used in practice.

CASE 1

Allison, age 7, entered the Women's Shelter with her mother, 9-year-old brother, and 3-year-old sister, appearing very frightened as she clung to her mother. This was Allison's second stay at the shelter in 2 years. A child advocate completed a children's intake with her mother and

TABLE 5.1   Crisis Intervention with Traumatized Preschoolers

	Stage I Establishing rapport and assessing danger	Stage II Identifying symptoms and problems	Stage III Providing support and addressing feelings	Stage IV Exploring alternative action plans	Stage V Follow-up
Problems and symptoms	Passivity or withdrawal Helplessness Fear of new environment Confusion Anxious attachment	Reexperiencing symptoms Avoidance symptoms Arousal symptoms Intervention fantasies	Posttraumatic play Disrupted sleep, eating, toileting Regression		
Child advocate roles and activities	Establishing rapport Assessing danger Assessing for maltreatment Assess mother's functioning	Assess for PTSD symptoms Assess for other problems	Provide support Facilitate verbal expression of feelings Maintain consistency of care and stability	Facilitate grief work Work with mother Establish limits for behavior Monitor play	Make referrals Prepare for leaving shelter
Techniques and aids	Intake process Introduction booklets Tour of shelter Severity of Violence Matrix	Direct observation Interview mother Evaluation interview (Arroyo & Eth, 1995)	Help child attach names to feelings Drawing Clay modeling Encourage telling of story	Facilitate play	

TABLE 5.2   Crisis Intervention with Traumatized School-Age Children

	Stage I Establishing rapport and assessing danger	Stage II Identifying symptoms and problems	Stage III Providing support and addressing feelings	Stage IV Exploring alternative action plans	Stage V Follow-up
Problems and symptoms	Responsibility and guilt Fear of new environment Confusion Safety concerns Concern for others, e.g., father	Reexperiencing symptoms Avoidance symptoms Arousal symptoms Intervention fantasies	Posttraumatic play Sleep disturbance Distractibility Somatic symptoms Fear of feelings	Close monitoring of mother's behavior Fear and confusion over grief responses Missing absent parent	Anger at being in shelter or leaving father or returning home Fear of returning home or unknown future
Child advocate roles and activities	Establishing rapport Assessing danger Assessing for maltreatment Assess mother's functioning	Assess for PTSD symptoms Assess for other problems	Provide support Facilitate verbal expression of feelings Maintain consistency of care and stability Encourage expression of fantasies Facilitate school entry	Facilitate grief work Work with mother to establish limits for behavior Monitor play Encourage talking to supportive adults	Make referrals Prepare for leaving shelter Prepare for return to home school or new school
Techniques and aids	Intake process Introduction booklets Tour of shelter Severity of Violence Matrix	Direct observation Interview mother Evaluation interview (Arroyo & Eth, 1995)	Listen to feelings and help child attach labels Drawing Clay modeling Encourage telling of story	Provide information	

TABLE 5.3   Crisis Intervention with Traumatized Adolescents

	Stage I Establishing rapport and assessing danger	Stage II Identifying symptoms and problems	Stage III Providing support and addressing feelings	Stage IV Exploring alternative action plans	Stage V Follow-up
Problems and symptoms	Anger at having to be at the shelter Embarrassment, shame Fear of new environment Confusion Protectiveness toward mother	Reexperiencing symptoms Avoidance symptoms Arousal symptoms Intervention fantasies	Posttraumatic acting out Aggression toward others Sleep disturbance Somatic symptoms Embarrassment about fears, shame	Self-destructive behavior Fear and confusion over grief responses Missing absent parent Acting older than years Depression Sense of hopelessness	Anger at being in shelter or leaving father or returning home Fear of returning home or unknown future
Child advocate roles and activities	Establish rapport Assess danger Assess for maltreatment Assess mother's functioning	Assess for PTSD symptoms Assess for other problems Validate losses associated with shelter stay Clarify responsibility for abuse	Provide support Facilitate verbal expression of feelings Maintain consistency of care and stability Encourage expression of fantasies Assist with grieving	Facilitate grief work Work with mother to establish limits for behavior Encourage talking to supportive adults Set limits Elicit actual plans for revenge and consequences Assist with coping	Make referrals Prepare for leaving shelter Prepare for return to home school or new school

TABLE 5.3 *(cont.)*

	Stage I Establishing rapport and assessing danger	Stage II Identifying symptoms and problems	Stage III Providing support and addressing feelings	Stage IV Exploring alternative action plans	Stage V Follow-up
Techniques and aids	Intake process Introduction booklets Tour of shelter Severity of Violence Matrix	Direct observation Interview mother Evaluation interview (Arroyo & Eth, 1995)	Drawing Use of journal Encourage telling of story Normalize emotions		

determined that Allison had seen her mother hit, pushed, and kicked by her father. She had witnessed this kind of violence for most of her short life. The first night Allison and her family came to the shelter, she received a tour of the shelter and entrance gifts. The child advocate met with Allison the next day to complete a "Get to Know You" form that addressed her favorite food, hobbies, school subjects, and so forth. In addition, Allison was asked if she knew why her family had come to the shelter and she replied, "Dad and Mom are always fightin' too much."

The "Get to Know You" form also served to identify symptoms and negative feelings Allison associated with the abuse and coming to the shelter. Allison disclosed that she was scared and worried about hitting and was afraid that her friends might get hurt. The advocate asked Allison to identify three wishes: If she could have anything she wanted, what would they be? The first wish was that her mom and dad would not fight. Children's staff noted other problem areas in Allison that included fighting with her siblings, displaying anger toward her mother, and refusal to obey her mother. Allison also seemed to be very protective of her mother, clinging to her and showing reluctance to participate in activities with the other children.

Allison's feelings and symptoms were addressed primarily through support groups held at the shelter. She attended a family violence group that emphasized that abuse is not acceptable and that children are not to blame for their parents' arguments and violence. During a feelings support group, Allison learned to understand and label the different feelings associated with family abuse. Subsequent groups that Allison attended were initiated with a discussion of how the children were feeling that day. Allison was taught that she has the right to feel many different things. In addition, Allison worked on developing a protection plan and specific safety skills by practicing calling 911 to protect herself. She wrote on an index card where she would hide and which adult she would talk to about the abuse.

While in the shelter, Allison also gained skills to cope with her anger. She learned to identify when she is becoming angry and worked on healthier ways to express her anger. She learned this in part through role plays with a partner where each took turns showing good and bad ways to express anger. Participation in a self-esteem group helped Allison to find qualities that she likes about herself and also gave other children the opportunity to compliment her. During Allison's stay in the shelter, she was able to develop friendships with other children and told the child advocate that making new friends was the best part about being at the shelter.

A follow-up evaluation allowed the child advocate to determine what Allison had learned while in the shelter and addressed continued concerns about safety. Overall, Allison showed an understanding of abuse, said she felt safe, and reported positive feelings about participation in the children's program. Allison's mother was accepted into the transitional living program that includes weekly outreach support groups for children focused on family violence, safety, self-esteem, and anger control.

CASE 2

Glen, age 4, and his mother were admitted into a shelter serving battered women and their children. Both were fleeing the abusive father for the first time. At admission, they were both experiencing anxiety. While the case manager and mother were completing an initial intake, Glen was fussy. The case manager introduced Glen and his mom to the child advocate, who encouraged him to pick out a stuffed animal. He smiled and clung to the animal tightly, while his mother completed the intake interview. Glen and his mother were taken on a tour of the shelter, with Glen continuing to hug his stuffed animal and staying close to his mother's side. The case manager met with Glen's mother the next day to complete more forms.

The mother completed the PTSD Semi-structured Interview and Observation Record for Infants and Young Children (Zeanah & Scheeringa, 1994). From the mother's observations, Glen appeared to exhibit symptoms in each of the three domains of reexperiencing, avoidance, and hyperarousal. For example, he engaged in traumatic play, had regressed to wetting the bed at night, and was having trouble sleeping. Glen's witnessing of domestic violence events caused terror and anxiety in him. As their stay continued, staff observed Glen behaving aggressively toward his mother, other children, and animals. He appeared to be re-enacting the violence he had seen his father direct toward his mother.

The child advocate talked to Glen's mother about his aggressive behavior, and they agreed to a time-out plan to be used any time Glen hit or otherwise behaved aggressively toward others. The advocate modeled appropriate parenting behavior when she imposed time-out on Glen by using eye contact, speaking softly, and validating his feelings of anger or frustration. This approach enabled Glen to feel safe and understand the limits and rules at the shelter. He was also encouraged to verbalize his feelings, rather than acting them out on others. Staff worked with his mother to use praise as positive reinforcement when Glen was able to express his feelings. Although it was difficult for his mother, she was able to remain calm while Glen was crying and angry. She talked softly to Glen, and her soothing voice seemed to calm and reassure him. Although still crying, he would hug her as she rocked him back and forth, whispering, "Mommy loves you."

When staff noticed Glen playing at the shelter, they would help him to express his feelings. When he engaged in trauma play, he seemed to be expressing revenge toward his father for hurting his mother. Staff would permit such play, intervening only if other children became involved or seemed to be at risk of getting hurt, and encouraging to talk about his fears.

The mother told the child advocate that Glen had been sleeping poorly while at the shelter. She stated that he would often wake up screaming in the middle of the night and would only go back to sleep if he could sleep in her bed. The advocate suggested maintaining a consistent routine at bedtime. She also suggested that the mother ask Glen about his bad dreams, which were based on his fears that this father would come and find them and hurt his mother. She was encouraged to let him describe his nightmares, followed by reassuring him that they were in a safe place now, and allowing him to remain in her bed.

Later in the shelter stay, Glen's mother received referrals to agencies that could help Glen come to terms with his experience. Glen attended several play therapy sessions outside the shelter, while his play at the shelter was monitored by the child advocate. Gradually, the staff and Glen's mother noticed a change in how Glen responded to his mother and others. He seemed to feel more comfortable in his surroundings and was able to express his feelings rather than acting them out. Eventually Glen and his mother moved to a new living arrangement, although Glen continued to visit the shelter to help him deal with the aggressive behaviors he had learned at home.

SUMMARY AND CONCLUSIONS

Witnessing domestic violence between one's parents can be a traumatic experience for a child. Such abuse is often recurrent, occurs in close proximity, and can lead to injuries in the adults or child himself or herself. The evidence of traumatic responses can be found in virtually all areas of children's functioning: physiological responses, such as hypervigilance and sleep disturbances; cognitive responses, such as confusion and revenge fantasies; emotional responses, such as intense fear, guilt, and anger; and behavioral responses, such as agitation, regression, and traumatic play. These reactions create a state of crisis for affected children and a need for crisis intervention services. Because traumatized child witnesses can be found in domestic violence shelters, shelters provide the ideal setting for crisis intervention work. Increasingly, shelters designate particular staff members, often called child advocates, to work with children.

We have presented a model of crisis intervention for child witnesses with a focus on trauma symptoms, based on the developmental model of child traumatic response of Pynoos and his colleagues. Their model recognizes that children's posttraumatic responses are influenced not only by the nature of the traumatic stressor itself, but also on the child's subjective responses to the event, and other concurrent stressors that are associated with the traumatic stressor. Examples of the latter include staying in a domestic violence shelter, moving to a new home, or changing schools. The five stages of the model are: Establishing rapport and assessing danger, identifying symptoms and problems, providing support and addressing feelings, exploring and formulating alternative action plans, and follow-up. Three tables are provided with suggestions for how the model can be used by child advocates and others to intervene with characteristic posttrauma symptoms exhibited by preschoolers, school-aged children, and adolescents. Finally, two case studies are presented to illustrate further how the model can to be applied in shelter settings.

ACKNOWLEDGMENTS

The authors would like to thank Lisa Schmidt-Estrella, LMSW, and Dana Grasso, MSSW, from the Women's Shelter, Arlington, Texas, for their case contributions.

REFERENCES

Aguilera, D. C., & Messick, J. M. (1984). *Crisis intervention: Theory and methodology.* St. Louis, MO: Mosby.

Alessi, J. J., & Hearn, K. (1984). Group treatment of children in shelters for battered women. In A. R. Roberts (Ed.), *Battered women and their families* (pp. 49–61). New York: Springer Publishing Company.

American Psychiatric Association. (1994). *Diagnostic and statistical manual of mental disorders* (DSM-IV) (4th ed.). Washington, DC: American Psychiatric Association.

Andrews, A. B. (1990). Crisis and recovery services for family violence survivors. In A. R. Roberts (Ed.), *Helping crime victims: Policy, practice and research* (pp. 206–232). Newbury Park, CA: Sage.

Arroyo, W., & Eth, S. (1995). Assessment following violence-witnessing trauma. In E. Peled, P. G. Jaffe, & J. L. Edleson (Eds.), *Ending the cycle of violence: Community responses to children of battered women* (pp. 27–42). Thousand Oaks, CA: Sage.

Caplan, G. (1964). *Principles of preventive psychiatry.* New York: Basic Books.

Carlson, B. E. (1990). Adolescent observers of marital violence. *Journal of Family Violence, 5,* 285–299.

Carlson, B. E. (1991). Outcomes of physical abuse and observation of marital violence among adolescents in placement. *Journal of Interpersonal Violence, 6,* 536–534.

Carlson, B. E. (1996). Children of battered women: Research, programs, and services. In A. R. Roberts (Ed.), *Helping battered women: New perspective and remedies* (pp. 172–187). New York: Oxford University Press.

Davis, L. V., & Carlson, B. E. (1987). Observation of spouse abuse: What happens to the children? *Journal of Interpersonal Violence, 2,* 278–291.

Domestic Abuse Intervention Project. (1997). *Creating a process of change for men who batter.* Unpublished manuscript.

Dziegielewski, S. F., & Resnick, C. (1996). Crisis assessment and intervention: Abused women in the shelter setting. In A. R. Roberts (Ed.), *Crisis management and brief treatment: Theory, technique, and applications* (pp. 123–141). Chicago: Nelson-Hall.

Dziegieliewski, S. F., Resnick, C., & Krause, N. (1996). Shelter based crisis intervention with abused women. In A. Roberts (Ed.), *Helping battered women: New perspectives* (pp. 159–171). New York: Oxford University Press.

Eth, S., & Pynoos, R. S. (1994). Children who witness the homicide of a parent. *Psychiatry: Interpersonal and Biological Processes, 57,* 287–306.

Fantuzzo, J. W., DePaola, L. M., Lambert, L., Martino, T., Anderson, G., & Sutton, S. (1991). Effects of interparental violence on the psychological adjustment and competencies of young children. *Journal of Consulting and Clinical Psychology, 59,* 258–265.

Hadley, S. M. (1992). Working with battered women in the emergency department: A model program. *Journal of Emergency Nursing, 18,* 18–23.

Haizlip, T. M., & Corder, B. F. (1996). Coping with natural disasters. In C. R. Pfeffer (Ed.), *Severe stress and mental disturbance in children* (pp. 131–152). Washington, DC: American Psychiatric Association.

Holden, G. W., & Ritchie, K. L. (1991). Linking extreme marital discord, child rearing, and child behavior problems: Evidence from battered women. *Child Development, 62,* 311–327.

Hudnall, B. (Ed.). (1996). *Measurement of stress, trauma, and adaptation.* Lutherville, MD: Sidran.

Hughes, H. M. (1988). Psychological and behavioral correlates of family violence child witnesses and victims. *American Journal of Orthopsychiatry, 58,* 77–90.

Hughes, H. M., & Marshall, M. (1995). Advocacy for children of battered women. In E. Peled, P. G. Jaffe, & J. L. Edleson (Eds.), *Ending the cycle of violence: Community responses to children of battered women* (pp. 121–144). Thousand Oaks, CA: Sage.

Hughes, H. M., Parkinson, D., & Vargo, M. (1989). Witnessing spouse abuse and experiencing spouse abuse: A "double whammy"? *Journal of Family Violence, 4,* 197–209.

Jaffe, P. G., Sudermann, M., & Reitzel, D. (1992). Working with children and adolescents to end the cycle of violence: A social learning approach to intervention and prevention programs. In R. DeV. Peters, R. J. McMahon, & V. L. Quinsey (Eds.), *Aggression and violence throughout the lifespan* (pp. 83–99). Newbury Park, CA: Sage.

Jaffe, P. G., Sudermann, M., & Reitzel, D. (1993). Child witnesses of marital violence. In R. T. Ammerman & N. W. Hersen (Eds.), *Assessment of family violence: A clinical and legal sourcebook* (pp. 313–331). Newbury Park, CA: Sage.

Jaffe, P. G., Wolfe, D. A., & Wilson, S. K. (1990). *Children of battered women.* Newbury Park, CA: Sage.

Jaffe, P. G., Wolfe, D. A., Wilson, S., & Zak, L. (1986). Similarities in behavioral and social maladjustment among child victims and witnesses to family violence. *American Journal of Orthopsychiatry, 56,* 142–146.

Janosik, E. H. (1984). *Crisis counseling: A contemporary approach.* Monterrey, CA: Wadsworth.

Jobes, D. A., & Berman, A. L. (1996). Crisis intervention and time limited intervention with high risk suicidal youth. In A. R. Roberts (Ed.), *Crisis management and brief treatment* (pp. 60–82). Chicago: Nelson-Hall.

Lehmann, P. (in press). The posttraumatic stress disorder responses in a sample of child witnesses to mother assault. *Journal of Family Violence.*

Lehmann, P., Rabenstein, S., Duff, J., & Van Meyel, R. (1994). A multidimensional model for treating families that have survived mother-assault. *Contemporary Family Therapy, 16,* 7–25.

MacLeod, L. (1987). *Battered but not beaten: Preventing wife battering in Canada.* Ottawa, Ontario, Canada: Canadian Advisory Council on the Status of Women.

Monahon, C. (1993). *Children and trauma: A parent's guide to helping children heal.* New York: Lexington.

Mowbray, C. T. (1988). Post-traumatic therapy for children who are victims of violence. In. F. Ochberg (Ed.), *Posttraumatic therapy and victims of violence* (pp. 196–212). New York: Brunner/Mazel.

Myer, R. A., & Hanna, F. J. (1996). Working in hospital emergency departments: Guidelines for crisis intervention workers. In A. R. Roberts (Ed.), *Crisis management and brief treatment: Theory, technique, and applications* (pp. 37–59). Chicago, IL: Nelson-Hall.

Nader, K. (1994). Countertransference in the treatment of acutely traumatized children. In J. P. Wilson & J. D. Lindy (Eds.), *Countertransference in the treatment of PTSD* (pp. 179–205). New York: Guilford.

Nader, K. O. (1997). Assessing traumatic experiences in children. In J. P. Wilson & T. M. Keane (Eds.), *Assessing psychological trauma and PTSD* (pp. 291–348). New York: Guilford.

Nader, K., & Pynoos, R. S. (1990). Drawing and play in the diagnosis and assessment of childhood post-traumatic stress syndromes. In C. Shaeffer (Ed.), *Play, diagnosis and assessment* (pp. 375–389). New York: Wiley.

Nader, K., & Pynoos, R. S. (1991). Drawing and play in the diagnosis and assessment of childhood post-traumatic stress syndromes. In C. Shaeffer (Ed.), *Play, diagnosis and assessment* (pp. 375–389). New York: Wiley.

National Clearinghouse on Family Violence, Health Promotion and Programs Branch Health. (1995). *The Transition Home Survey by Statistics Canada.* Ottowa, Canada: Author.

National Coalition Against Domestic Violence. (1991). *Directory of shelters and services for battered women.* Washington, DC: Author.

Osofsky, J. D., & Fenichel, E. (Eds.). (1994). *Hurt, healing, hope: Caring for infants and toddlers in violent environments.* Washington, DC: Zero to Three Publications.

Osofsky, J. D., & Fenichel, E. (Eds.). (1996). *Islands of safety: Assessing and treating young victims of violence.* Washington, DC: Zero to Three Publications.

Peled, E. (1996). "Secondary" victims no more: Refocusing intervention with children. In J. L. Edleson & Z. C. Eisikovits (Eds.), *Future interventions with battered women and their families* (pp. 125–153). Thousand Oaks, CA: Sage.

Peled, E. & Davis, D. (1995). *Group work with child witnesses of domestic violence: A practitioner's manual.* Thousand Oaks, CA: Sage.

Peled, E., & Edleson, J. L. (1994). Advocacy for battered women: A national survey. *Journal of Family Violence, 9,* 285–296.

Peled, E., & Edleson, J. L. (1995). Process and outcome in small groups for children of battered women. In E. Peled, P. G. Jaffe, & J. L. Edleson (Eds.), *Ending the cycle of violence: Community responses to children of battered women* (pp. 77–96). Thousand Oaks, CA: Sage.

Pynoos, R. S. (1996). Exposure to catastrophic violence and disaster in childhood. In C. R. Pfeffer (Ed.), *Severe stress and mental disturbance in children* (pp. 181–210). Washington, DC: American Psychiatric Press.

Pynoos, R. S., & Eth, S. (1984). The child as witness to homicide. *Journal of Social Issues, 40,* 87–108.

Pynoos, R. S., & Eth, S. (1985). Children traumatized by witnessing acts of personal violence: Homicide, rape, or suicide behavior. In S. Eth & R. S. Pynoos (Eds.), *Post-traumatic stress disorder in children* (pp. 17–44). Washington, DC: American Psychiatric Press.

Pynoos, R. S., & Eth, S. (1986). Witness to violence: The child interview. *Journal of the American Academy of Child Psychiatry, 25,* 306–319.

Pynoos, R. S., & Nader, K. (1988). Psychological first aid and treatment approach to children exposed to community violence: Research implications. *Journal of Traumatic Stress, 1,* 445–474.

Pynoos, R. S., & Nader, K. (1990). Children's exposure to violence and traumatic death. *Psychiatric Annals, 20,* 334–344.

Pynoos, R. S., & Nader, K. (1993). Issues in the treatment of posttraumatic stress in children and adolescents. In J. P. Wilson & B. Raphael (Eds.), *International handbook of traumatic stress syndromes* (pp. 535–549). New York: Plenum.

Pynoos, R. S., Steinberg, A. M., & Goenjian, A. (1996). Traumatic stress in childhood and adolescence: Recent developments and current controversies. In B. A. van der Kolk, A. C. McFarlane, & L. Weisaeth (Eds.), *Traumatic stress: The effects of overwhelming experience on mind, body, and society* (pp. 331–358). New York: Guilford.

Rhodes, R. M., & Zelman, A. B. (1986). An on-going multi-family group in a women's shelter. *American Journal of Orthopsychiatry, 56,* 120–130.

Roberts, A. R. (1984). Crisis intervention with battered women. In A. R. Roberts (Ed.), *Battered women and their families: Intervention strategies and treatment programs* (1st ed.) (pp. 65–83). New York: Springer Publishing Company.

Roberts, A. R. (Ed.). (1990). *Crisis intervention handbook: Assessment, treatment, and research.* Belmont, CA: Wadsworth.

Roberts, A. R. (1991). *Contemporary perspectives on crisis intervention and prevention.* Englewood Cliffs, NJ: Prentice-Hall.

Roberts, A. R. (Ed.). (1996). *Crisis management and brief treatment.* Chicago: Nelson-Hall.

Roberts, A. R., & Roberts, B. (1990). A comprehensive model for crisis intervention with battered women and their children. In A. R. Roberts (Ed.), *Crisis intervention handbook: Assessment, treatment and research* (pp. 105–123). Belmont, CA: Wadsworth.

Rossman, B. B. (1994). Children in violent families: Current diagnostic and treatment considerations. *Family Violence and Sexual Assault Bulletin, 10,* 29–34.

Rosenberg, M. S., & Rossman, B. B. (1990). The child witness to marital violence. In R. T. Ammerman & H. Hersen (Eds.), *Treatment of family violence: A sourcebook* (pp. 183–210). New York: Wiley.

Saakvitne, K. W., & Pearlman, L. A. (1996). *Transforming the pain: A workbook on vicarious traumatization.* New York: W. W. Norton.

Scheeringa, M. S., & Zeanah, C. H. (1995). Symptom expression and trauma variables in children under 48 months of age. *Infant Mental Health Journal, 16,* 259–270.

Silvern, L., & Kaersvang, L. (1989). The traumatized children of violent marriages. *Child Welfare, 68,* 421–436.

Silvern, L., Karyl, J., & Landis, T. Y. (1995). Individual psychotherapy for the traumatized children of abused women. In E. Peled, P. G. Jaffe, & J. L. Edleson (Eds.), *Ending the cycle of violence: Community responses to children of battered women* (pp. 43–76). Thousand Oaks, CA: Sage.

Terr, L. (1990). *Too scared to cry: Psychic trauma in childhood.* New York: Harper & Row.

Terr, L. (1991). Child traumas: An outline and overview. *American Journal of Psychiatry, 148,* 10–20.

Terr, L. (1992). Mini-marathon groups: Psychological "first aid" following disasters. *Bulletin of the Menninger Clinic, 56,* 76–86.

Udwin, O. (1990). Annotation: Children's reactions to traumatic events. *Journal of Child Psychology and Psychiatry, 34,* 115–127.

Wenckstern, S., & Leenaars, A. A. (1993). Trauma and suicide in our schools. *Death Studies, 17,* 151–171.

Wolfe, D. A., & Jaffe, P. G. (1991). Child abuse and family violence as determinants of child psychopathology. *Canadian Journal of Behavioral Science, 23,* 282–299.

Wolfe, D. A., Jaffe, P. G., Wilson, S. K., & Zak, L. (1985). Children of battered women: The relation of child behavior to family violence and maternal stress. *Journal of Consulting and Clinical Psychology, 14,* 95–104.

Wolfe, D. A., Jaffe, P. G., Wilson, S. K., & Zak, L. (1988). A multivariate investigation of children's adjustment to family violence. In G. Hotaling, D. Finkelhor, J. Kirkpatrick, & M. Straus (Eds.), *Family abuse and its consequences: New directions in research* (pp. 228–243). Newbury Park, CA: Sage.

Wolfe, D. A., Zak, L., Wilson, S. K., & Jaffe, P. G. (1986). Child witnesses to violence between parents: Critical issues in behavioral and social adjustment. *Journal of Abnormal Child Psychology, 14,* 95–104.

Wolfe, V. V., & Birt, J. Z. (1995). The psychological sequelae of child sexual abuse. *Advances in Clinical Child Psychology, 17,* 1–25.

Zeanah, C., & Scheeringa, M. (1994). *The PTSD Semi-Structured Interview and Observational Record for Infants and Young Children.* Unpublished assessment instrument, Louisiana State University, Department of Psychiatry.

CHAPTER 6

Integrating Domestic Violence Assessment into Child Protective Services Intervention: Policy and Practice Implications

Linda G. Mills

> Rosa is crying, collecting the remnants of shattered glass, making her way through the mess to the children. Lisa and Donnie are visibly shaken, but otherwise intact. Dad's gone, left, as he always does when his temper rages. They have been here before. Stains from the thrown spaghetti mark the walls, and Coke is dripping from the door. The silence following Dad's outburst is palpable. The chaos becomes their rallying point. The scars gather weight in their collective souls.

Domestic violence presents institutional, policy, and most of all, practice challenges to child protective services agencies already overburdened by reports of child abuse. Through an exploration of the interrelationship between intimate and child abuse, I argue for new policy and practice guidelines that would encourage child protective services agencies to explore the linkages between the

129

abuses. I begin by presenting an overview of domestic violence and make the case for considering intimate abuse in the assessment of child abuse. Fundamental to this inquiry is how battered women are viewed by child protective services workers. Toward this end, I examine the tensions that have emerged over the past 10 years between battered women's advocates and child protective services workers. In addition, I address the assumptions child protective services workers may hold regarding victims of domestic violence by exposing the reasons battered women stay in abusive relationships. I dispel the myth that battered women are to blame for the abuse afflicted on them and their children. To determine to what extent child protective services agencies have accepted domestic violence as an indicator of risk in child abuse cases, empirical data is presented on how the 58 counties in California currently address domestic violence in their child abuse assessment formats. These findings suggest that child protective services agencies have been reluctant to use domestic violence as an indicator of child abuse. I conclude by presenting a Model Assessment Method as it is applied to a case like Rosa's. This method should be adopted by child protective services agencies and explicitly acknowledges the interrelationship between domestic violence and child abuse. It presents a new assessment format for workers intervening in cases with both abuses.

OVERVIEW OF DOMESTIC VIOLENCE

Domestic violence describes a pattern of battering or abusive acts by men against women in the context of an intimate relationship. Domestic violence spans a continuum of severity and includes physical, emotional, and sexual abuse. Violence occurs in the context of asymmetrical power relations between men and women in the family and in the society at large.

Violence against women by their intimate partners is a leading cause of injury and death to women. Domestic violence causes more injuries among women than accidents, muggings, and cancer deaths combined (Nurius, Hilfrink, & Rifino, 1996). Indeed, domestic violence is the largest cause of injury to women ages 15 to 44 (Corsilles, 1994). Domestic violence is responsible for the death of an average of four women every day in the United States (Corsilles, 1994). Of all female homicides, 31% are attributed to domestic violence (U.S. Department of Justice, 1992). Acute domestic violence by a spouse or lover accounts for 11.7% of women who seek care in emergency departments (Abbott, Johnson, Koziol-McLain, & Lowenstein, 1995).

Domestic violence is prevalent among all racial, ethnic, and economic groups (Corsilles, 1994). In the United States, each year at least 8 million women of all races and classes are battered by an intimate partner (see chapters 1 and 2). Current patterns predict that 50% of women will be victims of domestic violence at some point in their lives (Corsilles, 1994).

Although startling, these statistics may underestimate the occurrence of domestic violence. Precise quantification is difficult because victims often hesitate to report incidents of domestic violence out of fear, love, lack of viable alternatives, or cultural commitment or pressure. Indeed, Straus and Gelles (1986) estimate that less than 15% of victims report domestic violence incidents. Unreported cases are unlikely to be recorded elsewhere because medical personnel often fail to question clients concerning sexual, emotional, or physical aggression by partners (Nurius et al., 1996). Similarly, child protective services workers lack adequate assessments to uncover domestic violence as well as methods to validate the mother's experiences. Thus, continuing education and better assessments are needed for professionals likely to encounter survivors of domestic violence.

RESEARCH FINDINGS: THE INTERRELATIONSHIP BETWEEN DOMESTIC VIOLENCE AND CHILD ABUSE

There is a direct link between domestic violence and child abuse. Batterers do not always limit abuse to adult partners, but sometimes abuse their children as well. Studies suggest that 45 to 70% of batterers who have children present also abuse their children (American Humane Association, 1994). Based on a sample of 184 ethnically diverse children, O'Keefe (1995) found that in 47% of families where a batterer abused his adult partner, the batterer also abused his children. Conservative estimates suggest that child abuse is 15 times more likely to occur in households where domestic violence is present than in those without adult violence (American Humane Association, 1994). The United States Advisory Board on Child Abuse and

Neglect (1995) found that domestic violence is the single major precursor to child deaths in the United States. Thus, children in a household with domestic violence are at an increased risk of experiencing abuse.

Domestic violence provides a context in which child abuse readily develops (Stark & Flitcraft, 1985). Children may be hurt accidentally, if they are in the "line of fire," and experience violence meant to harm the adult partner. In addition, children may be hurt, both emotionally and physically, when intervening to protect a battered parent (Jaffe, Wolfe, & Wilson, 1990). A batterer may also use child abuse to terrorize his adult partner (Zorza, 1995). The batterer's intent to hurt his adult partner can lead to child abuse.

Danger of a batterer escalating violent incidents against both the mother and the child increases when parents separate. According to Hart (1988), battered women who attempt to leave their abuser are most at risk of death, or what has been referred to as "femicide." Separated battered women report abuse 14 times as often as those still living with their partner (Harlow, 1991). When parents separate, children are also at risk for abuse, especially during contact visits. Hester and Radford (1992), and Hester and Pearson (1993) reported varying types of abuse during contact with a separated parent, including the witnessing of physical or verbal abuse at the drop-off point; abduction and use of the child to secure the partner's return to the marriage; and "grilling" the child for information on the mother, thereby exacerbating the child's feelings of divided loyalty.

Victims of domestic violence may also abuse their children. Walker (1984) found mothers are eight times more likely to hurt a child when battered than when safe. More recent statistics reveal that women who have been beaten by their spouses are twice as likely as other women to abuse a child (American Humane Society, 1994). Battered women may abuse their children to keep from escalating a situation, that is, to prevent the child from creating an excuse for the batterer to batter. The victim may be attempting to keep the children "in line," to prevent the batterer from abusing them. The victim may also abuse her children as an attempt to release her frustration from being abused. Understanding reasons for the abuse may help determine whether the battered mother would continue abusing her child if she were safe.

Another form of child abuse is the witnessing of domestic violence itself (Echlin & Marshall, 1995). The effect of witnessing domestic violence can be devastating. Children who witness domestic violence show symptoms similar to children who have been physically, sexually, or emotionally abused (Echlin & Marshall, 1995). Children exposed to domestic violence are at risk for internalized and externalized behavior problems (Carlson, 1996). Internalized behaviors include withdrawal, anxiety, and somatic complaints. Externalized behaviors include aggressive actions, delinquency, and noncompliance with parental and school requests. Children who are both witnesses of domestic violence and victims of physical abuse are at even higher risk for behavioral problems, specifically externalizing behaviors.

The intergenerational transmission of domestic abuse is alarming. Children exposed to domestic violence and children who are physically abused are more likely to use violence in their later relationships. In a study of attitudes concerning violence, Jaffe, Wilson, and Wolfe (1986) found that children exposed to violence condoned it to resolve relationship conflicts more readily than members of control groups. Boys who witness family violence are more likely, as adults, to batter female partners (Hotaling & Sugarman, 1986). Straus and Gelles (1986) found that in a comparison of violent men with a control group of nonviolent men, the sons of violent parents have a rate of wife-beating 900 times greater than that of sons of nonviolent parents. Donna Wills, Chief District Attorney of the Los Angeles County Family Violence Unit, reports that 90% of all death row offenders allege domestic violence or child abuse in their background (Wills, 1995). These examples suggest exposure to violence can have enormous long-term effects on a child.

Not all children who witness abuse or experience abuse adopt a pattern of abuse. There is mixed data concerning whether girls who grow up in homes with domestic violence experience violence in their adult relationships (Fantuzzo & Lindquist, 1989). Fantuzzo and Lindquist (1989) reviewed 29 published papers on children observing violence with a total sample of 1069 children. They found that externalized behaviors, such as aggression, appeared linked with exposure to violence in almost all studies, but not consistently across all ages and genders. In a 1985 study conducted by Wolfe, Jaffe, Wilson, and Zak, 26% of children remained well-adjusted despite living with abuse.

Because domestic violence creates a setting in which child abuse may develop, understanding the interrelationship of the two factors is crucial. Understanding the interrelationship can improve child protective services workers' ability to recognize the risks and develop viable child safety plans. However, before such partnerships can be forged, we must first examine the tensions that have emerged between battered women's and child abuse advocates.

BATTERED WOMEN'S ADVOCATES AND CHILD PROTECTIVE SERVICES WORKERS: THE TENSIONS

As the issues of domestic violence and child abuse have evolved in policy and practice arenas, tensions have developed between battered women's advocates and child protective services workers. Explanations for these tensions include high caseloads requiring crisis intervention, different philosophies, different terminologies, different mandates, and competition for funding (Schechter & Edleson, 1994). Indeed, battered women advocates and child protective services workers do not have a history of working together.

Child protective services workers and battered women's advocates may have different perceptions of the role of the batterer. Child protective services workers often place the burden of protecting the children on the mother. Child protective services workers also concentrate blame for child abuse on the mother, rather than on the batterer (Schechter & Edleson, 1994). Battered women's advocates on the other hand, believe that protecting the mother will help ensure protection of the children (Schechter & Edleson, 1994).

Although the foci of battered women's advocates and child protective services workers differ, these foci are not exclusive. While the child protective services community primarily focuses on the child, and the battered women's community primarily focuses on the woman, both groups are concerned with ensuring a safe environment for the mother–child unit. Child protective services workers focus this attention on the parents when agonizing over what is in the best interest of the child. Similarly, battered women's advocates struggle to ensure that battered women can keep their children safe.

Even with different mandates, child protective services workers and battered women's advocates have many goals in common. Both are concerned that children who witness violence may be at risk for developing a variety of problems, including a cycle of intergenerational and intrafamilial abuse. Both attempt to break the pattern of intergenerational transmission of violence by intervening in the abusive crisis. Recognizing these commonalties may help the two groups work together towards the safety of both the battered woman and the child. Pivotal to a constructive relationship between victim advocates and child protective services workers are these questions: Can the battered mother keep her children safe? What external circumstances keep her trapped in the violent relationship?

WHY DOES SHE STAY: THE UBIQUITOUS QUESTION

A commonly asked question is why would a battered woman stay in an abusive relationship. This question reflects several judgments. First, the question assumes that battered women generally do stay in abusive relationships. It also assumes that women should always leave an abusive relationship. In addition, by asking why she stays, the onus of leaving the relationship is placed on the woman, and the battered woman is blamed for allowing the abuse to continue. Women are viewed as weak because they remain in a relationship and endure the violence that threatens their lives and the lives of their children.

Without blaming them, reasons why women stay in abusive relationships merit attention. First, structural constraints limit the choices available to women. The current structure of society includes inequality in wages for men and women and more lucrative job opportunities for men. This structure forces some women into dependence on their male partners. In addition, women may lack the education necessary to pursue employment. Finally, institutions change at a slow pace and the acceptance of violence against women has strong roots in our society. An old English saying is illustrative: "A woman, a horse, and a hickory tree, the more you beat them the better they be."

A result of the structure of society is that women may lack the financial resources to leave a relationship. Women may not be able to afford housing, childcare, or basic life necessities (Sullivan, 1991). Women may worry that their children will lack financial security if they leave. Indeed, many batterers use their more lucrative financial position to control the women they abuse. Batterers commonly withhold finances, or control finances, in order to ensure their position of financial strength in the relationship.

Some women remain in an abusive relationship for cultural reasons. Orthodox Jewish women, for example, may feel trapped because Jewish law forbids filing for a divorce. Some African-American women and Latinas fear that if they leave a relationship they will be ostracized for contributing to racial stereotypes. African-American women may also resist intervention by a hostile police force (Crenshaw, 1991). Women living in cultures that value community over individuality, as well as those that hold women fundamentally responsible for the preservation of community—which includes most of the world's cultures—face enormous barriers when confronting domestic violence. Women may fear breaking up their families (Zambrano, 1985). Nilda Rimonte (1991) explains that in some Asian-Pacific cultures, a woman abused by her husband will "hesitate . . . a very long time before attempting to do anything about the violence at all" (p. 139). Rimonte continues:

> To some, her inaction and silence suggest collusion. In fact, it is an indication of the desperation induced by the limited vocabulary of self-definition permitted by her culture, and the terrible price she must pay to preserve her identity within her culture. (p. 139)

Women also stay in abusive situations because they are emotionally attached to the relationship. Battered women may feel that a family "should stay together" and that they should tolerate abuse to protect the nuclear family. Similarly, they may stay because their child, who has a good relationship with their father, expresses either directly or indirectly that he or she wants the mother to stay (Zambrano, 1985). Women may worry that leaving will disrupt their children's lives by forcing them to change their school and their friends.

Finally, battered women may be too afraid to leave. Often, batterers threaten survivors who threaten to leave. Indeed, women who leave are more at risk for death or femicide (Hart, 1988). As discussed above, risk of abuse increases for both the mother and the child when parents separate.

DOMESTIC VIOLENCE AND CHILD ABUSE: THE INSTITUTIONAL RESPONSE

Many battered women are deterred from reporting their abuse and their children's maltreatment because of fear of losing custody

(United States Advisory Board on Child Abuse and Neglect, 1995). The Board also found that many child abuse prevention programs direct their attention to mothers, failing to focus on the men who batter. The extent to which battered women actually lose custody of their children due to their status as battered women is unclear. However, the perception that reporting domestic violence could affect custody may effectively close communication between the child protective services worker and the battered woman (Felder & Victor, 1996).

To learn more about how child protective services agencies assess child abuse cases for domestic violence, the risk assessment formats of all 58 counties in California were collected and reviewed. In 47 counties in California, an actual form is used by child protective services workers when assessing risk in a child abuse case. Eleven counties do not require their workers to use any special form or format when assessing risk in a child abuse case. As one might expect, those counties that use forms ask questions regarding the "precipitating incident," "child characteristics," "caretaker characteristics," and "family factors." Some forms give further guidelines to workers such as whether or not the case presents a "low," "moderate," or "high" risk.

A further analysis of the forms reveals that only six counties, those using the "Los Angeles Risk Assessment Form," explicitly assess for "spousal abuse" and/or "marital conflict." Those counties include Los Angeles, San Bernardino, San Francisco, San Mateo, Tulare, and San Joaquin Counties (See Table 6.1). San Joaquin County, one of the six counties, only uses this form with children under 5 years old, and only when there is an allegation of physical abuse. Twenty-four counties in California use the "Fresno Risk Assessment Form," including Alameda, Butte, Colusa, Glenn, Humboldt, Kern, Lake, Lassen, Madera, Marin, Merced, Nevada, Plumas, Riverside, Sacramento, San Diego, San Joaquin (for children over 5 years of age, or under 5 years of age with no allegation of physical abuse), Santa Clara, Solano, Sutter, Trinity, Ventura, Yolo, and Yuba Counties (see Table 6.1). In this form there is no explicit reference to spousal abuse, only a generic reference to "History of Abuse/Neglect in Family" under the "Family Factors" section of the form. Sixteen counties in California use the "State Risk Assessment Form," including Alpine, Amador, Calaveras, Del Norte, Imperial, Inyo, Kings,

TABLE 6.1   Analysis of Risk-Assessment Forms

Form	Counties	Explicit reference to domestic violence	Possible implicit reference to domestic violence
Los Angeles Risk Assessment Form	Los Angeles, San Bernardino, San Francisco, San Mateo, Tulare, San Joaquin (child under 5)	Spousal Abuse	N/A
Fresno Risk Assessment Form	Alameda, Butte, Colusa, Glenn, Humboldt, Kern, Lake, Lassen, Madera, Marin, Merced, Nevada, Plumas, Riverside, Sacramento, San Diego, San Joaquin (child over 5), Santa Clara, Solano, Sutter, Trinity, Ventura, Yolo, and Yuba	None	History of Abuse/ Neglect in Family
State Risk Assessment Form	Alpine, Amador, Calaveras, Del Norte, Imperial, Inyo, Kings, Mariposa, Mono, Modoc, San Benito, Sierra, Siskiyou, Sonoma, Stanislaus, and Tuolumne	None	History of Abuse
No Form: "State" Model Training	El Dorado	N/A	N/A
No Form: "Fresno" Model Training	Contra Costa, Mendocino, Monterey, Napa, Orange, Placer, Santa Barbara, and Tehama	N/A	N/A
No Form: Own Training	Fresno and Shasta	N/A	N/A
Online Risk Assessment	Santa Cruz	No	No
Own Form	San Luis Obispo	No	No

Mariposa, Mono, Modoc, San Benito, Sierra, Siskiyou, Sonoma, Stani-slaus, and Tuolumne Counties (See Table 6.1). Again, no explicit reference to spouse abuse is made. A "History of Abuse" appears under the "Family Factors" section of the form.

One other county, El Dorado, was trained to use the "State" model, but uses no form. Eight counties, Contra Costa, Mendocino, Monterey, Napa, Orange, Placer, Santa Barbara, and Tehama were trained to the "Fresno" model, but use no form. Fresno and Shasta Counties use no form, and did not use the Fresno or State training as their guide. San Luis Obispo has gone online, using a form that asks no questions regarding incidents of spousal abuse, and Santa Cruz uses its own form that makes no mention of domestic violence (See Table 6.1).

Although the use of risk assessment forms is itself controversial (Nelson, 1994), a review of the forms used by nearly every county in California, except those six counties using the Los Angeles Risk Assessment Form, suggests that child protective services workers have not yet begun to factor domestic violence into their assessment of child abuse. Indeed, even the Los Angeles Risk Assessment Form falls far short of adequately determining the extent to which domestic violence is present in a family, and does not require the worker to discuss with a battered woman her experience of intimate abuse. Even the Los Angeles Risk Assessment Form does not instruct the child protective services worker to show any particular interest in the safety of the mother. The form only provides for the consideration of domestic violence in the assessment of the alleged child abuse. Without an explicit tool to help facilitate these discussions, battered women will continue to be reluctant to divulge the intimate abuse that is plaguing their and their children's lives.

DOMESTIC VIOLENCE AND CHILD ABUSE: A MODEL ASSESSMENT RESPONSE

In response to the dearth of available assessment instruments for child protective services workers to use when evaluating domestic violence, a Model Assessment Method was developed. The goal of the Method is to create a partnership between the mother and child protective services worker; to protect the child, and to empower the mother. Through this collaboration, both the child protective services worker and the mother can determine the best method of protecting the child and develop a safety plan to protect both the mother and the child. A collaborative approach facilitates communication between the mother and child protective services worker. It also involves the mother in the decision making process.

A case example involving Rosa and her children, Lisa and Donnie, was presented in the introduction to this chapter. It is useful to consider how the Model Assessment Method might be used by a child protective services worker called to this client's home.

The first step is for the child protective services worker—let's call her Doris—to assess whether domestic violence has occurred. Unlike the typical CPS case, the worker's first inquiry is not into the child's safety, but into the mother's ability to protect herself and her children. Assuming Doris is responding to an emergency call (made by a neighbor, by the police, or by Rosa herself), Doris must determine whether domestic violence is occurring and with what frequency and intensity.

Using the "Guidelines for Interview with Battered Woman," presented as Form A, Doris would begin the interview with Rosa by engaging her. To engage her, it is helpful for Doris to inform her that she wants to involve Rosa in the assessment process, and that as a CPS worker her commitment is not only to Rosa's children, but also to Rosa. Doris would also tell Rosa that what she shares will affect how Doris intervenes in her case. Full disclosure of reporting requirements can facilitate honesty and ensure trust.

Once Rosa is aware of the CPS worker's role, both as a social worker and a mandated reporter, Doris should try and engage Rosa, to encourage her to talk about her history. Using a direct approach, the worker would inquire whether Rosa had been physically hurt during a fight, or whether her husband had screamed at her. Explanations of these distinctions are often necessary, as battered women can sometimes become inured to the abuse. Doris might ask whether Rosa had ever been sexually abused by her husband or lover. Using an indirect approach, Doris might ask: "What happens when you fight?" This is the time to create a space in which the battered woman can tell her own story, to recreate her own history.

While listening, Doris should evaluate the risk Rosa and her children face, using the "Assessment of Threat," Form B. While assessing the threat, Doris might share with Rosa her insights and expose the seriousness of the danger posed by the abuse. Using a current or past-year calendar to facilitate the Assessment of Threat can be instrumental in assisting Rosa in remembering the range and frequency of abuse, and for assessing the potential for escalation. Throughout the interaction, Doris should avoid blaming Rosa for the domestic violence she has endured, and should stress the importance of working together. Hopefully, this collaboration can ameliorate the tension inherent in an interview when the child protective services worker has the power to remove the children from the household, and should stimulate a trust which can involve Rosa in designing her own future. At every step of the assessment process, Doris should be aware of any countertransference issues that might interfere with her assessment of the violence in Rosa's life. Such issues may include Doris' own history as a victim of intimate abuse, or as a survivor of a childhood history of domestic violence.

After providing Rosa a safe space to describe the violence, Doris can help her identify sources of support and develop a safety plan, using Form C. The child protective services worker and the mother together determine her safety options. A "Social Support Inventory" is used to list potential resources. In Rosa's case, if she has lived in this country her whole life, she is likely to have family or friends she might rely on, although it is also helpful to remember that women in abusive relationships are often isolated from loved ones and taught to believe they have no one they can trust. The worker can reassure the battered woman and help determine what realistic safety options exist. If she has no realistic options, a shelter may provide her only solace.

In Rosa's case, her lover and the father of her children has left the home by the time Doris arrives. Should he return, we'll call him Dave. While Doris is present in the home interviewing Rosa, several important steps should be taken. Doris should be aware that her own safety might be at stake when Dave learns why she is there. Doris needs to trust her instincts as to the dangerousness of the situation and heed her internal concerns (De Becker, 1997).

To assess the situation more accurately, Doris should refer to Form D, "Worker Safety Planning and Batterer Interviewing Guidelines." She would review the "Assessment of Threat," Form B, and synthesize what she knows about the batterer in light of his current reaction. If Rosa and her children are preparing to leave, or any other violence provoking action will be taken, this may exacerbate his anger. A backup call to law enforcement may be necessary. Otherwise, a worker may want to avoid contact with the batterer in his home altogether. Interviewing him at the CPS office might make more sense, where there is heightened security.

The content of Doris' interview with Dave, once worker safety issues have been resolved, would cover five domains: his beliefs about how intimate relationships resolve conflicts; the level of abuse (verbal and physical), according to Dave; his own view of his behavior, and the use of his violence to control Rosa; his perceived risk of the domestic violence to the children; and his willingness to address the violence. An assessment of Dave's threat to Rosa and his children, would assist Doris in evaluating, with Rosa's input, what interventions are most appropriate in this case.

In the final analysis, Doris would use the "Affirmative Action Plan," Forms E1 and E2, to determine what action she will need to take in relation to Lisa and Donnie. An Affirmative Action Plan is necessary when the child protective services worker determines that domestic violence is present (Form A) and there is a risk of threat (Form B). The Affirmative Action Plan is flexible and can be altered to meet local conditions. If Rosa was living in a county where there were several recent child deaths, the child protective services agency may be under intense political pressure to take action, removing all children from potentially abusive homes. Under these circumstances, the county may be "more restrictive" in its approach to working with battered women and in their assessment of child abuse (Form E1). Using a more restrictive approach, Rosa may be required to leave her husband immediately, either by entering a shelter with the children, or going to live with family members deemed qualified to protect her and her children. A restraining order would be obtained and the police would thereby monitor Rosa and her children's continuing safety. However, in a less restrictive environment, child protective services workers could give battered women a range of options, including the possibility of no immediate intervention. In Rosa's case, the county might issue a warning to the batterer, or ensure that he is arrested for this incident. A "less restrictive" approach (Form E2) may not require Rosa to act at all.

In sum, this Model Assessment Method helps child protective services workers create a safe, nonjudgmental space for mothers to discuss their story, with full disclosure of the CPS workers' accountability to their agency. In addition, it would assist the worker in assessing, with the battered woman, the batterer's threat and his willingness/availability to work with the system to change. It also helps everyone understand what social support is available to the battered woman and her children. Finally, the Method is designed to help child protective services workers respond to a "more" or "less" restrictive political environment, while taking into account the particular circumstance of this battered woman and her child. Without such support, Rosa, and battered women like her, would be reluctant to reveal their ongoing history of terror, and would be prevented from finding safety in a system too quick to blame the battered woman's previous inaction.

POLICY AND PRACTICE IMPLICATIONS

Child protective services agencies maintain a policy of ignoring or overlooking domestic violence. This policy impedes the ability of child protective services workers to gather information from the mother necessary to protect the child. Understanding the interrelationship between child abuse and domestic violence can help empower the mother as well as protect the child. Knowing why women stay in abusive relationships, and that in some cases this is a safer alternative than leaving the batterer, can help child protective services workers and battered women's advocates to work together. A policy shift which includes the practice of assessing for domestic violence in child abuse cases requires a focus on the mother-child unit, rather than the current focus of child protective services agencies solely on the child. In addition, it requires that child protective services workers hold both parents responsible for protecting the child, rather than placing the burden solely on the mother, especially in cases where the father is violent against his spouse. These policy and practice shifts are necessary not only to protect children, but also to protect the battered women, who might otherwise never have a chance to divulge their own histories of abuse.

FORM A: Model Assessment Method

GUIDELINES FOR INTERVIEW WITH BATTERED WOMAN

The step-by-step method outlined below will help guide you as you work to involve the woman in the assessment. This kind of investigation/ interview is very different. You are working with the battered woman, so that *together* you can formulate what is in the best interests of her and her child. *Remember that this assessment is an ongoing process.* Also, please try to be sensitive to the issues that this situation raises for you and your history.

I.   **Determine If Domestic Violence Is Present**
     Explain what is going to happen.
     • Explain that you are there to hear her perspective. Ask if she is alone and able to talk. If she is afraid to arrange to be alone (i.e., there would be repercussions), offer her options that would allow you to both operate within your time frame and honor her concerns.
     • Explain that CPS (Child Protective Services Agency) has developed this new program that is sensitive and understanding of the structural, emotional, cultural, and financial problems of women experiencing domestic violence.
     • Assess whether domestic violence is present using indirect/direct approach:
          ~ Indirect: "What happens when you fight."
          ~ More Direct: "Have you ever been physically, emotionally or sexually hurt in a fight?"
          ~ Direct: "Is there hitting, intimidation, etc., between you and your partner?"
     • Explain that you are available to help her develop a plan to help keep her and her children safe.
     • Clarify that you will not ask her to leave the abusive relationship permanently, if she doesn't want to leave. Instead, you are here to assure that she and the child(ren) are safe/protected.
     • Explain that this is an ongoing assessment process.
     • Let her know that the child(ren) will also be interviewed because you are interested in the well-being of both the mother and the child(ren). Let her know that you or a law enforcement officer will probably interview her husband or partner.
     • Explain that your primary purpose is not to take her child(ren) away but that it is a possibility. You will discuss this again at the last part of your interview. You need to address this directly, even if she does not raise it.
     • Explain that you want to establish a team relationship with her to prevent removal of her child(ren) from the home.
     • Make comments on affect and injuries you observe; don't collude with the batterer through silence. Use the batterer's first name when eliciting

information. Ask about both the positive as well as the negative aspects of the relationship.

- Inquire about the violent behaviors of all those people living in the household (to determine if there is elder abuse, sibling abuse, etc.).

II. Listen To Her Story

- Try to elicit her conceptualization of her situation. Use her terms when possible.
- Tell her that there are people who will listen to and believe her story. Try not to interrupt her, as she may experience this frequently.
- Once you have created a trusting relationship, she may be ready to tell you about the violence she has endured. Explain the limits of confidentiality and if the information must be used, you will advise her. Explain that you will not jeopardize her safety.
- Be patient and compassionate since you may be the first person she has ever told about the violence against her, or never told anyone who really listened.

III. Discuss Her Perspective

- Work together with her to determine her level of danger. If she appears to be experiencing a pattern of violent episodes, you should explain how you see the pattern unfolding.
- Give validating messages—it is often validating to explain how cultural, emotional, and financial barriers affect battered women. Be specific to her own cultural and socioeconomic background.
- Elicit from her what she has done so far in her efforts to protect herself and her child(ren). This is part of your ongoing assessment of her protective capacity and ability to make change.

IV. Issues of Responsibility

- Avoid blaming the battered woman for the actions of the abuser or her previous history of abuse. Previous abuse history should not automatically lead to an assessment of inability to protect. Legally, the parents are both responsible for the protection of minors.
- Ask yourself,
  - ~ "Am I being objective in my assessment of all parties?"
  - ~ "Have I provided all possible resources to this mother to facilitate her movement to an independent position?"

V. Assessment of Threat

- Explain that you are very interested in what her experience was with her husband or partner. State that because her safety is critical for both her and the child, you hope that she can be as honest as possible in sharing information; you need to convince her of your partnership in determining her and the child's safety.
- For a method to assess threat, see Form B.

VI. Conduct the Social Support Inventory I, II, III (Form C)

- Helps you and the battered woman make a joint assessment of supports that may become resources and part of her safety plan.

- Facilitates your assessment of strengths; and her view of herself as having some assets.
- Remember that battered women often don't realize that they have a support system as the batterer has often undermined her relationship with others. Don't penalize her for not responding positively.

FORM B: ASSESSMENT OF THREAT

The accuracy and consistency of predicting dangerousness and violence is a relatively young science that continues to evolve. The following serves as a guideline only, supplemented by professional(s)' judgements and the use of a shared decision making model on 3 levels: worker/client; worker/supervisor/management; worker and supervisor/outside professionals.

Directions: If you suspect domestic violence, directly ask the battered woman whether or not she has knowledge of the following:

I. DOES THE BATTERER:
   A. Have a history of abuse or demonstrated antisocial behavior both inside and outside of the home, including
      ~ sexual abuse (includes forcing sex with her)
      ~ physical abuse (including choking and abuse during pregnancy)
      ~ emotional abuse
      ~ destructive acts
      ~ mutilation of pets
      ~ violent criminal record
      ~ impulsive acts
   B. Have *evidence* of a mental health disorder (and/or previous psychiatric *diagnosis*), including
      ~ threatened or fantasized suicide
      ~ been acutely or unusually depressed with little hope for moving beyond it
      ~ consumed alcohol or drugs, elevating his despair, or is an ongoing substance abuser
      ~ obsessed with partner or with controlling and regulating the partner's contacts outside of the relationship
   C. Have access to or demonstrated propensity to use weapons against the partner
      ~ threatened or fantasized homicide
      ~ possess or have access to weapons (includes threatening to use or demonstrated a propensity to use household kitchen or other knives, scissors, etc. in a threatening manner)
   D. Have difficulty maintaining consistent employment/ or is currently unemployed

II. DOES THE VICTIM:
   A. Have a history of visits to
      ~ the emergency room for domestic violence injuries
      ~ a shelter
      ~ a therapist or clergy for help with domestic violence related problems
      ~ a friend or relative for help with domestic violence related problems
   B. Have a history of thoughts of suicide; have a history of attempting suicide.

NOTE: Use a current and past year calendar to help your client get a sense of the *range, frequency,* and potential escalation in severity of abuse. Calendars can facilitate consciousness-raising in domestic violence cases.

FORM C: SOCIAL SUPPORT INVENTORY, PART I

Social support networks are an important and critical factor in battered women's ability to recover from violence. This inventory will:

* help her identify her sources of support,
* help her identify where she may have been isolated, and
* help her identify where she may want to target her network efforts.

The information on this inventory may also become part of her safety and action plan.

NAME: _____

Directions: List as many people you can think of in each category. First, list your personal allies and resources, then you can also list people in organizations who might be considered professional helpers. Remember to think of people you can easily reach by phone, and in the neighborhood. Do these individuals know about your situation? If not, can you tell them?

<u>Note</u>: *On these inventories, references to the first person (you and I) refer to the client.*

List the names and relationship of adults who:

1. *You feel really care about you and listen to you:*
   Name: _____   Relationship: _____
   _____   _____
   _____   _____

2. *You count on for advice or information on personal matters or resources:*
   Name: _____   Relationship: _____
   _____   _____
   _____   _____

3. *You depend on when you need help:*
   Name: _____   Relationship: _____
   _____   _____
   _____   _____

4. *You can count on for favors:*
   Name: _____   Relationship: _____
   _____   _____
   _____   _____

SOCIAL SUPPORT INVENTORY, PART II

* Were you able to list personal social support allies in all categories?
* Of those listed, which can you count on to be part of your safety plan?
  - A key issue may be whether or not the batterer would have access to you/the children if you were temporarily living with the person.

– Also consider, *what other resources* I can count on from this person, other than a place to live. List them as a resource on part III.
• If not, is there value in trying to develop supports in the *general areas* where you have none or few?
  – Companionship, what do you need?
  – Advice & information, what do you need?
  – Practical assistance, what do you need?
  – Emotional support, what do you need?
• How would you go about doing that?
  – Plan for developing support and alliances in the identified areas.

SOCIAL SUPPORT INVENTORY, PART III

The following is a list that battered women need to consider in developing a safety and action plan. This can also serve as a checklist to help her take stock where she is, if independent survival is her goal. The list can also help CPS workers work with battered women in considering realistic options.

RESOURCE	I Have This/Identify Resource	I Need to Develop
Housing		
Material Goods & Resources		
Cash on Hand/Finances		
Employment		
Education/Job Training/Skills		
Transportation		
Social Support		
Legal Assistance/ Protection		
Child Care		
Health Care/Mental Health Care		

FORM D: Worker Safety Planning & Batterer Interviewing Guidelines*

1.   Recognize that while all batterers are *potentially* dangerous, not all will demonstrate that behavior with you. We want to encourage you to trust your instincts, but also heed these tips which are useful in *high risk* situations.

2.   What is a high risk situation is not always clear-cut. The assessment of dangerousness is an infant science. Consider the following:
   a.   Review *Assessment of Threat* list (Form B). What do you know about the batterer's history at this point?
      ~ Conduct a criminal records check; determine if courts or probation, etc., are currently involved.
   b.   Are you involved in confronting/negotiating any of the following potentially high risk situations?
      ~ Victim is preparing to leave.
      ~ Children are going to be removed.
      ~ Batterer has just been released from jail and serious criminal charges are pending (if batterer is unemployed this may increase risk).
      ~ Allegations regarding child abuse/neglect are being made directly.
      ~ Batterer is inquiring about family's secret whereabouts.
      ~ Reunification services are being terminated.
      ~ History of alcohol use/abuse.

3.   Engage in active prevention planning; consider the following in your planning:
   a.   Contact law enforcement if necessary.
   b.   Do not meet alone with batterer; have him come to office.
   c.   Have security officer accompany you to your car.
   d.   Notify office security and co-workers of a potentially dangerous client visit.
   e.   Explore multiple exits ahead of time.
   f.   Know the procedure to follow in an emergency situation, i.e., how do you access help, is there a "call button" in the interview room?
   g.   In an interview room, position yourself close to the door.

4.   Should you find yourself in a dangerous situation:
   a.   Again, trust your instincts. Many workers let the situation escalate too far *before* reacting/seeking help.
   b.   Stay calm yourself. Use your active listening and allow for ventilation. While you can validate angry feelings, you should also set some clear guidelines should behavior escalate.
   c.   Assess your ability to provide control, and be prepared to escape, if necessary.

    d.   Later, notify the battered woman if you become aware that the batterer's anger is increasing.

5. The content of your interview with an alleged batterer covers the following domains (below are sample questions only; note the "process": from the general to the specific):

    a.   Current relationship and beliefs about relationships.
- ~ Describe your relationship with wife/partner and family.
- ~ What do you like/dislike about wife/partner and family?
- ~ What do you do when you disagree?
- ~ What do you do when you are angry?

    b.   Level of abuse—verbal & physical.
- ~ Does anyone think your temper is a problem? Who?
- ~ Have police ever come to your home? When? Who called? Why did they call? What happened as a result?
- ~ Have you ever forcefully had to touch someone?
- ~ Have you ever been so angry you wanted to hurt someone?
- ~ Have you ever stopped your wife/partner from leaving? What happened?

    c.   View of his own behavior and violence in general.
- ~ When is it okay to (incident) ?
- ~ How do you think your partner reacted to (incident) ?
- ~ Who is responsible for (incident) ?

    d.   Risk to the children.
- ~ Describe the children.
- ~ What are your expectations?
- ~ How do you discipline?
- ~ How do you think kids are affected when they see or hear you and your wife/partner fighting?

    e.   Willingness to address the violence.
- ~ What will you do when the problems we identified come up again?
- ~ What changes are you willing to make to:
  - – keep CPS out of your life?
  - – keep your family safe?
- ~ Remember, batterers can be charming. They may say that they are willing to change and have no intention. Assess the seriousness of their commitment through action, including attendance to meetings and treatment.

---

*Adapted from County of San Diego, Department of Social Services, Children's Services Bureau, December 1996, Domestic Violence Protocol.

FORM E1:   *SAMPLE* AFFIRMATIVE ACTION PLAN

More Restrictive Approach

- An Affirmative Action Plan is necessary when you have determined that domestic violence is present and there is risk of threat. The remaining parent becomes the focus of your interventions.
- *REMEMBER*: AVOID BLAMING THE BATTERED WOMAN FOR THE ACTIONS OF THE ABUSER. THE PARENTS *SHARE* RESPONSIBILITY FOR THE SAFETY OF THE CHILDREN.
- Always try to make a safety plan with the battered woman regardless of her level of cooperation.
- Ask yourself—have you done all that you can to ensure that the batterer experiences consequences.

Once you have assessed Threat and Social Support, you will develop an Affirmative Action Plan. Please note that many of the identified social supports are also *strengths* and should be factored into your Affirmative Action Plan. If the children are to remain with her and she goes to a relative/friend, assess all parties for risk of child abuse.

Low Risk		
An Assessment of *low risk* is appropriate if the batterer does not have access to the battered woman and/or family members. (Is he living there or not? Ex- or current partner? Does he have legal custody?) Use the Assessment of Threat as a guide for your individual assessment of dangerousness.		
		CPS worker options include:
Battered woman is willing to:	Do nothing to change the situation; make a safety plan for woman.	(1) make a safety plan for woman; and/or (2) continue ongoing assessment.
	Obtain an EPO* or TRO** (presumes police report and potential arrest of the batterer).	(1) continue ongoing assessment (includes compliance with EPO/TRO).
	Leave the home and go to a shelter (includes getting a EPO/TRO).	(1) depending upon the shelter, children may be able to go with mother; and (2) ongoing assessment.
	Leave the home and go to a safe friend/family home (includes EPO/TRO).	(1) children may go with the mother; and (2) ongoing assessment.

High Risk An Assessment of *high risk* is appropriate if the batterer has access to the battered woman and/or family members; use the Assessment of Threat as a guide for your individual assessment of dangerousness.		
		CPS worker options include:
Battered woman is willing to:	Do nothing to change the situation.	(1) remove the children.
	Obtain an EPO* or TRO** (no arrest made).	(1) make a safety plan for woman and child(ren); and/or (2) remove the children.
	Make a police report which results in the batterer's arrest (which includes obtaining an EPO/TRO).	(1) leave children with the mother; and (2) continue ongoing assessment (includes compliance with EPO/TRO).
	Leave the home and go to a shelter (includes getting an EPO/TRO).	(1) depending upon the shelter, children may be able to go with mother; and (2) ongoing assessment.
	Leave the home and go to a safe friend/family home (includes EPO/TRO).	(1) children may go with the mother; and (2) ongoing assessment.

In every case, the battered woman:

1. should be given a copy of a Safety Handbook, which describes how she needs to respond in a crisis and encouraged to use it. A Safety Plan should be developed in all cases.
2. should be given additional resource material according to her need and at the discretion of the CPS worker.
3. should be advised that any assessment is preliminary and needs to be discussed with a supervisor, and in some cases, an administrator. If there is a need to separate the mother and remove the child(ren), the police may need to be involved.
4. deserves to be evaluated on individual and case merits (strengths/risks). Some things are hard to itemize and weigh, but this assessment process should be helping both the battered woman and CPS worker think concretely, logically and in an organized fashion about these complex issues. Your training and experience are components of your professional judgment; these are critical elements of your assessment.

---

*Emergency Protective Order.
**Temporary Restraining Order.

FORM E2: *SAMPLE* AFFIRMATIVE ACTION PLAN

Less Restrictive Approach

- *REMEMBER*: AVOID BLAMING THE BATTERED WOMAN FOR THE ACTIONS OF THE ABUSER. THE PARENTS *SHARE* RESPONSIBILITY FOR THE SAFETY OF THE CHILDREN.
- Always try to make a safety plan with the battered woman regardless of her level of cooperation.
- Ask yourself—have you done all that you can to assist the battered woman AND ensure that the batterer experiences consequences.

Once you have assessed Threat and Social Support, you will be developing a plan of action. This includes eliciting from her what she thinks would help her and her child(ren) become more safe. Ask her to explain her reasons as they may not be obvious. Please note that many of the identified social supports are also *strengths* and should be factored into your Risk Assessment.

Risk Assessment

Assessment is always appropriate when safety for the mother and child is at issue.
1. First, consider *access* to her and her child(ren)
   ~ Does he live there; Is he an ex- or current partner?
   ~ Is he a current legal custody holder?
2. How dangerous is the batterer (refer to Assessment of Threat)? Given that the clinical prediction of dangerousness is not always reliable, CPS workers are encouraged to assess risk in collaborative decision-making. Include your supervisor.
3. What needs to be done to assure safety?

		CPS worker options include:
Battered woman is willing to:	Do nothing to change the situation.	(1) remove the children; and/or (2) continue ongoing assessment.*
	Obtain an EPO or TRO (presumes police report and potential arrest of the batterer).	(1) continue ongoing assessment (includes compliance with EPO/TRO).*
	Leave the home and go to a shelter (includes getting a EPO/TRO).	(1) depending upon the shelter, children may be able to go with mother; and (2) ongoing assessment.*
	Leave the home and go to a safe fiend/family home (includes EPO/TRO).	(1) children may go with the mother;* and (2) ongoing assessment.*

In every case, the battered woman:

1. should be given a copy of a Safety Handbook, which describes how she needs to respond in a crisis and encouraged to use it.
2. should be given additional resource material according to her need and at the discretion of the CPS worker.
3. should be advised that any assessment is preliminary and needs to be discussed with a supervisor, and in some cases, an administrator. If there is a need to separate the mother and remove the child(ren), the police may need to be involved.
4. deserves to be evaluated on individual and case merits (strengths/risks). Some things are hard to itemize and weigh, but this assessment process should be helping both the battered woman and CPS worker think concretely, logically and in an organized fashion about these complex issues. Your training and experience are components of your professional judgment; these are critical elements of your assessment.

If the children are to remain with the mother and she goes to a relative/friend, assess all parties for risk of child abuse. Using a less restrictive approach, ongoing assessment includes a range of options including voluntary family maintenance. When children "go with mothers," consider requesting an accelerated hearing and release of children to the mother or other relative.

These forms were adapted from Linda G. Mills and Colleen Friend, UCLA School of Public Policy & Social Research, Department of Social Welfare, Center for Child & Family Policy Studies, 3250 Public Policy Building, Los Angeles, CA 90095-1656; Health & Human Services Grant #: 09CT0206/01. If you would like to adapt or use these forms in your agency, please contact Dr. Linda Mills.

REFERENCES

Abbott, J., Johnson, R., Koziol-McLain, J., & Lowenstein, S. (1995). Domestic violence against women: Incidence and prevalence in an emergency department population. *Journal of the American Medical Association, 273,* 1763–1767.

American Humane Association. (1994). *Child protection leader: Domestic violence and child abuse.* Englewood: American Humane Association.

Carlson, B. (1996). Children of battered women: research, programs and services. In A. Roberts (Ed.), *Helping battered women: New perspectives and remedies* (pp. 172–187). New York: Oxford University Press.

Corsilles, A. (1994). Note: No drop policies in the prosecution of domestic violence cases: Guarantee to action or dangerous solution. *Fordham Law Review, 63,* 853–881.

Crenshaw, K. (1991). Mapping the margins: Intersectionality, identity politics, and violence against women of color. *Stanford Law Review, 43,* 1241–1299.

De Becker, G. (1997). *The gift of fear: Survival signals that protect us from violence.* Boston: Little, Brown.

Echlin, C., & Marshall, L. (1995). Child protection services for children of battered women. In E. Peled, P. Jaffe, & J. Edleson (Eds.), *Ending the cycle of violence: Community responses to children of battered women.* Thousand Oaks, CA: Sage.

Fantuzzo, J., & Lindquist, C. (1989). The effects of observing conjugal violence on children: A review & analysis of research methodology. *Journal of Family Violence, 4*(1), 77–94.

Felder, R., & Victor, B. (1996). *Getting away with murder: Weapons for the war against domestic violence.* New York: Simon and Schuster.

Hart, B. (1988). Beyond the duty to warn: A therapist's "duty to protect" battered women's children. In K. Yllo & M. Bogard (Eds.), *Feminist perspectives on wife abuse* (pp. 334–348). Beverly Hills, CA: Sage.

Harlow, C. (1991). *Female victims of violent crime.* Washington, DC: Bureau of Justice Statistics.

Hazel, D. (1995). Presentation at the 1995 San Diego Conference on Child Maltreatment. San Diego, CA.

Hester, J., & Pearson, C. (1993). Domestic violence, mediation, and child contact arrangements: Issues from current research. *Family Mediation, 3*(2), 3–6.

Hester, J., & Radford, L. (1992). Domestic violence and access arrangements for children in Denmark and England. *Journal of Social Work and Family Law, 1,* 57–70.

Hotaling, G., & Sugarman, D. (1986). An analysis of risk markers in husband to wife violence: The current state of knowledge. *Violence and Victims, 1,* 101–124.

Jaffe, P., Wilson, S. K., & Wolfe, D. (1986). Specific assessment and intervention strategies for children exposed to wife battering: Preliminary empirical investigations. *Canadian Journal of Behavior Science, 18,* 356–366.

Jaffe, P., Wolfe, D., & Wilson, S. (1995). *Children of battered women.* Newbury Park, CA: Sage.

Nelson, K. (1994). Do services to preserve the family place children at risk? In E. Gambrill & T. Stein (Eds.), *Controversial issues in child welfare.* Boston, MA: Allyn and Bacon.

Nurius, P., Hilfrink, M., & Rifino, R. (1996). The single greatest health threat to women: Their partners. In P. Raffoul & C. A. McNeece, *Future issues for social work practice.* Boston, MA: Allyn & Bacon.

O'Keefe, M. (1995). Predictors of child abuse in maritally violent families. *Journal of Interpersonal Violence, 10*(1), 3–25.

Rimonte, N. (1991). A question of culture: Cultural approval of violence against women in the pacific-asian community and the cultural defense. *Stanford Law Review, 43,* 1311–1326.

Schechter, S., & Edleson, J. L. (1994). *In the best interest of women and children: A call for collaboration between child welfare and domestic violence constituencies.* Unpublished manuscript.

Stark, E., & Flitcraft, A. (1985). Women and children at risk: A feminist perspective on child abuse. *International Journal of Health Services, 181,* 97–118.

Straus, M., & Gelles, R. J. (1986). Societal change and family violence from 1975 to 1985 as revealed by two national surveys. *Journal of Marriage and the Family, 48,* 465–479.

Sullivan, C. (1991). The provision of advocacy services to women leaving abusive partners: An exploratory study. *Journal of Interpersonal Violence, 6*(1), 41–54.

U.S. Advisory Board on Child Abuse and Neglect. (1995). *A nation's shame: Fatal child abuse & neglect in the U.S.* Washington, DC: U.S. Department of Health and Human Services.

Walker, L. (1984). *The battered women's syndrome.* New York: Springer Publishing Co.

Wills, D. (1995). *The Criminal Justice Response: Domestic Violence.* Los Angles, CA: Publication of the District Attorney's Office.

Wolfe, D. A., Jaffe, P., Wilson, S. K., & Zak, L. (1985). Children of battered women: The relation of child behavior to family violence and maternal stress. *Journal of Consulting and Clinical Psychology, 53,* 657–665.

Zambrano, M. (1985). *Mejor sola que mal acompanada: For the Latina in an abusive relationship.* Seattle, WA: Seal Press.

Zorza, J. (1995). How abused women can use the law to help protect their children. In E. Peled, P. Jaffe, & J. Edleson (Eds.), *Ending the cycle of violence: community response to children of battered women* (pp. 147–169). Thousand Oaks, CA: Sage.

CHAPTER 7

Group Treatment of Children in Shelters for Battered Women

Joseph J. Alessi and Kristin Hearn

A new treatment population has recently emerged. This population consists of the children who find themselves in shelters for victims of domestic violence. In recent years there has been a dramatic increase in these shelters. A recent publication (*Programs Providing Services to Battered Children*, 1981) cited the number of such shelters in the United States as 394. There are 325 shelters reported to accept children. Of those, 172 stated that they had some form of program for those children. The type of program was generally described as "child care." Counseling for these children was reportedly offered as a service in only three of the shelters, despite the fact that children who come to shelters are experiencing crisis.

The purpose of this chapter is to identify this new population and its special needs and characteristics; to establish, based on the literature and on our clinical experience, the need to treat these children; to identify problems inherent in treating these young people; and to offer a treatment style that we have developed to treat this group of children.

NATURE OF THE PROBLEM

The children who find themselves in shelters are in crisis. Their normal coping patterns (which were probably not initially that healthy) and their support systems are disrupted. They have experienced the loss of school, friends, neighborhood, home, and usually the significant adult male in their lives. These children are experiencing acute feelings of separation, loss (anger, fear, and emotional pain), and they have difficulty coping with these feelings in a healthy fashion (Davidson, 1978; Fleming, 1979). As Myers and Wright (1980) report, these children "are in as much crisis as their mothers" (p. 4).

It is our contention that appropriate services for children in shelters are lacking. A publication of the New York State Department of Social Services (1980) states:

> Although the primary focus of a Special Care Home program (shelter) is the adult victim, children often outnumber adult residents by a factor of two to three. Some shelter programs have planned inadequately for child care and supervision. This results in more stress and frustration for both residents and staff, thereby undermining the real work that should be going on in the shelter. (p. 4)

It appears, from the statement, that the work of the shelter is defined merely as treating the adult victim with little appreciation for the child as victim.

Kinard's (1980) review of the literature, primarily focusing on abused children, makes note of the same dilemma: "Although concern with the problems of abused children has increased dramatically in the last decade, the primary target of intervention, particularly in the mental health field, has been the abusing parents. The impact of abuse on the child's future emotional development has seldom been considered." He goes on to state:

> Recent studies of emotional development in abused children indicate that these children have serious emotional problems despite the ser-

vices provided to their families. Knowledge about these problems is necessary in order to develop intervention and treatment strategies for ameliorating them. (p. 4)

Walker (1979), Martin (1976), Pizzey (1977), the Justices (1976), and Myers and Wright (1980) have all commented on and documented the nature of the problems and characteristics of children who find themselves in shelters. In her book *The Battered Woman*, Walker writes:

> that children who live in a battering relationship experience the most insidious form of child abuse. Whether or not they are physically abused by either parent is less important than the psychological scars they bear from watching their fathers beat their mothers. They learn to become part of a dishonest conspiracy of silence. They learn to lie to prevent inappropriate behavior, and they learn to suspend fulfillment of their needs rather than risk another confrontation. . . . They do expend a lot of energy avoiding problems. They live in a world of make-believe. (p. 46)

Martin explains how children suffer "simply because they exist" in a battering household and how they run the risk of being battered themselves, or, at least, being scapegoated by the mother who has been scapegoated by her mate. Martin goes on to note how the child suffers emotional trauma—shock, fear, and guilt. Not only is the young person terrified because he/she is at a loss as to what to do, but also the child feels responsible and guilty. Pizzey (1977) offers countless examples of how the "children of battered women cannot win." Subject to and witnesses of rejection, inconsistency, and violence, boys and girls come to shelters passive and withdrawn, as well as aggressive and destructive. The Justices' (1976) characterization of abused children's behavior coincides with those of Kinard, Walker, Martin, and Pizzey. Myers and Wright (1980) echo these characterizations. They have noticed the withdrawal and passivity, the use of aggression to solve problems, impaired peer relations, and immature and regressive behavior, as well as a "pseudo-maturity" resulting from their being made to play an adult role, encouraged by parents who are themselves emotionally immature. Myers and Wright also explain that not only do children feel responsible and guilty about violence, but they tend to see themselves as responsible for their mother leaving.

The characteristics of the children we have treated and observed mirror those described in the literature. The shelter where we are working has served more than 700 women and more than 900 children (ranging from infants to teenagers) since it opened in May 1979. Haven House is a shelter in Buffalo, New York for victims of domestic violence. It was founded by the Erie County Coalition for Victims of Domestic Violence. Treatment for children is provided by the Adult, Child and Family Clinic (formerly the Child Guidance Clinic), Department of Psychiatry, Erie County Medical Center, Buffalo, New York. The women sheltered here have been battered by husbands, boyfriends, adult sons, fathers, brothers, mothers, and sisters-in-law. There have also been children who have been abused by fathers and/or mothers. Several of these children have been incest victims. Most of the children who come to the shelter have witnessed violence and other abusive behavior (for example, verbal and sexual abuse, sleep and nutritional deprivation) in their homes. By the time a woman and her children come to the shelter, they have usually left the abusive household several times.

As stated earlier, coming to a shelter precipitates a crisis in the children's lives. Based on our observations and clinical experience, we have classified, according to age, the characteristic ways in which children react to this crisis. Infants tend to be irritable, to have difficulty sleeping, to suffer and diarrhea, and to become ill frequently. Preschool aged children tend to be irritable, reluctant to leave their mothers, fearful of being alone, and yet open about violence in their families. Elementary school aged children vacillate between being eager to please adults and eager to make new friends and being hostile and aggressive. They are also verbal about their home life. Children 11 years and older are very protective of mother and very guarded and secretive about their family situations. They often deny that violence ever occurred in their homes.

There are several characteristics which these shelter children, ages 2 through 17, share. Their initial method of solving problems is by hitting. They do not seem aware of other alternatives. They tend to be aggressive with each other as well as with adults, animals, and inanimate objects. They often use abusive language. Children as young as 2 years old have been heard voicing abusive words in adult contexts. The children of this particular population attribute their own faults and mistakes to other people and to inanimate objects. They tend to regress in areas where they had previously made developmental gains. The children exhibit a high degree of anxiety—biting their fingernails, pulling their hair, and somaticizing feelings as manifested by complaints of headaches and "tight" stomachs. They often verbalize feelings of responsibility for their parents' fighting and separation. They are confused about their feelings for their father. They hate him and love him at the same time.

TREATMENT

After working with children in the shelter and becoming familiar with the literature, the need for treatment was obvious. Supportive activities were being done with all children in the shelter. These included encouraging children to talk about their family situations and to express feelings through art, puppetry, dramatic play, creative writing, music, and creative movement. Children's "house meetings" were scheduled in which all children had an opportunity to discuss complaints, problems and suggestions. However, there was no specifically structured treatment program for these children.

Obstacles

Once the decision was made to provide treatment, it became clear there were a number of obstacles inherent in working with children in a shelter. The shelter population is unique for the following reasons:

1. The population is transient. Families are there for varying lengths of time (a few days to several months).
2. The age range of the children is wide (infants to teenagers). This results in a variety of developmental stages.
3. The availability of shelter staff to provide treatment is often limited. This is due to fiscal constraints, time limitations and/ or lack of expertise.

4. An appropriate place to provide treatment is often hard to find. Privacy, space and accessibility must be considered.

Treatment of Choice. We overcame these obstacles by first deciding that group treatment would be the treatment of choice. A group not only enabled us to work with a greater amount of children in a limited amount of time but also offered support and was less threatening than was individual counseling for these children. It helps them to feel more secure and enhances their sense of being supported and accepted. To deal with the transient nature of this population we developed a highly structured, time limited, intensive group model. This model will be described in detail later in the chapter.

Age. We chose to limit the children treated to ages 8 through 16. Our rationale was to provide the older children with a group experience structured to their cognitive and maturational needs since the supportive activities in the shelter provided an avenue for younger children to express themselves (in nonverbal and symbolic ways) and because there were staff and time limitations.

Staffing. The problem of availability of staff for leading the group was resolved by using the expertise available in working with children in groups. This was found at a local clinic providing services to families and children. Thus a mutual process of identifying the need, realizing fiscal constraints, combining resources and responding to a critical problem in the community was realized. In this case, the child care coordinator of the shelter teamed with a clinical social worker from the clinic. This team approach was done in recognition of the social worker's expertise in treating children in groups and the child care coordinator's expertise in child development and in working with the children in the shelter. It was very valuable that one of the group leaders was from the shelter. This provided the children with a sense of continuity and grounding from which a successful group experience might spring.

Location. We dealt with the problem of finding an appropriate place to provide treatment by experimenting with available rooms in the shelter and at the clinic. We also learned to cope with such problems as the children's school schedules and limited transportation. This meant working together in a creative and cooperative fashion to find a location which is private, has adequate space, and is easily accessible to the children and to the leaders of the group.

Goals

The goals of the treatment group were to give children living in the shelter the opportunity to:

1. have the necessary support to resolve the crisis they were experiencing;
2. learn to identify and express feelings;
3. learn problem solving skills; and
4. learn modes of healthy coping behaviors.

Treatment Components

A Crisis Model Component. This component allows for the ventilation of feelings, the reestablishment of equilibrium, and a focus on problem-solving skills. What equilibrium existed in these children's lives has been disrupted (Lindemann, 1961). First and foremost, the function of the group is to help children find some stability; they have a need to express feelings in an atmosphere of support. It is important for them to correct distortions in thinking that may have arisen following their abrupt departure from home. Crisis theory (Parad et al., 1976; Rapoport, 1970) provides the structure for these tasks.

An Accelerated Model Component. This means there is a time-limited contract, an ahistorical here and now focus, an avoidance of the mental illness model, an emphasis on the individual for taking responsibility for solving his or her problems, a focus on the future, and emphasis on an individual's potential rather than on the difficulties (Garvin, Reid, & Epstein, 1976; Stoller, 1972). These children are only with us for a short period of time. We want to offer them an intensive experience that is immediately of value to them. We are not interested in, nor do we expect, personality change. We are pragmatic. We hope these children can take away tools with which to cope more effectively in the future whether they return to their home and father (which happens frequently) or start a new life living with mother and siblings separate from their father.

An Educational Component. This is essential to this model. Children are either misinformed or uninformed as to how to cope with their present problems in healthy ways. Children need information, not only about distortions and misconceptions that have arisen from their present trauma, but about how to cope with unpleasant feelings and problems in the future (Slavson & Schiffen, 1975). Children need to know that there are healthy as well as unhealthy ways to respond to their feelings of anger, fear, and pain. They are taught how to problem solve and are encouraged to choose healthy solutions (Somers, 1976).

This group model includes the ten curative factors of groups that have been identified by Yalom (1970):

1. *The imparting of information* (as explained in the Educational Component).

2. *The instillation of hope.* The message is "you can do it." The children are told that they have some control over their lives. There are things they can do to feel better and protect themselves.

3. *Universality.* Knowing that other children are experiencing the same feelings and similar family situations can be immensely helpful to children. This is fostered by a group situation where trust and sharing are encouraged. The messages are "you're not alone" and "you're normal."

4. *Altruism.* Giving and receiving are fostered. Children are discouraged from negatively criticizing each other and are encouraged, primarily through leader modeling, to give each other positive "strokes." This experience of giving and receiving positive feedback has proved very rewarding and therapeutic for these children.

5. *The corrective recapitulation of the primary family group.* While corrective changes do not take place on a par with long-term treatment groups, the limit setting that takes place on our parts, the constructive way that we, as male and female authority figures,

work together, and the support and nurturance we offer in these roles trigger positive responses from these children. They have the experience that there are male and female adults who can work together without violence and arguments and even adults who can be supportive and nurturing.

6. *Development of socializing techniques.* Exercises designed to help children share feelings and information in the group are prime times for them to act out when anxiety is increased. Inappropriate expression of feelings (displacement and scapegoating) are common. It is at these times that socialization takes on unhealthy aspects. We are quick to confront and foster a more appropriate interaction.

7. *Imitative behavior.* As authority figures we model appropriate behavior and reinforce desired behavior in the children.

8. *Interpersonal learning.* Each moment is an opportunity for interpersonal learning as each group member is asked to respond and react to other members as well as participate themselves. Whenever the opportunity arises, we comment appropriately on the interaction at hand.

9. *Group cohesiveness.* This is achieved very quickly. Sharing, support, and ventilation help to quickly form a bond among the group members as children express their feelings and reveal the circumstances which brought them to the shelter. This bond carries over in the shelter where the children can be a source of support for each other outside the group.

10. *Catharsis.* The group is an opportunity for children to relieve themselves of feelings that they have been carrying with them. More than one child has stated how good it was "to get things off my chest."

Treatment Sequence

Treatment is comprised of a sequence of six sessions, each with its own focus: (1) the identification and expression of feelings; (2) violence; (3) unhealthy ways to solve problems; (4) healthy ways to solve problems; (5) sex, love, and sexuality; and (6) termination and saying goodbye. We chose these focal areas because we found they best met the needs of the children given the limited amount of time they are at the shelter.

The Identification and Expression of Feelings.   The purpose of this session is to introduce the children to the therapist from the clinic, explain the reasons for the group, identify and express feelings, and teach the children why identifying and expressing feelings is important.

Since the children already know the child care coordinator who works full-time at the shelter (and who has already prepared the children with general information about the group), time is spent, initially, getting the children acquainted with the clinical social worker. This is also a time to observe the children and get a sense of each child (how to approach and interact with him or her). We explain to the children that they need a special time to discuss things that they have on their mind. We introduce feelings and name them: Mad, Glad, Sad, and Scared. It is explained that there are lots of other words for feelings, like lonely for sad, frustrated for mad, and frightened for scared. We explain that if we use these simple words we will all understand what the other is saying. We tell the children that the reason we name and express feelings is to feel better and to use feelings to solve problems.

A variety of exercises are used to facilitate learning: faces are drawn on paper or chalkboard to express the four basic feelings; we make faces at each other—sad ones, angry ones, and so forth; children are asked to print the feeling words expressively (for example, one child drew the word "sad" three dimensionally, colored it blue with tears dripping, and another drew the word "mad" with each letter having teeth and colored it red); the children are given sentences to complete ("I feel sad when _____" or "When I feel mad I _____"). We, as leaders of the group, always participate in all of the exercises. When we risk and share it is easier for the children to trust us and share themselves. The exercises are designed to provide structure which decreases anxiety, and to involve the children in active learning. This facilitates retention. We always assign homework, the purpose of which is to keep the session alive for the children during the week. After this session we ask each child to return the following week with a poem or short essay about a particular feeling they had and what they did to take care of that feeling. In addition, these exercises are usually a positive experience for the children and set the tone for the rest of the group sessions.

Violence.   The purpose of the session on violence is to give children an opportunity to explore and express feelings about the violence in their families and how it has affected them. This helps children break down their denial and minimization of the problem. It also gives children a chance to learn that other families have similar problems and that many families do not. The following questions are presented to each of the children for reflection and discussion:

1. Why did you come to Haven House?
2. Do you think it's right for a man to hit a woman or a woman to hit a man, and why?
3. Do you think it's right for a parent to hit a child, and why?
4. How do you think you've been affected by the violence in your family?
5. Do you think you'll grow up to be violent or accept violence in intimate relationships?

The homework for this session is to create a minidrama about family violence and present the play the following week.

Unhealthy Ways to Solve Problems. The goal of this session is to help the children realize that when they have a problem, and its accompanying unpleasant feelings, one choice they have is to solve the problem using unhealthy solutions. Using brainstorming techniques (and a chalkboard), children are encouraged to think of unhealthy ways to solve problems. Some of the ways identified by the children are: using drugs (including alcohol), sex, getting married very young, problems with the court system and police (stealing, vandalizing), running away from home, skipping school, getting poor grades, eating too much or too little, sleeping too much or too little, losing friends, fighting, day dreaming, and so on.

We have found that the children have no problem thinking of many unhealthy solutions to problems. Their homework is to bring back a list of the unhealthy ways that they each try to solve problems. We think that this process helps children become aware of their individual coping patterns and aids them in terms of having choices in responding to problems.

Healthy Ways to Solve Problems. The goal of this session is to teach problem solving and to help group members think of healthy ways to cope with problems. We are honest with the children. We tell them that we know that sometimes young people have to live in bad situations and that there are times that parents do not change. We encourage them not to try to solve their parents' arguments and not to get caught between their parents, literally and figuratively. We have found that children spend a great deal of time and energy in efforts to solve their parents' problems. We encourage the children to devote this time and energy, instead, to solving their own problems. We teach that problem solving means connecting one's feelings with one's thinking, exploring available options and choosing the best option—the healthy one.

We encourage the children to think on their own and explain that there are healthy ways to make themselves feel better. Some of the healthy solutions that children have identified are: In an emergency (when someone in the family is going to get hurt), leave the house (don't try to stop an angry, violent adult) and get help or call for help; talk with friends, counselors, clergy, relatives; when sad listen to music, exercise, draw, write in a diary, talk with friends, write stories or poems; and when angry exercise, play sports, hit a pillow or punching bag in controlled situations.

It is important to communicate to children that they have some control over their lives and they can do things to feel better. Their homework is to bring a list to the next session of healthy ways that each of them can use to cope with their feelings and their problems.

Sex, Love, and Sexuality.   This topic is included because we have found it to be an important concern of preadolescents and adolescents. They need information and want clarification not only about sex but also about relationships. The children in the shelter tend to come from families who poorly model all aspects of a loving, caring relationship, including sex. Several of the children have experienced incest and sodomy. The group provides a confidential and trusting setting for children to discuss their thoughts and feelings and to ask questions on this subject. Age related films such as Sol Gordon's "How Can I Tell When I'm Really in Love?," together with other films on sexuality, provoke questions and vivid discussions. After such films, we have the children write anonymous questions for us to answer.

Termination and Saying Goodbye.   This session is a summary and review of the five previous sessions. Group members might bring cookies and we will have a party. We end on a positive note, showing by example that goodbyes can be a positive experience. We also give the children a short written evaluation of nine questions for them to complete.

1. How did you like this group?
2. How did this group help you?
3. What will you remember from the group that will help you?
4. Will you use those things you remember to help you in the future (yes/no)? Which things?
5. What did you like about the group?
6. What didn't you like about the group?
7. How would you like the group to be different?
8. Do you talk to your parents about this group? If yes, what do they think about the group?
9. Tell us anything else about the group or yourself that you want to.

In this way we get feedback about what they learned and our actions and words say "you're important and what you say is important."

SUMMARY

Based on our observations, clinical experience, and the literature, it is clear that children in shelters for victims of domestic violence are in need of treatment. We propose a short-term treatment model that helps these children cope with the crisis they are experiencing as well as providing them with information and problem-solving skills that will be useful once they leave the shelter. This treatment approach includes a crisis model component, an accelerated model component, an educational component, as well as the ten curative factors of groups as identified by Yalom. The treatment group involves a sequence of six sessions.

REFERENCES

Back, S. M., Blum, J., Nakhnikian, E., & Stark, S. *Spouse Abuse Yellow Pages.* Social Systems Research and Evaluation Division, Denver Research Institute, University of Denver, Colorado.

Davidson, T. (1978). *Conjugal crime.* New York: Hawthorn Books.

Fleming, J. B. (1979). *Stopping wife abuse.* Garden City, New York: Anchor Press.

Garvin, C. D., Reid, W., & Epstein, L. (1970). A task centered approach. In R. W. Roberts & H. Northern (Eds.), *Theories of social work with groups.* New York: Columbia University.

Gordon, S. (1979). *How can I tell when I'm really in love?* Freeport, New York: Educational Activities, Inc., Filmstrip and cassette.

Johnson, N. *Primary objectives for adults working with sheltered children.* Information published by Volunteers Against Violence Technical Assistance Program, the American Friends Service Committee, New York Metropolitan Region, 15 Rutherford Place, New York, New York.

Justice, B., & Justice, R. (1976). *The abusing family.* New York: Human Sciences Press.

Kinard, E. M. (1980). Mental health needs of abused children. *Child Welfare, 59,* 8.

Lindemann, E. (1961). Symptomatology and management of acute grief. In H. J. Parad (Ed.), *Crisis intervention: Selected readings.* New York: Family Services Association of America.

Littner, N. (1970). *Separation of the child from his natural family grouping.* Address to the Annual 1970 Conference of the Ontario Association of Children's Aid Societies.

Martin, D. (1976). *Battered wives.* New York: Simon & Schuster.

Myers, T., & Wright, L. (1980, November). *Raised in violence.* Paper presented at the 32nd Annual Meeting of the American Association of Psychiatric Services for Children, New Orleans, Louisiana.

New York State Department of Social Services. (1980). *Special care homes . . . A new beginning,* Pub. #1080.

Parad, H. J., et al. (1976). Crisis of intervention with families and groups. In R. W. Roberts & H. Northern (Eds.), *Theories of social work with groups.* New York: Columbia University Press.

Pizzey, E. (1977). *Scream quietly or the neighbors will hear.* Short Hills, NJ: Ridley Enslow Publishers.

Programs Providing Services to Battered Children (3rd ed., 2nd revision). Domestic Violence information series, No. 1, 1981. P.O. Box 2309, Rockville, MD.

Rapoport, L. (1970). Crisis intervention as a mode of brief treatment. In R. W. Roberts & R. H. Nee (Eds.), *Theories of social casework.* Chicago: University of Chicago Press.

Slavson, S. R., & Schiffen, M. (1975). *Group psychotherapies for children* (pp. 388–390). New York: Industrial Press.

Somers, M. L. (1976). Problem-solving in small groups. In R. W. Roberts & H. Northern (Ed.), *Theories of social work with groups.* New York: Columbia University Press.

Stoller, F. S. (1972). Accelerated interaction: A time-limited approach based on the brief, intensive group. In C. J. Sager & H. S. Kaplan (Eds.), *Progress in group and family therapy*. New York: Brunner/Mazel.

U.S. Department of Health and Family Services. *Family violence: Intervention strategies*. Office of Human Developmental Services, Administration for Children, Youth and Families, Children's Bureau.

Walker, L. E. (1979). *The battered woman*. New York: Harper & Row.

Yalom, I. D. (1970). *The theory and practice of group psychotherapy*. New York: Basic Books.

CHAPTER 8

Intervention and Treatment Strategies with Adolescents from Maritally Violent Homes

Maura O'Keefe and Shirley Lebovics

Dad was always really mean. He blamed us whenever anything went wrong at home. He would hit all of us when he was mad, but Mom got most of it. He drank, but hit her when he was sober too. Once he beat her so badly, she could barely get up. We thought he might have killed her. Billy [Susan's brother, age 14] often tried to stop him, but it didn't help. It only made Dad hit Billy too. I tried to stay out of it. I wish I'd been tougher and done something, but I just couldn't get up the nerve.

Dad never let me and Billy have time to be with friends. Billy always had to help Dad with things around the house. I spent a lot of time at home too. I thought helping Mom would be a good idea so there'd be less to make Dad upset. My worst fear right now is that Mom will go back to Dad. I hate him for what he did to Mom, but sometimes I get real mad at Mom too. Billy and me talk about how great it would be for all of us if Dad died. We've been away from home at this shelter for 3 weeks now, and I still hate him. I hope this time Mom never goes back. I don't know what I'll do if she does.

—from Susan, age 13

I t is estimated that between 3.3 million and 10 million children in the U. S. witness physical violence between their parents each year (Carlson, 1984; M. A. Straus, 1991). The types of violence children observe may range from overhearing some form of violent behavior from their bedrooms to seeing severe acts of violence such as beatings, chokings, or assaults with guns and knives directed at their mother by their father or father-substitute. In many cases, these children observe repeated acts of violence perpetrated by multiple partners throughout their childhood.

Although the high number of children witnessing wife-battering is not a new phenomena, it is only relatively recently that the effects of witnessing interparental violence have been documented. Adverse effects have been found in a number of domains of child functioning. Both clinical case reports and empirical studies indicate that children who witness marital violence exhibit a high frequency of externalizing behavior problems (e.g., aggression, noncompliance, and delinquency) (Holden & Richie, 1991; Jaffe, Wolfe, Wilson, & Zak, 1986; O'Keefe, 1994; Sternberg et al., 1993) as well as internalizing behavior problems (e.g., depression, anxiety, and somatic complaints) (Christopoulos et al., 1987; Davis & Carlson, 1987; O'Keefe, 1994).

On measures of social competence, such as participation in social activities, these children scored significantly below their peers (Fantuzzo et al., 1991; Hughes, 1988; Wolfe, Zak, Wilson, & Jaffe, 1986). Other problems noted among these children included school adjustment difficulties (e.g., poor academic performance, difficulties in concentration, and school phobia), deficits in problem solving, low self-esteem, and lack of empathy (Hinchey & Gavelak, 1982; Hughes, 1988; Jaffee, Wolfe, & Wilson, 1990; Rosenberg, 1987). Posttraumatic stress disorder symptomatology, such as sleep disturbances, fear and helplessness, denial, psychic numbing, and behavioral regression has also been identified among children exposed to severe marital aggression (Mowbray, 1988; Silvern & Kaersvang, 1989). Further, children growing up in violent homes learn that violence is an appropriate and acceptable means of resolving conflict in intimate relationships, a lesson that may have both short- and long-term consequences (Jaffe et al., 1990).

The vast majority of studies documenting the effects of witnessing marital violence on children's functioning have sampled preschool-

and latency-age children residing with their mothers at battered women's shelters. However, there is little research on adolescents exposed to marital violence, or on effective treatment interventions to help them cope with the trauma of the violence. This lack of information may be partly due to the fact that adolescents often do not to stay with their mothers at shelters. Also, many battered women shelters exclude male children over the age of 13. Further, adolescents, by virtue of their age, physical size, and greater independence, may be viewed as less in need of protection and therefore perhaps less deserving of concern.

The little that is known about the effects of marital violence on adolescents reveals a positive association between witnessing marital violence and aggression toward parents, running away, delinquency, and suicide (Carlson, 1990; Elze, Stiffman, & Dore, 1996; Grusznski, Brink, & Edelson, 1988). Further, there is considerable empirical support for the cycle of violence or intergenerational transmission of violence hypothesis—the notion that children from violent families carry violent and violence-tolerance roles to their adult intimate relationships. Numerous studies have found that witnessing interparental violence places individuals (particularly males) at high risk for perpetrating as well as being the recipient of violence, not only in their dating relationships, but in their marriages as well (Foo & Margolin, 1995; Gwartney-Gibbs, Stockard, & Bohmer, 1987; Kalmus, 1984; O'Keefe, in press).

Clearly, the critical nature of the consequences of exposure to interparental violence on adolescents' adjustment underscores the need for accurate assessment of marital violence as well as for effective intervention and treatment. The goals of this chapter are severalfold. First, we review some of the developmental tasks of adolescence. Second, we discuss common reactions to witnessing marital violence, and some of the ways in which exposure to marital violence may impede adolescent development. Third, we provide guidelines for assessment and intervention with adolescents from maritally violent homes when domestic violence is not disclosed as well as when the presenting problem is wife abuse. Finally, primary violence prevention programs for adolescents are discussed.

ADOLESCENCE

Adolescence is a developmental period, spanning the years 12 through 21, characterized by numerous and rapid changes. These changes include biological (e.g., physiological changes associated with puberty), cognitive (e.g., the acquisition of abstract reasoning skills that are part of formal operational thought), psychological (e.g., greater capacity for self-awareness and the formation of stable identity), social (e.g., identification with a peer group), educational (e.g., the development of educational and vocational goals); sexual (e.g., identification of sexual preference) and familial (e.g., leaving home) (M. B. Straus, 1994).

Developmental theorists vary in the emphasis they place on the tasks that must be accomplished in order for an individual to success-fully negotiate one stage of development and move on to the next. For Blos (1967), the developmental tasks of adolescence involve separating from childhood relationships and using the newfound energy to form more peer-appropriate relationships. He refers to the turning away from parents as the second step in the individuation/separation process. During this time, the adolescent frequently expe-riences an increase in narcissism, self-preoccupation, and moodiness.

Erikson (1963) coined the term "identity crisis" and viewed the primary task of adolescence as the development of an ego identity. During adolescence, individuals work to consolidate their personal, occupational, and ideological identities. In contrast to the more psychodynamic theorists, Erikson stressed the importance of the adolescent's social environment in facilitating identity formation. Thus, identity is based not only on one's internal sense of sameness and continuity in time and space, but also from others' recognition and affirmation of that self. If the adolescent is unable to develop a sense of personal identity, or if the environment does not assist the individual in constructing an identity, he/she may experience identity confusion or develop a negative identity—one based upon hostility and rebellion against parents and society.

Life-cycle theorists view adolescence as a period involving the negotiation of tasks such as identity clarification, coping with sexual-ity, and separation, but stress the necessity of looking at this stage of development in the context of the family (Carter & McGoldrick, 1980). The family is viewed as having its own life cycle, with predict-able and identifiable transitions that are usually accompanied by a normal degree of crisis. Thus, two vectors must be considered: the individual developmental demands of adolescence, and the family's position in its own life cycle. The ways in which the family accom-plishes its developmental tasks influence the individual development of family members and may serve to facilitate or inhibit this development. As children move into adolescence and become increasingly independent, parental roles must accommodate and become more flexible, allowing for experimentation, yet providing protection (M. B. Straus, 1994).

Following are two case vignettes that illustrate some common concerns, issues, and reactions of adolescents who witness marital violence.

CASE ILLUSTRATION I

Jimmy, age 13, was the oldest of three children to an intact family. His sisters were ages 9 and 7. Father worked as an accountant and mother worked as a nurse. Jimmy attended 8th grade at a local public school. Jimmy was referred for treatment by his teacher due to a long-standing history of defiant behavior. His grades included C's and D's and had worsened considerably since 7th grade. Jimmy's acting out involved lying, stealing from peers, and extreme rudeness to all of his teachers. He would often disrupt the classroom with various pranks, or by disturbing other students.

Jimmy was described by his teachers as socially isolated and unpopular due to his aggressive behavior. He spent most of his time alone. His mood was usually sullen and angry. He was also reported to "pick fights" with classmates which led to physical violence and injuries on the school yard. These led the principal to suspend Jimmy on two occasions.

During the intake session with Jimmy and his parents, marital tension was noticeable. Father was dominating and voiced loud and harsh statements about how Jimmy's behavior was not to be tolerated. Father was openly critical of both Jimmy and mother. He blamed his wife for Jimmy's misbehavior because she was "too easy on him." Mother appeared noticeably uncomfortable with her husband's manner and accusations, but said little.

Attempts by the clinician to address any difficulties between the parents were met with resistance by the father. The father insisted he was paying for therapy only to "get Jimmy to shape up." The father refused to participate in future sessions, and made no ongoing contact with the therapist. Mother assumed responsibility for bringing Jimmy in, and occasionally discussed her difficulties disciplining Jimmy at home.

Jimmy formed a positive relationship with the therapist, who was a male in his mid-thirties. Jimmy eventually referred to the terrible shouting matches at home. However, Jimmy voiced high regard for his father and defended his angry outbursts. He continually made excuses for his father, referring to how hard his father worked to support the family, and all the bad breaks he had in life.

Jimmy's love and admiration for his father were the few emotions he voiced with any conviction. He idealized his father, despite his father's physical and verbal abuse of the entire family. Jimmy said little about his feelings about his mother, but regarded her as lazy and as a "bad wife." He blamed his mother for the fights that went on at home, stating she always provoked his father. He wished his parents would divorce so that he could live with his father.

After several months of treatment, Jimmy's mother began seeing the therapist for her own individual sessions. She eventually referred to a disagreement between her and her husband and broke down crying. She finally stated that her husband had hit her, resulting in severe bruises, and that this had happened on numerous occasions throughout their marriage.

CASE ILLUSTRATION II

Lenny, age 16, was one of four sons of a Spanish-speaking mother who was separated from her husband. Siblings were ages 13, 6, and 4. After 17 years of a severely abusive marriage, the mother left home and sought safety at a local shelter with her two younger children. Since adolescents were not admitted there, Lenny and his 13-year-old brother were placed at a crisis youth shelter for children aged 12 through 18. Services between the two sites were coordinated so that family sessions were possible.

Lenny presented as a soft-spoken, sensitive, and gentle young boy. He was engaging, likeable, and communicated well. He maintained a realistic and mature view of people and the world. He never engaged in the power struggles with authority that were typical of many other adolescents at the shelter.

During the intake interview, Lenny relayed examples of the wife abuse he had witnessed. His father would reportedly not only beat his mother, but force her to dress like a prostitute. He would rarely allow her out of the house or to spend time with her family. The threats to harm or even kill his wife were frequently heard by all the children.

Lenny's role at home was that of a parentified child. He took pride in being the protector and caregiver to his mother and siblings. He was consistently focused on offering them reassurance, assistance, or affection. His adoration and high degree of concern for his mother was quite pronounced. One example was his attempt to hide the knife his father used when making threats.

Lenny's protective and caring manner was apparent at the shelter as well. He was often seen holding and kissing his younger brothers. During one incident in which another teenager argued with Lenny's brother, Lenny immediately ran to his brother's defense in an attempt to "rescue" him. He also enjoyed serving as the interpreter for his mother during family counseling sessions.

During another incident at the shelter, Lenny heard screaming from a resident and immediately jumped to offer assistance to staff. He later mentioned in session that whenever he would hear conflict he would respond "automatically." He felt a sense of duty to be helpful by mediating.

In subsequent sessions with his counselor Lenny stated that he loved his father, but felt that his father was "really messed up." He voiced dismay that his mother didn't have the "husband she really deserved." Lenny also expressed his pervasive fear of his father, which did not abate during his shelter stay. He was concerned that despite the protection of the shelter, his father would eventually find and kill them.

ADOLESCENT OBSERVERS OF INTERPARENTAL VIOLENCE

Adolescents vary in their feelings, defense mechanisms, and strategies employed to cope with the trauma of growing up in a maritally violent home. Common reactions to witnessing violence may include feelings of shame, rage, fear, and anxiety. The consequences of the violence, however, may be far-reaching and reverberate throughout many areas of the adolescent's life, including school performance, social relationships, personal safety, self-esteem, and future stability.

Shame

Domestic violence is a family secret. Last night's fight which resulted in mother's black eye is not discussed openly among family members and must never be mentioned outside the family. Adolescents carry these secrets, and are often burdened by the responsibility of censoring any remarks about their parents' relationship.

Because adolescents are self-conscious about both their physical and social appearance, anything that calls attention to themselves as different from peers may be experienced as embarrassing or as a threat to their self-esteem. A home life which includes a father who batters and a mother who shows the physical and emotional consequences of being battered may be a source of great shame. The adolescent may be reluctant to invite friends home due to fear of exposure. The need for secrecy may lead to social isolation at a time when acceptance and support from peers is especially essential to social development.

Maria, a 17-year-old adolescent, who for most of her childhood witnessed her stepfather severely beat her mother, recalled: "I thought violence only occurred at my house. I always felt there was something wrong with me—that I was messed up just like my family. I was good at keeping the secret, but I felt that any minute I would be found out—that somehow I would be exposed and that others would judge me for what my family was like."

Fear and Anxiety

The general climate in homes where domestic violence occurs is often one of apprehension, tension, and a feeling of "walking on eggshells," as evidenced in the vignettes of both Jimmy and Lenny. The family is frequently in a state of disequilibrium, never knowing when the next violent incident may recur. The adolescent may fear being the next target of attack or doing something that will provoke their father to attack their mother. Some adolescents may become paralyzed with feelings of anxiety that may not only permeate the family atmosphere, but affect other areas of the adolescent's life, such as their ability to cope with normative stresses or plan future education or career goals.

Traumatic Reactions

Adolescents may develop symptoms of posttraumatic stress disorder (PTSD) as a result of observing repeated or severe interparental violence. This is not surprising, in that seeing one's mother being beaten can be a terrifying event at any age. PTSD symptoms identified in children of battered women include: a re-experiencing or preoccupation with the traumatic event (e.g., nightmares or distressing recollections of the violence); increased arousal symptoms (e.g., somatic complaints, sleep disturbances, fears, and temper outbursts); and avoidance or psychic numbing (Arroyo & Eth, 1995; Mowbray, 1988; Silvern, Karyl, & Landis, 1995). These symptoms are also found in adolescents and may manifest in ways that are more difficult to discern, particularly if chronic. For example, psychic numbing may present as emotional constriction, flat affect, or withdrawal and disinterest in activities (Jaffe et al., 1990; Pynoos & Eth, 1984). Other symptoms, for example, running away from home or delinquency, may be expressed in a manner that disguises their origin and etiology (Jaffe et al., 1990). Because disclosure of family violence is unlikely, there may be little opportunity for resolution of the trauma.

Alliances with the Batterer

It is not uncommon for children of battered women to develop an alliance with the batterer. Some, like Jimmy, may blame their mother for the tension at home and feel angry at her for provoking the abuse. This alliance with the father against the mother may even manifest itself in assaults directed at the mother. These assaults often begin during adolescence, when the child becomes physically stronger than his or her mother. One study of adolescents who were physically abusive towards their parents found that in households where there was wife-battering, a high pattern of abuse directed at mothers was reported (Cornell & Gelles, 1982).

A factor that may account for the adolescent's alliance with the batterer is fear. In any fearful situation, a paradoxical attachment and unconscious collusion may develop between victim and aggressor. This phenomenon, originally described by Anna Freud (1974) as "identification with the aggressor," is a process wherein a child may unconsciously identify with the perpetrator as a means of warding off danger. This defense mechanism is never fully effective; even when a strong alliance exists with the father, it is usually accompanied by underlying feelings of ambivalence, confusion, or guilt.

Parentification

Adolescents who have grown up in maritally violent homes may feel responsible for maintaining safety and peace in the home. As in the case of Lenny, they may assume a parental role, defending their mother from their father's abuse or providing younger siblings with support and reassurance, particularly during violent episodes.

One of the tasks that adolescents face is individuation from the family system. Due to the dysfunctional nature of a violent family system, however, this becomes a difficult if not impossible task for the adolescent. The parentified adolescent may be concerned about who will take care of the family if he or she leaves. The assumption of a parental role frequently precludes the child from having his/her own dependency needs met, and may interfere with the development of a healthy sense of self, as well as the achievement of independence from parents.

Aggression

The relationship between witnessing interparental violence and aggression in children and adolescents has been substantiated by a number of empirical studies (Holden & Ritchie, 1991; Kempton, Thomas, & Forehand, 1998; O'Keefe, 1994; Sternberg et al., 1993). Research also indicates that violent youth are more likely than nonviolent youth to have witnessed or been victims of violence in their homes (Kratcoski, 1985). Modeling has been proposed as one means by which aggression develops (Bandura, 1971). Children from violent homes learn to imitate both the physical expression of anger and the types of problem-solving strategies evidenced by their parents, and thus develop aggressive behaviors and poor conflict resolution skills of their own. Physical aggression is often first directed at siblings and peers and later used in their own family of procreation (Cornell & Gelles, 1982).

Rage

Like their mothers, adolescents from maritally violent homes may be the recipients of physical, sexual, and emotional abuse. A child growing up in such an abusive home may initially use denial to cope with their strong feelings. As the years progress and the violence increases, the feelings of pain and anger may increase in intensity to the point where they cannot be denied effectively. The adolescent may then become overwhelmed by anger and rage.

Since adolescents have a strong need to feel a sense of control over their world, they may experience a deep sense of rage not only about the violence, but about their powerlessness to remedy the situation. They may also feel rage at their mother for her power-lessness and for her tolerating abuse or staying in the marriage. Like their mother, they may harbor fantasies and wishes that their father would somehow disappear or die. One 15-year-old teen who wit-nessed his mother's severe abuse spent long hours fantasizing about ways in which he would eventually get even. Another boy, age 13, who was residing at a battered women's shelter with his mother and three younger siblings reported that he and his mother attempted to kill the batterer by poisoning him. This boy reported that after a particularly violent incident, he and his mother bought rat poison, ground it up, and served it to the batterer in his dinner.

Depression

Adolescents from maritally violent homes are at high risk for depres-sion and suicidal behavior (Carlson, 1990; O'Keefe, 1996). Many possible factors contribute to this. The adolescent's experience of wife abuse as a traumatic, uncontrollable, and pervasive stressor may lead to feelings of helplessness, apathy, and despair. Second, chronic or severe battering may result in the mother's psychological unavail-ability, lack of nurturance, or diminished parenting ability, that leaves the child or adolescent vulnerable to depression (Jaffe et al., 1990). Third, the adolescent may experience the loss of the idealized and wished-for family, as well as the real loss of one parent, should a divorce take place.

Characteristic symptoms associated with depression in adolescents may include a loss of interest in activities, sluggishness, inability to concentrate, and/or changes in sleeping and eating patterns. He/she may be unable to set goals, achieve them, or feel a sense of satisfaction when they are achieved. Depression in the adolescent may also be manifested by displays of anger, as it is often the underly-ing emotion in the adolescent's acting out behaviors (Mishne, 1986).

Runaways

As children move into adolescence, they may become increasingly unwilling to live with the violence. Some may seek relief by running away from home. One study reported that witnessing marital violence was an important predictor of runaway behaviors among adolescent females (Elze et al., 1996). Another study found that adolescent males in residential placement who had witnessed marital violence were more likely to have run away from home than were males who had not witnessed such violence (Carlson, 1990). Although their unwillingness to live in an unhealthy situation may be viewed as a sign of strength, adolescent runaways are extremely vulnerable to other dangers, such as drug abuse, rape, pregnancy, and sexually transmitted diseases, to name only a few.

Delinquency

As children from violent homes move into adolescence, they may begin to engage in behaviors serious enough to come to the attention of the juvenile justice authorities. These behaviors may include: substance abuse, truancy, gang involvement, assaults, robbery, use of weapons, setting fires, or other illegal activity (Gruzsnski et al., 1988). Considering the lack of positive role models, it is not surprising to find the adolescent rebelling against authority figures.

Researchers have identified numerous family factors consistently associated with delinquency, including child physical abuse, marital conflict, inconsistent and inappropriate discipline, maternal depression, and criminal behavior of parents (Office of Technology Assessment, 1991). Many of these factors are also present in families in which domestic violence occurs. One researcher noted that delinquent adolescents almost always have another violent member in their family (Kratcoski, 1985).

Dating Violence

There are several unique aspects of adolescence that may make teenagers particularly vulnerable to dating violence. Because they are generally inexperienced in relationships, adolescents may have difficulty managing the complexity of feelings and conflicts that arise in intimate relationships. They may romanticize these relationships and interpret jealousy, possessiveness, and abuse as signs of love. Additionally, peer pressure may require that the adolescent have a boyfriend or girlfriend; the fear of being different or violating peer norms can create enormous stress and rigid conformity to gender-role stereotypes. Finally, due to their struggle for independence or conflicts with parents, many adolescents may not ask for any help from adults to cope with conflict or frightening experiences in their dating relationships (Levy, 1991).

Dating violence has been called a training ground for marriage and a link between witnessing violence in one's family of origin and using it in one's family of procreation (Jorgensen, 1986). A recent study of high school students living in an urban area found alarmingly high rates of dating violence: 42% report they had used physical aggression against their dating partners and 45% reported that they were victims of that violence (O'Keefe, 1997; O'Keefe & Treister, in press). Further, adolescents, particularly males, from violent homes have been found to be at increased risk for inflicting violence in dating relationships (DeMaris, 1987; Foo & Margolin, 1995; O'Keefe, 1997). It has been postulated that the intergenerational transmission of violence may be the result of modeling aggressive parental behaviors, learning aggression as a coping or problem-solving strategy, and increased frustration and sensitivity to power imbalances as a result of growing up in a coercive, conflictual, and low-warmth family environment (Langhinrichsen-Rohling & Neidig, 1995).

It should also be noted that whereas witnessing interparental violence may influence the later use of violence in dating relationships, it does not fully explain it. Other factors, such as being the victim of parental abuse, low socioeconomic status, poor self-esteem, acceptance of violence in dating relationships, and exposure to violence in one's community, have been found to differentiate high-risk adolescents who inflicted violence in dating relationship from those who did not (O'Keefe, in press).

Other Issues

Gender-Related Differences in Children's Adjustment. Gender differences in children's reactions to witnessing interparental violence have been examined by several researchers. Some studies have noted that males from maritally violent homes exhibit high levels of externalizing behaviors (e.g., aggression, temper outbursts, and disruptive behaviors), while females exhibit high levels of internalizing behaviors (e.g., withdrawal, passivity, and clinging behaviors) (Wolfe, Jaffe, Wilson, & Zak, 1985; Wolfe et al., 1986). Other researchers, however, have detected no such gender differences, indicating that both boys and girls from violent homes are at high risk for developing externalizing as well as internalizing behaviors (Davis & Carlson, 1987; Fantuzzo et al., 1991; O'Keefe, 1994). It has been hypothesized that as children approach adolescence and begin to develop heterosexual relationships, they may begin to conform to more rigid sex roles and more closely model parental behaviors. One study, however, examining the effects of different types of domestic violence (i.e., being the victim of parent child violence and witnessing interparental violence) on adolescent adjustment found that family violence did not adversely impact males more than females; that is, both males and females developed aggressive as well as depressive symptomatology as a result of experiencing parent-child violence and/or witnessing interparental violence (O'Keefe, 1996). Although more research on adolescents is needed, results call into question a simple gender-role modeling explanation for the effects of violence on children's or adolescents' adjustment.

Coexistence of Other Problems and the Effects of Mediating Variables.   Not all children who grow up in maritally violent homes are behaviorally disturbed, nor do all become involved in abusive relationships in adolescence or adulthood. In fact, adjustment problems of children and adolescents who have witnessed marital violence have been shown to be highly variable. Children who grow up in maritally violent homes may experience a number of risk factors simultaneously, including marital discord, parental alcohol and drug use, poverty, stress, maternal impairment, and physical abuse and neglect (Wolfe, 1997). It is likely that the combined effects of these stressors are cumulative; that is, those who experience multiple stressors are likely to have more behavioral problems.

Assessing for the presence of these or other risk factors, as well as for the presence of protective factors, is important in understanding both the unique effects of violence exposure on child adjustment and for explaining why some children from violent homes appear to function well, while other children exhibit severe behavioral and emotional problems. One study found that protective factors such as positive child temperament (low emotionality and high sociability), positive feelings of self-worth, school competence, and a positive relationship with the mother all served to mitigate the deleterious effects of exposure to marital violence. Vulnerability factors that exacerbated the effects of violence exposure included high levels of interparental violence, high mother-child violence, and frequent stressful life events in the child's life (O'Keefe, 1994). Results like these underscore the need to assess other variables that mediate the effects of exposure to marital violence on child and adolescent adjustment.

ASSESSMENT AND TREATMENT OF ADOLESCENTS WHO WITNESS SPOUSE ABUSE

Assessment

An adolescent is often referred to treatment by a parent or teacher because of difficulties such as failing grades, acting-out behaviors, or depression. The occurrence of spouse abuse may never be disclosed to the clinician, since both the parents and the adolescent might view the marital violence as having nothing to do with the problem. The clinician's careful attention and screening for spouse abuse therefore becomes critical in conducting an assessment of adolescents and their families, regardless of what the presenting problem appears to be.

The case of Jimmy demonstrated an example of an adolescent referred for treatment due to acting-out behaviors. The clinician in that case did not learn of the violence until several months later. Considering the impact of the home situation on Jimmy's behavior, earlier knowledge of the violence would have been helpful. The following are several guidelines that may assist clinicians with early and effective assessment in similar situations.

Guidelines for Assessment of Spousal Abuse

1. Assess for Spouse Abuse as a Routine Part of an Evaluation.   Clinicians may be reluctant to approach the subject due to their own fears about how to intervene effectively. Other concerns may be about offending the parents or endangering the mother and/or adolescent. Failure to address the spousal abuse, however, ignores a significant factor that may be causing, maintaining, or contributing to the adolescent's problem.

2. Maintain an Awareness that Abuse May Not Be Readily Disclosed.   When a family comes in for treatment, they generally do not acknowledge that family violence is a problem. The battered woman may be reluctant to do so because she believes that the violence is her fault. In addition to feeling shame and guilt, she may fear retribution from the batterer. The batterer also may engage in denial and minimization of the severity of the problem and its impact on the children. The adolescent may be hesitant to disclose the violence due to his/her own shame and embarrassment, pressure to keep it a secret, or fear of the consequences.

3. Watch for Subtle Indicators of Abuse.   During the intake interview with the family, the clinician should be alerted to possible indicators of wife abuse, especially signs of control in the marital relationship. Such signs may include the following:

- suspicious injuries seen on the mother that are accounted for as accidental;
- the mother's lack of access to money or a car that is not attributable to low income;
- the family's isolation from friends or extended family;
- the mother's references to her partner's temper or fear of getting him angry;
- the mother's reluctance to speak or disagree in the presence of her partner;
- the father's humiliating, insulting, and/or dominating behavior;
- a history of physical abuse toward the children.

4. Meet with the Mother Alone. If wife abuse is suspected, the clinician should ask to interview the parents separately, so that the mother or adolescent is not in danger of an assault when the interview is over. Meeting separately should be explained to the family as a routine procedure, for example, "When I see adolescents I usually get a thorough history from each parent." The clinician's comfort and confidence in making this recommendation will communicate to the family that it is a necessary part of the evaluation process.

The mother is more likely to disclose the violence after she has developed some rapport with the clinician. A technique called "funneling" can be a productive way to ask questions about violence, particularly when it is not the presenting problem. This technique is designed to bring up the subject of abuse gradually, thus diminishing the client's potential defensiveness. The clinician begins by asking clients how conflict is handled in the home, and gradually moves to more specific probes such as: "Is your husband ever jealous of you?" or "Does he ever try to control what you do or where you go?" and "Has your husband ever hit you?"

5. Explain the Relevance of the Abuse to Her. If wife abuse is disclosed, it important to ascertain the degree of immediate danger to her and her children. The clinician should inform her that wife-battering is a crime, that she is not to blame for his violent behaviors, and that children and adolescents who witness interparental violence are negatively affected by it, even if they are not the direct targets of abuse. The relevance of the violence to the adolescent's problem should be made clear. Additionally, the clinician should provide her with information regarding community resources. The clinician needs to decide whether he/she will work with the battered woman or refer her to another counselor. Follow-up in terms of the intervention for the mother should be offered. In addition, periodic conjoint sessions with the mother and adolescent may be helpful.

Treatment

As noted, adolescents may present for treatment in situations in which the marital violence has not been disclosed, or may be seen in a crisis state when the marital violence is the identified problem;

for example, when they accompany their mother to a battered women's shelter. The following section describes a short-term crisis treatment approach that may be used with adolescents in various settings in which wife abuse is identified.

Crisis Intervention

Crisis intervention models emphasize brief, time-limited, focused treatment that is action-oriented (Roberts, 1996). Roberts' Seven-Stage Model of crisis intervention (1996) has been applied to a broad range of crisis situations, including battered women in crisis, and is clearly applicable to the treatment of adolescents who witness domestic violence. As described by Roberts, the model is a guide to be used flexibly and differentially as the particular situation requires.

The seven stages of the Crisis Intervention Model are as follows:

1. make psychological contact and rapidly establish the relationship;
2. identify the major problems;
3. encourage expression of feelings and emotions;
4. explore and assess coping skills;
5. provide alternatives and specific solutions;
6. formulate an action plan;
7. closure and followup.

Stage 1: Make Psychological Contact and Rapidly Establish the Relationship. Developing rapport and establishing a therapeutic alliance with adolescents can be challenging. Because they often have mixed feelings about adults in positions of authority, clinicians must make an extra effort to establish themselves as trustworthy and create a safe and therapeutic environment. Adolescents need to feel that the clinician is concerned about them, respects them, and is trying to help them maximize their own potential for growth (Gil, 1996). A supportive, nonjudgmental working relationship is essential to enable adolescents to reveal and begin to cope with painful feelings that are often too difficult for them to cope with alone. Most adolescents in crisis will value the opportunity to be heard, understood, and have an ally.

Stages 2 and 3: Identify the Major Problems and Encourage Expression of Feelings and Emotions.   It is important to help adolescent witnesses recount the recent episode of violence which precipitated the crisis or brought their family to a battered women's shelter. A recounting of the violence will help them achieve greater psychosocial mastery of the traumatic event. Thus, clinicians should facilitate a full description of the violence, its antecedents, and its aftermath. For example, adolescent witnesses should verbalize what they may have heard or seen, what they were thinking and feeling at the time, what they did, and whom they blame for the violence. It is often helpful to have them discuss the worst moment of the violence for them and how they felt at that time (Arroyo & Eth, 1995).

The clinician should listen closely and ask for clarification or elaboration when needed. Responding empathetically will assist the adolescent to ventilate painful or overwhelming emotions such as fear of harm, a wish for revenge, or intense anger at the batterer or at their mother. It is essential for the therapist to provide emotional support and to normalize the adolescent's feelings by communicating that their emotions are a natural reaction to an extremely distressing situation. The clinician should be particularly attentive to any feelings of guilt or self-reproach the adolescent may have for not being able to prevent or stop the violence. The therapist may help diminish such feelings by providing the adolescent with a more realistic sense of his/her self-efficacy.

If the adolescent is living at a battered women's shelter, it is important for the clinician to inquire what it is like for them to be there, away from their familiar environment, including home and possessions, school, peers, and even pets. For some adolescents, leaving their home and personal possessions to stay at a crowded shelter may be as much or more of a crisis as the trauma of the violence itself. Problems such as having to attend a new school or deciding what to tell friends may be overwhelming. Some adolescents, with permission from their mother, may elect to stay with relatives or friends. However, this will depend upon a careful assessment of the degree of danger they or their mother might face from the batterer.

Stage 4: Explore and Assess Coping Skills.   As the adolescent's anxiety level lessens, a more comprehensive assessment of major areas of their functioning should be obtained by the clinician. The frequency and intensity of past family violence and previous coping mechanisms should be determined. It is important to obtain a fuller understanding of the roles the adolescent plays in relation to the violence, the meaning they attribute to the violence, and how they have been affected by it.

The nature and quality of the adolescent's relationship with each parent should be explored, as well as whether they have been the target of abuse either directly or indirectly from attempting to intervene in their parent's battles. In addition, the adolescent's characteristic response styles in interactions with parents, teachers, and peers should be determined. The clinician should engage the adolescent in a discussion of how conflicts are handled and how he or she generally copes with anger. Many adolescent from violent homes have poor communication skills, as well as poor problem-solving skills, which interfere with conflict resolution.

The adolescent's relationships with peers and his/her attitudes regarding violence in dating relationships should also be explored. For example, adolescents might be asked whether they believe it is ever justifiable for a boy to hit his girlfriend, or conversely, whether it is ever justifiable for a girl to hit her boyfriend. If they are dating, the clinician should inquire about how problems and conflicts in their dating relationships are handled.

Throughout this process, the clinician should recognize and focus on the client's strengths and positive coping abilities. Adolescents from violent homes often suffer from low self-esteem and self-efficacy as a result of growing up in a violent, nonsupportive home. Consequently, they may need extra help defining areas of strengths, as well as building on these strengths.

Stages 5 and 6: Provide Alternatives and Formulate an Action Plan. Since adolescents from maritally violent homes present with such a variety of problem behaviors, cognitive behavioral strategies are frequently needed to help them gain new perspectives on their problems, correct faulty cognitions, and increase behavioral competencies (Zarb, 1992). One important component of such treatment is providing the adolescent with information on the prevalence of wife abuse. Simply recognizing that they are not alone and that other families experience the trauma of violence may lessen feelings of shame and isolation.

Another important component of cognitive behavioral treatment is the identification and restructuring of the adolescent's erroneous beliefs regarding family violence. The adolescent may believe that violence is a normal part of relationships, or that violence, intimacy, and love are enmeshed. Another distorted belief may be that someone other than the batterer is responsible for the abuse, i.e., their mother or themselves. Interventions that challenge these presumptions should be part of the treatment. It may be useful to explain the dynamics of abuse, power and control, and the cycle of violence in terms the adolescent can understand.

Cognitive behavioral techniques may also be effective in treating anxiety or phobic responses conditioned during the violence. Those who experience overwhelming anxiety may benefit by relaxation training. The adolescent is instructed to sit in a comfortable position, close his/her eyes, and follow instructions as the clinician guides the client through various steps of the relaxation exercise. The client may then be given a homework assignment of practicing relaxation these skills by listening to a relaxation tape (Zarb, 1992).

The angry or acting-out adolescent may be helped through interventions such as anger management techniques, which combine relaxation training, cognitive self-instruction, and behavioral rehearsal (Meichenbaum, 1977; Zarb, 1992). First, the client is familiarized with the concept of anger as being maintained by negative self-statements made in situations of provocation. The adolescent's anger pattern is then carefully assessed. The therapist might ask the adolescent to describe specific situations in which he/she got angry and to report accompanying thoughts and somatic affective factors. The therapist then helps the client to analyze the content of these cognitions. Any dysfunctional cognitions and faulty information-processing styles that maintain their aggressive responses are challenged. For example, erroneous attributions leading to anger arousal, for example, "The teacher is trying to make me look like a fool," or self-evaluative statements, for example, "I have be tough and prove myself," are pointed out. The client is then helped to consider alternate interpretations of the situation. Additional skills taught might include relaxation skills, humor, or nonhostile responses, such as leaving the scene or agreeing with the other person in a neutral way. Finally, the adolescent is asked to practice and role-play new behavioral skills during the session, and then to try out newly learned skills in real-life situations.

Some adolescents are drawn into marital conflicts by one parent to punish or manipulate the other. In such cases, the adolescent might be taught to examine dysfunctional family patterns and to practice techniques for avoiding being drawn into the conflict. In situations of ongoing marital violence, the goal of therapy may be analogous to helping the adolescent "be sane in an insane place" (Jaffe et al., 1990). In some cases, the only feasible goal may be to help the adolescent learn not to imitate aggressive acts and to make educational and vocational plans that will eventually allow him/her to become independent and successfully move out of the stressful family home. Meanwhile, they may need help structuring activities that will get them away from the home situation as much as possible, such as a part-time job, sports, or other extracurricular school activities.

As noted, many adolescents from violent homes frequently experience low self-esteem and may view themselves as undesirable and inadequate. Consequently, they may avoid setting goals or engaging in constructive pursuits. Treatment should include interventions to promote self-esteem and increase positive self-statements. The adolescent may be taught to identify self-blaming or self-critical thoughts and how to replace them with positive counter-thoughts.

Implementing a safety plan is a crucial goal in the treatment of adolescents from violent homes. The adolescent may have strong feelings of guilt, ambivalence, and conflict about what his/her role ought to be when the marital violence erupts. One adolescent reported that she was told by a counselor at a battered women shelter to call 911 during a violent episode. When the mother and daughter returned to the batterer, however, the mother warned her against taking this action, fearing that this would only antagonize the batterer. Although the instruction to call the police may seem reasonable, this is not a simple issue. Such an assignment places an inordinate sense of responsibility and pressure on the adolescent and may endanger the adolescent or jeopardize his/her relationship with one or both parents.

Each family's safety plan must be individualized to provide the maximum protection to both the mother and children. The plan should focus on what the adolescent should do during a violent episode and where he/she can go to get help. The plan should be laid out in terms of very specific behavior, including which phone she/he would use, who to call, where to go, and whether the adolescent should call 911.

Stage 7: Closure and Follow-up Measures.   In the final sessions, the clinician and the adolescent might review progress in terms of tasks covered, goals reached, and any unfinished work. An atmosphere that engenders hope and fosters greater independence should be maintained. Treatment has been effective if the adolescent has greater understanding of the dynamics of wife abuse, has greater self-esteem and increased coping skills, and is better able to identify his/her own strengths.

If adolescents reside at a shelter, their concerns and feelings about their mother's decision to leave the abusive relationship or return to the batterer should be discussed. If the mother should decide to return to the abuser, it is helpful to have a conjoint session with the mother and adolescent to review the safety plan. If the mother leaves the abuser, conjoint therapy may also be helpful focusing on defining new roles, rules, or realigning of boundaries as well as planning for the future. A followup phone call to discuss how things are going may be helpful if it does not place the adolescent or mother in any danger. The adolescent may be given referrals for individual or group counseling, if warranted.

GROUP INTERVENTION WITH ADOLESCENTS

The most widely recommended intervention for children of battered women is a group counseling program. Most of these, however, are housed in shelters for battered women, and are targeted for latency-age children or younger (Carlson, 1995). As more mental health agencies accurately assess for family violence among their caseloads, more adolescents may be identified and targeted for referrals for group counseling to cope with the trauma related to growing up in a maritally violent home.

There is a growing body of literature on group work with younger children of battered women. The majority of programs involve highly structured sessions which meet 60 to 90 minutes weekly for approximately 10 weeks. The goals of the program are clearly outlined with specific educational activities designed to achieve these goals. Some of the goals of group treatment include understanding family violence, emotional labeling, increased coping skills and self-esteem, procurement of social support, and safety enhancement (Peled & Edleson, 1995). Clearly, many of these same goals are applicable to treating adolescents. The reader is referred to some excellent children's group programs (Grusznski et al., 1988; Peled & Davis, 1995; Wilson, Cameron, Jaffe, & Wolfe, 1986) which can be easily adapted to fit adolescents' needs. An additional component of a program for adolescents should include a discussion of dating violence as well as teaching skills for coping with conflict in dating relationships.

PRIMARY PREVENTION PROGRAMS

Clinicians and researchers in the field of family violence have emphasized the importance of primary prevention programs to change attitudes and behaviors that may sanction or encourage violence in intimate relationships. The problem of violence in intimate relationships is one that concerns high-school students. Teen dating violence is almost as widespread and frequent as violence in adult relationships (Girshick, 1993) and this finding becomes more worrisome if one considers dating relationships as the training ground for partners to rehearse future marital roles (Jorgensen, 1986). The extent of violence in intimate relationships and its ensuing mental health problems make prevention a critical priority (Sudermann, Jaffe, & Hastings, 1995).

Several authors have suggested that schools should play a more important role in promoting awareness about violence and teaching alternative forms of conflict resolution in intimate relationships. High schools are uniquely positioned to reach a large proportion of youth and challenge sex-role stereotypes or beliefs that violence in intimate relationships is acceptable or justifiable (Sudermann et al., 1995). Curricula can be incorporated into high school family life education courses and should include discussion of the normalcy of tension and conflict in relationships, what constitutes violence and sexual assault, how violence can escalate in relationships, and skills for resolving relationship conflict nonviolently. A number of excellent school-based violence prevention programs are currently being offered. Some examples include In Touch With Teens (Aldridge, Friedman, & Guiggans, 1993), Skills for Violence Free Relationships (Levy, 1984), the Relationship Abuse Prevention Project (Marin Abused Women's Program, 1986), and the Minnesota Coalition for Battered Women School Curriculum Project (Jones, 1987).

SUMMARY

Little attention has been focused on adolescents who have been exposed to interparental violence. This may be partly due to the fact that adolescents tend not to stay with their mothers at shelters as frequently as do younger children, and are therefore unavailable as research subjects. Yet adolescents may be a particularly vulnerable population, since they may have witnessed severe interparental violence throughout their childhood, and the changes associated with this life stage may further add to their vulnerability.

The present chapter discussed some common reactions of adolescents who witnessed interparental violence. A treatment approach based on careful assessment, crisis intervention, and cognitive behavioral strategies was presented. This approach may be applied to adolescents at shelters or those seen at mental health outpatient settings where domestic violence is not the presenting problem. The need for primary prevention measures with this age group was also discussed.

ACKNOWLEDGMENTS

The authors would like to thank Claudia Petrozzi from Klein Bottle Youth Shelter, Santa Barbara, CA for her help.

REFERENCES

Aldridge, L., Friedman, C., & Guiggans, P. O. (1993). *In touch with teens: A relationship violence prevention curriculum for youth ages 12–19.* Los Angeles, CA: The Los Angeles Commission on Assaults Against Women.

Arroyo, W., & Eth, S. (1995). Assessment following violence-witnessing trauma. In E. Peled, P. G. Jaffe, & J. L. Edleson (Eds.), *Ending the cycle of violence: Community responses to children of battered women* (pp. 27–42). Thousand Oaks, CA: Sage.

Bandura, A. (1971). *Social learning theory.* Morristown, NJ: General Learning.

Blos, P. (1967). The second individuation process of adolescence. *Psychoanalytic Study of the Child, 22,* 162–186.

Carlson, B. E. (1984). Children's observation of interparental violence. In A. R. Roberts (Ed.), *Battered women and their families: Intervention strategies and treatment program* (pp. 147–167). New York: Springer.

Carlson, B. (1990). Adolescent observers of marital violence. *Journal of Family Violence, 5,* 285–299.

Carlson, B. (1995). Children of battered women: Research, programs, and services. In A. R. Roberts (Ed.), *Helping battered women: New perspectives and remedies* (pp. 172–187). New York: Oxford University Press.

Carter, B., & McGoldrick, M. (1980). *The changing family life cycle: A framework for family therapy* (2nd ed.). Needham Heights, MA: Allyn & Bacon.

Christopoulous, C., Cohen, D. A., Shaw, D. S., Joyce, S., Sullivan-Hanson, J., Kraft, S. P., & Emery, R. (1987). Children of abused women: 1. Adjustment at time of shelter residence. *Journal of Marriage and the Family, 49,* 611–619.

Cornell, C. P., & Gelles, R. J. (1982). Adolescent to parent violence. *The Urban and Social Change Review, 15,* 8–14.

Davis, L. V., & Carlson, B. E. (1987). Observation of spouse abuse: What happens to the children? *Journal of Interpersonal Violence, 2,* 278–291.

DeMaris, A. (1987). The efficacy of a spouse abuse model in accounting for courtship violence. *Journal of Family Issues, 8,* 291–305.

Elze, D., Stiffman, A. R., & Dore, P. (1996, June). *Family violence as a predictor of runaway behavior among adolescent females.* Paper presented at the First National Conference on Children Exposed to Family Violence, Austin, TX.

Erikson, E. (1963). *Childhood and society.* New York: Norton.

Fantuzzo, J. W., DePaola, L. M., Lambert, L., Martino, T., Anderson, G., & Sutton, S. (1991). Effects of interparental violence on the psychological adjustment and competencies of young children. *Journal of Consulting and Clinical Psychology, 59,* 258–265.

Foo, L., & Margolin, G. (1995). A multivariate investigation of dating violence. *Journal of Family Violence, 10,* 351–375.

Freud, A. (1974). *The psychoanalytical treatment of children* (4th ed.). New York: Schocken.

Gil, E. (1996). *Treating abused adolescents.* New York: Guilford.

Girshick, L. B. (1993). Teen dating violence. *Violence Update, 3,* 1–6.

Grusznski, R. J., Brink, J. C., & Edelson, J. L. (1988). Support and education groups for children of battered women. *Child Welfare, 67*, 431–444.

Gwartney-Gibbs, P. A., Stockard, J., & Bohmer, S. (1987). Learning court-ship violence: The influence of parents, peers, and personal experiences. *Family Relations, 36*, 276–282.

Hinchey, F. S., & Gavelak, J. R. (1982). Empathic responding in children of battered mothers. *Child Abuse and Neglect, 6*, 395–401.

Holden, G. W., & Ritchie, K. L. (1991). Linking extreme marital discord, child rearing and child behavior problems: Evidence form battered women. *Child Development, 62*, 311–327.

Hughes, H. M. (1988). Psychology and behavior correlates of family violence in child witnesses and victims. *American Journal of Orthopsychiatry, 58*, 77–90.

Hughes, H. M., Parkinson, D., & Vargo, M. (1989). Witnessing spouse abuse and experiencing physical abuse: A "double whammy?" *Journal of Family Violence, 4*, 197–209.

Jaffe, P., Wolfe, D., & Wilson, S. K. (1990). *Children of battered women.* Newbury Park, CA: Sage.

Jaffe, P., Wolfe, D. A., Wilson, S. K., & Zak, L. (1986). Family violence and child adjustment: A comparative analysis of girls' and boys' behavioral symptoms. *American Journal of Psychiatry, 143*, 74–77.

Jones, L. E. (1987). *Dating violence among Minnesota teenagers: A summary of survey results.* St. Paul, MN: Minnesota Coalition for Battered Women.

Jorgensen, S. R. (1986). *Marriage and the family: Development and change.* New York: Macmillan.

Kalmus, D. (1984). The intergenerational transmission of marital aggression. *Journal of Marriage and the Family, 46*, 11–19.

Kempton, T., Thomas, A. M., & Forehand, R. (1988). Dimensions of interparental conflict and adolescent functioning. *Journal of Family Violence, 4*, 297–307.

Kratcoski, P. C. (1985). Youth violence directed toward significant others. *Journal of Adolescence, 8*, 145–157.

Langhinrichsen-Rohling, J., & Neidig, P. (1995). Violent backgrounds of economically disadvantaged youth: Risk factors for perpetrating violence? *Journal of Family Violence, 10*, 379–397.

Levy, B. (1984). *Skills for violence-free relationships.* Long Beach, CA: Southern California Coalition for Battered Women.

Levy, B. (1991). *Dating violence: Young women in danger.* Seattle, WA: Seal.

Marin Abused Women's Services. (1986). *Relationship Abuse Prevention Project.* San Rafael, CA: Author.

Meichenbaum, D. (1977). *Cognitive behavioral modification: An integrative approach.* New York: Plenum.

Mishne, J. M. (1986). *Clinical work with adolescents.* New York: The Free Press.

Mowbray, C. T. (1988). Post-traumatic therapy for children who are victims of violence. In F. M. Ochberg (Ed.), *Post-traumatic therapy for children who are victims of violence* (pp. 196–212). New York: Brunner/Mazel.

Office of Technology Assessment. (1991). Delinquency: Prevention and services. In D. Dougherty (Ed.), *Adolescent health, Vol. II, Background and the effectiveness of selected prevention and treatment services.* Washington, DC: Congress of the United States.

O'Keefe, M. (1994). Adjustment of children from maritally violent homes. *Families in Society, 75,* 403–415.

O'Keefe, M. (1996). The differential effects of family violence on adolescent adjustment. *Child and Adolescent Social Work Journal, 13,* 51–68.

O'Keefe, M. (1997). Predictors of dating violence among high school students. *Journal of Interpersonal Violence, 12,* 546–568.

O'Keefe, M. (in press). Factors mediating the link between witnessing interparental violence and dating violence. *Journal of Family Violence.*

O'Keefe, M., & Treister, L. (in press). Victims of dating violence among high school students: Are the predictors different for males and females? *Violence Against Women.*

Peled, E., & Davis, D. (1995). *Groupwork with children: A practitioner's manual.* Thousand Oaks, CA: Sage.

Peled, E., & Edleson, J. L. (1995). Process and outcome in small groups for children of battered women. In E. Peled, P. G. Jaffe, & J. L. Edleson (Eds.), *Ending the cycle of violence: Community responses to children of battered women* (pp. 77–96). Thousand Oaks, CA: Sage.

Pynoos, R. S., & Eth, S. (1984). The child as witness to homicide. *Journal of Social Issues, 40,* 87–108.

Roberts, A. R. (1996). Epidemiology and definition of acute crisis in American society. In A. R. Roberts (Ed.), *Crisis management and brief treatment: Theory, techniques, and applications* (pp. 16–33). Chicago, IL: Nelson-Hall.

Rosenberg, M. S. (1987). Children of battered women: The effects of witnessing violence on their social problem solving abilities. *Behavior Therapies, 10,* 85–89.

Silvern, L., & Kaersvang, L. (1989). The traumatized children of violent marriages. *Child Welfare, 68,* 421–436.

Silvern, L., Karyl, J., & Landis, T. (1995). Individual psychotherapy for the traumatized children of abused women. In E. Peled, P. G. Jaffe, & J. L. Edleson (Eds.), *Ending the cycle of violence: Community responses to children of battered women* (pp. 43–75). Thousand Oaks, CA: Sage.

Sternberg, K. J., Lamb, M. E., Greenbaum, C., Cicchetti, D., Dawud, S., Cortes, R. M., Krispin, O., & Lorey, F. (1993). Effects of domestic violence on children's behavior problems and depression. *Developmental Psychology, 29,* 44–52.

Straus, M. A. (1991, September). *Children as witness to marital violence: A risk factor for life-long problems among a nationally representative sample of American men and women.* Paper presented at the Ross Roundtable titled "Children and Violence," Washington, DC.

Straus, M. B. (1994). *Violence in the lives of adolescents.* New York: Norton.

Sudermann, M., Jaffe, P. G., & Hastings, E. (1995). Violence prevention programs in secondary (high) schools. In E. Peled, P. G. Jaffe, & J. L. Edleson (Eds.), *Ending the cycle of violence: Community responses to children of battered women* (pp. 232–254). Thousand Oaks, CA: Sage.

Wilson, S. D., Cameron, S., Jaffe, P. G., & Wolfe, D. (1986). *Manual for a group program for children exposed to wife abuse.* London, Ontario: London Family Court Clinic.

Wolfe, D. A. (1997). Children exposed to marital violence. In O. W. Barnett, C. L. Miller-Perrin, & R. D. Perrin (Eds.), *Family violence across the lifespan* (pp. 136–157). Thousand Oaks, CA: Sage.

Wolfe, D. A., Jaffe, P. G., Wilson, S. K., & Zak, L. (1985). Children of battered women: The relation of child behavior to family violence and maternal stress. *Journal of Consulting and Clinical Psychology, 51,* 702–708.

Wolfe, D. A., Zak, L., Wilson, & Jaffe, P. (1986). Child witnesses to violence between parents: Critical issues in behavioral and social adjustment. *Journal of Abnormal Child Psychology, 14,* 95–104.

Zarb, J. M. (1992). *Cognitive behavioral assessment and therapy with adolescents.* New York: Brunner/Mazel.

Health Care and Welfare Policies and Practices with Battered Women

Battered Women in the Emergency Room: Emerging Roles for the ER Social Worker and Clinical Nurse Specialist

Mary E. Boes

Although many health care organizations in the United States have called for a new response to domestic violence, in view of the staggering numbers of victims and historical lack of medical recognition and response, determination must be made if actual health care interventions are changing. A national health objective for the year 2000 is for at least 90% of hospital emergency rooms to have protocols for routinely identifying, treating, and referring victims of spouse abuse. The Joint Commission on Accreditation of Health Care Organizations (JCAHO, 1992) has also recommended that accredited ERs have policies, procedures, and education in place to guide staff in the treatment of battered adults. As domestic violence is a public health problem, every woman must be effectively screened for level of risk for abuse in every ER in the United States. This chapter seeks to profile the efficacy of use of adult abuse protocols for selected ERs and the emerging roles of the ER Social Worker and Clinical Nurse Specialist in the implementation and coordination of these initiatives. It is argued that social work and clinical nurse specialist intervention strategies and treatment goals improve the quality of both emergency and ongoing care for this growing and often at-risk population.

STATISTICS AND TRENDS

The most prevalent cause of trauma in women treated in emergency rooms is wife abuse. Retrospective chart reviews in hospital ERs indicate that although 30–35% of women seen in the emergency room have symptoms or injuries secondary to battering, the cause of the problem is identified in only 5% of those cases (Randall, 1990). Although it is generally believed that domestic violence is seriously underreported and undiagnosed, within the past year at least 7% of American women (3.9 million) who are married or living with someone as a couple were physically abused, and 37% (20.7 million) were verbally or emotionally abused by their spouse or partner. In the U.S. every 9 seconds a woman is physically abused by her husband (The Commonwealth Fund, 1993). The U.S. Department of Justice estimates that 95% of assaults on spouses or ex-spouses are committed by men against women (Douglas, 1991). Domestic violence is the leading cause of injuries to women between the ages of 15 and 44 and is more common than muggings, auto accidents, and cancer deaths combined (U.S. Senate Judiciary Committee, 1992). Sixty percent of all female homicides are due to domestic violence (DelTufo, 1995).

Domestic violence is repetitive in nature: about 1 in 5 women victimized by their spouse or ex-spouse reported that they had been a victim of a series of at least 3 assaults in the last 6 months (Zawitz et al., 1993).

Pregnancy is a risk factor for battering; as many as 37% of obstetrics patients are physically abused during pregnancy (Council on Scientific Affairs, 1992). The level of injury resulting from domestic violence is severe: Of 218 women presenting at a metropolitan emergency department with injuries due to domestic violence, 28% required major medical treatment, and 40% had previously required medical care for abuse (Berrios & Grady, 1991).

A study conducted at Rush Medical Center in Chicago found that the average charge for medical services provided to abused women, children, and older people was $1,633 per person per year. That would amount to a national annual cost of $857.3 million (Meyer, 1992).

Ninety-two percent of women who were physically abused by their partners did not discuss these incidents with their physician; 57% did not discuss the incidents with anyone (The Commonwealth Fund, 1993). Mooney's (1994) study reports that women told friends (46%) and relatives (31%) and only 22% of doctors about domestic violence.

> The data suggest that health care settings provide services to many women affected by domestic violence. Unfortunately, many of these settings are unaware of the incidence and prevalence data that make them ideal sites to develop a response. (Edleson & Eisikovits, 1996, p. 56)

The ER is a vital entry point into the health care system, especially for some of the more severely abused women who may be at greatest risk for serious impairment and/or death (McLeer & Anwar, 1987).

Many battered women also seek medical care for problems like depression, anxiety, suicide attempts, and substance abuse, although medical providers are often unaware of the connection of the presenting problem to recurrent domestic abuse (Edleson & Eisikovits, 1996). Albert R. Roberts (1996b) dispels the myth that only a small percentage of battered women who suffer severe beatings for years experience symptoms of posttraumatic stress disorder (PTSD). He details three clinical studies of battered women with PTSD rates ranging from 45 to 84%. Women are frequently misdiagnosed with affective disorders, anxiety disorders, and personality disorders as the primary diagnosis because the trauma that causes the symptoms is unidentified (Keller, 1996).

REASONS VIOLENCE IS MISDIAGNOSED OR UNDIAGNOSED

The reasons violence so often is misdiagnosed—or goes undiagnosed—are multitude. Part of the problem is that physicians are not trained to view violence the way they do bacteria and viruses. Despite its vast medical consequences, domestic abuse is included in only 53% of all U.S. medical school curricula, and most of those devote no more than 90 minutes to the topic. Until the current decade, for the most part, major medical journals ignored it. A study of how emergency room (ER) personnel dehumanize battering victims was reported in *The Journal of the American Medical Association* in 1990 only after it was published in a journal called *Gender and Society*. Early theory-building studies on domestic abuse were prejudiced by the researchers' inability to study batterers. They then turned their attention to "the wife-beater's wife." She would talk to them. Undeterred by having only one side of the story, and the victim's side at that, the researchers found that she had brought on her own suffering because she was masochistic, frigid, and controlling. Someone had to be at fault. More recent research takes a more sympathetic view of the abused woman.

Some hospitals have nothing more than ad hoc protocols. When treating battered women, ER physicians may lose their only chance for early intervention because they have no guidelines for identifying and dealing with abuse victims, nor is it considered their medical obligation.

In many hospitals that do have established procedures for dealing with abuse victims, the medical staff simply does not follow them. In one study done at a Chicago hospital (Warshaw, 1989), nurses who were supposed to refer abuse victims for social work consultations did so less than 10% of the time. Though many of their patients were seriously hurt by their attackers, the nurses filed police reports in less than half the cases.

The reluctance of physicians to see and treat intimate violence is explained by tradition. Physical and sexual abuse of women has been regarded as something of a private matter or one better left to the law or the psychiatrists. Many physicians feel it's not part of their job to treat a "social problem."

For various reasons, many physicians simply do not want to see violence. In a study of a New Haven, Connecticut ER, a team of researchers combing medical records easily identified 340 abuse cases ER personnel had missed. Physicians identified 1 in 35 women they saw as a victim of intimate violence; the researchers found the reality was closer to 1 in 4.

In 1990, researcher Nancy Kathleen Sugg, M.D., of the University of Washington in Seattle, asked 38 family care physicians in a large health maintenance organization why they didn't intervene in cases of domestic violence (Sugg & Inui, 1992). Many told Sugg they were afraid of offending their patients if they broached the subject. Most had never had any training in dealing with domestic violence. The largest majority—71%—told Sugg they were simply too busy. Their greatest fear was that domestic violence would eat up too much of their scarce time.

The extent to which physicians try to distance themselves from victims of violence is clearly detailed in a 1989 study done by Carole Warshaw, M.D., at Cook County Hospital in Chicago. Warshaw began her research with the hypothesis that the notations physicians and nurses made on ER charts would reveal the way they thought about their patients. Warshaw read all of the charts for women trauma patients during a 2-week period, identifying those who specifically mentioned being deliberately harmed by someone else. Medical personnel dutifully recorded the extent of the women's injuries, but in only one case was abuse mentioned as a cause (Warshaw, 1989).

Warshaw believes the "medical model" contributes to what appears to be callous disregard for the victim. Doctors are taught to remain detached and learn to objectify. Medical school tends to dehumanize doctors, who then dehumanize their patients.

It is not a way for doctors to be better doctors. Physicians may have personal reasons for maintaining a psychological distance from the victim. Many resort to victim-blaming as a form of self-preservation: "If you can discount the victim, you can preserve your belief in your own invulnerability," says Harvard psychiatrist Judith Herman (personal communication, April 4, 1997).

Research by psychologist Diana Russell (1986) found that the risk of rape and battering is double for incest victims. This is frequently misunderstood by physicians and therapists who are likely to see it as a "character flaw," a propensity for choosing abusive relationships, rather than the result of victims being rendered helpless by repeated traumatization.

Physicians are products of a social milieu in which women are devalued and violence against them is not only tolerated but is a form of entertainment. Recent studies of male college students found that as many as 30% admit they have committed rape and up to 70% could envision themselves striking a spouse.

Women have always been on the periphery but not part of the research or theory-building class (Judith Herman, personal communication, April 4, 1997).

> They were allowed to care for victims but not pose the hypotheses or do the research. From initial denial we've come to recognize that yes, battering occurs, but there's still a tendency to see it as unusual and deviant and to not recognize how endemic it is and how pervasive its effects are.

It has taken 20 years of chiding by women's groups to produce even a flicker of medical attention to violence as a public health problem.

PROVISION OF SUPPORT, ASSISTANCE, OR PROTECTION IN ERs

The Joint Commission on Accreditation of Healthcare Organizations (JCAHO, 1992), addressing victims of possible abuse or neglect, states in its "Emergency Services" chapter that the intent of the guideline is to have emergency service personnel be made more alert to the identification and needs of victims of possible abuse or neglect. A plan for educating appropriate staff about criteria for identifying and the procedures for handling child, adult, and elder victims of possible abuse or neglect is required. The JCAHO standards require that procedures for the evaluation of patients who meet the criteria address patient consent, examination, and treatment; the hospital's role in the collection, retention, and safeguarding of specimens, photographs, and other evidentiary material released by the patient; and, as legally required, notification of and release of information to the proper authorities. The standard also requires that a list is maintained in the emergency department/service of private and public community agencies that provide or arrange for evaluation and care for victims of abuse, and referrals are made as appropriate. The items listed in the required characteristic are documented in the medical record. The medical record includes documentation of examinations, treatment given, any referrals made to other care providers and to community agencies, and any required reporting to the proper authorities. JCAHO has mandated a plan for education of appropriate staff about the criteria for identifying and the procedures for handling possible victims of abuse.

GUIDING PRINCIPLES FOR HEALTH CARE CLINICAL INTERVENTION

A set of guiding principles for health care clinical intervention is described by the Family Violence Prevention Fund (Warshaw & Ganley, 1996):

1. Respecting safety of victims and their children as a priority.
2. Respecting the integrity and authority of each battered woman over her own life choices.
3. Holding perpetrators responsible for the abuse and for stopping it.
4. Advocating on behalf of victims of domestic violence and their children.
5. Acknowledging the need to make changes in the health care system to improve the health care response to domestic violence.

Many health care organizations in the United States have called for a response to domestic violence. The American Medical Association has held national meetings calling for a new response to domestic violence and has issued diagnostic and treatment guidelines for physicians. The Nursing Network Against Violence Against Women has also coordinated national conferences and training seminars about domestic violence.

FRAGMENTED CARE IN ER: ORIENTED TOWARD LIFE AND DEATH

Within emergency rooms alone, at least 16%–18% of women presenting with trauma have been abused (Boes, 1997; Tilden, 1989). Care in the emergency room is often fragmented and necessarily oriented toward life-and-death situations. Therefore, women are not adequately assessed for prior physical or sexual abuse and so receive little or no emotional support or intervention specific to their needs (Campbell, 1991; Roberts, 1996). It can be surmised that the cost to the health care system is phenomenal, with little or no positive outcome. A cycle persists in which women seek care and receive either no intervention or interventions that are grossly ineffective (Campbell & Sheridan, 1989).

Nursing research has established that at least 8% of women in prenatal and primary care settings are abused by a male partner and approximately 20% of women in emergency departments have a history of abuse (Bullock, McFarlane, Bateman, & Miller, 1989; Goldberg & Tomlanovich, 1984; Helton, McFarlane, & Anderson, 1987; Stark et al., 1981). Other nursing studies indicate that such violence is usually not documented correctly in medical records so that they could be used in court, and that abused women do not feel they have been appropriately assessed and treated (Brendtro & Bowker, 1989; Drake, 1982). However, Tilden and Shepherd (1987) demonstrated that training of emergency room personnel about abuse can significantly increase the accurate identification of abused women.

ASSESSMENT

Assessment for all forms of violence against women should take place for all women entering the health care system, regardless of their point of entry. At each contact clients should be assessed on the following points: physical safety, legal needs, support needs and options, economic status, feelings of blame, isolation, fear, and responsibility, resources available, community shelters, support groups and counseling, legal options, safety plan, and economic assistance.

Women can be categorized into three groups in terms of abuse: no risk, low risk, or moderate-to-high risk. Women with no signs of current or past abuse are considered at no risk. Women at low risk show no evidence of recent or current abuse. Assessment of moderate-to-high risk status includes evaluation of a woman's fear of both psychological and physical abuse.

Lethality potential should be assessed (Campbell, 1986). Risk factors for homicide in abusive relationships include: physical abuse increasing in frequency and/or severity; abuser has used a weapon (gun, knife, baseball bat) against her; abuser has threatened to kill her; abuser chokes or attempts to choke her; gun in the home; she is forced into sex; children abused; abuse during pregnancy; abuser is violent outside of the home; abuser uses crack, amphetamines, "ice," or combination drugs; abuser is drunk every day or almost every day or is a "binge" drinker; abuser is violently and constantly jealous; abuser makes statements such as "If I can't have you, no one can"; abuser controls most or all of her daily activities, money, and so on; and either partner has threatened or tried to commit suicide. The determined risk level should also be documented, and any past or present physical evidence of abuse from prior or current assault should be either photographed or shown on a body map as well as described narratively. It is important that the assailant be identified in the record, which can be accomplished by the use of quotes from the woman or subjective information. These records can be very important for women in future assault and/or child custody cases, even if she is not ready to make a police report at the present time.

Indicators of Actual or Potential Abuse

Included in the client's history will be her primary reason for contact, which may include vague information about the cause of the problem, discrepancies between physical findings and the description of the cause, minimizing the injuries, inappropriate delay between time of injury and treatment, and inappropriate family reactions (e.g., lack of concern, overconcern, threatening demeanor).

Information from a family genogram may reveal family violence in history (child, spouse, elder), history of violence outside of the home, incarcerations, violent deaths in the extended family, and alcoholism or drug abuse in the family history.

The health history may also give an indication of actual or potential abuse. The client may have a history of traumatic injuries, spontaneous abortions, psychiatric hospitalizations, or a history of depression or substance abuse.

Sexual history may note prior sexual abuse, use of force in sexual activities, venereal disease, a child with sexual knowledge beyond that appropriate for his or her age, and promiscuity.

Actual or potential abuse indicators included in the social history may include unwanted or unplanned pregnancy, adolescent pregnancy, social isolation (difficulty naming persons available for help in a crisis), lack of contact with extended family, unrealistic expectations of relationships or age-appropriate behavior, extreme jealousy by spouse or partner, rigid traditional sex-role beliefs, verbal aggression, belief in use of physical punishment, difficulties in school, truancy, and running away.

The psychological history would indicate feelings of helplessness/hopelessness, feeling trapped, difficulty making plans for the future, tearfulness, chronic fatigue, apathy, and suicide attempts.

Included in the financial history as indicators of actual or potential abuse may be poverty, finances rigidly controlled by one family member, unwillingness to spend money on health care or adequate nutrition, complaints about spending money on family members, unemployment, and use of elders' finances for other family members.

Family beliefs and values which may indicate actual or potential abuse may include a belief in the importance of physical discipline, autocratic decision making, intolerance of differing views among members, and mistrust of outsiders.

Finally, family relationships may show a lack of visible affection or nurturing between family members, extreme dependency between family members, autonomy discouraged, numerous arguments, temporary separations, dissatisfaction with family members, lack of enjoyable family activities, extramarital affairs, and role rigidity (inability of members to assume nontraditional roles).

INTERVENTIONS

Immediate care for a woman in a potentially harmful or present abusive situation involves the development of a safety plan. Questions that are important to ask include the following: "How can we help you be safe? Do you have a place to go?" A woman can be assisted to look at the options available to her. Shelter information and access to counseling and legal resources should be discussed. If a woman wants to return to her spouse or partner, she can be helped in the development of plans that can be carried out if the abuse continues or becomes more serious.

When there are no obvious injuries, assessment for abuse is best included with the history about the patient's (both genders) primary intimate attachment relationship. Answers to general questions on the quality of that relationship should be assessed for feelings of being controlled or needing to control. A relationship characterized by excessive jealousy (of possessions, children, jobs, friends, and other family members, as well as potential sexual partners) is more likely to be violent. The patient can be asked about how the couple solves conflicts, for example, if one partner needs to have the final say; frequent and forceful verbal aggression also can be considered a risk factor. Finally, the patient should be asked if arguments ever involve "pushing or shoving." Questions about minor violence within a couple's relationship help to establish the unfortunate normalcy of battering and to lessen the stigma of disclosure. If the patient hesitates, looks away, displays other uncomfortable nonverbal behavior or reveals risk factors for abuse, she or he can be asked again later in the interview about physical violence.

If abuse is revealed, the professional's first response is critical. It is important that an abused woman realize that she is not alone; important affirmation can be given with a statement about the frequency of spouse/partner abuse.

A COMPARISON OF THE PATERNALISTIC AND EMPOWERMENT MODELS OF INTERVENTION WITH BATTERED WOMEN

Using the paternalistic model, the professional is perceived to be more knowledgeable than the survivor. In contrast, the professional using the empowerment model sees that there is a mutual sharing of knowledge and information. When the paternalistic model is used, responsibility for ending the violence is placed on the survivor. When the empowerment model is used, the professional strategizes with the survivor. Survivors are assisted to recognize societal influences. Using the paternalistic model, advice and sympathy are given rather than respect, whereas using the empowerment model, the survivor's competence and experience are respected.

FOUR STEPS TO SUCCESSFUL INTERVENTION WITH BATTERED WOMEN

These steps build on Roberts' (1996a) Seven-Stage Crisis Intervention Model. The first step according to Roberts is assessment of domestic violence severity, injuries, and lethality. Schecter (1987) in step 1 focuses on identification.

Identification includes the use of clinical indicators: central injury pattern; patterned injuries (injuries look like the object that caused them); and injury (injuries) inconsistent with patient's or accompanying partner's explanation. The patient may claim to be "accident prone" or "clumsy"; or there may be multiple injuries in various stages of healing (pattern of injury), a history of trauma-related injuries, unexplained delay between injury occurrence or severe symptom onset and seeking medical treatment, history of depression, tranquilizer and/or sedative use, eating disorders, substance abuse, or suicide attempts. The patient may have had multiple visits to the emergency room for anxiety and/or depression symptoms (Boes, 1997). The patient is accompanied by an overly attentive or aggressive partner and the partner is insistent on staying with the patient or refuses to leave the patient alone. The patient displays an inappropriate affect, appears fearful of partner; the patient has a flat affect, avoids eye contact, etc. The final clinical indicator is that the accompanying partner has injuries to their hands and/or in other areas such as face or arms.

To facilitate identification, the mental health practitioner can place posters, wallet-sized cards, or brochures on domestic violence in bathrooms, patient-examining areas, or wherever other patient information is displayed. They must interview her alone and out of earshot and eyesight of any accompanying partner. Using nonverbal communication when assessing the patient is also helpful. Ask the patient directly if she is being hurt or threatened by her partner. Show comfort in asking questions about domestic violence. Practice with co-workers.

The second step to successfully intervening with battered women is to validate her experience. Believe what the battered woman tells you. Be prepared to hear information which may shock you or may be painful to listen to. Empathize with her experience and validate her feelings of fear, confusion, love, and hope; reassure her that her feelings are legitimate and normal. Offer positive messages to counter harmful past messages she may have received. The following messages are very simple and powerful: "You are not alone"; "This happens to many women"; "You are not to blame for the things your partner does"; "You are not crazy"; "You do not deserve to be abused"; "You don't deserve to be treated this way"; and "What happened to you is a crime."

Advocating for the woman's safety and expanding her options is the third step to successful intervention with battered women. The woman's safety must be the primary goal of all interventions. Ensure that your actions do not in any way compromise her safety, regardless of any other perceived benefits of those actions. Recognize that she is likely to be the best judge of what is safe for her. Offer information about the formal network of services that may be available. In particular, provide specific information about the local domestic violence services/shelter. Explore informal resources and supports to which she may have access.

Provision of ongoing, unconditional support is the final step. Recognize that you, as a health care professional, may feel frustrated, angry, fearful, or helpless when dealing with battered women. Find support for yourself, and avoid transferring your feelings of frustration onto the victim. Remember: It takes battered women an average of 6–8 times of leaving before a final separation occurs, and that ending the relationship doesn't necessarily mean that the violence will end. Recognize that it is a "success" that she is talking about the violence and beginning to explore options. Tell yourself you have done a great job if you have utilized these four steps in your intervention.

AMERICAN MEDICAL ASSOCIATION GUIDELINES FOR INTERVIEWING BATTERED WOMEN

The American Medical Association (AMA) (as well as many other professional organizations) recommends routine screening of all women patients in emergency, surgical, primary care, pediatric, prenatal, and mental health settings for domestic violence. The AMA recommends starting with a statement such as, "Because abuse and violence are so common in women's lives, I've begun to screen for it routinely." This kind of statement lets the patient know that you are concerned and knowledgeable about battering. The AMA recommends that health care professionals be aware of the following pitfalls in interviewing. Avoid questions such as: "Are you the victim of domestic violence?," "Are you being battered?/abused?" Many victims do not identify themselves with those labels. Avoid "why" questions: "Why didn't you call the hotline?" "Why didn't you call the police?" "Why" questions sound accusatory and tend to be victim-blaming.

MEDICAL DOCUMENTATION FOR VICTIMS OF DOMESTIC VIOLENCE

The medical record is a legal document. Appropriate documentation can provide concrete evidence of violence and abuse and may be critical to the outcome of any legal case. Always write legibly. This can help keep you out of court and/or provide strong support if you are required to testify. Document the patient's explanation for the injuries. Whenever possible, use the patient's own words in quotes. Ask the patient to be as specific as possible. For example: documenting "Patient states: My boyfriend, Joseph Smith, hit me with his belt," is better than "Patient has been abused."

When circumstances allow, elicit and document if there were any witnesses to the incident, where the incident occurred, and when it occurred. Document any other agency representatives involved. For example, document any prehospital care and transport and police response. If the police are called, document the responding police agency and incident report number and any police action taken.

The author was a medical social worker for 8 years at The Graduate Hospital, an affiliate of the Hospital of the University of Pennsylvania. The practice regarding confidentiality in Pennsylvania was that health care professionals should call the police only if the patient requests this or exhibits a reportable injury. If you call the police without the request or permission of the adult victim, you are violating patient confidentiality.

MEDICAL PHOTOGRAPHY OF DOMESTIC VIOLENCE VICTIMS

Photographs are an extremely valuable way of documenting intentional injuries. It is helpful to tell the patient, particularly those patients who do not wish to call the police or press charges, that the medical record is a legal document and a confidential record and that it is maintained for a period of 6 years or 3 years past age 18, the age of maturity. Explain that if the patient decides to divorce and/or seek child custody or support, and the abuser denies ever hurting him/her, there will be visual proof of the injuries.

GENERAL EVIDENCE COLLECTION GUIDELINES FOR HEALTH CARE PROFESSIONALS

Based on Virginia Lynch's "Clinical Forensic Nursing: A New Perspective in the Management of Crime Victims from Trauma to Trial" (1995), health care professionals are responsible under the law to maintain physical evidence in all cases of gunshot or stab wounds and injuries serious enough to result in death; however, they are urged to provide appropriate evidence collection for all crime victims. Appropriate evidence collection assists in proving that a crime was committed, that a certain person committed the crime, and how the crime was committed. A solid chain of evidence should be maintained to insure the integrity of every specimen or piece of evidence collected. Failure to maintain the "chain of custody"—the identity of the individuals having control or custody over evidentiary, potentially evidentiary, or other property—may render potentially important evidence worthless or inadmissible in a court of law.

CLINICAL CLUES OF BATTERING DURING PREGNANCY

Based in part on The March of Dimes "Abuse During Pregnancy: A Protocol for Prevention and Intervention" (McFarlane & Parker, 1994), in which battering is said to frequently start or escalate during pregnancy, health care professionals who are engaged in the delivery of prenatal care, perinatal care, and/or childbirth education are told that they have a unique opportunity to identify and assist battered women. While many of the clinical clues of battering during pregnancy are the same as for nonpregnant women, there are additional clues which may occur during pregnancy. Some of these clues may be central injury pattern which include injuries to the head, neck, pregnant abdomen, breasts, back, buttocks, and genitalia; late entry or no prenatal care; or partner engages in "teasing" behavior with his pregnant partner, calling her "fat," "a cow," or "a blimp."

POLICY ON DOMESTIC VIOLENCE: ST. VINCENT'S HOSPITAL AND MEDICAL CENTER

The purpose of St Vincent's Hospital and Medical Center's Policy on Domestic Violence is to comply with the New York State Department of Health Regulations and to assist the staff in the treatment of domestic violence victims by following an established protocol. In order to ensure appropriate treatment referral and support, their protocol states that a referral should be made to the Social Work Department. Staff are reassured that if the situation has been acknowledged and validated and appropriate referrals have been made, everything has been done to help.

BATTERED WOMEN—IDENTIFICATION, TREATMENT AND REFERRAL OF; DEPARTMENT OF EMERGENCY SERVICES—RUSH–PRESBYTERIAN–ST. LUKE'S MEDICAL CENTER, CHICAGO, IL

This protocol identifies the person responsible (i.e., physician, R.N., Family Violence Program (FVP) staff and/or Clinical Coordinator) for each procedure. The Chicago Police Department is notified when a patient presents to Emergency Service with injuries incurred as a victim of crime. It is noted that a battered woman can make a police report without having to sign a criminal complaint and that she will be informed of this right.

RADAR: A DOMESTIC VIOLENCE INTERVENTION OF THE MASSACHUSETTS MEDICAL SOCIETY

RADAR action steps were developed by the Massachusetts Medical Society in 1992.

R = Routinely screen female patients. Although many women who are victims of domestic violence will not volunteer any information, they will discuss it if asked simple, direct questions in a nonjudgmental way and in a confidential setting. Interview the patient alone.

A = Ask direct questions. "Are you in a relationship in which you have been physically hurt or threatened?" If no, "Have you ever been?" "Have you ever been hit, kicked, punched by your partner?" "Do you feel safe at home?" "I notice you have a number of bruises; did someone do this to you?"

D = Document your findings. Use a body map to supplement the written record. Offer to photograph injuries. When a serious injury or sexual abuse is detected, preserve all physical evidence. Document an opinion if the injuries are inconsistent with the patient's explanation.

A = Assess patient safety. Before she leaves the medical setting, find out if she is afraid to go home. Has there been an increase in frequency or severity of violence? Have there been threats to her children?

R= Review options and referrals. If the patient is in imminent danger, find out if there is someone with whom she can stay. Does she need immediate access to a shelter? Offer her the opportunity of a private phone to make a call. If she does not need immediate assistance, offer information about hotlines and resources in the community. Remember that it may be dangerous for the woman to have this information in her possession. Do not insist that she take it, but make a follow-up appointment to see her.

FAMILY SAFETY

The usefulness of couples' counseling or family intervention in the presence of domestic violence is under debate. Attempts to implement family therapy in the presence of ongoing violence may increase the risk of serious harm. The first concern must be for the safety of the patient and any children.

Often, patients are not the only victims at home: Child abuse has been reported to occur in 33% to 54% of families where adult domestic violence occurs. In situations where children are also being abused, coordinated liaisons between advocates for victims of domestic violence and child protective service agents should be used to ensure the safety of both the patient and any children. Otherwise, the reporting and investigation of alleged child abuse may increase the patient's risk of abuse.

CRITICAL/CLINICAL PATHWAYS

Developed by Linda Dyar (Personal communication, May 12, 1997) of the Women's Center and Shelter of Montgomery County for Abington Memorial Hospital, PA, the critical/clinical pathway clearly outlines social worker and nursing interventions and when they are likely to occur (Figure 9.1). She notes that the patient comes to the ER, is triaged, registers, and is taken to the exam room, at which point family and friends are asked to leave the room. The nurse and doctor then do the screening. If the patient identifies herself as abused, she is referred to the social worker. If she denies abuse and identifying factors exist, she is also referred to the social worker. In the situation where domestic violence is suspected and the patient states that the abuse is occurring, she is placed in a room with a door. The doctor and nurse then obtain the patient's history. The doctor diagnoses and manages the patient's current medical and surgical problems, documents, and then either admits or discharges the patient. The social worker discusses options (safety plan, hotlines, legal advocacy, shelters) and provides supportive/empowerment counseling and resources/referrals. The social worker will be available to the patient throughout her ER visit, and upon admission or discharge there will be patient follow-up.

CONCLUSION

It should be the role of the ER Social Worker and the main function of the Social Work Department to coordinate and ensure that the ER protocols to identify and treat victims of abuse are effectively utilized.

Paramount to any coordinated initiative is the interdisciplinary education of the entire ER team, which should be initiated by an appointed coordinator from the Social Work Department.

The best programs involve and enlist intercommunity resource cooperation, in which the ER team is a vital link: from paramedics to police, shelters, and other community resources.

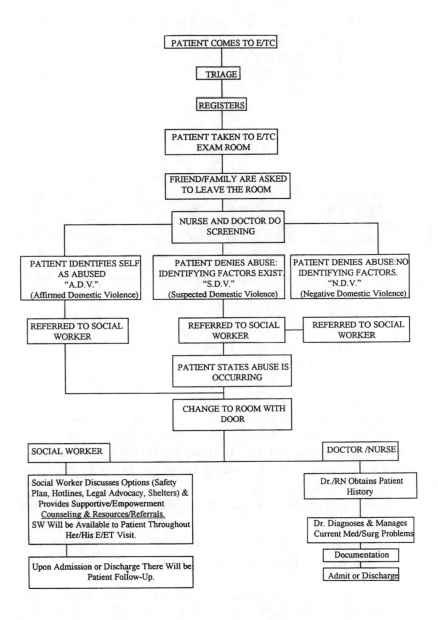

FIGURE 9.1   Critical/clinical pathways.

Source: Linda Dyar, Women's Center and Shelter of Montgomery County Medical Advocacy
Project for Abington Memorial Hospital, PA.

Unfortunately, most ERs in the country today are not in compliance with the JCAHO recommendations; only 29% of all California ERs have policies for domestic violence.

St. Vincent's Hospital, New York, N.Y., includes a note of encouragement to their ER staff:

> Don't judge the success of the intervention by the patient's actions. A person is most at risk of serious injury and even homicide when they attempt to leave an abusive partner and it may take them a long time before they can finally do so. It is frustrating for the treating staff when a patient stays in an abusive situation. Staff should be reassured that if the situation has been acknowledged and validated and appropriate referrals have been made, everything has been done to help. (1996, p. 6)

To intervene effectively, social workers and nurses must understand that abuse is a cumulative process that must be examined as a continuum. During this process, the abuse, the relationship, and a woman's view of her self change, requiring time-specific interventions. It is mandatory that all women be effectively screened for domestic violence in every ER in the U.S.

It is critically important that there be immediate referral when necessary to emergency shelter, community mental health center, family service agency, or a community support group. Many of the women are in crisis and transition needs to be developed. Roberts' (1990) Seven-Stage Crisis Intervention Model (Figure 9.2) can facilitate early identification of crisis precipitants, problem solving, and effective crisis resolution.

The seven stages of the crisis intervention model are as follows:

1. *Plan and conduct a thorough assessment* (including lethality, dangerousness to self or others, and immediate psychosocial needs).

2. *Establish rapport* and rapidly establish the relationship (conveying genuine respect and acceptance of the client while also offering reassurance and reinforcement that the client, like hundreds of previous clients, can be helped by the therapist).

3. *Identify major problem(s)*. This step includes identifying the "last straw" or precipitating event that led the client to seek help

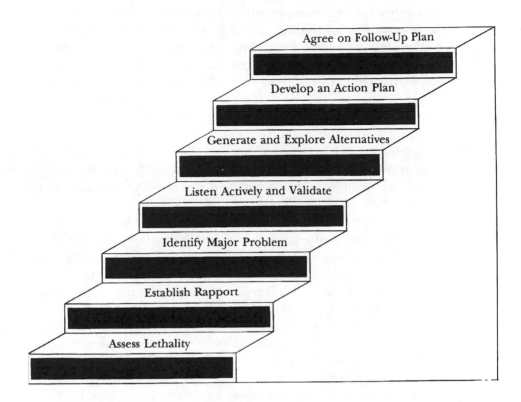

FIGURE 9.2 Roberts' Seven-Stage Crisis Intervention Model.

at this time. The clinician should help the client to focus on the most important problem by helping the client to rank order and prioritize several problems and the harmful or potentially threatening aspect of the number one problem. It is important and most productive to help the client to ventilate about the precipitating event or events; this will lead to problem identification.

4. *Deal with feelings and emotions.* This stage involves active listening, communicating with warmth and reassurance, nonjudg-

mental statements and validation, and accurate empathetic statements. The person in crisis may well have multiple mood swings throughout the crisis intervention. As a result, nonverbal gestures, such as smiling and nodding, might be distracting and annoying to the person in acute crisis. Therefore, Roberts suggests the use of verbal counseling skills when helping the client to explore his or her emotions. These verbal responses include reflecting feelings, restating content, using open-ended questions, summarizing, giving advice, reassurance, interpreting statements, confronting, and using silence.

5. *Generate and explore alternatives.* Many clients, especially college graduates, have personal insights and problem-solving skills, as well as the ability to anticipate the outcomes of certain deliberate actions. However, the client is emotionally distressed and consumed by the aftermath of the crisis episode. It is therefore very useful to have an objective and trained clinician assist the client in conceptualizing and discussing adaptive coping responses to the crisis. "In cases where the client has little or no introspection or personal insights, the clinician needs to take the initiative and suggest more adaptive coping methods" (Roberts, 1990, p. 13). During this potentially highly productive stage, the therapist/crisis intervenor and client collaboratively agree upon appropriate alternative coping methods.

6. *Develop and formulate an action plan.* Developing and implementing an action plan will ultimately restore cognitive functioning for the client. This active stage may involve the client agreeing to search for an apartment in a low-crime suburban area, for example, or it may involve the client making an appointment with an attorney who specializes in divorce mediation, or agreeing to go to a support group for widows or persons with sexually transmitted diseases (STDs). Many clients have great difficulty mobilizing themselves and following through on an action plan. It is imperative that the client be encouraged and bolstered so that he or she will follow through. Clients in crisis need to hear that you have had other clients who have failed and have been lethargic, yet have made an all-out effort to overcome the obstacle and were successful in resolving the crisis.

7. *Follow-up.* Stage seven in crisis intervention should involve an informal agreement or formal appointment between the thera-

pist and the client to have another meeting at a designated time, either in person or on the phone, to gauge the client's success in crisis resolution and daily functioning 1 week, 2 weeks, or 1 month later.

REFERENCES

Berrios, D. C., & Grady, D. (1991, August). Domestic violence: Risk factors and outcomes. *Western Journal of Medicine, 155*(2), 133–135.

Boes, M. (1997). A typology for establishing social work staffing patterns. *Crisis Intervention and Time-Limited Treatment, 3*(3), 171–188.

Brendtro, M., & Bowker, L. H. (1989). Battered women: How can nurses help? *Issues in Mental Health Nursing, 10*, 169–180.

Bullock, L., McFarlane, J., Bateman, L., & Miller, V. (1989). Characteristics of battered women in a primary care setting. *Nurse Practitioner, 14*, 47–55.

Campbell, J. C. (1986). Nursing assessment for risk of homicide with battered women. *Advances in Nursing Science, 8*, 36–51.

Campbell, J. C. (1991). Public health conceptions of family abuse. In D. Knudson & J. Miller (Eds.), *Abused and battered* (pp. 35–48). New York: Aldine de Gruyter.

Campbell, J. C., & Sheridan, D. (1989). Emergency nursing with battered women. *Journal of Emergency Nursing, 15*, 12–17.

The Commonwealth Fund. (1983, July 14). *First comprehensive national health survey of American women finds them at significant risk.* New York: Author.

Council on Scientific Affairs, American Medical Association. (1992). Violence against women: Relevance for medical practitioners. *Journal of the American Medical Association, 267*, 3184–3189.

DelTufo, A. (1995). *Domestic violence for beginners* (pp. 525–535). New York: Writers and Readers Publishing.

Douglas, H. (1991, November). Assessing violent couples. *Families in Society.*

Drake, V. K. (1982). Battered women: A health care problem. *Image, 19*, 40–47.

Edleson, J. L., & Eisikovits, Z. C. (1996). *Future interventions with battered women and their families.* Thousand Oaks, CA: Sage.

Goldberg, W. G., & Tomlanovich, M. C. (1984). Domestic violence victims in the emergency department. *Journal of the American Medical Association, 251*, 3259–3264.

Helton, A., McFarlane, J., & Anderson, E. (1987). Prevention of battering during pregnancy: Focus on behavioral change. *Public Health Nursing, 4*, 166–174.

Joint Commission on Accreditation of Healthcare Organizations. (1992). *Accreditation Manual: 1. Standards.* Oakbrook Terrace, IL: Author.

Keller, L. E. (1996). Invisible victims: Battered women in psychiatric and medical emergency rooms. *Bulletin of the Menninger Clinic, 60,* 1–21.

Lynch, V. A. (1995). Clinical forensic nursing: A new perspective in the management of crime victims from trauma to trial. *Critical Care Nursing Clinics of North America, 7,* 489–507.

McFarlane, J., & Parker, B. (1994). Nursing Module *"Abuse during pregnancy: A protocol for prevention and intervention"* (pp. 1–44). White Plains, NY: March of Dimes.

McLeer, S., & Anwar, R. (October, 1987). The role of the emergency physician in the prevention of domestic violence. *Annals of Emergency Medicine, 16,* 1155–1161.

Meyer, H. (1992, January). The billion dollar epidemic. *American Medical News,* p. 7.

Mooney, J. (1994). *The hidden figure: Domestic violence in North London.* London: Islington Police and Crime Prevention Unit.

Randall, T. (1990). Domestic violence intervention calls for more than treating injuries. *Journal of the American Medical Association, 264,* 939–940.

Roberts, A. R. (Ed.). (1990). *Crisis intervention handbook: Assessment, treatment and research.* Belmont, CA: Wadsworth.

Roberts, A. R. (Ed.). (1996a). *Crisis management and brief treatment.* Chicago: Nelson-Hall.

Roberts, A. R. (Ed.). (1996b). *Helping battered women.* New York: Oxford University Press.

Russell, D. E. H. (1986). *The secret trauma: Incest in the lives of girls and women* (pp. 103–105). New York: Basic Books.

Saint Vincent's Hospital and Medical Center. (1996). *Administrative Manual, Executive Committee of the Medical Staff* (pp. 1–6). Policy No. 248. New York: Saint Vincent's Hospital and Medical Center.

Schechter, S. (1987). *Guidelines for mental health practitioners in domestic violence cases* (p. 9). Washington, DC: The National Coalition Against Domestic Violence.

Sheridan, D. J. (1987). Advocacy with battered women: The role of the emergency room nurse. *Response to the Victimization of Women and Children, 10,* 14–15.

Stark, E., & Flitcraft, A. H. (1991). Spouse abuse. In M. L. Rosenberg & M. A. Fenley (Eds.), *Violence in America: A public health approach* (pp. 138–139). New York: Oxford University Press.

Stark, E., Flitcraft, A., Zuckerman, D., Grey, A., Robison, J., & Frazier, W. (1981). *Wife abuse in the medical setting.* (Domestic Violence Monograph No. 7). Rockville, MD: National Clearinghouse on Domestic Violence.

Sugg, N., & Inui, T. (1992). Primary care physicians' response to domestic violence: Opening Pandora's box. *Journal of the American Medical Association, 267,* 3157–3160.

Tilden, V. P. (1989). Response of the health care delivery system to battered women. *Issues in Mental Health Nursing, 10,* 309–320.

Tilden, V. P., & Shepherd, P. (1987). Increasing the rate of identification of battered women in an emergency department: Use of a nursing protocol. *Research in Nursing and Health, 10,* 209–215.

U.S. Senate Judiciary Committee. (1992). *Violence against women.* Washington, DC: Government Printing Office.

Warshaw, C. (1989). Limitations of the medical model in the care of battered women. *Gender and Society, 3,* 506–517.

Warshaw, C., & Ganley, A. (1996). Identification, assessment, and intervention with victims of domestic violence. In *Improving the health care response to domestic violence: A response manual for health care providers* (2nd ed., pp. 49–86). San Francisco: Family Violence Prevention Fund.

Zawitz, M., Klaus, P. A., Bachman, R., Bastian, L. D., De Berry, M., Jr., Rand, M. R., & Taylor, B. M. (1993). *Highlights from 20 years of surveying crime victims: The National Crime Victimization Survey, 1973–92.* Washington, DC: U.S. Department of Justice.

CHAPTER 10

Intimate Partner Violence: Intervention in Primary Health Care Settings

Bonnie E. Carlson and Louise-Anne McNutt

INTRODUCTION

This chapter has two objectives: To discuss the association between intimate partner violence and women's physical and emotional health, and to present a model for domestic violence screening and intervention in primary care settings. Abuse of women is a major public health, medical, and social problem. There are many definitions of woman abuse and many terms used to describe it. For purposes of this chapter we will use the definition of the American Medical Association (AMA), which characterizes intimate partner violence as a "pattern of coercive behaviors that may include repeated battering and injury, psychological abuse, sexual assault, progressive social isolation, deprivation, and intimidation" (American

Medical Association, 1994, p. 5). This definition encompasses three major forms of abuse of women: physical violence, psychological or emotional abuse, and sexual abuse. To date, the consequences of physical violence have been studied more extensively than those resulting from emotional or sexual abuse by an intimate partner, with few if any studies considering the simultaneous and independent effects of the three types of abuse. Thus, the emphasis of the literature reviewed here will be on physical violence and associated health outcomes, due to the limitations of existing research, rather than a belief that physical abuse is more harmful than sexual or emotional abuse. On the contrary, preliminary data suggest that emotional abuse and sexual assault by an intimate partner may be equally or even more harmful than physical violence.

Of the three health care sectors, primary, secondary, and tertiary, primary care settings are distinguished by providing direct patient access, addressing relatively common health problems in community-based settings, and focusing attention on prevention of health problems. Primary care settings include physicians' offices, health maintenance organizations (HMOs; prepaid plans that combine insurance with medical services), public health clinics, and community health centers. Providers include physicians with specializations in family practice, internal medicine, and obstetrics and gynecology, as well as physicians' assistants and nurse practitioners in these areas (Oktay, 1995). The term "physician/provider" will be used to refer to these health care professionals.

INTIMATE PARTNER ABUSE

Prevalence of Intimate Partner Violence

Each year, it is estimated that approximately 8% to 11%, or about 4 million married or cohabiting women, are physically assaulted by a male partner; 3% to 4%, or about 2 million women, experience severe violence (Plichta, 1996; Straus & Gelles, 1990; Teske & Parker, 1983). Emotional abuse is estimated to affect between 3% and 20% of women who are not physically assaulted (Follingstad, Rutledge, Berg, Hause, & Polek, 1990; McNutt, Carlson, Winterbauer, & Gagen,

1997; O'Leary & Curley, 1986). Prevalence estimates of sexual violence vary widely, with estimates centering around 15% to 20% of women in the general population and as many as 50% of physically abused women (Kilpatrick, Saunders, Veronen, Best, & Von, 1987; Koss & Oros, 1982; Russell, 1990).

Studies based in primary care practices typically report slightly higher prevalences of intimate partner violence than do general population studies, with the most common estimates between 10% and 25% of women physically abused within the previous year, and up to 50% of women having experienced physical abuse at some time (Freund, Bak, & Blackhall, 1996; Hamberger, Saunders, & Hovey, 1992; Hillard, 1985; Plichta & Abraham, 1996). Two studies found particularly low prevalence rates: a study of internal medicine patients (McCauley et al., 1995) and a study of women with gastrointestinal disorders, which used a very conservative definition of physical abuse (i.e., "*often* hit, kicked, or beaten") and found a very low prevalence rate of only 4% (Drossman et al., 1990). Although definitions of intimate partner violence vary substantially across studies, the most likely explanations for the typically higher prevalence reported in primary care practice studies is first that they focus on samples of low-income women who tend to have higher rates of abuse, and second, that the negative health sequelae of abuse are likely to bring abused women into the medical setting more often than nonabused women.

Sequelae of Intimate Partner Violence

Medical sequelae of intimate partner violence include injuries, symptoms of psychological stress, and a wide range of physical symptoms. The most obvious health outcomes of physical violence are acute traumatic injuries. Injuries are reported by approximately 50% of women who are physically assaulted (Hale-Carlsson, Hutton, Fuhrman, McNutt, & Morse, 1996). However, only 20% of women who are injured seek medical attention for the injuries (Hale-Carlsson et al., 1996). Thus, most women who are physically assaulted do not see health care professionals for injuries.

Often, the cause of injuries leaves distinct characteristics. Injuries that are unintentional tend to affect the extremities. For example, someone who falls may hurt her wrist because she instinctively reached out with her hand to break her fall. Although any type of injury is possible from a physical assault, these intentional injuries tend to occur most commonly on the head, face, neck, and torso (Helton, McFarlane, & Anderson, 1987; McFarlane, Parker, Soeken, & Bullock, 1992). Also, injuries caused by domestic violence have other trademarks, including bruises in different stages of healing and explanations of the causes of injuries that do not match the injuries' presentations.

Nonspecific Physical Symptoms and Symptoms of Psychological Stress

Numerous studies evaluating the association between domestic violence and health outcomes have found that abused women tend to report multiple emotional and nonspecific physical symptoms (see Table 10.1). Physically abused women also have higher utilization of health care than nonabused women, although not necessarily for injuries (Drossman et al., 1990; McNutt, Hutton, Fuhrman, Hale-Carlsson, & Morse, 1997; Webster, Chandler, & Battistutta, 1996). In addition, abused women report more sick days and poorer physical and mental health than nonabused women (Gelles, 1990; McNutt, Hutton, et al., 1997; Plichta, 1996). A study of primary care, internal medicine patients had a typical study design and results (McCauley et al., 1995). A total of 1952 consecutive, female patients completed a questionnaire while they were alone in an examination room. The questionnaire asked, "Within the last year, have you been hit, slapped, kicked, or otherwise physically hurt by someone?" An affirmative answer identifying the abuser as a husband, boyfriend, ex-husband, or relative was counted as domestic violence. Compared to women not physically assaulted during the previous year, the 108 (5.5%) physically assaulted women were over three times as likely to experience anxiety, five times as likely to be depressed, and over six times as likely to have a low self-esteem. Of the 20 nonspecific physical symptoms measured, 15 symptoms were 1.5 to 3.5 times more common for physically assaulted women, including problems with eating, sleeping, breathing, gastrointestinal symptoms, and pain (i.e., chest, abdominal, breast, and headaches). These symptoms are

TABLE 10.1   Health Outcomes Associated with Intimate Partner Violence

Injuries	*Pain*
Bruises	Choking sensation
Lacerations and cuts	Breast pain
Fractured and broken bones	Chest pain
Sprains	Back pain
Hematomas	Abdominal pain
Black eyes	Pelvic pain
Detached retinas	Headaches

Nonspecific Symptoms

Problems eating	Problems sleeping
Loss of appetite	Nightmares
Binging	Problems falling asleep
Purging	
Intestinal and urinary problems	Problems breathing
Diarrhea	Shortness of breath
Constipation	Asthma
Problems passing urine	Choking sensation
Gynecology problems	Other nonspecific symptoms
Vaginal discharge	Seizures (epilepsy)
Menstrual problems, endometriosis	Fatigue
Reproductive problems	Pain or irritation of eyes
Sexually transmitted diseases	Fainting and passing out

Symptoms of Psychological Stress and/or Psychiatric Disorders

Depression	Substance abuse
Anxiety	Alcohol abuse
Interpersonal sensitivity	Illegal drug use
(low self-esteem)	
Panic attacks	Prescription drug abuse
Post-traumatic stress disorder	Smoking
Attempted suicide	
Suicidal ideation	

Death

References: Bailey et al., 1997; Cascardi, Langinrichsen, & Vivian, 1992; Drossman et al., 1990; Dumas, Katerndahl, & Burge, 1995; Hillard, 1985; McCauley et al., 1995; Mercy & Saltzman, 1989; Plichta, 1996; Stark & Flitcraft, 1996; Webster et al., 1996.

often more common than injuries. All four emotional symptoms and 13 of the 20 physical symptoms were more common than injuries (i.e., frequent or serious bruises) among physically assaulted women (McCauley et al., 1995). Other studies based in family practice (Saunders, Hamberger, & Hovey, 1993), obstetrics and gynecology (Hillard, 1985; Webster et al., 1996), internal medicine (Freund et al., 1996), gastroenterology (Drossman et al., 1990), psychiatry (Hilberman & Munson, 1978), pain clinics (Walling, O'Hara, Reiter, Milburn, Lilly, & Vincent, 1994), emergency departments (Abbott, Johnson, Koziol-McLain, & Lowenstein, 1995) and in the general population (Plichta & Abraham, 1996) also have found that abused women report more symptoms and poorer health than women who have not experienced abuse.

Intimate partner violence has also been associated with a wide variety of negative psychological or mental health outcomes. Studies conducted in primary care practices and clinics have consistently found that physically assaulted women report more symptoms of psychological stress than other women (Drossman et al., 1990; McCauley et al., 1995; Stark, Flitcraft, & Frazier, 1979). Being physically abused has been found to be associated with elevated levels of psychiatric disorders, including dysthymia and major depression (Cascardi, O'Leary, Lawrence, & Schlee, 1995; Sato & Heiby, 1992), generalized anxiety (Gleason, 1993), obsessive compulsive disorder (Gleason, 1993), and posttraumatic stress disorder (Cascardi et al., 1995; Astin, Lawrence, & Foy, 1993; Saunders, 1994). In general, the research indicates that the more severe the violence and abuse, the more negative the mental health outcomes experienced (Gelles & Harrop, 1989).

A substantial body of literature has documented the short- and long-term effects of sexual assault, although most studies have not examined sexual assault by an intimate partner. Sexual assault has been associated with poor physical and mental health outcomes, such as chronic pain disorders and gastrointestinal complaints, poor self-esteem, suicidal behavior, anxiety and posttraumatic stress, and substance abuse, leading to increased health care utilization (Gelles & Harrop, 1989; Koss, Gidcyz, & Wisniewski, 1987; Shields & Hanneke, 1983). The few studies that examine rape by an intimate partner have found that such sexual assault can be traumatic and contribute to negative outcomes such as psychosomatic illness, independent of the effects of physical abuse (Shields & Hanneke, 1983).

Emotional abuse, too, can have harmful effects on well-being, although its impact has not been well studied. Among women experiencing both physical and emotional abuse, emotional abuse is frequently reported by victims and researchers as more difficult to cope with or harmful (Follingstad et al., 1990; Herbert, Silver, & Ellard, 1990; Marshall, 1994; Tolman, 1992). Emotional abuse has been found to be associated with lowered self-esteem, which may be the mechanism through which it affects other aspects of well-being. Victims of emotional abuse are also said to suffer from somatic problems such as headaches and stomach aches, as well as posttraumatic effects (Loring, 1994).

Does intimate partner violence cause poorer mental and physical health? Data suggest this is a distinct possibility; however, with the exception of acute traumatic injuries, causality has not been proven because most studies are cross-sectional in design. That is, women are asked if they experienced abuse and specific symptoms during the last year. Because abuse and symptoms are measured at the same time, it is impossible to ascertain from these studies that the intimate partner violence occurred before the onset of symptoms.

Second, most analyses have not been adjusted for possible confounding factors. Two potential confounders are socioeconomic status and childhood abuse. One study that focused on the association between physical assault and sexual assault with depression, anxiety and physical symptoms scale and did adjust for socioeconomic factors and childhood abuse found that intimate partner violence was associated with somatization and anxiety among patients in pain, dental, and gynecology clinics (Walling et al., 1994). Most other studies do not adjust for potential confounders.

Third, most studies have measured only the physical violence component of intimate partner violence and found associations between these assaults and health outcomes. However, most women who have been physically assaulted have also experienced emotional abuse, and some were sexually abused. Thus, health outcomes associated with physical violence may actually be due to emotional abuse, sexual abuse, or some combination of the three forms of abuse.

In our own pilot research on a sample of female primary care patients and women using domestic violence services in the community, we found that physical violence, emotional abuse, and sexual abuse made independent contributions to four reported symptoms:

fatigue, insomnia, shortness of breath, and stomach pain. Furthermore, sexual violence appeared to make an even greater contribution to these symptoms than did physical violence (McNutt, Carlson, Winterbauer, & Gagen, 1997).

Recognizing the interconnectedness of physical, emotional, and sexual abuse and their possible joint effects on well-being is important, because most papers focus only on the effects of physical abuse and reducing physical violence. Physicians/providers are informed primarily about the consequences of physical violence and thus may focus on only these acts. It may well be that reducing physical violence can lead to increased emotional abuse. That is, an abuser who beats his partner to control her and finds that the costs are too high to continue using physical abuse may shift to increasing emotional and/or sexual means of control. Thus, overlooking the possibility of emotional or sexual abuse while focusing exclusively on physical violence has the potential for causing more harm.

Pregnancy and Intimate Partner Violence

Intimate partner violence has been found to be prevalent during pregnancy, with 0.9% to 20.1% of pregnant women reporting physical abuse (Gazmararian et al., 1996). This relatively high prevalence may be attributable to the fact that young age is associated with both pregnancy and intimate partner violence (Gelles, 1990). For some women abuse increases or starts during pregnancy, whereas for many others abuse may decrease during pregnancy (Hillard, 1985). Common sites for physical abuse during pregnancy include the face and torso (the most common sites for nonpregnant abused women) as well as the abdomen, breasts, and genital areas (Helton et al., 1987). Abuse during pregnancy creates a variety of health risks for both the woman and the developing fetus, including miscarriage, preterm labor, chorioamnionitis, low birth weight, fetomaternal hemorrhage, abruptio placentae, and in some cases fetal death or neonatal death (Goodwin & Breen, 1990; McFarlane & Parker, 1996; McFarlane, Parker, & Soeken, 1996; Webster et al., 1996).

Intimate Partner Violence and Primary Care

Primary care physicians are likely to see abused women in all practice settings, as women seeking help for abuse often turn first to the health care system and see physicians as an appropriate person with whom to discuss abuse-related problems (Stark & Flitcraft, 1991). Women age 15 to 44 have an average of three office visits per year, the majority of which are to primary care practices (Schappert, 1992). Abused women may be even more likely than nonabused women to seek medical care, and those who do seek care have higher utilization rates than nonabused women (American Medical Association, Council on Internal Affairs, 1992; Drossman et al., 1990; Stark & Flitcraft, 1991). However, intimate partner violence has tended to be underdetected in medical settings. Part of the reason for this lack of identification is undoubtedly due to the fact that woman abuse has traditionally been a taboo topic, shrouded by shame and disbelief, which atmosphere has interfered with honest discussions about abuse between its victims and medical providers. And yet health care professionals may be the only professionals to recognize and be in a position to intervene on behalf of many abused women, because such women are very likely to see them for abuse-related injuries and other medical sequelae, as well as for routine health care (Hadley, Short, Lezin, & Zook, 1995). In a 1991 telephone survey conducted by the AMA, the majority of those surveyed reported that physicians could be helpful in controlling or reducing family violence (American Medical Association, 1991). Hadley et al. (1995) have noted that

> Health professionals are in a pivotal position to identify injuries or symptoms caused by abuse relatively early in the victim's process—in many cases, years before the violence has become so extreme and unrelenting that it may drive someone to a shelter or result in death. It is thought that the critical timing of this early identification and intervention may not only prevent or reduce further suffering and violence in victim's lives, but may also reduce significant health care and productivity costs associated with domestic violence. (p. 190)

Barriers to Identification of Intimate Partner Violence in Primary Care

A variety of barriers to detection of domestic violence in medical settings exist, especially in primary care settings. These barriers exist on the part of both providers and patients.

Physician Barriers.   First, over two-thirds of all primary care physician-patient contacts last fewer than 15 minutes (Schappert, 1992), during which time numerous issues must be addressed in addition to physical complaints. For a domestic violence intervention to become a regular component of primary care practice, the intervention must take into account these time constraints. Second, the long-term nature of domestic violence—the lengthy process that some women experience in identifying abuse, deciding what to do about it, and ultimately leaving if that is their only alternative to get the abuse to stop—presents a perplexing challenge for many medical professionals who have been taught to ameliorate problems as expeditiously as possible (Hadley et al., 1995). Third, although rates of abuse are fairly stable across a wide range of medical practices, many physicians believe they do not see domestic violence in their practices and fail to recognize how prevalent intimate partner violence is (American Medical Association, 1994; Flitcraft, 1995). Fourth, many—perhaps most—physician/providers are not knowledgeable about intimate partner abuse and have not been trained in methods to screen and intervene with abused women (American Medical Association, 1994). This lack of awareness and training may leave them feeling ineffectual and pessimistic about the likelihood of their being able to do anything constructive on behalf of abused women. Fifth, physician/providers are under the misconception that patients do not want to be asked about abuse (Friedman, Samet, Roberts, Hudlin, & Hans, 1992). Sixth, some providers believe that it is not part of their role to identify abuse and make appropriate referrals, or fear opening a "Pandora's Box" (Sugg & Inui, 1992). Seventh, personal experiences with domestic violence may interfere with the provider's ability to be objective and effective with abused patients (deLahunta & Tulsky, 1996). And finally, the provider may himself be an abusive partner.

Patient Barriers.   Significant barriers also exist on the part of abused female patients that can interfere with their ability or willingness to initiate discussions of abuse or even acknowledge abuse when it is brought up by a physician or other provider. Much shame, humiliation, and embarrassment is associated with being abused, with many women assuming responsibility for their victimization. Some battered women are not aware they are being abused, believe they are not deserving of assistance, or pessimistically assume that nothing can be done about the abuse. Others are so fearful of their partners that they cannot risk disclosure to anyone outside the family, even with guarantees of confidentiality. Many fail to connect the health and mental health symptoms they suffer with the abuse. Still others are protective of the abusive partner because he is their only source of support or because they fear how he will be treated by criminal justice or social service agencies that have traditionally discriminated against and oppressed men from ethnic minority groups. Finally, some women are fearful that disclosure of abuse will lead to the health professional contacting law enforcement authorities, as they are required to do by law in some states (See discussion below on mandatory reporting).

Because of the high prevalence of woman abuse, its negative health consequences, and the high health-related costs of domestic violence, several influential individuals and organizations in the health community have recognized the importance of primary care practices identifying and aiding abused women. These individuals and organizations include two Surgeons General (Everett Koop and Antonia Novello); Secretary of Health and Human Services Donna Shalala; the Centers for Disease Control and Prevention (CDC); the AMA; the American Public Health Association; the American College of Obstetricians and Gynecologists (ACOG); and the American Nurses Association (American College of Obstetricians and Gynecologists, 1995; American Medical Association, 1994; American Nursing Association, 1991).

A COMPREHENSIVE/DIFFERENTIATED MODEL OF IDENTIFICATION, SCREENING AND INTERVENTION: MEDICINE, NURSING, AND SOCIAL WORK

Since Surgeon General Everett Koop first convened a workshop on violence in 1985, a substantial amount of activity has occurred in the medical community to address domestic violence. In addition to recommendations by national professional health organizations, almost half of state medical societies have developed efforts to address woman abuse, such as protocols or clinical pathways, task forces, or specific educational programs (Flitcraft, 1995). Because the primary care setting offers an ideal place to screen women for intimate partner violence, the AMA, the ACOG, the American Nurses Association and most other national and state medical associations suggest that physicians and nurses screen female patients for possible abuse. Primary care practices take many forms. The focus of intimate partner violence intervention discussed here is the multi-physician/provider practice that is becoming predominant in health care. However, the basic concepts can be applied across other types of primary care practices.

The proposed integrated model is based not only on recommendations from the AMA and ACOG, but also on suggestions from experts in the field of domestic violence; abused women themselves; and female patients. The model also takes into account the following premises:

1. physicians/providers do not have time to implement an entire intimate partner screening and intervention protocol in the primary care setting;
2. nurses typically work as a team with physicians/providers, and this team approach is well suited for domestic violence screening and intervention;
3. abuse screening will not be sustained in most settings unless resources are readily available to assist abused women; and
4. primary care practices are appropriate settings to identify women experiencing abuse and provide basic interventions, whereas for more comprehensive social services, abused women will be better served by community programs that specialize in domestic violence. Thus, a partnership between primary care practices and community programs is essential to serving abused women.

Although the recommendations from the various organizations are diverse, the content is fairly consistent: Screen routinely for intimate partner violence, validate that abuse is a serious problem, provide information, and make referrals to community resources. In addition, some have suggested that abused women be hospitalized if no other safe options are available (American Medical Association, Council of Ethical and Judicial Affairs, 1992). The model we present recognizes the complex nature of intimate partner abuse. It also takes into account the unique roles, training, and skills of physicians/

providers, nurses and social workers, and attempts to make the best use of the unique talents of each type of professional.

Goals and Objectives

- Identification of cases of physical, emotional, and/or sexual abuse, through routine and targeted screening by physician/providers or nurses;
- Documentation of patient abuse by nurses and/or physician/providers;
- Validation of the abused woman's experience by physician/providers, nurses, and/or social workers;
- Increased patient knowledge of domestic violence;
- Enhanced patient safety, through interventions by a nurse and/or social worker;
- Reduced patient isolation, through interventions by a nurse and/or social worker;
- Increased patient knowledge of community resources, through interventions by a nurse or social worker; and
- Make appropriate referrals through social worker interventions.

Screening for Intimate Partner Violence

Because domestic violence has so often been overlooked in clinical practice, the development of protocols has been suggested as a useful tool to assist physician/providers in addressing domestic violence in primary care (Flitcraft, 1995; McLeer & Anwar, 1989). In developing a screening protocol, four questions need to be addressed:

1. Under what conditions should women be screened?
2. What kinds of questions need to be asked?
3. Which health professionals should be designated to ask questions about intimate partner violence? and
4. When should health care professionals screen women for intimate partner violence?

Environment. In every interaction related to intimate partner violence, safety is a primary consideration. A woman should be asked about intimate partner violence only when she is alone with a health care professional, due to the concern that information about the conversation may reach the perpetrator (American Medical Association, 1994). It may be obvious to most professionals that asking about intimate partner violence while a perpetrator is present could result in harm to the patient. However, the presence of persons not presumed to be the perpetrator may also be harmful. For example, if a friend, relative, or ally of a perpetrator is present when a woman discusses abuse, then a report of that information may reach the perpetrator and result in further abuse. Children, especially young children, may state what happened at the visit without understanding the ramifications of the information repeated.

Additionally, harm may not necessarily manifest itself as physical violence. If a perpetrator suspects that a woman is speaking about abuse to health care professionals, then he or she may make it difficult for a woman to access medical care due to the fear that the violence will be disclosed and the victim counseled. Additionally, an abused woman speaking in the presence of others may state that no abuse is occurring simply because she is fearful or ashamed. The result is that the abused woman may end up feeling helpless rather than validated and supported.

For the same reasons, patients who do not speak English need an interpreter who can facilitate an open discussion about very private experiences. Children, family members, and friends should be avoided in translating conversations about intimate partner violence. Ideally, the interpreter would be a member of the primary care practice staff or someone with training in intimate partner violence.

Thus, it is advisable to create a standing policy that all patients be seen unaccompanied for at least part of their history and/or physical. In that way, health care professionals will not find themselves in the awkward position of having to isolate individual women whom they suspect to be abused. In addition, because there is no one defining characteristic of abused women, a standing policy of seeing all women alone for at least part of the visit alleviates the problem of trying to predict who is being abused and who is not.

There will be times when a patient refuses to be seen alone or when a person accompanying a patient refuses to leave her—a difficult situation if abuse is suspected. In general, questions about abuse should not be asked if a patient is accompanied. Therefore, the decision usually will be either to allow the visitor to stay with the patient and omit questions about intimate partner violence, or to insist that the patient be seen alone. Each of these situations needs to be evaluated individually, recognizing that potential benefit or harm may result from either decision. Thus, the health care professional must weigh the benefits against the risks in each situation.

Intimate Partner Violence Screening Questions.   Many types of screening questions for intimate partner violence have been suggested (e.g., ACOG, 1995; AMA, 1994). The types of questions most commonly recommended use nonjudgmental language that feels comfortable to the provider. For example, a health care professional might ask, "Are you in a relationship in which you have been physically hurt or threatened by your partner?" or "Are you in a relationship in which you felt you were treated badly? In what ways?" (American Medical Association, 1994). The best questions emphasize explicit behaviors, events, and feelings, avoiding terms open to varying interpretation, such as "abuse" or "victimization." Suitable questions might include: "During fights or arguments, are you frightened that your partner may hurt you?" or "During the last year, has your intimate partner hit, kicked, beat or otherwise hurt you?" A question such as "Are you being abused?" may elicit a negative response from a woman who does not perceive herself as being abused, even though she is being hit or threatened by her partner.

Our own research asked primary care patients and abused women about the types of questions they thought health care professionals should ask patients (McNutt, Carlson, Gagen, et al., 1997). Whereas nonabused women suggested rather general questions such as "Is everything OK at home?" abused women typically suggested more specific questions, consistent with the recommendations in the literature. Perhaps a combination of general and specific questions would be ideal, beginning with the general and ending with the specific. The addition of one to three questions to a standard history interview appears to be sufficient to increase dramatically the number of women reporting intimate partner violence (Freund et al., 1996; Hillard, 1985). For example, in an internal medicine practice, the addition of one question to a written history form (i.e., "At any time, has a partner ever hit you, kicked you, or otherwise physically hurt you?") increased identification of women reporting physical violence from 0% to 11.6% (Freund et al., 1996). In a cohort of 742 obstetrics patients, 10.9% of women asked "Has anyone at home hit or tried to hurt you?" answered yes. Further questions identified 3.9% of the women who were abused during their current pregnancies (Hillard, 1985). A slightly longer set of questions form the Abuse Assessment Screen (McFarlane et al., 1992). Three questions focusing on physical and sexual violence by an intimate partner identified that 17% of 691 low-income women seeking prenatal care had been abused. The brief Abuse Assessment Screen performed similarly to the longer Conflicts Tactics Scale and the Index of Spouse Abuse (McFarlane et al., 1992).

Caution is needed in using a written history form to stimulate discussion of intimate partner abuse. Although these forms identify many women experiencing abuse not previously identified, at least one study suggests that even more women may be missed. A study by McFarlane, Christoffel, Bateman, Miller, and Bullock (1991) found that 8% of prenatal women reported physical violence on a written history form, in contrast to 29% of the women reporting physical violence when asked by a health care professional. Thus, it appears that in at least some patient populations, written histories are not a good alternative to verbally screening female patients for abuse.

Most studies of intimate partner violence in primary care settings have focused questions primarily on physical violence and occasionally on sexual violence. Less attention has been paid to screening for emotional abuse, despite studies suggesting that many health consequences may be as strongly related to emotional abuse as physical violence. Inclusion of a question about emotional abuse and/or isolation should be considered in any primary care screening program. The SAFE questions recommended by Ashur (1993) include questions on stress and fear in relationships in addition to questions about physical violence and assessments of social supports and emergency plans. Other sets of questions that may be useful for screening patients in the primary care setting may be found in Brown, Lent, Brett, Sas, and Pederson (1996) and McLeer, Anwar, Herman, and Maquiling (1989).

Who Should Screen Patients? The two obvious choices for initial intimate partner violence screening of female patients are nurses and physicians/providers. The American Nurses Association position paper suggests that nurses screen patients for abuse (American Nurses Association, 1991), whereas the AMA, ACOG and other physician organizations clearly recommend that physicians screen all female patients for intimate partner violence. Screening by nurses and physicians/providers each have advantages. Nurses often have more time to discuss health topics; for example, while taking vital signs or inquiring about the primary reason for the office visit. This time can be structured so that the patient and nurse are alone in the examination room and thus in a safe environment. Some abused women would prefer to be asked about abuse by a nurse (McNutt, Carlson, Gagen, et al., 1997), which may reflect the supportive-care nature of nursing and the likelihood that the nurse is also a woman. Additionally, because nurses are usually paid less than physicians/providers, using nursing time for the preliminary screening may be more cost-effective. The primary strength of physician/provider screening over nurse screening is the position of authority that physicians hold in our society. Sometimes called the ''physician-God connection,'' it is hypothesized that physicians taking the time to discuss abuse with a patient may sent a strong signal that abuse is not acceptable and that no one deserves to be victimized (Flitcraft, 1995).

Clearly, a case can be made for either nurses or physicians to screen. Perhaps the group of professionals who is most interested and willing in a particular setting should be designated as the ones to be responsible for screening.

When to Screen for Intimate Partner Violence. Medical guidelines recommend screening all women in the primary care setting, but do not specify when to screen (American Medical Association, 1994). Clearly, screening for any risk factor cannot be successfully maintained if the screening occurs at all visits. Thus, developing a policy to screen for intimate partner violence consistently at specific types of appointments is needed. Routine screening for abuse is necessary, because most abused women do not present with physical injuries or other clear indicators of abuse. The screening plan needs to identify appointment types that virtually all women have on a yearly basis to provide complete coverage. Additionally, the appointments chosen need to have a structure conducive to domestic violence screening and be acceptable both to patients and health care providers. Initial visits, gynecology and obstetrics visits, and routine physical examinations appear to meet these criteria. All of these examinations are commonly extended visits with longer time periods allotted, and usually include questions about multiple risk factors, such as smoking, substance use, and sexually transmitted disease risk factors. Inquiries about intimate partner violence would fit well within a set of sensitive questions such as these.

Most women are likely to have at least one of these routine appointments during a year-long period. While abused women report barriers in accessing health care (Plichta, 1996), a population-based study found that approximately 80% of women 18 to 44 years of age who reported physical violence by a partner had a gynecology examination during the previous year and 90% did so during the previous two years (McNutt, Hutton et al., 1997). Another study found that most women, both abused and nonabused, agreed that asking about intimate partner violence would be acceptable at gynecology, prenatal, and routine physical examinations, although most participants did not favor intimate partner screening at sick visits (McNutt, Carlson, Gagen, et al., 1997).

In addition to routine screening for intimate partner abuse targeted screening should occur when there are signs and symptoms of abuse. Such signs may include presentations of injuries that appear intentionally inflicted, clusters of nonspecific symptoms and symptoms of psychological stress without a clear etiology, and other presentations that suggest abuse as a possibility to the health professional. Screening at these visits is not only necessary to identify women experiencing abuse, but also is needed to alleviate the harm that could occur by being silent and ignoring potentially obvious signs.

Caution should be exercised to create a feasible abuse-screening approach. Being overzealous during the planning stage could result in a screening protocol that interferes with the medical practice and is subsequently abandoned as infeasible. Creation of a practical screening protocol is essential. A lesson can be learned from one intimate partner violence screening protocol that was highly successful in the short run but failed in the longer term. A study on identifying patients in an emergency department showed that staff education about abuse and a standardized protocol for a trauma history had a positive short-term effect, increasing identification of abused women from 5.6% to 30% of the female trauma patients (McLeer & Anwar, 1989). However, no monitoring of the protocol's use occurred, and 8 years later the emergency department staff identified only 7.7% of female trauma patients as abused women (McLeer et al., 1989). Thus, it appears the program fell victim to the commonly dreaded "disease-of-the-year" phenomenon, where a short-term successful program disappears when interested individuals either move on or change their focus. This experience teaches us that staff education about intimate partner violence and a protocol are not sufficient to integrate intimate partner violence screening into the practice long-term.

In summary, screening for intimate partner violence in the primary care setting should address issues of the necessary context for screening; the kinds of questions that should be asked of patients; which health care professionals are in the best position to screen patients for abuse; and at what types of visits patients should be screened. The ideas described above are not proposed as the only approaches to intimate partner violence screening in primary care, but rather are presented as suggestions and to highlight the practical issues that need consideration when incorporating intimate partner violence screening into primary care practice.

In our model, intimate partner abuse screening is conceived as a two-phase process, with nurses as the primary screeners and physician/providers providing additional screening under certain circumstances. Nurses and physician/providers will provide basic and time-limited interventions, such as validation and offering preliminary information. Then referrals will be made to the onsite social worker or domestic violence advocate. The social worker will perform a comprehensive assessment, provide detailed information, assist with safety planning, and make referrals to community services.

Before implementing domestic violence screening and intervention into a practice, education on intimate partner abuse and community resources is necessary, especially since intervention efforts can place women at increased risk for harm. Education programs totaling about 4 hours appears to be feasible for HMOs. Such programs should include background on intimate partner violence and its causes and dynamics, types of abuse, characteristics of abusers and victims, dangers related to intimate partner abuse, health and mental health sequelae of abuse, and relevant resources in the community. Ideally, domestic violence education should be available to all staff at a practice. While the interventions are focused on nursing and medical staff, support staff often may also benefit from such training if they have substantial patient contact. For example, receptionists may be less judgmental when a patient cancels an appointment for the third time if they understand the difficulties some women have in accessing health care.

SCREENING PHASE I: NURSING

All patients over a specified age should be seen unaccompanied for at least part of the history and physical, allowing time with both the nurse and physician/provider to discuss intimate partner abuse and other sensitive topics in private. The nurse will be the primary person to screen female patients for abuse. Using a standardized set of questions, the nurse will ask about abuse experiences. If a patient confirms she is being abused or abuse is suspected even though she denies it or evades the questions, the nurse will

1. discuss what intimate partner violence is;
2. provide relevant information, including supportive validation;
3. mention that a social worker or domestic violence advocate is available in the office; and
4. communicate that the patient is abused to the physician/provider so that he or she can briefly follow up.

Since nurses and physicians/providers do not always interact directly when seeing patients, communication using the medical record is practical. This communication can be as simple as placing a removable color-coded tag on the cover of the chart (e.g., blue for no abuse reported or suspected; yellow for abuse suspected but denied; red for abuse reported by the patient; and a "see me" tag if there is specific information that needs to be communicated).

In these interactions, the goal is to conduct what Flitcraft calls a "patient-centered interview" (Stark & Flitcraft, 1996). It is important to listen to the patient and let her know that she can discuss any problem with the nurse or physician/provider on this or future visits.

There should be no pressure to discuss the abuse, unless you perceive she may be in imminent danger.

SCREENING PHASE II: PHYSICIAN/PROVIDER

Physician/providers will follow up on patients that report experiencing abuse or when the nurse suspects abuse may be occurring. For patients who deny abuse but present signs consistent with abuse, physicians/providers need to initiate gently a brief discussion about intimate partner violence, noting that many women who are abused do not recognize it at first, that once violence or emotional abuse occurs a few times, it may reoccur and get worse, and that there is someone on site to talk to about abuse or any other need related to social services. It is important that the patient knows she is in charge of if, when, and how to discuss intimate partner abuse. There is a delicate balance between providing an environment that will allow women to choose to discuss abuse and letting women know that they don't need to say anything they are not comfortable with—especially since some may not have been abused.

Intimate Partner Violence Screening as an Intervention

Screening for abuse can itself serve as an intervention. Many women do not perceive that they are abused until they are asked objective questions and hear themselves answering "yes." Often, abused women minimize the severity of physically abusive acts and attribute violent behavior to alcohol or stress rather than the perpetrator. Emotional abuse appears to be even more difficult to identify for some women. The insidious nature of the undermining insults and progressive isolation from family, friends, and other social networks can make the abuse difficult to identify until it becomes severe. At that point, a woman may have significantly decreased self-esteem and few individuals to help her.

An example of how questions about abuse can raise awareness occurred when a blank intimate partner abuse questionnaire developed for the medical setting was used by students developing a computer program for data. One student subsequently stated privately she didn't realize she had been abused for more than 10 years until she read the questions and found herself answering yes to most of them.

In addition to being asked about physical violence, a list of questions may help women evaluate their experiences with intimate partners. To help educate women, the New York State Coalition against Domestic Violence has developed a brochure with a list of questions that can help women assess whether abuse may be present in their relationship (see Figure 10.1).

The following intervention activities can be performed either by nursing or social work staff: validation of abuse, providing information on domestic violence, making referrals.

FIGURE 10.1   Questions to ask yourself: Are you being abused?

DOES YOUR PARTNER*

- Hit, punch, slap, kick, shove or bite you?
- Threaten to hurt you and your children?
- Threaten to hurt friends or family members?
- Have sudden outbursts of anger or rage?
- Behave in an overprotective manner?
- Become jealous without reason?
- Prevent you from seeing family or friends?
- Prevent you from going where you want when you want, without repercussions?
- Prevent you from working or attending school?
- Destroy personal property or sentimental items?
- Deny you access to family assets such as bank accounts, credit cards or car?
- Control all finances and force you to account for what you spend?
- Force you to have sex against your will?
- Force you to engage in sexual acts you do not enjoy?
- Insult you or call you derogatory racial or sexual names?
- Use intimidation or manipulation to control you or your children?
- Humiliate you in front of others?
- Turn minor incidents into major arguments?
- Abuse or threaten to abuse pets?

If you have answered yes to one or more of the above . . . you might be abused! You are not alone! Domestic violence is a CRIME. For help call . . .

*Developed by the Battered/Formerly Battered Women's Task Force of the New York State Coalition Against Domestic Violence, funded by a grant from the NYS Children & Family Trust Fund, and used with permission.

Documentation.   The AMA (1994) and others have noted the importance of documenting instances of intimate partner violence in the
medical record to have concrete evidence of the abuse in the hopes
of preventing future abuse. Both chapter 9 in this volume (Boes)
and the AMA's *Diagnostic and Treatment Guidelines on Domestic Violence*
offer technical details on how documentation is best accomplished.
Objective summaries are recommended, including quotes of the
patient's statements (e.g., "Patient said, 'My husband punched me
in the face and pushed me against the wall so hard my head has a
bump' "), description of all injuries, and photographs if possible.

Although documentation is very important for legal proceedings,
there are many anecdotal reports that documentation of intimate
partner abuse in the medical record can lead to discrimination
in medical insurance and employment for some women. Because
intimate partner violence can be associated with increased utilization
of health care, abused women are vulnerable to denial of coverage
by insurance companies. Although some states have laws that prohibit
discrimination against victims of domestic violence, these laws do
not cover all insurance companies, such as large companies that self-
insure. In these situations, the employer may receive the employee's
medical records. Anecdotal reports of abused women being fired
due to abuse exist. Some fired employees are reluctant to file a
formal complaint out of fear that it will jeopardize their chances of
securing future employment. One potential way to minimize the
risk of a woman losing insurance coverage or a job is to keep documentation of intimate partner violence in a relatively protected portion of the medical chart, such as with substance abuse records, and
not including domestic violence in any billing record.

Validation of Abuse.   Recommendations universally suggest that
health care professionals validate a woman's experience, beginning
with believing what a woman tells you. Validation should take place
by whomever discovers abuse during the screening process as well
as by staff who work with a patient subsequently, such as nurses or
social workers. It is important to state that what she has experienced
is abuse, that abuse is serious and a crime, and that abuse is not the
victim's fault (American Medical Association, 1994; ACOG, 1995).
Flitcraft has stated that "The very acknowledgment that domestic
violence is going on, and that you and she agree it is a serious

problem, is a very powerful and therapeutic first step" (Randall, 1990, p. 940). For an abused woman, understanding that the abuse is a serious problem and that she is a victim may initiate a process that leads ultimately to finding safety.

Providing Information.   Battered women, female patients who have not experienced abuse, and staff at community domestic violence programs all agree that providing information about intimate partner abuse and resources is an important part of intimate partner abuse intervention at the primary care setting (McNutt, Carlson, Gagen, et al., 1997). Providing information about domestic violence and services for women who are abused is a fairly inexpensive intervention that can be used by nurses and/or social workers. Several types of information about intimate partner violence are now available in many primary care offices. Common information resources include domestic violence hotline telephone numbers placed on business-size cards (small enough to be hidden) and pamphlets about intimate partner violence and community resources for abused women.

The placement of these materials has been found to affect their use. Some providers found that when materials were placed in a common waiting room they were taken infrequently; however, when they were moved into private spaces, such as restrooms and examination rooms where they could be taken unobtrusively, the supplies disappeared quickly. Another form of information is posters, again usually placed in examination rooms or adjacent restrooms. It may be advisable to keep these posters in patient areas only, because if abusers accompany their partners to the office visit and see posters about domestic violence in the waiting room, it may influence their willingness to allow their partners to return for medical services in the future.

Both patients who acknowledge abuse and those for whom it is merely suspected can benefit from the following kinds of information about intimate partner abuse:

- Definitions and examples of what intimate partner violence is, especially emotional abuse (see Figure 10.1 for one example of a brochure that is used in New York State that could be placed in bathrooms or examination rooms in a clinic);

- That abuse cuts across all economic, educational, and cultural categories;
- That physical violence is a crime, even if perpetrated by one's spouse;
- That witnessing abuse can be harmful to children; and
- That abuse causes a wide variety of physical and mental health consequences.

While providing information about intimate partner violence and related services is becoming more common in primary care offices, it is important to note that the availability of this information is not without risk. It is commonly believed that abused women are at heightened risk for severe violence when they are in the process of leaving an abusive relationship or shortly thereafter (American Medical Association, 1994). Information about intimate partner violence and resources in the health care system or community may be particularly threatening to abusers. It is therefore important that women are informed about the heightened risk of abuse associated with leaving an abusive relationship and be cautioned about leaving printed information in places where an abuser may find it. This is especially important for women who are just beginning to identify their relationship as abusive and who are relatively uninformed about intimate partner violence and how dangerous it can be. Some practices now use cards listing only the domestic violence hotline telephone number, where its only identification is a domestic violence hotline phone number located over the card stack in the office. Another approach used by one health maintenance organization is a general health and social services resource directory that also includes information about domestic violence as just one of many sections, thus masking the intended purpose of the directory.

Reports indicate that women do take information made available in private settings, and thus providing written and verbal information about intimate partner abuse and associated resources may be an effective form of patient education. Providing informational materials also communicates to women patients that the primary care practice is aware of intimate partner violence and committed to addressing it.

Referrals. Another standard recommendation is that abused patients be referred to needed resources. It is essential for health care professionals to be aware of services available, and the practical limitations of these resources (e.g., space availability, cost, language, and transportation). In communities with established domestic violence services, a referral to the local domestic violence program will connect the patient with shelter, legal, and supportive programs. In communities without an established domestic violence program, multiple referrals may be needed, requiring education about community resources and time to explain options and assist the patient in making the connections. We assume that health care professionals will be more willing to refer patients to a resource with which they are familiar. In addition, referrals may be more likely to be utilized if the staff member can tell the patient that he or she is familiar with the program and its staff. Thus, having staff from relevant community agencies introduce themselves and discuss exactly what happens when a woman is referred to the program can improve referrals.

The time and knowledge required to make referrals may be one of the main reasons physicians are hesitant to screen for intimate partner abuse, because making helpful referrals can be time-consuming. The individual needed at a community service may not available at the time of the call because she is busy helping others. Sometimes the first phone call merely identifies further calls that need to be made. Merely suggesting that a patient call agencies without helping to lay the groundwork can do more harm than good by creating frustration and the fear that there is no effective help available. Referrals to community resources are probably best made by knowledgeable nurses or social workers.

SCREENING PHASE III: SOCIAL WORK

When Ross (1995) observed that "the persistent involvement of social work with health can be attributed to the fact that many health problems are inseparably linked to social factors and that certain behaviors can lead to disease" (p. 1366), she could easily have been referring to domestic violence. Social work and social welfare principles and values are compatible with public health perspectives, such as an emphasis on multicausal explanations for problems, the role of the community, and the importance of prevention. Although social workers have long been involved in primary health care settings, they are currently not being utilized in most such settings, perhaps because their services are not perceived as being cost-effective (Oktay, 1995; Resnick & Tighe, 1997). However, because so many presenting problems in primary care settings—some say a majority—have psychosocial origins, an expanded social work role can reduce the need for medical staff to address social and psychological concerns rather than the medical problems they are trained to ameliorate, especially in managed care settings (Resnick & Tighe, 1997).

Social workers in primary health care settings are likely to encounter intimate partner violence when a patient is referred from a physician/provider or nurse. Such referrals will occur when the health care professional has seen a patient who acknowledges abuse upon being asked or whom they suspect is being abused despite a denial that abuse is occurring. A variety of social work roles may be performed, including:

- Educator for patients as well as nurses and physicians, especially regarding the role of family and environmental factors as influences on patient behavior (Oktay, 1995; Resnick & Tighe, 1997; Ross, 1995);
- Counselor/case manager in areas including assessment; safety planning; individual or group counseling; linking patient to community services (Oktay, 1995);
- Collaborator; and
- Advocate.

In the performance of these various roles, a variety of skills, methods, and activities will be required. With regard to education, the social worker may be in the position to take the lead in obtaining needed information on domestic violence and setting up educational or training sessions for physician/providers and nurses, as discussed above. Training materials such as videotapes and written materials are readily available from a wide variety of sources that are listed in the section below on resources. Patient education is also important, as discussed above.

A wide range of counseling and case management activities can be performed by social workers in primary health care settings to address intimate partner violence. Crisis intervention may be necessary if the patient has recently experienced a violent incident and is being seen for injuries resulting from the abuse. Much has been written about crisis intervention in general and with abused women in particular, and that will not be duplicated here. Roberts (1990, 1991, 1996) has written extensively about crisis intervention for social workers. His Seven-Stage Model encompasses specific tasks that should be accomplished and are relevant for intimate partner abuse identified in the primary care setting: Assess lethality; establish rapport; identify major problems; deal with feelings; explore alternatives; and follow up (Roberts, 1996).

If the patient is not being seen for abuse-related injuries, the social worker should begin by conducting a psychosocial assessment. The extent of information collected will depend on whether the worker is able to engage in counseling beyond one session, assuming the patient wishes to receive such counseling, or whether a referral needs to be made to mental health counseling within the primary care setting itself or in the community. It will not be helpful to engage the client to form a close treatment alliance and collect detailed information about the abuse if the worker will not have the opportunity to see the patient for multiple sessions. However, at the very least, one should obtain enough information to assist in developing a safety plan.

Much has been written about safety planning, which is the cornerstone of intervention with abused women. The purpose of a safety plan is to develop collaboratively a concrete plan designed to prevent future violence and abuse toward a woman and her children, or at least minimize such violence, and to inform her about what her options are. The purpose is *not* to encourage a woman to leave the abusive relationship, but rather to empower her to make whatever decisions are in her best interest, recognizing that she, and not you, is the expert on her own situation. Furthermore, it is dangerous to recommend that a woman leave her partner without having a safety plan in place (Buel, 1995), despite recommendations by the ACOG to encourage abused patients to terminate abusive relationships. Minimally, a safety plan should include attention to (1) cues that a violent incident may be imminent; (2) a place to go where the patient and her children can be safe; and (3) a means to travel to that safe place.

Discussion can begin by inquiring about past violence, the kinds of things that appear to have triggered it, and what she has done in the past to try to stay safe. The safe place might be the home of a friend or relative, a motel, or a battered women's shelter. If the patient thinks she might want to use a shelter, it is important for her to know how to contact it and to have a means of transportation to get there. If she does not own or have access to an automobile, this might mean hiding sufficient money to get to her destination via a taxicab or public transportation. It is also important to think about what forms of identification or legal documents she will need. For example, she may need copies of her children's birth certificates or immigration papers in order to be admitted to a shelter or to enroll her children in a new school. The appendix to the Buel (1995) article includes safety tips, and Figure 10.2 provides a sample form that can be used for safety planning. Buel suggests providing blank copies of such a form in bathrooms and examination rooms at the health center.

If brief or more extended counseling with abused women is possible, it is important for the social worker to become familiar with the growing literature on counseling issues and techniques. Examples can be found in Carlson (1997), Dutton (1992), Petretic-Jackson and Jackson (1996), and Walker (1994).

Groupwork is another type of intervention that has been found to be extremely valuable to abused women because it can be a powerful means to reduce the social isolation that so often accompanies or is caused by intimate partner abuse. Several group models have been described in the literature for those wishing to offer support or therapeutic groups in the primary care setting (e.g., Brown & Dickey, 1992; Hartman, 1987; Tutty, Bidgood, & Rothery, 1993; Wood & Middleman, 1992). Volunteers have been used in some settings to offer support groups (e.g., Hadley et al., 1995). If it is not possible to offer support groups for abused women in the primary care setting, virtually all community-based domestic violence programs offer such groups.

For women who have identified themselves as abused, it is important to follow them, particularly if referrals have been made to other services within the primary care setting or the community. Abused women may have difficulty pursuing referrals to other professionals or agencies due to their ambivalence about acknowledging

FIGURE 10.2   Safety plan.

I.   Safe place:
    ____ Has a place to go if danger is threatened
    ____ with a family member
    ____ with friend or neighbor
    ____ hotel or motel
    ____ domestic violence shelter
    ____ other

II. Transportation:
    ____ Has access to automobile
    ____ Has own set of keys
    ____ Has money hidden for cab
    ____ Has other plans for transportation _____

III. Necessary items:
    ____ Has suitcase packed with essentials for self (e.g., ID, medication, house and car keys, Social Security card, driver's license, medical records, etc.)
    ____ Has suitcase packed with essentials for children (e.g., birth certificate, clothing, medication, special toy)
    ____Has financial resources
    ____ cash
    ____ checkbook
    ____ credit cards

Case Summary:
_____
_____
_____
_____

and seeking help for abuse as well as because of learned helplessness that they may be experiencing (Walker, 1979). In recontacting the patient to see if she was able to access a particular service, caution is needed to avoid disclosing to others in her home that she has acknowledged abuse and is seeking assistance and to avoid being perceived as pressuring her to do something she is not ready for.

It is important for social workers to collaborate with other health professionals in the primary care setting. Developing a multidisciplinary team approach, using a model such as the one described here, is an ideal way of addressing domestic violence because it is both efficient and effective. All professionals know their roles and perform the functions they have been trained to perform. Communication among members of the team is extremely important so that cases neither fall through the cracks or are overlooked because one staff member thinks another is addressing the problem, nor are different staff working on a particular case working at cross purposes to one another. When social workers are following a domestic violence case, it is important to communicate that information back to nurses and physician/providers, unless the patient explicitly states that she wants certain information to be kept confidential. Ground rules for confidentiality within the clinic should be discussed, perhaps treating domestic violence cases in ways similar to mental health or substance abuse cases, and bearing in mind the potential for an abusive partner to discover that intimate partner violence has been acknowledged to health care professionals.

Social workers in health care often function in the nexus between the health care setting and the community (Ross, 1995). Collaboration with community-based professionals such as domestic violence shelter staff is essential to develop professional relationships that will facilitate referrals on behalf of patients. Examples of ways to foster such collaboration include having the social worker or nurse visit the shelter or domestic violence program and inviting shelter staff to the primary care setting to address staff about intimate partner abuse as a problem and the services offered by their program. Developing a relationship with relevant law enforcement officials who have jurisdiction is another way to interface with community services on behalf of abused patients.

The role of advocate for abused women is also important. Although domestic violence shelters now exist in many communities nationally, clearly some communities are more service-rich than others. The social worker in primary care should become knowledgeable not only about services available for abused patients in her community, but also about gaps in needed services. When gaps are identified, the social worker should become willing to take action with other professionals to develop new services (Edinburg & Cottler, 1995). One means of accomplishing this is through a domestic violence task force. Many communities have formed task forces to bring together professionals who are addressing different aspects of domes-

tic violence and to coordinate services to avoid unnecessary duplica-
tion of services and maximize scarce domestic violence resources.
It may be useful to become a member of the local task force or to
be placed on its mailing list and attend meetings, when possible, to
become knowledgeable about domestic violence issues and services
in the local community. If no task force has been formed and service
gaps or coordination problems exist, initiating a domestic violence
task force can be a valuable way of addressing these difficulties on
a community level. The statewide domestic violence coalition, the
Family Violence Prevention Fund, or the National Coalition Against
Domestic Violence may be able to offer technical assistance (see
Resources, below).

Cultural Factors

Culture can exert a significant influence on a person's values,
thoughts and perceptions, and behaviors, including coping strategies. Thus, culture can affect how intimate partner violence is viewed
and the possible solutions a woman is willing to pursue if she is
being abused (Bohn, 1993; Coley & Beckett, 1988; Lockhart & White,
1989; Torres, 1993). Research findings on the incidence and prevalence of domestic violence have yielded inconsistent findings about
whether there is significant variability according to ethnic group
(e.g., Straus & Smith, 1990). However, the important issue for health
care providers is not whether African-American or Hispanic women
are more or less likely to be abused than White women, but rather
how patients from various ethnic groups perceive such abuse when
it occurs, and what potential solutions are viewed as culturally congruent. For example, Native American and Hispanic women tend to be
very closely connected to extended family systems for support, and
may risk alienating such systems if they seek assistance to address
intimate partner violence from professionals (Bohn, 1993; Torres,
1993). And both Black and American Indian women may wish to
avoid involving law enforcement agencies if they are being abused,
in order to protect themselves and their partners from possible
discrimination (Bohn, 1993). Lacking knowledge of the history of
oppression and discrimination by people of color, a well-meaning
White, middle-class social worker or health care professional may

have difficulty understanding how fear of discrimination might keep a woman from accessing needed police protection or social services.

Cultural sensitivity is also extremely important in approaching potentially abused patients for purposes of screening and intervention. Social workers and health care professionals who work with significant numbers of patients from diverse cultural groups should become knowledgeable about not only how such groups view health and illness, but also about effective ways of approaching patients from diverse groups in the health care setting. Lack of such knowledge can cause well-intended professionals to inadvertently offend or alienate a patient by being overly familiar. For example, in traditional Hispanic families, the husband is considered to be responsible for the health care of all family members, including his wife (Torres, 1993). Not knowing this might lead to an assumption that a husband who is taking care of his wife's health care is being overly controlling in order to hide his abuse, when in fact he may be performing his culturally approved role as husband.

The importance of language cannot be overemphasized. It is especially important to communicate respect and value self-determination when interacting with patients from cultural groups different from one's own. Bohn (1993) notes that professionals working with Native American women, who tend to be rather reticent, need to become comfortable with periods of silence and avoid physical contact or embraces until a trusting relationship has been established. And Hispanic women may prefer being addressed by their surnames (Torres, 1993).

Risk Management: Mandatory Reporting and the Duty to Warn

Recently, a number of states have passed legislation requiring that health professionals report domestic violence to various authorities. Mandatory reporting, as it is often called, is controversial because many battered women's advocates believe that contacting law enforcement or other authorities can place an abused woman and her children at even greater risk. In addition, such reporting undermines a woman's right to self-determination, is seen as fundamentally paternalistic, and may actually discourage women from seeking medical attention for abuse-related injuries or symptoms (Hyman & Chez,

1995). Although one justification for mandatory reporting is that it helps to document the incidence of intimate partner violence, such statistics are often inaccurate, as experience with mandatory reporting of child maltreatment has taught us. Although most states currently require health care professionals to report certain injuries that appear to be inflicted by weapons, as of 1995 only six states require reporting of domestic violence (California, Colorado, Kentucky, New Hampshire, New Mexico, and Rhode Island; Hyman & Chez, 1995). These states vary in what must be reported and to whom such reports should be made. Social workers and health care professionals in these states should familiarize themselves with these laws, as should workers in seven other states that require reporting of injuries that appear to be inflicted violently (Florida, Hawaii, Michigan, Nebraska, North Carolina, Ohio, and Tennessee; Hyman & Chez, 1995).

Another issue pertains to the responsibility of mental health professionals such as psychologists and social workers to warn potential victims of the possibility of their being harmed, sometimes referred to as the Tarasoff decision of 1976. Because this requires that professionals make predictions about the likelihood of a person using violence and requires that guarantees of confidentiality be set aside in the hopes of protecting a potential victim, the decision has been controversial. Sonkin (1986) discussed these issues and offers helpful suggestions to clinicians who work in the domestic violence arena to help them prepare themselves for this possibility.

SUMMARY AND CONCLUSIONS

Intimate partner violence is a serious and costly social problem that has been associated with a wide variety of medical sequelae in addition to injuries, such as intestinal, urinary and gynecological problems and problems eating, sleeping, and breathing. These health problems are likely to bring abused women to primary care settings for medical services, although intimate partner violence has traditionally been overlooked in many health care settings due to barriers on the part of both providers and patients. Because of the prevalence of woman abuse and its health consequences, numerous national medical organizations have recommended that women patients be systematically screened for abuse and that we intervene on behalf of abused women in health settings.

We have presented an integrated model of intimate partner violence screening and intervention for use in primary health care settings such as HMOs and community clinics. It proposes an interdisciplinary team of physician/providers, nurses, and social workers with the goals of identifying cases of intimate partner abuse, documenting the abuse, validating the woman's experience, increasing patient knowledge about intimate partner abuse, enhancing patient safety while reducing isolation, increasing patient knowledge of community resources, and making appropriate referrals to these resources.

RESOURCES

- National Domestic Violence Health Resource Center, (888) RXABUSE (792-2873)
- Family Violence Prevention Fund, San Francisco, (415) 252-8900
- *Diagnostic and Treatment Guidelines on Domestic Violence,* American Medical Association, Chicago, IL (312) 464-5000.
- National Domestic Violence Hotline (800-333-SAFE)
- Statewide coalitions against domestic violence
- Local domestic violence programs, shelters, and rape crisis centers

REFERENCES

Abbott, J., Johnson, R., Koziol-McLain, J., & Lowenstein, S. R. (1995). Domestic violence against women: Incidence and prevalence in an emergency department population. *Journal of the American Medical Association, 273,* 1763–1767.

American College of Obstetricians and Gynecologists. (1995). *Domestic violence (ACOG technical bulletin).* Washington, DC: Author.

American Medical Association. (1991). *American Medical Association survey on violence and the role of physicians in controlling it.* Chicago, IL: Author.

American Medical Association. (1994). *Diagnostic and treatment guidelines on domestic violence.* Chicago, IL: Author.

American Medical Association, Council on Ethical and Judicial Affairs. (1992). Physicians and domestic violence: Ethical considerations. *Journal of the American Medical Association, 263,* 3190–3193.

American Medical Association, Council on Internal Affairs. (1992). Violence against women: Relevance for medical practitioners. *Journal of the American Medical Association, 267,* 3184–3189.

American Nurses Association. (1991). *Position statement on physical violence against women.* Washington, DC: Author.

Ashur, M. L. (1993). Asking about domestic violence: SAFE questions. *Journal of the American Medical Association, 269,* 2367.

Astin, M. C., Lawrence, J. J., & Foy, D. W. (1993). Posttraumatic stress disorders among battered women: Risk and resiliency factors. *Violence and Victims, 8,* 17–28.

Bailey, J. E., Kellermann, A. L., Somes, G. W., Banton, J. G., Rivara, F. P., & Rushforth, N. P. (1997). Risk factors for violence death of women in the home. *Archives of Internal Medicine, 157,* 777–782.

Bohn, S. (1993). Nursing care of Native American battered women. *AWHONN's Clinical Issues, 4,* 424–436.

Brown, P. A., & Dickey, C. (1992). Critical reflection in groups with abused women. *Affilia, 7,* 57–71.

Brown, J. B., Lent, B., Brett, P.J., Sas, G. & Pederson, L. L. (1996). Development of the Woman Abuse Screening Tool for use in family practice. *Family Medicine, 28,* 422–428.

Buel, S. M. (1995). Family violence: Practical recommendations for physicians and the medical community. *Women's Health Issues, 5,* 158–172.

Carlson, B. E. (1997). A stress and coping approach to intervention with abused women. *Family Relations, 46,* 1–8.

Cascardi, M., Langhinrichsen, J., & Vivian, D. (1992). Marital aggression: Impact, injury, and health correlates for husbands and wives. *Archives of Internal Medicine, 152,* 1178–1184.

Cascardi, M., O'Leary, K. D., Lawrence, E. E., & Schlee, K. A. (1995). Characteristics of women physically abused by their spouses and who seek treatment regarding marital conflict. *Journal of Consulting and Clinical Psychology, 63,* 616–623.

Coley, S. M., & Beckett, J. O. (1988). Black battered women: A review of empirical literature. *Journal of Counseling and Development, 66,* 266–270.

deLahunta, E. A., & Tulsky, A. A. (1996). Personal exposure of faculty and medical students to family violence. *Journal of the American Medical Association, 275,* 1903–1906.

Drossman, D. A., Leserman, J., Nachman, G., Li, A. M., Gluck, H., Toomey, T. C., & Mitchell, C. M. (1990). Sexual and physical abuse in women with functional or organic gastrointestinal disorders. *Annals of Internal Medicine, 113,* 828–833.

Dutton, M. A. (1992). *Empowering and healing the battered woman.* New York: Springer.

Dumas, C. A., Katerndahl, D. A., & Burge, S. K. (1995). Familial patterns in patients with infrequent panic attacks. *Archives of Family Medicine, 4,* 863–867.

Edinburg, G. M., & Cottler, J. M. (1995). Managed care. *Encyclopedia of social work* (19th ed.) (pp. 1635–1641). Washington, DC: National Association of Social Workers.

Flitcraft, A. (1995). Project SAFE: Domestic violence education for practicing physicians. *Women's Health Issues, 5,* 183–188.

Follingstad, D. R., Rutledge, L. L., Berg, B. J., Hause, E. S., & Polek, D. S. (1990). The role of emotional abuse in physically abusive relationships. *Journal of Family Violence,* 107–120.

Freund, K. M., Bak, S. M., & Blackhall, L. (1996). Identifying domestic violence in primary care practice. *Journal of General Internal Medicine, 11,* 44–46.

Friedman, L. S., Samet, J. H., Roberts, M. S., Hudlin, M., & Hans, P. (1992). Inquiry about victimization experiences: A survey of patient preferences and physician practices. *Archives of Internal Medicine, 152,* 1186–1190.

Gazmararian, J. A., Laxorick, S., Spitz, A. M., Ballard, T. J., Saltzman, L. E., & Marks, J. S. (1996). Prevalence of violence against pregnant women. *Journal of the American Medical Association, 275,* 1915–1920.

Gelles, R. J. (1990). Violence and pregnancy: Are pregnant women at greater risk of abuse? In M. A. Straus & R. J. Gelles (Eds.), *Physical violence in American families: Risk factors and adaptations to violence in 8,145 families* (pp. 279–286). New Brunswick, NJ: Transaction.

Gelles, R. J., & Harrop, J. W. (1989). Violence, battering, and psychological distress among women. *Journal of Interpersonal Violence, 4,* 400–420.

Gleason, W. J. (1993). Mental disorders in battered women: An empirical study. *Violence and Victims, 8,* 53–68.

Goodwin, T. M., & Breen, M. T. (1990). Pregnancy outcome and fetomaternal hemorrhage after noncatastropic trauma. *American Journal of Obstetrics and Gynecology, 162,* 665–671.

Hadley, S. M., Short, L. M., Lezin, N., & Zook. E. (1995). WomanKind: An innovative model of health care response to domestic violence. *Women's Health Issues, 5,* 189–198.

Hale-Carlsson, G., Hutton, B., Fuhrman, J., McNutt, L. A., & Morse, D. (1996). Physical and injuries in intimate relationships: New York State Behavioral Risk Factor Surveillance System. *Morbidity and Mortality Weekly Report, 45,* 765—767.

Hamberger, L. K., Saunders, D. G., & Hovey, M. (1992). Prevalence of domestic violence in community practice and rate of physician inquiry. *Family Medicine, 24,* 283–287.

Hartman, S. (1987). Therapeutic self-help groups: A process of empowerment for women in abusive relationships. In C. M. Brody (Ed.), *Women's therapy groups: Paradigms of feminist treatment* (pp. 67–81). New York: Springer.

Helton, A., McFarlane, J., & Anderson, E. (1987). Battered and pregnant: A prevalence study. *American Journal of Public Health, 77,* 1337–1339.

Herbert, T. B., Silver, R. C., & Ellard, J. H. (1990). Coping with an abusive relationship: I. How and why do women stay? *Journal of Marriage and the Family, 53,* 311–325.

Hilberman, E., & Munson, K. (1978). Sixty battered women. *Victimology, 2,* 460–470.

Hillard, P. J. (1985). Physical abuse in pregnancy. *Obstetrics and Gynecology, 66,* 185–190.

Hyman, A., & Chez, R. A. (1995). Mandatory reporting of domestic violence by health care providers: A misguided approach. *Women's Health Issues, 5,* 208–213.

Kilpatrick, D. G., Saunders, B. E., Veronen, L. J., Best, C. L. & Von, J. M. (1987). Criminal victimization: Lifetime prevalence, reporting to police, and psychological impact. *Crime and Delinquency, 33,* 479–489.

Koss, M. P., Gidcyz, C. A., & Wisniewski, N. (1987). The scope of rape: Incidence and prevalence of sexual aggression and victimization in a national sample of higher education students. *Journal of Consulting and Clinical Psychology, 42,* 162–170.

Koss, M. P., & Oros, C. (1982). The sexual experiences survey: A research instrument investigating sexual aggression and victimization. *Journal of Consulting and Clinical Psychology, 50,* 455–457.

Lockhart, L., & White, B. W. (1989). Understanding marital violence in the black community. *Journal of Interpersonal Violence, 4,* 421–436.

Loring, M. T. (1994). *Emotional abuse.* New York: Lexington.

Marshall, L. L. (1994). Physical and psychological abuse. In W. R. Cupach & B. H. Spitzberg (Eds.), *The dark side of interpersonal communication* (pp. 281–311). Hillsdale, NJ: Lawrence Erlbaum.

McCauley, J., Kern, D. E., Kolodner, K., Dill, L., Schroeder, A. F., DeChant, H. K., Ryden, J., Bass, E. B., & Derogatis, L. R. (1995). The "Battering Syndrome": Prevalence and clinical characteristics of domestic violence in primary care internal medicine practices. *Annals of Internal Medicine, 123,* 737–746.

McFarlane, J., Christoffel, K., Bateman, L., Miller, V., & Bullock, L. (1991). Assessing for abuse: Self report versus nurse interview. *Public Health Nursing, 8,* 245–250.

McFarlane, J., & Parker, B. (1996). Physical abuse, smoking, and substance use during pregnancy: Prevalence, interrelationships, and effects on birth weight. *Journal of Obstetric Gynecologic and Neonatal Nursing, 25,* 313–320.

McFarlane, J., Parker, B., & Soeken, K. (1996). Abuse during pregnancy: Associations with maternal health and infant birth weight. *Nursing Research, 45,* 37–42.

McFarlane, J., Parker, B., Soeken, K., & Bullock, L. (1992). Assessing for abuse during pregnancy: Severity and frequency of injuries and associated entry into prenatal care. *Journal of the American Medical Association, 267,* 3176–3178.

McLeer, S. V., & Anwar, R. (1989). A study of battered women presenting in an emergency department. *American Journal of Public Health, 79,* 65–66.

McLeer, S. V., Anwar, R. A. H., Herman, S., & Maquiling, K. (1989). Education is not enough: A systems failure in protecting battered women. *Annals of Emergency Medicine, 18,* 651–653.

McNutt, L. A., Carlson, B. E., Gagen, D., & Winterbauer, N. (1997). *Domestic violence screening and intervention in the primary care setting: Female patients and battered women's experiences and perspectives.* Unpublished manuscript.

McNutt, L. A., Carlson, B. E., Winterbauer, N., & Gagen, D. (1997). *The relationship between physical, emotional and sexual abuse with health: A complex picture.* Manuscript in preparation.

McNutt, L. A., Hutton, B., Fuhrman, J., Hale-Carlsson, G., & Morse, D. (1997). *Health care utilization practices of abused women: An opportunity for intervention.* Manuscript in preparation.

Mercy, J. A., & Saltzman, L. E. (1989). Fatal violence among spouses in the United States, 1976–1985. *American Journal of Public Health, 79,* 595–599.

Oktay, J. S. (1995). Primary health care. *Encyclopedia of social work* (19th ed.) (pp. 1887–1894). Washington, DC: National Association of Social Workers.

O'Leary, D. K., & Curley, A. D. (1986). Assertion and family violence: Correlates of spouse abuse. *Journal of Marriage and Family Therapy, 12,* 282–289.

Petretic-Jackson, P. A., & Jackson, T. (1996). Mental health interventions with battered women. In A. R. Roberts (Ed.), *Helping battered women: New perspectives and remedies* (pp. 188–221). New York: Oxford University Press.

Plichta, S. B. (1996). Violence and abuse: Implications for women's health. In M. M. Falik & K. S. Collins (Eds.), *Women's health: The Commonwealth Fund Study* (pp. 237–270). Baltimore, MD: The Johns Hopkins University Press.

Plichta, S. B., & Abraham, C. (1996). Violence and gynecologic health in women <50 years old. *American Journal of Obstetrics and Gynecology, 174,* 903–907.

Randall, T. (1990). Domestic violence intervention calls for more than treating injuries. *Journal of the American Medical Association, 264,* 939–940.

Resnick, C., & Tighe, E. G. (1997). The role of multidisciplinary community clinics in managed care systems. *Social Work, 42,* 91–98.

Roberts, A. R. (1990). *Crisis intervention handbook: Assessment, treatment and research.* Belmont, CA: Wadsworth.

Roberts, A. R. (1991). *Contemporary perspectives on crisis intervention and prevention.* Englewood Cliffs, NJ: Prentice-Hall.

Roberts, A. R. (1996). *Crisis management & brief treatment: Theory, techniques, and applications.* Chicago, IL: Nelson-Hall.

Ross, J. W. (1995). Hospital social work. *Encyclopedia of social work* (19th ed.) (pp. 1365–1377). Washington, DC: National Association of Social Workers.

Russell, D. E. H. (1990). *Rape in marriage.* Bloomington, IN: Indiana University Press.

Sato, R. A., & Heiby, E. M. (1992). Correlates of depressive symptoms among battered women. *Journal of Family Violence, 7,* 229–245.

Saunders, D. G. (1994). Posttraumatic stress symptom profiles of battered women: A comparison of survivors in two settings. *Violence and Victims, 9,* 31–44.

Saunders, D. G., Hamberger, L. K., & Hovey, M. (1993). Indicators of woman abuse based on a chart review at a family practice center. *Archives of Family Medicine, 2,* 537–543.

Schappert, S. M. (1992). *National ambulatory medical care survey: 1989 summary.* Hyattsville, MD: U. S. Department of Health and Human Services (DHHS Publication (PHS) 92–1771).

Shields, M. E., & Hanneke, C. R. (1983). Battered wives' reactions to marital rape. In D. Finkelhor, R. J. Gelles, G. T. Hotaling, & M. A. Straus (Eds.), *The dark side of families: Current family violence research* (pp. 131–148). Beverly Hills, CA: Sage.

Sonkin, D. (1986). Clairvoyance vs. common sense: Therapist's duty to warn and protect. *Violence and Victims, 1,* 7–22.

Stark, E., & Flitcraft, A. (1996). *Women at risk: Domestic violence and women's health* (pp. 3–42). Thousand Oaks, CA: Sage.

Stark, E., & Flitcraft, A. H. (1991). Spouse abuse. In M. L. Rosenberg & M. A. Fenley (Eds.), *Violence in America: A public health approach* (pp. 123–157). New York: Oxford University Press.

Stark, E., Flitcraft, A., & Frazier, W. (1979). Medicine and patriarchal violence: The social construction of a "private" event. *International Journal of Health Services, 9,* 461–493.

Straus, M. A., & Gelles, R. J. (1990). How violent are American families? Estimates from the national Family Violence Survey and other studies. In M. A. Straus & R. J. Gelles (Eds.), *Physical violence in American families: Risk factors and adaptation to violence in 8,145 families* (pp. 95–112). New Brunswick, NJ: Transaction.

Straus, M. A., & Smith, C. (1990). Violence in Hispanic families in the United States: Incidence rates and structural interpretations. In M. A. Straus & R. J Gelles (Eds.), *Physical violence in American families: Risk factors and adaptations to violence in 8,145 families* (pp. 341–367). New Brunswick, NJ: Transaction.

Sugg, N. K., & Inui, T. (1992). Primary care physicians' response to domestic violence: Opening a Pandora's box. *Journal of the American Medical Association, 267,* 3157–3160.

Teske, R. H. C., & Parker, M. L. (1983). *Spouse abuse in Texas: A study of women's attitudes and experiences.* Huntsville, TX: Criminal Justice Center, San Houston State University.

Tolman, R. M. (1992). Psychological abuse of women. In R. Ammerman & M. Hersen (Eds.), *Assessment of family violence: A clinical and legal sourcebook* (pp. 291–308). New York: Wiley.

Torres, S. (1993). Nursing care of low-income battered Hispanic pregnant women. *AWHONN's Clinical Issues, 4,* 416–423.

Tutty, L. M., Bidgood, B. A., & Rothery, M. A. (1993). Support groups for battered women: Research on their efficacy. *Journal of Family Violence, 8,* 325–343.

Walker, L. E. (1994). *Abused women and survivor therapy.* Washington, DC: American Psychiatric Association.

Walker, L. E. A. (1979). *The battered woman.* New York: Harper and Row.

Walling, M. K., O'Hara, M. W., Reiter, R. C., Milburn, A. K., Lilly, G., & Vincent, S. D. (1994). Abuse history and chronic pain in women: II. A multivariate analysis of abuse and psychological morbidity. *Obstetrics and Gynecology, 84,* 200–206.

Webster, J., Chandler, J., & Battistutta, D. (1996). Pregnancy outcomes and health care use: Effect of abuse. *American Journal of Obstetrics and Gynecology, 174,* 760–767.

Wood, G. G., & Middleman, R. R. (1992). Groups to empower battered women. *Affilia, 7,* 82–95.

CHAPTER 11

Domestic Violence Against Women with Mental Retardation

Leone Murphy and Nancy J. Razza

Women who are mentally retarded are frequently victimized and sexually or physically abused. The incidence of abuse is much higher in this population because of their vulnerability, low self-esteem, and lack of assertiveness. The Arc of Monmouth County has developed a unique and comprehensive model of identification of victims of abuse, therapeutic intervention, and treatment. Many of the women seen in the program are typified by the victim in the following case vignette.

CASE VIGNETTE

Maryann is a 26-year-old woman who has mild mental retardation and lives in a small apartment with her 5-year-old son and her boyfriend. Her boyfriend is not the child's father and her son has developmental disabilities. She was referred to the Arc clinic for counseling by her job

271

coach because of ongoing problems at her fast food placement. Issues of concern were unexplained absences, tardiness, and symptoms of depression. After several weeks of counseling, Maryann confided that her boyfriend was verbally abusive to her but denied physical abuse. On more than one occasion she appeared at the clinic with bruises, but continued to deny any physical abuse.

Since Maryann's family lived out of state and she was without friends and other support services, a referral was initiated for social work services at the Arc's Program Support Unit. The social worker was able to arrange for a summer day camp program, including transportation, for Maryann's son. This was a tremendous benefit for the mother, since she had previously relied on her boyfriend for babysitting while she worked. The boyfriend had not been reliable and frequently let the little boy wander around the apartment complex by himself. Maryann confided that her boyfriend would often threaten her as she was leaving for work, saying that he was not going to watch her son. Her son had a speech impediment, and Maryann said that her boyfriend would often ridicule and mock her son's behavior.

Finally, after many months of group therapy, Maryann trusted the women in the therapy group enough to admit to being physically abused by her boyfriend. She was supported by these other women and then she was able to initiate changes to improve her situation. She was hesitant to go to a women's shelter because she felt they would not be able to manage her son's disabilities and the problems associated with her own disability such as being unable to read, having no means of transportation, and having difficulties communicating. The Arc's social worker assisted Maryann in obtaining a restraining order against her boyfriend and the Arc provided access to services such as day care, budgeting assistance, meal planning, and parenting skills.

ASSESSMENT AND DETECTION OF ABUSE

A growing concern for advocates of women who are mentally retarded is the sexual and physical abuse of this population. No exact figures have been kept on the incidence of abuse of women with mental retardation who live in the community, but leading advocates estimate the incidence to be four to ten times that of the general population. It is widely believed by developmental disability experts that 90% of women who are mentally retarded will be sexually or physically victimized in their lifetime (Sgroi, 1989). The actual reporting of abuse and violence is low, since many of the women have difficulties communicating or can become easily confused about times, places, and details.

In addition to the visible signs of physical or sexual abuse, the victim often may have sleep problems, depression, increased aggression, or self-injurious behaviors. Our initial health assessment is comprehensive and includes a family history, an extensive medical history, records of any hospitalization or surgeries, and a medication profile. It is sometimes difficult to obtain this information, because many women who are mentally retarded were placed in institutions early in their lives and they may not know of their families. With the current movement to close large institutions and relocate the residents back into the community, medical records and information are often missing. The woman herself, because of her cognitive limitations, may give conflicting information. For example, she may know that she had a surgical procedure, but may not understand what surgery was done.

Factors such as unemployment, alcohol or drug abuse, and social isolation are carefully screened for, since they contribute to abusive situations. Most of the referrals we receive are from day program or group home staff who suspect that the woman may be being abused. It is in everyone's best interest to proceed slowly and collect as much evidence as possible. In the past when staff have moved too quickly, there have been situations where the person doing the abuse has taken the victim out of the Arc's programs and even moved her to another state.

A medical file is slowly and carefully documented. Interviews with staff, caregivers, and family members are conducted cautiously. Guardianship of the woman is also of concern, since the state or a family member may have been previously declared the woman's legal guardian. The victim does not usually admit to being abused. Any bruises, lacerations, or injuries are carefully documented and photographed. We try to have two staff present for the examinations and interviews to corroborate the evidence. We frequently need to build a trusting relationship with the victim before she will admit to being abused. It then takes more effort, and cultivation of more trust, before the victim will allow staff to help her alter the situation.

The Arc's model of care integrates staff from a variety of disciplines. A clinical nurse specialist and a family practice physician carefully examine and document the medical and physical evidence of abuse. The Arc's psychologist and the clinical nurse specialist then conduct carefully selected interviews to verify the abusive situation. The findings are shared with the Arc's social worker, who completes the victim's team of health care professionals. This team then develops a plan for intervention, therapy, and support services.

SCOPE OF PROBLEM AND INTERVENTION APPROACHES

Although no data has been collected as of this writing on the prevalence rates of domestic violence against individuals with mental retardation, Carlson states that experts in the field estimate that women with mental retardation are believed to be at even greater risk for domestic violence than are women from the general population. This thinking is consistent with preliminary studies that show that women with mental retardation are more frequently victimized by sexual abuse than are women in the general population (Furey, 1994). For example, from data collected by the Wisconsin Council on Developmental Disabilities (1991), it is estimated that up to 83% of women and 32% of men with developmental disabilities suffer sexual abuse at some point in their lives. Additionally, in a survey of 162 individuals with disabilities who experienced sexual abuse, Sobsey and Doe (1991) found that 81.7% were women, and that the majority of these women had intellectual impairments as their disability.

It is important to consider that women with mental retardation often live in dependent situations, not just with a husband or boyfriend, but with nuclear or extended family or in government or agency-sponsored homes (described later in greater detail). As a result, there is a greater range of experiences which may be considered domestic abuse. For example, we worked with one woman who was repeatedly the target of physical battering by one of her fellow group home residents. She very much displayed the complex of behaviors seen in battered women. As might be imagined, intervention at the systems level is paramount in such a case.

Carlson (1997) describes a three-tiered approach to work with domestic violence victims who have developmental disabilities. Her approach reflects the importance of assessing the unique characteristics, abilities, and history of the individual, as well as of the immediate social/familial context in which the violence takes place. Finally, Carlson addresses the need for looking at the larger cultural and societal systems which impact on the individual in question. She makes recommendations for intervening in each of these three areas.

This multilevel approach is supported by models of clinical work with nonhandicapped domestic violence victims as well. Pioneering work done by Almeida (Wiley, 1996) involves the concerned parties in individual and group sessions, including groups for both the offending and the victimized partner. Police, the court system, and extended family members are also involved. In keeping with McGoldrick's focus on the individual along with his or her social/cultural context, Almeida's work "widens the lens" through which the problem is viewed and addressed in marked contrast to more traditional models of psychopathology with an intra-individual focus. Importantly, Almeida's work has yielded a measure of success not often found in domestic violence treatment.

Work with individuals who have mental retardation is often approached in a similar fashion. That is, individual issues are addressed while at the same time interventions are being made within the individual's surrounding system. This is fairly common practice within agencies that provide services to persons with mental retardation for all manner of needs and problems. The nature of the disability is such that the individual's dependency on the surrounding network is more apparent (although, arguably no more—or less— significant than that of nonhandicapped persons). Experts in the treatment of mentally retarded persons with concomitant psychological disturbances have advocated for interventions that include the individual along with their natural family and professional caregivers (Petronko, Harris, & Kormann, 1994). These authors note that such interventions are not only beneficial to the individual, but have resulted in increased leisure time and satisfaction and decreased stress and depressive moods in family members and caregivers.

In considering how to approach the problem of domestic violence as it affects persons with mental retardation, then, there appears to be good support for the idea that a multilevel approach is essential. We will begin with a look at assessing the individual victim of domestic violence, followed by a discussion of the assessment process as it pertains to the familial and social systems that encompass the individual's life.

INDIVIDUAL ASSESSMENT

Performing clinical evaluations of individuals who have mental retardation poses certain challenges for mental health professionals. Nezu, Nezu, and Gill-Weiss (1992) specify potential obstacles, such as limited capacity for verbal expression, concrete thinking, stereotypic motor behaviors, and a poor understanding of time (e.g., an inability to be clear as to when events took place). Moreover, accurate assessment of mental disorder rests on the clinician's ability to differentiate between psychologically significant symptoms and predictable behaviors or deficits that are solely a function of the individual's level of cognitive development. An additional complicating factor is that with some individuals who have mental retardation, particularly those at the lower ends of the range, psychological symptoms are sometimes displayed in unexpected ways. For example, we treated a woman with mental retardation who also suffered from posttraumatic stress disorder. She would spontaneously act out traumatizing events she had experienced. These displays appeared to be essentially like those described in the DSM-IV criteria for children with this disorder, in which they are referred to as "trauma-specific reenactments." However, such displays—dramatic, sudden, and unexplained— would make the woman appear "crazy" to those around her, scaring involved staff members into thinking she was more unbalanced than she truly was. In addition, staff often got the impression that the traumatic abuses were currently taking place. It took a great deal of observation to put together the post-traumatic nature of this particular symptom.

A set of guidelines have been described by Nezu et al. (1992) which provide a helpful overview when making clinical assessments of individuals with mental retardation. Their recommendations outline a multifaceted assessment including the following:

> a clinical interview, in which the clinician questions and observes the individual with an eye toward his or her mental status, in much the same way as would be done with a nonhandicapped patient;

an observational analysis, in which the clinician observes the individual in his or her environment;

a caregiver interview, with a focus on gaining information about the individual as well as on assessing the quality of the caregiving relationship; and

psychological testing, along with the procurement of a neuromedical assessment to rule out possible neurological or physiological causes of symptoms.

In cases of suspected or known abuse, such symptoms may also represent the effects of abuse. The issue of neurological assessment is of particular importance, and can be complicated to assess in persons with mental retardation who may have been battered. In many cases, there is likely to be an intelligence test available in the individual's records, since documentation of impaired intellectual functioning is required for the individual to receive services. A prior neuropsychological battery is less commonly available. As trauma specialist Lenore Walker (1994) points out in discussing assessment of battered, nonhandicapped women, exposure to battering in the form of blows to the head may result in organic brain damage. Prolonged exposure to such battering may result in progressive deterioration in key areas of functioning, including feelings of disorientation, sensorimotor difficulties, language difficulties, and coordination problems. Care must be taken to determine if the individual's functioning has been compromised due to exposure to abuse; the individual's condition may not be solely the function of their mental retardation.

For clinicians unfamiliar with individuals who have mental retardation, it is important to be aware that the majority of these individuals have only mild mental retardation. Intelligence test scores, though not the sole criterion for determining mental retardation, tend to cluster around the average score of 100 for the population as a whole. Deviations from this average, both higher and lower, tend to fall close to the average range. Thus, profoundly retarded individuals are as rare as truly brilliant ones. Recent estimates of retardation in countries with advanced medical care put the prevalence rates of severe retardation at 2.5 to 5.0 per 1000, and that of mild retardation at 2.5 to 40.0 per 1000 (Durkin & Stein, 1996). This is important because individuals with mild mental retardation generally have verbal abilities that, while limited, are sufficient for the purposes of psychotherapy. Individuals with moderate mental retardation are also often capable of sufficient verbal exchange to make therapeutic dialogue possible. It is not responsible to exclude a person from a therapeutic service simply because the diagnosis of mental retardation comes with them. Individual assessment is needed to determine that person's capacity for self-expression. For those with a greater degree of impairment, assessing and intervening with key figures in the individual's environment takes on essential significance.

ASSESSMENT OF THE SOCIAL/FAMILIAL ENVIRONMENT

The next level of assessment, evaluating the individual's social/familial context, can be extremely challenging or relatively uncomplicated, depending on the clinician's access to reliable informants and on whether or not the clinician is able to observe the individual in his or her environment.

Due to the nature of their disability, individuals with mental retardation often live in situations in which they are, to varying degrees, dependent on others. The living arrangement may be one in which the family takes primary responsibility (living with parents, adult siblings, or, less commonly, their own apartment with assistance in daily living responsibilities), or in which the state or a state-supported agency takes primary responsibility (institution, group home, apartment with staff nearby who provide assistance, or with a family which the state pays to provide shelter and care for the individual, similar to a foster family). In each of these cases, it is important to make contact with one or more of the individuals who have some responsibility for the individual's care, being mindful that the caregiver could be the abuser. The other party's perspective can offer valuable insights.

It is important, however, to keep in mind that even well-meaning caregivers can be a part of the individual's problem. For example, we worked with one woman who had moderate mental retardation and who was generally characterized by a sweet demeanor and was well-liked. She displayed sudden and intense self-biting and tantrum-like behavior under certain conditions of frustration, such as being teased. Staff would respond to this behavior by rushing to her aid and encouraging her to talk, thinking she was upset about her father who had recently died. The woman would engage in talks with them about her feelings, and the episode would end. Additionally, the staff brought her to a therapist who, though unfamiliar with individuals with mental retardation, helped her talk further about her feelings. The self-abusive episodes continued to increase in frequency, however. When staff agreed to try actively withdrawing their attention from her following these self-abusive episodes, and engaging her in nurturing, supportive discussions on a regular basis during periods of nonabusive behavior, the episodes eventually made a significant decrease. The staff had unintentionally been "reinforcing" her episodes of self-injurious behavior by their increased attentiveness at such times. Thus, when the staff made the effort to supply her with their attention when she was peaceful, the instances of self-abuse decreased. This intervention was carried out along with the introduction of individual and, later, group, therapy in which the focus was directed toward helping the woman become aware of the types of situations which triggered her self-abusive behavior, and of adaptive alternatives she could employ. We often treat women who are aggressive towards themselves rather than towards others.

It is often very helpful to obtain information from more than one source. Most people spend the majority of their time in two distinct environments, residential and vocational. For example, staff who work with an individual in a vocational training program may refer her because they suspect she is being abused or battered in her home environment. If the clinician feels that the individual cannot provide clear information concerning her experiences, it is important that an effort be made to observe and assess the dynamics in both environments.

CASE MANAGEMENT AND DELIVERY SERVICES

Ideally, interventions in the lives of women with mental retardation who experience domestic violence are the product of a team effort, and affect the individual woman, as well as the immediate and extended systems of which she is a part. Following a comprehensive assessment of the individual and her situation, an effort should be made to connect with the various parties involved with the individual for the purposes of planning and executing a strategy to address the particular woman's needs.

Individuals with mental retardation in New Jersey are entitled to services through the Division of Developmental Disabilities. The Division assigns them a case manager who is responsible for seeing that the full gamut of the individual's needs are met, e.g., for appropriate housing, medical concerns, vocational preparation, and so on. This case manager is involved with staff members from various agencies who provide such services. Traditionally agencies, such as the many Arcs (formerly Association for Retarded Citizens) across the country, have supplied primarily vocational and residential support, while medical services were generally sought on a case-by-case basis from clinics and individual practitioners. This has been and continues to be an arduous task, as many practitioners do not welcome patients with mental retardation, and because only those practitioners who accept Medicaid can usually even be considered. (Most adults with mental retardation have only Medicaid for their insurance coverage.) Our work in providing medical and mental health treatment to people with mental retardation has occurred in the context of an innovative project in the State of New Jersey.

Meeting with the individual's case manager is a key step toward intervention, as this person is in a position to convene the other important figures in the person's life for a planning meeting. For example, with respect to the woman who was being battered by a fellow group home resident, a multilevel intervention was developed and then carried out with the help of various parties. The woman and her father advocated for her to be moved, and the agency was able to find a home for her in which she was safe from abuse. (They had previously worked quite hard to prevent the violence from occurring in the home, but proved unable to stop it entirely.) Also, the woman was evaluated for psychological services, and proved to be quite symptomatic, with an anxiety disorder that predated the battering experience, and was, of course, exacerbated by it. (Unfortunately, her agitated expressions of anxiety seemed to trigger the battering resident's attacks.) The woman's father was able to engage a private psychiatrist who prescribed medication which helped with her anxiety, and finally, the project of which we are a part was able to provide the woman with individual and then group psychotherapy. This woman, who has moderate mental retardation, has been able to receive support through the therapy not only to manage her anxiety, but to redevelop her sense of herself; that is, to begin to see herself as being able to make good decisions for herself and take action for herself. Her sense of self-efficacy had been extremely damaged because of her lifelong experience of shame as she saw herself failing at school, being made fun of by peers, and unable to do the growing number of things her sisters could do. Added to this, her experience of victimization in her group home made her feel even more that there was little she could do for herself. Much of her treatment has been, and continues to be, aimed at helping her to see that she has done much to help herself (for example, complaining when she was unhappy, repeatedly asking to be moved until she was listened to). Even steps she takes to lessen her experience of anxiety, which often sound eccentric to us, are acknowledged and affirmed because they build her sense of self-efficacy. Her growing sense of herself as an effective person, even though she knows she has limitations, seems to hold the most promise for her to function optimally and enjoy her life. It is apparent in even this one case that the intervention effort must involve the individual in a process of her own recovery, as well as systems-level change.

Another woman with whom we still work has always managed to live in apartments of her own and functions with a fair degree of independence. She manages her SSI income, and utilizes local medical clinics for her health care. She makes use of food stamps, and will seek assistance as she feels the need.

She was referred to us for treatment of depression. At the time she was living alone and reported that her son, then age 4, had been taken by DYFS and placed with her sister. She continued to have contact with him via visits, but was very unhappy. As we uncovered the details of her life, we eventually learned that she had been living with her boyfriend (not the child's father), and that they had gotten into such raucous fights that neighbors had called the police, who in turn called DYFS. We also learned that the boyfriend would become abusive to her at times, and that these fights occurred in the context of her efforts to protect herself.

The woman became less depressed with the help of therapy, and was assisted by our project in connecting with a social worker at the Arc to help her in her efforts to regain custody of her son, or at least increase visitation to include weekends at her home. Soon after, the woman began seeing the boyfriend again. She was very happy about this, and was starting to believe that he would help her to get custody of the son. During this time he treated her quite well. Although we were unable to evaluate him ourselves, we got the impression that he had some type of mental health problems, as the woman told us that he went for regular monthly appointments at a mental health clinic and was taking medication. She eventually decided to marry him, stating she thought this would certainly help her to get back her son. Those of us involved with her reminded her that this man had been instrumental in her losing custody of the child, but to no avail. Her husband, perhaps with good intentions, would talk to her about how he would help her get the boy back, and the woman reported that her son had gotten quite attached to him, and that he was good to the boy.

Eventually the woman's husband stopped taking his medication. He began behaving in what sounded like a psychotic fashion, and became abusive and threatening to her at times. On one occasion, he began to choke her, but she was able to get away. After this incident, she was able to end the relationship with him. Since that time she has been somewhat more amenable to accepting support services again for her custody issues. She remains in therapy, and has begun a relationship with another man who appears to be non-abusive. We focus our efforts in the therapy on affirming her actions on her own behalf, which gives her a sense of herself that buffers her against the depression. It seems that when she is depressed she is particularly vulnerable to engaging in a relationship with a man in an effort to make herself feel better, even if that man is periodically hurtful to her.

A BRIEF HISTORY OF MENTAL HEALTH TREATMENT

Within recent years there has been increasing recognition that individuals with mental retardation both need and deserve mental health services (Hurley, Pfadt, Tomasulo, & Gardner, 1996; Nezu et al., 1992; Petronko et al., 1994). During the 1980s significant advances were made in promoting the use of psychotherapeutic techniques with persons who have mental retardation, and in assessing their utility (Hurley & Hurley, 1986). The literature reflects a growing interest in the provision of specialized mental health treatment for individuals with this disability. Moreover, preliminary outcome research suggests that individuals with mental retardation are able to benefit from certain therapeutic experiences. For example, Tomasulo, Keller, and Pfadt (1995) report on a study that provides the first wave of outcome research on the development of therapeutic factors in groups being run with individuals having mental retardation (Keller, 1995). Raters familiar with group psychotherapy procedures and processes observed videotapes of selected sessions without knowledge of whether they were viewing initial or advanced sessions. They were able to identify the presence of eight distinct therapeutic factors in the advanced groups, supporting the idea that groups with persons who have mental retardation are able to make the same types of therapeutic gains as are found in groups with nonhandicapped members.

The success of such therapeutic endeavors is particularly important in that it has been established in recent years that the mental health needs of individuals with mental retardation are considerable. With reference again to the extensive volume by Nezu et al. (1992), their comprehensive review of the existing literature makes clear that persons with mental retardation experience the full spectrum of psychiatric disorders, and in very similar ways as nonretarded individuals. Importantly, these authors have found that psychiatric disorders are, in fact, even more prevalent among persons with mental retardation than in the general population.

It is clear that mental health treatment for individuals with mental retardation is a field that is still quite young. It is not surprising, then, that the literature reveals a lack of published work on the treatment of domestic violence issues in the lives of persons with mental retardation.

We will now turn to some of the broader policy areas which bear on the issues of abuse and domestic violence in the lives of people with mental retardation, and we will briefly discuss the role of our project in this context.

POLICY

Most research and educational efforts regarding people with developmental disabilities have been directed at those who live in institutional settings. In 1962, President Kennedy's Committee on Mental Retardation initiated the shift to mainstreaming people into the community. Advocacy efforts have continued for inclusion into schools and "person-centered" planning. Many state institutions have closed, and there is a long-range plan to return as many individuals as possible to the community. The survival of these people depends on the strength of the support services in the community (Furey, 1994).

The New Jersey Division of Developmental Disabilities (DDD, 1994) has a policy designed to protect the rights of those they serve and to insure that people who have a developmental disability are not exploited, or abused physically or sexually (Division Circular # 4). However, DDD has not specifically addressed the problem of domestic violence. The return of many individuals to the community from state institutions will no doubt create a need for such a policy to be drafted.

Paul Stavis' (1991) landmark position paper advocates for the right of people with a developmental disability to express their sexuality but still be protected from harm. This progressive philosophy is new to those who work in the field of developmental disabilities, and one that many families find difficult to accept. People who have a developmental disability have the right to develop intimate relationships, but need education on the process. Families, staff, and other caregivers also need education in this area. Marchetti and McCartney (1990) explain that inadequate staff training, poor administrative practices, and inadequate supervision of staff and clients contribute to the lack of reporting of abuse of people who have a developmental disability.

People who have lived in institutions are more vulnerable than those who have been exposed to others in the community. They are easily coerced and preyed upon by abusers and batterers (Marchetti & McCartney, 1990). Many of them were abused in the institution, and this makes them more easily victimized in the community. Many may have a lower cognitive level that makes them less assertive and less informed of their rights. Women who have a developmental disability are usually not familiar with community resources, and often do not know how to seek assistance. Many of them are dependent on others for financial support and this dependency creates more opportunities for abuse. Their credibility is easily attacked, because they can be confused about facts such as dates and times. They often believe they deserve the abuse and feel powerless against their attackers. Carlson (1997) describes the learned helplessness that may cause the victim to give up because her actions appear ineffective.

It is our policy at the Arc that if a woman reports that she has been sexually or physically abused in any way, she is supported totally and provided with every available resource to address the situation. Many women with mental retardation have poor or nonexistent relationships with their families, and find it impossible to extricate themselves from abusive relationships without this tremendous support by our staff. Many women have been conditioned to accept abuse and it is only when the abuse reaches beyond themselves to their children that they find the strength to remedy the situation. Conditions that they have been able to tolerate for many years become suddenly intolerable when one of their children is abused. McFarlane and Parker (1994) have done extensive research on the frequency of abuse in pregnant women. Their abuse assessment screen focuses on three key areas: physical abuse; physical abuse during pregnancy; and sexual abuse. Abuse during pregnancy may also act as an impetus to cause the victim to seek assistance.

In a recent case we were treating, the woman became pregnant and her boyfriend would not believe the child was his. We often see the male partners deny that they are responsible and they then accuse the woman of seeing other men. The abusive situations escalate and the woman may decide to terminate the pregnancy.

TREATMENT ISSUES

The Arc of Monmouth provides a comprehensive array of services that includes educational, vocational, residential, recreational, supported employment, and health care programs. Approximately 1000 adults who have a developmental disability and live in the community receive these services. For the past 6 years The Arc of Monmouth's Ambulatory Care Center has provided primary health care and mental health services to men and women who have mental retardation and other disabilities.

A team of dedicated health care professionals with expertise in meeting the needs of this population has developed an integrated model of care that includes the disciplines of medicine, psychiatry, psychology, nursing, and social work. Care coordination is a key component of this model of care, and exceeds the limitations of the well-known concept of case management. Care coordination is a more involved form of case management that is needed because of the individual's complex needs. It is not unusual to coordinate care for a person who is mentally retarded, has seizures, a cardiac condition, and needs psychotropic medications.

Initially, in providing medical care to men and women with developmental disabilities, the growing incidence of sexual abuse of this population became apparent. Women who have a developmental disability are viewed by perpetrators as easily preyed upon due to the very nature of their disability (Furey, 1994). These women have difficulty communicating, have low self-esteem, are easily confused, and are desperately seeking affection. Many of them have spent years in state developmental centers and other institutions where they were taught to be obedient and compliant. These behaviors contribute to their sense of helplessness and vulnerability. They may never have had someone in their lives who was able to protect and advocate for them. They are frequently abused by those who are closest to them, and they are often unable to develop trust. Many of the situations we are involved with include incest with brothers and fathers, sexual abuse by stepfathers or their mothers' boyfriends, and sexual abuse by staff members or peers. Physical abuse or assault is also a problem because of crowded day programs and the congregate living situations in which many of these women must live on a permanent basis. The decision of where and with whom they will live is made for them, and is often developed out of what living situation is available at the time it is needed. Residential options include group homes, skilled sponsor homes, boarding homes, supervised apartments, and living with their parents or other relative. Men and women usually live together in residential service settings. Also of concern is the fact that few agencies have guidelines for regulating intimacy between two individuals with developmental disabilities. Residents of these living arrangements tend to get little, if any, education on the topic of sexuality. They may also get mixed messages from staff who approve and those who disapprove of sexual contact between two adults with developmental disabilities. This lack of education about sexuality and intimacy contributes to this population's being unprepared to deal with life experience issues such as sexual abuse (Furey, 1994).

Women in the Arc's vocational programs are often referred by staff for sexuality education and sexual abuse prevention training prior to their referral for community job placements. Families voice concerns that the woman will be easily coerced into sexual activity, and the families feel unprepared to deal with the issues themselves.

Women who have a developmental disability and have been abused find it difficult to locate health care professionals who will be willing and comfortable in providing therapy. Their need for therapy is often dismissed by professionals because of the woman's mental retardation and lack of assertiveness. Available, accessible, and appropriate services to address violence and abuse are seriously limited. If the woman's limitations and specialized needs have to be accommodated, services are practically nonexistent. Many victims who have mental retardation need accommodations that acknowledge their disability (Carlson, 1997).

The Arc of Monmouth's Ambulatory Care Center has addressed this unmet need and provides individual and/or group counseling for these women. The woman is first evaluated by our psychologist and a treatment plan is developed. Frequently, these women need individual therapy before they are ready to benefit from group therapy. Assertiveness training is an integral part of the therapy, and the woman is empowered to assert herself in abusive situations. The Arc of Monmouth has a rich array of services that the woman is taught to access to improve her situation. For example, she may need a job coach to assist her to explore better employment and financial opportunities. The Program Support Unit with its social workers is available to help her obtain a restraining order, find day care for her children, or search for a new living arrangement. The woman is supported by staff in every effort she makes to alter the current abusive situation. Medical care and psychiatric services are readily available if indicated.

Treatment issues that often need to be addressed are guardianship, financial resources, transportation, and insurance coverage. Most of the women we see do not drive and rely on public transportation. So even a factor as simple as transportation can require coordination by our professionals to ensure that the woman can access therapy, work, and child care. A major goal of therapy is empowerment of the victim. Areas to be developed with the client include self-esteem, independence, coping skills, and decision making. The woman who is mentally retarded needs to develop a self-protection plan for when the abuse occurs. One of the best options for women in domestic violence situations is a women's or family shelter. However, staff at these shelters are not usually trained to meet the needs of women with mental retardation (Carlson, 1997). It is necessary to advocate for this training and to ensure that the needs of these women can be met.

The Arc of Monmouth Ambulatory Care Center currently provides group therapy sessions for four different groups of approximately forty individuals. The groups meet every week. One group is for women only; two groups are exclusively for men; and one group is mixed equally with men and women. All of the participants are initially screened and evaluated by the Arc's lead psychologist. The psychologist determines the major treatment issues and develops the treatment plan. If psychiatric care with medication monitoring is needed, that is scheduled. In some cases, individual therapy may be indicated before the person will benefit from the group process.

Women who have been abused participate in two of the ongoing groups. The women are at different stages in the treatment process, and the progress at times may seem slow. The women receive tremendous support from others in the group, and sometimes continue a friendship with other group members outside of the group relationship. They exchange telephone numbers and call each other in between the group sessions. They are able to learn from each other's experiences and develop a sense of empowerment from the knowledge that someone else was able to leave the abusive situation. The women are challenged by each other to set goals for themselves, and they receive feedback each week on what they did or did not accomplish. A psychologist and a clinical nurse specialist facilitate the groups, but the majority of the feedback comes from the group members themselves.

EDUCATING PROFESSIONALS

It is imperative that physicians, nurses, psychologists, and social workers be educated in meeting the needs of victims of physical and sexual abuse who have a developmental disability. Many professionals voice concerns over managing the complexities of the person's situation. This unfamiliarity with the population, coupled with the low reimbursement rate offered by Medicaid, discourages most professionals from developing expertise in this area. The national movement towards managed health care will integrate those with developmental disabilities into generic service providers such as community mental health clinics. Carlson (1997) advocates for coleaders in group therapy models, where one leader is experienced in developmental disabilities and the other has expertise in domestic violence. It must also be impressed upon generic service providers that progress for those with a developmental disability is slow and that more therapy sessions need to be allocated for this population.

Graduate schools need to include information about people with developmental disabilities in the curricula and offer clinical training sites that provide experiences with this population. Graduate students in nursing and psychology spend time in the Arc's Ambulatory Care Center learning from skilled clinicians, and actually participate in the care of people with developmental disabilities. Medical students elect to do their community clinical rotation at the Ambulatory Care Center and often select a second semester of studies at the center. The students enjoy the experience and develop a comfort level working with this population. It is hoped that this improved comfort level will encourage the students to provide treatment to people with developmental disabilities when they open their own practices.

Several of our staff have positions as professors or adjunct faculty at area colleges and universities, and introduce the concepts surrounding care for individuals who have a developmental disability. Areas currently being taught include primary health care, women's health care, sexual abuse prevention, and mental health care. It is our staff's belief that these educational efforts will result in more professionals being trained to provide quality services to men and women who have a developmental disability. It is imperative that the needs of this vulnerable population be addressed and that community providers be prepared to treat them.

REFERENCES

Carlson, B. (1997). Mental retardation and domestic violence: An ecological approach to intervention. *Social Work, 42,* 70–89.

Durkin, M. S., & Stein, Z. A. (1996). Classification of mental retardation. In J. W. Jacobson & J. A. Mulick (Eds.), *Manual of diagnosis and professional practice in mental retardation* (pp. 67–73). Washington, DC: American Psychological Association.

Furey, E. (1994). Sexual abuse of adults with mental retardation: Who and where. *Mental Retardation, 32,* 173–180.

Hurley, A. D., & Hurley, F. J. (1986). Counseling and psychotherapy with mentally retarded clients: The initial interview. *PAMR Review, 5,* 22–26.

Hurley, A. D., Pfadt, A., Tomasulo, D., & Gardner, W. (1996). Counseling and psychotherapy. In J. W. Jacobson & J. A. Mulick (Eds.), *Manual of diagnosis and professional practice in mental retardation* (pp. 371–378). Washington, DC: American Psychological Association.

Keller, E. (1995). *Process and outcomes in interactive-behavioral groups with adults who have both mental illness and mental retardation.* Unpublished doctoral dissertation, Long Island University, Glen Head, NY.

Marchetti, A. G., & McCartney, J. R. (1990). Abuse of persons with mental retardation. *Mental Retardation, 28,* 367–371.

McFarlane, J., & Parker, B. (1994). *Abuse during pregnancy: A protocol for prevention and intervention* (March of Dimes Nursing Monograph). White Plains, NY: March of Dimes.

Nezu, A., Nezu, C., & Gill-Weiss, M. J. (1992). *Psychopathology in persons with mental retardation.* Champaign, IL: Research Press.

Petronko, M., Harris, S. L., & Kormann, R. (1994). Community-based behavioral training approaches for people with mental retardation and mental illness. *Journal of Consulting and Clinical Psychology, 62,* 49–54.

Sgroi, S. (1989). *Vulnerable populations.* Lexington, MA: Lexington Books.

Sobsey, D., & Doe, T. (1991). Patterns of sexual abuse and assault. *Sex Disability, 9,* 243–259.

State of New Jersey, Department of Human Services, Division of Developmental Disabilities. (1994). *Manual for case management.* Division Circular #4.

Stavis, P. (1991). Harmonizing the right to sexual expressions. *Sexuality and Disability, 9,* 131–141.

Tomasulo, D., Keller, E., & Pfadt, A. (1995). The healing crowd: Process, content, and technique issues in group counseling for people with mental retardation. *The Habilitative Mental HealthCare Newsletter, 14,* 43–50.

Walker, L. E. A. (1994). *Abused women and survivor therapy.* Washington, DC: American Psychological Association.

Wisconsin Council on Developmental Disabilities. (1991). *Greater risk: Legal issues in sexual abuse of adults with developmental disabilities (A training guide for caregivers).* Madison, WI: Author.

Wylie, M. S. (1996, March/April). It's a community affair. *Family Therapy Networker,* pp. 58–96.

CHAPTER 12

Women, Welfare, Work, and Domestic Violence

Patricia Brownell

> [After six years of marriage], I left [my attacker] and applied for assistance. My children were 18 months and five and a half years. . . . My life on welfare was very hard. There were times the three of us did not have enough to eat. . . . But I was able to go to school and develop the kind of skills that enabled me to make a better life for me and my children
>
> —*Jensen*

Rita Henley Jensen, a journalist, speaks for the multitude of women who were able to escape abusive intimate relationships with the assistance of Aid to Families with Dependent Children (AFDC). This was a public assistance program for poor families enacted during the Great Depression as part of the Social Security Act [Public Law No. 271, 74th Congress, II.R. 7260], which was approved August 14, 1935. It was one of the legislative agenda items of Frances Perkins, a settlement house reformer from the Progressive era who became the first woman cabinet member when appointed as Secretary of Labor under President Franklin Delano Roosevelt.

Aid to Dependent Children, as it was then known, was enacted as an entitlement program for all families who met categorical and financial criteria defined by federal and state law. It afforded a minimum level of financial security to primarily poor women and children deprived of a male breadwinner, by virtue of death, illness, or abandonment. By the 1970s, in the wake of the great civil rights and women's movements, it had also become an important source of support for women and children made destitute through fleeing domestic violence situations.

Domestic violence is defined as abuse of spouses and others in the home in which one's property, health, or life are endangered or harmed as a result of the intentional behavior of another family member (Barker, 1995). Since domestic violence was defined as a significant social problem in the 1960s, startling statistics have emerged about its impact on domestic life in the United States. Overwhelmingly victims are women (95%). As documented in chapters 1–3 of this book, recent estimates indicate that over 8 million women are beaten each year by their present or former intimate partners. Each year, more than a million women seek medical assistance for injuries caused by battering, and 37% of pregnant women are battered (see chapter 9 by Dr. Mary Boes).

State statistics also demonstrate the impact of domestic violence on children. Children were present or involved in 50% of New Jersey's 1993 police-reported domestic violence incidences. Fifty-five% of all female victims of domestic violence are children under the age of 11. Children from violent homes have higher risks of alcohol/drug abuse. Children in homes where domestic violence occurs are physically abused or seriously neglected at a rate 1,500% higher than the national average in the general population. As violence against women becomes more severe and frequent, children experience a 300% increase in physical violence by the male batterer (Bowker, 1995).

WELFARE AND DOMESTIC VIOLENCE

Studies have demonstrated a strong relationship between domestic violence and AFDC. According to Dr. Ruth Brandwein, Professor of Social Work at the State University of New York at Stony Brook and Chair of the National Association of Social Workers' (NASW) Welfare

Reform Response Network, from 50% to 80% of AFDC recipients have been found to have a past or current history of domestic violence. This is defined as abuse by a partner or spouse, parent, relative, or family friend (Brandwein, 1996).

A National Symposium sponsored by the University of Utah Graduate School of Social Work in May 1996 identified at least four types of linkages between family violence and the use of welfare (Brandwein, 1996).

First, many battered women are forced to turn to public assistance in order to extricate themselves from a violent relationship. The choice such women may face is to return to the batterer and a style of life to which they may have become accustomed—even if subjected to repeated violence and psychological abuse—or leave and enter a life of poverty, at least temporarily.

Second, many women are coerced by their partners (husbands or boyfriends) not to attend education or job programs, or not to show up at jobs. Some studies have suggested that abusive partners fear loss of control, and are threatened by their partner becoming independent of them.

Third, child abuse, particularly child sexual abuse, provides another pathway to welfare. In cases of child sexual abuse or incest, the nonoffending parent—usually the mother—is required to protect the child from the family offender—often the boyfriend, stepfather, or father. If losing the financial support of the offender means destitution for her and her family, a mother may be forced to turn to welfare.

Fourth, the route to welfare may stretch over a longer period of time. Girls who have been sexually abused are more likely to act out sexually, which can result in pregnancy during adolescence (Navarro, 1996). In one shelter for unwed mothers in New York State, social worker interns found that every girl there had been previously sexually abused. Although only about 12% of welfare recipients at any one point in time are teenage mothers, a large proportion of welfare recipients had their first child when teenagers (Brandwein, 1996).

ELIMINATION OF THE FEDERAL GUARANTEE TO ASSISTANCE FOR POOR FAMILIES WITH CHILDREN

The Aid to Families with Dependent Children Program was eliminated by President Bill Clinton on August 22, 1996, when he signed into law the Personal Responsibility and Work Opportunity Reconciliation Act (the PRA or Public Law 104-193). This ended the 60-year federal guarantee of a minimum level of social assistance for poor families with dependent children, established by Title IV of the Social Security Act in 1935. The PRA changed Aid to Families with Dependent Children (AFDC) from an entitlement program to a block grant—renamed Temporary Assistance to Needy Families (TAN-F). A primary purpose of TAN-F is to move heads of AFDC households into the workforce.

The PRA also denies benefits to teen unwed mothers until they turn 18, based on the belief that this will serve as a warning to other young girls not to become pregnant or to marry if they do (Gillespie & Schellhas, 1994). Two drug-related provisions of the PRA include terminating access to TAN-F for life for anyone convicted of a drug-related felony (including women of child-bearing age or with dependent children), unless state legislatures pass affirmative legislation to the contrary. A second—at state option—permits mandatory drug testing of TAN-F applicants and recipients. The PRA also eliminates access to federally funded public benefits—including TAN-F—for immigrant women with dependent children.

PERSONAL RESPONSIBILITY AS PUBLIC POLICY IN HISTORICAL CONTEXT

The term "personal responsibility" as a social welfare concept suggests a value shift away from social responsibility (Uchitelle, 1997). To talk about welfare and domestic violence in this era of defining welfare reform as "personal responsibility" is a contradiction. It harkens back to an earlier time in U.S. history—to the Colonial era, when members of the agrarian European settlements spoke of values such as "pulling oneself up by one's bootstraps" because that was all the social support that existed. This was a time when it was legal for a husband to beat his wife with a stick no thicker than a thumb (the so-called "rule of thumb") (Pleck, 1987).

Reform eras in United States social welfare history have served to focus public attention on social injustices and domestic ills beyond the control of the individual. During the Progressive era of the late 19th century to World War I, social reformers such as Charles Loring

Brace (1872), a worker for the charity organization movement and founder of the Children's Aid Society, and Jane Addams (1911), a founder of the settlement house movement in the United States, documented spouse abuse and domestic violence in the communities they served. Brace, a leader of the early child-saving movement, and Addams, a Progressive era maternalist who believed that women's primary role was in raising children and maintaining family life, not only documented incidences of family violence but also advocated for policies to protect women and children against abuse by male household heads (Gordon, 1988).

While not an explicit purpose of the Social Security Act of 1935, Perkins and others envisioned the Aid to Dependent Children program as a new form of "outdoor relief"—based on the concept of government entitlement, and not charity—that could sustain mothers with dependent children in the community without the support of a male breadwinner if necessary. The Great Depression served to underscore the belief that poverty was not necessarily the result of individual deficiencies and moral failings of the afflicted, but could result from systemic forces outside the control of the individual.

Wife-beating was redefined as domestic violence and a significant social problem during the 1960s and 1970s in the wake of the civil rights movement (Pleck, 1987). Domestic violence, like institutionalized racial discrimination, was framed in communitarian terms as a social issue of concern to everyone in society. Feminists framed the issue of domestic violence as one that affected women of all social classes. This reflected a conscious strategy designed to ensure that it was not perceived as a problem specific to the poor and communities of color, and—as a result—marginalized. While welfare policies and protocols were changed to ease access to AFDC programs and domestic violence shelters funded through Emergency Assistance to Families (EAF or Title IV of the Social Security Act), this was not widely publicized (Schechter, 1982).

The passage of the Personal Responsibility Act, ending Aid to Families with Dependent Children as an entitlement program, has focused new attention on the relationship between domestic violence and public welfare. The block grant replacing AFDC by the Personal Responsibility Act is named Temporary Assistance to Needy Families or TAN-F to emphasize the transitory nature of the program. In addition, the federal requirement is eliminated that all families who meet the categorical and financial requirements must receive assistance. Available funds can be used for other purposes in addition to cash assistance, including the reduction of state budget deficits.

TAN-F AND WORK REQUIREMENTS

Requirements that women receiving Aid to Families with Dependent Children participate in work or work-related activities as a condition of continuing eligibility for assistance is not new. The Work Incentive Program, legislated during the Nixon administration, was one of the first such welfare-to-work programs. Most recently, the Family Support Act of 1988 required states and localities to enroll AFDC heads of households in work-related programs, ranging from remedial literacy and training to job clubs to college programs. Ensuring adequate day care and transitional benefits such as Medicaid were the responsibility of the state. The federal safety net remained for those AFDC heads of households who were unable to attach or sustain attachment to the job market (U.S. House of Representatives, 1991, 1992).

Under the new TAN-F legislation, women must comply with rigid work or workfare requirements in order to maintain benefits for themselves and their children (U.S. House of Representatives, 1996). Missing time from workfare or job training can result in loss or reduction of benefits, even if this was due to a battering incident in the home, the need to seek medical attention for domestic violence-related injuries, or obtaining an order of protection. The burden of making child care arrangements is transferred under TAN-F from the state to the head of the household receiving assistance. By establishing a maximum 5-year lifetime cap on federal TAN-F benefits per family, the PRA has effectively eliminated the federal safety net for poor women and children.

This has important implications for a battered woman's access to needed emergency services for herself and her children. For example, many domestic violence shelters are funded through emergency Assistance to Families (EAF), now part of the TAN-F block grant, or the Social Services Block Grant (SSBG or Title XX of the Social Security Act), the funding for which has been cut as well. If in a domestic violence shelter, a TAN-F recipient may be required by shelter protocols to stop work. These protocols are intended to ensure that the batterer does not discover the location of the shelter by following the victim home from work. However, she could risk being found out of compliance with work regulations, or experience loss or reduction of benefits by not reporting to a mandated work assignment.

WOMEN, WELFARE, WORK AND ABUSE

In terms of "welfare reform," what we need to do is look at domestic violence victims as individuals, and the welfare system actually has to be flexible and responsive to the needs of individual women. Instead of . . . asking "Why doesn't she leave?," we have to reframe the issue to "What does she need to leave and become self-sufficient?" . . . The greatest antidote to poverty is jobs and well-paying jobs. (Women Fighting Poverty, 1996, p. 19)

One important reason that women stay in or return to abusive relationships is that often they cannot afford to support themselves and their children alone (Horn, 1994). Even public assistance programs, while traditionally an important safety net program for women who are victims of domestic violence and their children, do not raise families out of poverty (U.S. House of Representatives, 1996). For welfare recipients to successfully make the transition from welfare to work, they may require a continuum of supportive services flexible enough to meet individual needs, as well as access to an array of educational opportunities that allow them to secure long-term, stable jobs that provide family health benefits as well (Brandwein, 1997).

STUDIES ON DOMESTIC VIOLENCE AND JOB TRAINING PROGRAMS

One factor associated with success in permanently ending an abusive relationship for a woman with dependent children is education and training leading to stable employment, self-sufficiency, and a sense of personal efficacy (Jensen, 1995). However, studies on domestic violence and welfare-to-work programs conducted by the Taylor Institute in Chicago, the National Organization of Women Legal Defense and Education Fund in New York City, the Center for Urban Affairs and Policy Research at Northwestern University, and the Washington State University for Policy Research have identified significant barriers to achieving the goal of self-sufficiency through employment for women on public assistance involved in abusive relationships (Kenney & Brown, 1996; Raphael, 1995, 1996).

In 1995, the Taylor Institute, a public policy research and advocacy organization in Chicago, published a groundbreaking study examining welfare-to-work public policies and found them to be based on a number of misconceptions (Raphael, 1995). Cited as primary among them was a misconception that women on welfare did not have relationships with men. Furthermore, it was the male in the picture who frequently sabotaged the woman's efforts to become self-sufficient.

The Taylor Institute study, *Domestic Violence: Telling the Untold Welfare-to-Work Study* (Raphael, 1995), was based on a nationwide telephone survey of grass-roots welfare-to-work programs to determine the extent of this problem as noted by program case managers and administrators. Anecdotal evidence reported by those surveyed included sabotaging ploys of male partners, such as hiding or ripping work clothing; failing to appear as promised to care for children; revealing jealous fantasies about men at work sites; behaving seductively toward program participants; inflicting visible bruises, including black eyes, broken teeth, and cigarette burns; and picking fights prior to examinations and critical job interviews. Respondents stated that they believed that estimates of such incidents were low, as the women involved were often reluctant to report them.

Findings from the Taylor Institute study are corroborated by studies by other welfare-to-work programs. The Manpower Demonstration Research Corporation (MDRC), at the forefront of welfare-to-work demonstrations in the country, in 1991 reported on a study of 617 young women (ages 16–22) participating in the New Chance program designed for recipients at high risk of long-term welfare dependency. Of these, 16% of participants across the program sites reported being battered by boyfriends while in the program; 15% reported being actively discouraged from attending by a boyfriend; and another 15% reported being abused or discouraged from attending by other family members (Raphael, 1995). Estimates from other programs were higher. The Women's Employment Network in Kansas City, Missouri, estimated that 70%–80% of welfare-to-work program participants self-reported domestic violence during program participation. The Family Support and Education Center in Maryland reported that at least 20% of its participants were affected by this problem.

The second report by the Taylor Institute, *Prisoners of Abuse: Domestic Violence and Welfare Receipt: A Second Report of the Women, Welfare and Abuse Project* (Zorza, 1996), continues to emphasize the barriers domestic violence poses for women transitioning from welfare to work. In addition to continuing to document male partners' efforts to sabotage women's efforts to achieve self-sufficiency through education and job training, this report also documents the risks women face in cooperating with child support enforcement efforts (Raphael, 1996).

The extreme dangers posed by child support collections from violent noncustodial fathers are notorious. In the early 1990s, several government workers in the Watkins Glen, New York, Child Support Enforcement Office were murdered by an irate father ordered to pay back child support. In New York City, bulletproof plexiglas and a buzzer system prevent casual access to the Child Support Enforcement Office workforce. The 1996 Personal Responsibility Act mandates cooperation with child support enforcement for TAN-F recipients as another condition of their continued eligibility for assistance (U.S. House of Representatives, 1996).

The National Organization of Women (NOW) Legal Defense and Education Fund published a study, *Report from the Front Lines: The Impact of Violence on Poor Women*, based on interviews with New York City direct service staff, including job training and job placement program coordinators, vocational counselors, and job developers (Kenney & Brown, 1996). This survey "involved interviewing knowledgeable informants to determine the scope and extent of the problem of domestic violence for women in welfare-to-work programs" in New York City (p. 6).

Like the Taylor Institute studies, the NOW Legal Defense and Education Fund study found that high proportions of women in welfare-to-work programs are being abused by partners. Reported estimates ranged from 30 to 75% (Kenney & Brown, 1996). Respondents reported that the abuse took many forms (including physical and emotional abuse, stalking, and harassment), and it appeared intended to undermine women's efforts to develop employment-related skills. Unfortunately, it was successful in a number of cases. Study respondents reported that women in training programs who were being abused were more likely to drop out prior to completion of programs than those who did not report abuse (Kenney & Brown, 1996). These findings are consistent with other studies that suggest a correlation between battering and weak employment histories for women (Shepard & Pence, 1988).

The NOW report points out that under the enriched job training and educational opportunities provided through the Family Support Act of 1988, battered women may have been advantaged by the availability of case management services that improved detection and intervention for domestic violence as a barrier to participant self-sufficiency. Under TAN-F, the low-cost "jobs-first" strategy that emphasizes movement into entry-level jobs and workfare over training and education for recipients could place women at greater risk of abuse or—alternatively—increase the sanctions for lateness and absenteeism that penalize the TAN-F heads of household as well as their children.

The "welfare reform" social experiment initiated by the 1996 PRA is being closely tracked by conservative and liberal "think tanks," journalists, academics, and advocates (Harwood, 1997). Three indicators that would suggest failure of the PRA as a public policy include increased homelessness among families, increased numbers of children entering the foster care system, and increased mortality of women and their children at the hands of their abusers.

Wife-battering has already been cited as a major cause of homelessness among poor families (Zorza, 1991). In 1987, the New York State Office for the Prevention of Domestic Violence found that battered women and their children comprised 40% of the state's homeless shelter residents. HUD has reported that one half of adult clients in U.S. shelters that serve families with children have experienced domestic violence (U.S. Department of Housing and Urban Development, 1988). More recently, advocates in Milwaukee, Wisconsin, have reported an off-season increase in use of family homeless shelters among welfare recipients affected by the Wisconsin new highly-touted "welfare reform" program.

Public child welfare systems have been bracing for over a year for the impact of "welfare reform" on child abuse and neglect reports, as well as foster care caseloads (Kilborn, 1996). Concerns have been raised on the part of public child welfare officials about the availability of foster care families—including kin—if TAN-F work requirements are not relaxed or waived for foster care parents, who may be receiving public assistance in order to remain home to care for dependent children. While the PRA permits states to exempt up to 20% of the TAN-F caseload from the work requirements without penalty, a number of recipient categories far exceeding the 20% allotted cap are competing for exemption (Swarns, 1997).

A recent study on women murdered during the past 5 years in New York City was conducted by New York City Department of Health epidemiologist Dr. Susan Wilt. Wilt found that more women are killed by their husbands and boyfriends than in robberies, disputes, attacks, or any other crime in cases where the relationship between victim and murderer is known (Belluck, 1997). When they were killed by their husbands, one-third of the time the women appeared to be trying to end the relationship. Also, in one-quarter of the cases where husbands or boyfriends were the killers, children were either killed, injured, were onlookers, or found their mothers' bodies.

Challenging the often-cited belief that domestic violence affects women of all economic classes and ethnicities equally, two-thirds of the domestic violence killings were in the poorest boroughs—the Bronx and Brooklyn—and three-quarters of the women killed by husbands or boyfriends were Black or Hispanic. Dr. Jeff Fagan, director of the Center for Violence, Research and Prevention at Columbia University's School of Public Health was quoted in the article as noting that domestic violence is a problem of poverty, associated with other characteristics like high unemployment (Belluck, 1997).

The correlation between poverty and domestic violence comes as no surprise to advocates such as Brandwein (Brandwein, 1996; Raphael, 1995, 1996; Women Fighting Poverty, 1996). While domestic violence has been cited as a primary reason that women with children enter public assistance programs, it has also been documented as a significant barrier to leaving public assistance for stable, long-term employment.

For those battered women fortunate enough to find a job, there is no guarantee that they will sustain it in the face of a determined batterer. A 1988 study revealed that close to 75% of battered women are harassed by their abusers at work, causing 20% to lose their jobs (Brandwein, 1996). The danger that battered women face on the job after leaving violent partners was underscored in 1996 by the deaths of Falina Komar and Helen Coppola, both murdered in their place of work by their abusers (Gonnerman, 1997a; Krauss, 1996).

Domestic violence in the workplace is an issue of growing concern to corporations, government, and policy makers (Brownell, 1996). While some corporations and agencies are making workplace security for domestic violence victims a priority (Hardeman, 1995), women in low-wage service sector jobs remain vulnerable to assault (U.S. Department of Labor, 1996). Public policies that force a population known to be at risk of domestic violence—women with dependent children on public assistance—into unprotected community service and entry-level service jobs are courting disaster for those families.

TAN-F AND THE 5-YEAR LIFE TIME CAP ON BENEFITS

With the passage of the PRA and the 5-year maximum lifetime cap on benefits, the stakes have been raised considerably on ensuring the employment—as well as the employability—of poor women with dependent children currently receiving welfare benefits. In addition to those women with active or past histories of domestic violence— including incest and child abuse—another vulnerable group of public assistance recipients is the population with active substance abuse problems.

Many domestic violence victims and substance abusers have been found to experience long-term chronic or episodic periods of need for support and treatment (Burgess & Roberts, 1996; Van Den Bergh, 1991). Batterers, for example, may not be so considerate as to confine themselves to a 5-year lifetime limit of domestic abuse per victim. Relapse among substance abusers is generally viewed as an integral part of the recovery and healing process.

WOMEN, WELFARE, AND SUBSTANCE ABUSE

According to Joseph Califano, President of the National Center on Addiction and Substance Abuse at Columbia University in New York

City and former Secretary of Health, Education and Welfare in the Carter Administration, "Substance abuse and addiction have changed the nature of poverty in America. But the welfare reform legislation that . . . President Clinton signed . . . ignores this grim truth" (Califano, 1996, p. A23). Califano states that at least 20% of women on welfare—or as many as 1 million mothers—have drug or alcohol problems that are severe enough to require treatment. However, far from mandating that states provide treatment, the PRA permits—at state and county discretion—mandatory drug testing of TAN-F applicants and recipients. This may serve as a deterrent to eligible heads of households from seeking needed benefits. It also stipulates that unless state legislatures pass affirmative legislation to the contrary, anyone convicted of drug-related felonies after August 22, 1996, can be denied TAN-F benefits for life. This includes women of childbearing age or with dependent children

Studies by the National Center on Addiction and Substance Abuse (CASA) have demonstrated that, like women who are victims of domestic violence, substance-abusing women are largely victims of their own poverty. Although low-income women are less likely to try an illegal drug than high-income women, the low-income women are four times more likely to become addicted when they do (National Center on Addiction and Substance Abuse, 1996). However, the PRA does not require states to finance substance abuse treatment for TAN-F recipients.

The link between women's alcohol consumption and domestic violence has been well documented. A study by Miller, Downs, and Gondoli (1989) on spousal abuse among alcoholic and nonalcoholic women found

> [that] alcoholic women nine times more likely to be slapped by their husbands, five times more likely to be kicked or hit, five times more likely to be beaten and four times more likely to have their lives threatened. (National Center on Addiction and Substance Abuse, 1996, p. 51)

While most research has focused on the link between domestic abuse and alcoholism, violence is most lethal when linked to illegal drug use by women. For example, 70% of drug-addicted, low-income pregnant women in methadone treatment programs have been beaten—86% of them by husbands or partners, many of whom are also drug users (National Center on Addiction and Substance Abuse, 1996).

The National Center for Addiction and Substance Abuse (1994) is currently designing several projects as a follow-up to its 1994 study, *Substance Abuse and Women on Welfare*. There are at least three follow-up studies in various stages of planning and implementation. One is intended to study the relationship between the frequency with which a woman cycles on and off welfare, the cumulative length a woman is on welfare, and her patterns of drug and alcohol abuse. The second is a demonstration program to provide welfare recipients with substance abuse, health, employment, and other services through community-based organizations, with the goal of enabling recipients to remain drugfree and off welfare. The third is a study of the ways in which states intend to meet the treatment, job training, and health care needs of substance-abusing welfare recipients with dependent children (National Center on Addiction and Substance Abuse, 1995). Incorporated into planned demonstration project models are social work interventions intended to address domestic violence experienced by participants (M. Nakashian, personal communication, March 4, 1997).

New York State Senator Catherine Abate has identified a relationship between domestic violence and drug-related felony convictions for women. She cites surveys of the prison population that found some women convicted on drug related charges are coerced into drug dealing by abusive partners (G. Sharwin, personal communication, August 13, 1997). As noted, the Personal Responsibility Act eliminates access to TAN-F benefits and food stamps for life for anyone with a drug-related felony conviction, unless states pass affirmative legislation to the contrary.

IMMIGRANTS, WELFARE AND DOMESTIC VIOLENCE

The Personal Responsibility Act eliminates access to TAN-F, food stamps, and Medicaid for many legal immigrants. Battered immigrant women—both legal and nondocumented—face all the problems that citizen victims of domestic violence face, and more besides. In addition to the loss of home and income, they may also face ostracism and stigmatization from families and communities when they attempt to leave battering spouses. However, not to leave is to risk losing their children to the child welfare system if the children are found to be at risk due to the domestic violence in the household. Some states, such as New Jersey, have restored some benefits to the legal immigrant community using state tax levy funds. This remains an important advocacy issue in states that have not yet submitted their state plans for use of the TAN-F block grant.

WELLSTONE-MURRAY FAMILY VIOLENCE AMENDMENT TO THE PERSONAL RESPONSIBILITY ACT

The Wellstone-Murray Family Violence Amendment to the Personal Responsibility Act (Subsection 402 (A) (7)) authorizes (although it does not mandate) states to establish and enforce procedures to screen and identify victims of domestic violence, and refer them to counseling and supportive services. The amendment also allows for a waiver of program requirements that make it difficult for victims to escape domestic violence, unfairly penalize those who have been victims, or increase their risk of domestic violence (Weinstein, 1997).

As an example, requirements that TAN-F applicants or recipients must comply with the mandate to establish paternity, provide information on how to contact the legally responsible spouse—who may be the batterer—or cooperate with collection of child support may be waived under the Wellstone-Murray amendment if this could endanger a woman's safety (Gonnerman, 1997b). A growing number of states have elected to adopt this amendment, which can include waiving work requirements and exempting domestic violence victims from the 5-year lifetime cap on receipt of TAN-F benefits. A growing number of advocacy organizations are lobbying the Department of Health and Human Services to allow exemptions for victims of domestic violence in addition to, not included in, tabulations of 20% of the TAN-F caseload exempted for reasons of hardship (National Association of Social Workers [NASW], 1997a).

Advocates are targeting appeals to President Bill Clinton, who disclosed that his mother was a victim of domestic violence during an address in October 1996 for National Domestic Violence Awareness Month. However, most advocacy groups note that advocacy efforts must be targeted to state legislators from those states that have not yet finalized their state plan for submission to Health and Human Services for approval. The advocacy goal has been to fully adopt the Wellstone-Murray Amendment. In addition, governors and state legislators have been contacted on a regular basis by the advocacy community to urge passage of legislation to provide—as in the State of New Jersey—state-funded social welfare benefits for legal immigrants. Finally, social workers—particularly those working with the forensic substance-abusing population—are advocating for passage of state legislation permitting access to TAN-F and food stamp benefits for women with histories of domestic violence who are convicted of drug-related felonies.

IMPLICATIONS FOR SOCIAL WORK PRACTICE

With the passage of the new National Association of Social Workers Code of Ethics in 1996 (NASW, 1996), the mandate for social workers to advocate for policies that benefit clients is significantly strengthened. Social workers, who are experts in the interactions between people and their environments, are more attuned than most to the implications of irresponsible public policies such as the Personal Responsibility and Work Opportunity Reconciliation Act of 1996.

Clinicians who work with battered women and their families, victims of incest and child abuse, substance abusers struggling with feelings of powerlessness, and families without homes or dependable sources of income know the toll these social pressures take on the health and mental health of family members and their ability to remain together in the community. As noted by Belle (1990):

> Poverty is a complex phenomenon, with wide-ranging implications for the well-being of individuals. Future research [and practice] must build connections to therapies and public policies designed for poor women. The tragically increasing prevalence of poverty among women [and children] gives these issues particular urgency. (p. 388)

Women and children receiving public assistance are by definition poor. Public policy that mandates work for TAN-F recipients without consideration of circumstances that may limit achieving this goal—

such as domestic violence—can only doom large numbers of women and children to a Hobson's choice of life-threatening abuse or life-threatening destitution.

There is another alternative. A coherent national family policy to include social supports like adequate housing, child care, job training and development, and guaranteed jobs, as well as workplace security, and effective intervention programs for domestic violence victims and batterers, could go a long way to breaking the link between poverty and domestic abuse. Finally, more practice research is needed into the dynamics of domestic violence—including interventions that prove successful and the time and supports needed to ensure their success. Social workers have the expertise, as well as the ethical obligation, to inform and shape enlightened public policy that severs, not tightens, the link between family abuse and poverty.

REFERENCES

Addams, J. (1911). *Twenty years at Hull House.* New York: Macmillan.

Barker, R. L. (1995). *The social work dictionary* (3rd ed.). Washington, DC: NASW Press.

Belle, D. (1990). Poverty and women's mental health. *American Psychologist, 385–388.*

Belluck, P. (1997, March 31). Women's killers are very often their partners, a study finds. *The New York Times,* p. B1.

Bowker, L. B. (n.d.). *Domestic violence: The shameful facts.* Trenton, NJ: State of New Jersey, Department of Community Affairs, New Jersey Division on Women.

Brace, C. L. (1872). *The dangerous classes of New York and twenty years' work among them.* New York: Wynkoop & Hallenbeck. (Reprinted by NASW Classic Series)

Brandwein, R. (1996, May). *Family violence and welfare reform: What are the links?* Proceedings from the National Invitational Symposium Sponsored by the University of Utah Graduate School of Social Work, Salt Lake City, Utah.

Brandwein, R. (1997). *Statement Presented to New York State Assembly Standing Committee on Ways and Means, Assembly Standing Committee on Social Services and Assembly Standing Committee on Children and Families on Behalf of NASW New York State Chapter,* January 23, 1997.

Brownell, P. (1996). Domestic violence in the workplace: An emergent issue. *Crisis Intervention, 3,* 129–141.

Burgess, A. W., & Roberts, A. R. (1996). Family violence against women and children: Prevalence of assaults and fatalities, family dynamics, and interventions. *Crisis Intervention, 3,* 65–80.

Califano, J. A. (1996, August 24). Welfare's drug connection. *New York Times,* p. A23.

Gillespie, E., & Schellhas, B. (Eds.). (1994). *Contract with America.* New York: Times Books.

Gonnerman, J. (1997b, March 10). Welfare's domestic violence. *The Nation,* pp. 21–23.

Gonnerman, J. (1997a, January 28). The judge of abuse. *Village Voice,* p. 28.

Gordon, L. (1988). *Heroes of their own lives: The politics and history of domestic violence: Boston, 1880–1960.* New York: Viking.

Hardeman, J. (1995, October). *Domestic violence in the workplace.* Conference Sponsored by the Human Resources Administration, New York, NY.

Harwood, J. (1997, January 30). Think tanks battle to judge the impact of welfare overhaul. *The Wall Street Journal,* p. A1.

Horn, P. (1994). Creating a just economy will reduce violence against women. In K. L. Swisher & C. Wekisser (Eds.), *Violence against women* (pp. 182–188). San Diego, CA: Greenhaven.

Jensen, R. H. (1995, July/August). Welfare. *Ms.,* p. 56.

Kenney, C. T., & Brown, K. R. (1996). *Report from the front lines: The impact of violence on poor women.* New York: NOW Legal and Educational Defense Fund.

Kilborn, P. T. (1996, November 30). Shrinking safety net cradles hearts and hopes of children. *The New York Times,* p. A1.

Krauss, C. (1996, November 2). Man fatally shoots his wife in her Manhattan office. *The New York Times,* p. 27.

Miller, B. A., Downs, W. R., & Gondoli, D. M. (1989). Spousal violence among alcoholic women as compared to a random household sample of women. *Journal of Studies on Alcohol, 50,* 533–540.

National Association of Social Workers. (1996). *NASW code of ethics.* Washington, DC: Author.

National Association of Social Workers. (1997a). States eye domestic abuse welfare option. *NASW News, 42,* 3.

National Association of Social Workers, New York State Chapter. (1997b). *Testimony the New York State Assembly from NASW Welfare Reform Response Network by Dr. Ruth Brandwein, Chair,* January 23, 1997.

National Center on Addiction and Substance Abuse at Columbia University. (1994). *Substance abuse and women on welfare.* New York: Columbia University.

National Center on Addiction and Substance Abuse. (1995). *Annual report.* New York: Columbia University.

National Center on Addiction and Substance Abuse. (1996). *Substance abuse and the American woman.* New York: Columbia University.

Navarro, M. (1996, October 31). Teen-age mothers viewed as abused prey of older men. *The New York Times,* p. A1.

Pleck, E. (1987). *Domestic tyranny: The making of American social policy against family violence from colonial times to the present.* New York: Oxford University Press.

Raphael, J. (1995). *Domestic violence: Telling the untold welfare to work story.* Chicago: Taylor Institute.

Raphael, J. (1996). *Prisoners of abuse: Domestic violence and welfare receipt.* Chicago: Taylor Institute.

Schechter, S. (1982). *Women and male violence: The visions and struggles of the battered women's movement.* Boston: South End Press.

Shepard, M., & Pence, E. (1988). The effect of battering on the employment status of women. *Affilia, 3,* 55–61.

Swarns, R. (1997, March 29). Welfare family advocates, once allies, become rivals. *The New York Times,* p. A1.

Uchitelle, L. (1997, January 5). The shift toward self-reliance in the welfare system. *The New York Times,* p. A15.

U.S. Department of Housing and Urban Development, Division of Policy Studies. (1988). *Report on the 1988 National Survey of Shelters for the Homeless.* Washington, DC: Author.

U.S. Department of Labor. (1996). *Guidelines for preventing workplace violence for health care and social service workers-OSHA 3148-199.* Washington, DC: Occupational Safety and Health Administration.

U.S. House of Representatives, Committee on Ways and Means. (1991). *Green book.* Washington, DC: U.S. Government Printing Office.

U.S. House of Representatives, Committee on Ways and Means. (1992). *Green book.* Washington, DC: U.S. Government Printing Office.

U.S. House of Representatives, Committee on Ways and Means. (1996). *Green book.* Washington, DC: U.S. Government Printing Office.

Van Den Bergh, N. (1991). *Feminist perspectives on addictions.* New York: Springer Publishing Company.

Weinstein, H. E. (1997, February 10). Weinstein calls on governor to protect domestic violence victims from potentially dangerous welfare requirements and urges full adoption of Wellstone/Murray. *News from Assemblywoman Helene E. Weinstein,* pp. 1–2.

Women Fighting Poverty. (1996, March 16). *Organizing for Economic Justice* (Miriam Friedlander, Chair). New York, NY.

Zorza, J. (1991). Women battering: A major cause of homelessness. *Clearinghouse Review, 25,* 421–429.

High-Risk Groups and Vulnerable Populations

CHAPTER 13

Elder Abuse: Protective and Empowerment Strategies for Crisis Intervention

Patricia Brownell and Irvin Abelman

An estimated 4 to 10% of Americans age 60 or above will experience elder abuse in their lifetime (U.S. House of Representatives, 1990). The elderly can be victimized by adult sons or daughters, spouses, grandchildren, siblings, other relatives, informal companions, and significant others (Dundorf & Brownell, 1995). The purpose of this chapter is to provide an overview of elder abuse as a form of domestic violence; describe the evolution of three key social welfare systems that address elder abuse today; and discuss crisis intervention techniques to address the problem of elder abuse in the community.

Professionals in the field of aging are increasingly aware that abuse or neglect may threaten the well-being and safety of elderly clients on their caseload. While this is important, it is essential that they are also aware of the interrelationship among a number of different variables, usually studied and reported upon in isolation from one another. For example, definitions of elder abuse and neglect, profiles of abuse, populations at risk, and services available and utilized to address the problem of abuse and neglect are often discussed as separate issues. All are of critical significance for professionals in crisis intervention and the developing and implementing of service plans for clients who are victims of elder abuse.

DEFINITION OF ELDER ABUSE

Elder abuse or mistreatment, as a form of domestic violence, includes:

- Physical abuse, or the infliction of pain, injury or coercion, such as confinement against one's will. This may also include unwanted sexual attention.
- Psychological or emotional abuse, such as verbal insults or threats and menacing.
- Financial abuse, such as illegal or improper use or exploitation of funds, possessions, or other resources.
- Neglect, which may be either an intentional or unintentional failure to perform caregiving obligations such as providing medication, toileting, and other needed functions (Brownell, 1996).

PROFILES OF ABUSE

Media coverage of elder abuse is often characterized by exposure of the most severe occurrences, involving homicide, severe physical abuse, or abandonment of elderly relatives with dementia in public places. Such highly dramatic cases of elder abuse are relatively rare. Nonetheless, these situations occur, along with others that are less dramatic but result in diminished quality of life and compromised safety of older victims. Case profiles may include that of a healthy, competent older adult caring for an impaired adult child or grandchild; an impaired older adult abused by a caregiver, who may be overstressed, incapable of providing needed care, or intent on exploitation; or an older victim of spouse or partner abuse.

Exploitation and Abuse of Elderly Family Member by Dependent and Impaired Adult Child or Grandchild

Older adults who are competent and healthy can be at risk of abuse and exploitation by adult children or grandchildren who have one or more impairments, including mental illness, developmental disability, and alcohol or drug abuse. An example, reported in *The New York Times*, is that of Mrs. B., who was murdered by a substance-abusing granddaughter (Dugger, 1991).

> *Mrs. B., a 66-year-old retired civil servant, helped to raise her granddaughter because of the break-up of her daughter's marriage when she was young. Even after the granddaughter dropped out of a substance abuse program she was attending because of a crack cocaine addiction, Mrs. B. continued giving her granddaughter money and emotional support, and allowed her and her boyfriend to live rent-free in her apartment—against the advice of her family, including her daughter. Mrs. B. stated her belief that her granddaughter would eventually successfully complete the treatment program and move on with her life. She refused to press charges against her granddaughter for removing household possessions without her permission; she did not want her granddaughter to have a criminal record. One night—with a boyfriend who was also a substance abuser—the granddaughter murdered Mrs. B., after she finally stated she would press charges against her granddaughter for stealing her pension check.*

Neglect, Exploitation, and Abuse of a Frail Dependent Elderly Relative by an Overwhelmed, Impaired, or Exploitative Caregiver

> *Mrs. C., an 82-year-old former schoolteacher, moved in with her son and his live-in girlfriend after the death of her husband. She had been suffering from depression and aphasia, for which she had been treated in another state prior to her move. After living with her son and girlfriend for a year, she was brought into the emergency room of a local*

hospital with bedsores, severe dehydration, malnourishment, and an inability to speak coherently. There were marks around her ankles that appeared to be rope burns. She seemed to be struggling to communicate something to hospital staff, but was unintelligible. Her son said she was just agitated, that she had longstanding emotional problems, she refused to eat even though he tried to feed her, and he wanted her treated and returned home, where he and his girlfriend would continue to care for her. The son had recently transferred considerable resources from her bank account to his, showing a power of attorney form she had signed when she moved in with him (Lam, 1996).

Spouse Abuse Resulting from an Inability to Deal with Caregiving Responsibilities, Acting-Out Behavior Associated with Dementia, a Life Event such as Retirement, or Aging-out Spouse Abuse

Exploitation by Spouse of Alzheimer's Victim

Mr. M. is a 72-year-old man suffering from Alzheimer's disease. He was living with his wife of 5 years; she is 20 years younger than he and married him before the effects of his illness were apparent. While the couple's income and resources were adequate to meet their needs, there were significant rent arrears, and Mr. M. complained to neighbors of being constantly hungry. Mr. M. had over $75,000 in a bank account, which was now depleted. His wife had rented a room in the apartment to a younger male tenant, and neighbors witnessed both the tenant and Mrs. M. being verbally abusive to Mr. M. at times. Mr. M.'s daughter by a first marriage lived out of state and had not visited her father since his remarriage. Finally, the landlord issued a dispossess order for nonpayment of rent, and moved to evict Mr. and Mrs. M., along with their tenant. Mr. M. appeared unaware of his financial status, or the implications of the eviction. He expressed fear that his wife would leave, however, as he perceived himself to be dependent on her for support.

Aging-Out Spouse Abuse.   Aging-out spouse abuse refers to a domestic violence situation involving a long-time battered woman who—with her husband batterer—has now reached or surpassed the age of 60 years.

Mrs. S., age 74, was referred to a group for older abuse victims run by a social worker at a community-based agency serving older adults. She stated that she was ready to leave her abusive husband of 30 years, as she had been diagnosed with breast cancer. While her doctor had assured her it was operative, this made her realize how little support she received from her husband, and she was determined to make her physical illness the precipitating factor in her leaving him and beginning life anew. Because he threatened to kill her if she left, she chose to consider a domestic violence shelter. When the social worker made inquiries about shelters, however, she was told that none in the vicinity would accept an older woman, particularly if she had a health problem.

ELDER ABUSE PREVENTION

Prevention of elder abuse is possible with prior planning and careful safeguards (Douglass, 1987, 1991; New York City Department for the Aged, n.d.). Financial resources can be safeguarded through powers of attorney and other legal arrangements made by older adults with the assistance of an attorney. Protective payment mechanisms for public benefits and pensions and guardianship can be highly effective in preventing abuse of functionally incapacitated elders.

Maintaining strong social networks through active membership in senior clubs and centers can mitigate against loneliness and isolation, both risk factors for elder abuse and exploitation. Living alone or with an impaired adult child or abusive spouse can also make an older adult more vulnerable to abuse and exploitation, while sharing a residence with more than one relative or friend can mitigate against this. Community-based services, including protective services for adults, home care, financial management services, and community guardianship programs can be effective in alleviating isolation and reducing vulnerability.

It is possible to organize an elder abuse prevention network in the community (Nerenberg & Garbuio, n.d.). The planning for a community-based prevention network includes conducting a needs assessment. This should include the scope of the problem and available services, deciding on the membership, establishing tasks, designing a service delivery program, and formalizing the program. A task force or coalition can address problems of fragmentation among service systems such as Adult Protective Services (APS), the local Area Aging Agency, and the domestic violence service network. It can also improve linkages with health and mental health service providers, law enforcement, and other community institutions. Finally, a community-based elder abuse prevention network can raise community consciousness about elder abuse, and advocate more effectively than can single agencies for funding from state and other government agencies and foundations (Nerenberg & Garbuio, n.d.).

DETECTION

If elder abuse or exploitation occurs, victims are often reluctant to share this information, out of shame or fear (Breckman & Adelman, 1988; Quinn & Tomita, 1997). It is often left to the professional with whom the older adult may have contact to assess whether abuse or exploitation may be a factor in the older person's life.

An initial step for the professional in detection of elder abuse is eliminating stereotyped beliefs about victims and abusers. Both victims and perpetrators come from every racial, ethnic, and economic group. "Although obvious physical symptoms may exist, often the injuries are emotional and psychological, especially triggering feelings of fear and powerlessness" (Dundorf & Brownell, 1995, p. 81).

When violence, threats or financial exploitation does occur, common symptoms include:

- Unexplained bruises or cuts;
- Uncharacteristic withdrawal and evasiveness;
- Inability to pay bills, keep food in the house, or engage in normal activities, in spite of apparently sufficient income to do so;
- Visible manifestations of fear, particularly in the presence of certain family members (Douglass, 1987; Quinn & Tomita, 1997).

Symptoms of elder abuse can be detected by health and mental health professionals, community-based agencies serving the elderly and their families, law enforcement agents, family members, friends, and neighbors. In addition, banks and other financial institutions in the community, mail carriers, and superintendents and doormen are important frontline detectors of possible elder mistreatment.

SOCIAL WELFARE SYSTEMS AND SERVICES FOR ELDER ABUSE VICTIMS

Once possible elder abuse is detected, one of three social welfare systems may be engaged as part of an intervention strategy: Protective Services for Adults or Adult Protective Services (APS), as it is also known; Area Aging Agencies (Triple As), and local domestic violence (DV) networks. Often, however, professionals, including social workers, do not understand the historical roots of these systems, and so have difficulty understanding the distinctions among them. This can result in difficulties in determining what elder abuse situations should be referred to which service system. A brief historical overview is given here to deepen the professional worker's understanding of each service system.

Public Welfare and Deinstitutionalization

Elder mistreatment has been a concern of social workers even before it was identified as a distinct form of domestic violence in the late 1970s by sociologists, psychologists, and medical professionals. This is due to the unique interrelationship between social work and public welfare that began with the New Deal and the passage of the Social Security Act of 1935 (U.S. Department of Health and Human Services, 1982).

Through the enactment of Title I of the Social Security Act, which implemented Old Age Assistance, states were required to provide social support as well as financial benefits to indigent elderly incapable of protecting themselves from abuse and exploitation due to mental and physical infirmities.

This initiated the framing of elder mistreatment as a protective services issue related to mental and physical impairments of the elderly victim. Social workers and social service workers employed by state and county public welfare departments were charged with the responsibility of protecting frail elders receiving public welfare benefits. Thus began an initially ill-defined but new direction for social service delivery to older adults in the United States.

Inspired in part by the social work ideals of the 19th-century settlement house movement, the Social Security Act of 1935 provided a federally guaranteed subsidy for indigent elderly choosing to remain living in their communities (Axinn & Levin, 1997). Prior to the passage of this legislation, American public policy reflected English Poor Law tenets mandating familial or local responsibility for indigent dependents who were categorized as unemployable (the so-called "worthy poor"). Most indigent elders lived with families who were legally responsible for their care, in county "homes"— early 20th century versions of the almshouse—or in institutions for the mentally insane (Grob, 1994).

In the 19th century, the development of specialized institutions for dependents with what was then considered deprivation factors (orphaned children, the blind, the mentally ill, including older people with dementia, and others) reflected a significant social welfare trend. This trend was paralleled in the 20th century with a movement toward deinstitutionalization, community-based care, and in-home support for those unable to care for themselves due to age, impairments, or other infirmities.

The Social Security Act of 1935 (P.L. 271-74, II. R. 7260, August 4, 1935) (Axinn & Levin, 1997) established social insurance for selected retirees and their dependents, as well as social assistance for dependent children living with indigent single mothers, indigent elderly, and indigent blind. The trend toward community-based services continued with foster care in private homes for orphaned, abandoned, and abused children. Advances in psychotropic medications made in the 1950s led to deinstitutionalization policies for the institutionalized mentally ill, including many elderly inpatients, in the 1960s.

A growing advocacy movement for the elderly culminated in the White House Conference on Aging in 1961 and the passage of the Older Americans Act of 1965 (U.S. Senate Special Committee on Aging, 1997). A key purpose of this act was to provide funding for programs enabling older adults to remain in the community as long as possible with nutritional, recreational, social service, and in-home supports. Area Aging Agencies were established to serve as government planning and coordinating entities, as well as conduits for Older Americans Act funding, and for community-based services to older adults aged 60 and above by not-for-profit service providers (Gelfand, 1988).

In addition, the Social Security Act was amended in 1956 to include social assistance for the disabled, including the noninstitutionalized mentally disabled (Axinn & Levin, 1997). In 1962, social assistance for the indigent disabled, aged, and blind was combined into one program, which was administered by the federal government beginning 1974, called Supplemental Security Income (SSI). With the passage of the Title XX Amendment to the Social Security Act in 1974, states were provided with federal funding for non-means tested social services to adults and children in need of care and protection, including day care, domestic violence services, and Adult Protective Services (APS).

As a result of 20th-century social welfare trends, many initiated by social work professionals, a broad array of social welfare institutions have evolved in the community to address domestic violence across the lifespan. These include protective and preventive child abuse and neglect services, both residential and nonresidential emergency domestic violence programs, community-based programs for the elderly funded by Older Americans Act dollars, and Adult Protective Services (APS).

The latter category of service was intended to provide case management and access to an array of social, legal, and health services, on an involuntary basis if necessary, to adults living in the community who were at risk of harm due to mental or other impairments. Services are designed to prevent or remedy abuse by strengthening, to the extent possible, the elder's capacity to function as independently as possible. State and county protective services for adults programs were begun in the mid 1970s by state and county welfare agencies operating under new state statutes and regulations (Biggs, Phillipson, & Kingston, 1995).

For one particularly vulnerable category of abuse victims—the incapacitated and judgment-impaired elderly—Adult Protective Services (APS) stands out as a major public welfare program in which social workers intervene in situations where older adults are mistreated by family members, significant others, and neighbors.

Overview of Protective Services Response to Elder Abuse

Protective Services for Adults (also known as Adult Protective Services or APS) is a system of services aimed at maintaining incapacitated adults who are at risk of harm in the community as long as possible to prevent institutionalization (New York Elder Abuse Coalition [NYEAC], 1996). Services delivered through APS systems are designed to prevent or remedy the neglect, exploitation, or abuse of adults by strengthening—to the extent possible—the adult's ability to be self-directing, and the capacity of the affected adult and their immediate support systems to function optimally in the community.

The access point to APS services for impaired elder abuse victims is the state- or county-operated Adult Protective Service (APS) program. All 50 states have APS programs that operate under state statute and regulation. Most state and county APS programs were initiated in the mid-1970s, with the passage of the Title XX amendment to the Social Security Act (changed to the Social Services Block Grant in 1981 under the Reagan Administration) that provides federal-state matching funds for personal social services to vulnerable client populations. The ability of states and localities to serve impaired adults in the community was further strengthened by the assumption of federal responsibility for administering public assistance for the disabled, aged, and blind (DAB) categories through the Supplemental Security Income (SSI) program beginning in 1974.

In the 1980s, when abuse and mistreatment of older adults began to be framed as a significant social problem (Wolf, 1988), many state legislatures began to pass state laws mandating reporting of suspected elder abuse to state registers, modeled after child abuse central registries. As with mandatory reporting of child abuse, certain categories of professionals, such as physicians, nurses, and social workers, were required to report suspected cases of abuse and exploitation of adults aged 60 years and over to a central coordinating agency (generally an adult protective services or law enforcement office staffed by APS workers).

In the eight states that do not require mandatory reporting of elder abuse, provisions are made to professionals as well as nonprofessionals and the lay public for voluntary reporting of elder abuse. In APS systems in states like New York—which does not have a mandated reporting system for elder abuse—the emphasis is on educating professionals and the public about the problem of elder abuse and services that are available for elder abuse victims, and on encouraging the public to access county-administered APS and other services.

To protect reporters from breach of confidentiality or lawsuits, most states without elder abuse reporting mandates have statutes such as Section 473-b of the New York State Social Services law, that specifically provide immunity from civil liability to persons who, in good faith, report an adult whom they believe may be endangered or in need of protection (Abelman, 1997). Most states also have laws that enable APS programs to withhold information about people making referrals if a determination is made that this may be detrimental to their safety or interests.

A distinguishing factor of service provision by APS, as opposed to nongovernmental service programs—such as those provided through community-based organizations funded by Older American Act dollars, or established to address partner abuse—is the ability to provide services on an involuntary basis to adults who are assessed as incapable of making informed choices to avoid a serious threat to their safety and well-being. Professional assessment of the extent of risk or danger to an impaired adult living in the community can be made without the consent of an adult reported as a victim of abuse or neglect that places them seriously at risk.

Two legal principles provide APS, representing the state, with the authority to intervene in suspected cases of mistreatment or abuse of impaired adults. One is the police power of the state, giving the state authority to regulate activities that endanger the health and safety of others. The second is *parens patriae*, a legal principle adopted from English common law, that gives the state authority to act in a parental capacity for people who cannot care for themselves, or whose incapacitated state renders them a danger to themselves or others.

Actions taken against the wishes of abused elders generally require formal judicial proceedings and are monitored by the courts. Examples of interventions that APS can use without the consent of the incapacitated adult in crisis situations include:

Access Orders, where APS cannot investigate a referral because access is denied by that person or someone else in the household;

Short-term Involuntary Protective Services Orders, where APS can request a court order to provide involuntary emergency services, including involuntary commitment to a medical or psychiatric institution, for a defined period of time, for a nonconsenting adult at imminent risk of death or serious physical harm;

Orders of Protection, instructing an abusive person to refrain from harming a victimized adult unable to protect themselves from harm, preventing needed services (such as home care) from being provided, or to participate in a substance-abuse or counseling program;

Referrals to a law enforcement agency or district attorney's office without the consent of the incapacitated adult being abused or exploited, if the actions of the abuser constitute a criminal offense; and

Guardianships, as a last resort, may be requested by APS through petitioning the court when long-term management of impaired adults and/or their property is required.

An Overview of the Administration on Aging and Aging Agencies' Response to Elder Abuse

The Older Americans Act (P.L. 89-73, July 14, 1965, 79 Stat. 218), legislated during Lyndon Johnson's presidency in 1965, authorized the formation of state and area aging agencies to plan and serve as funding conduits for a coordinated network of services to assist older adults age 60 and above in remaining in the community as long as possible (Gelfand, 1988). Additional legislation passed in 1965 included Titles XVIII (Medicare) and XIX (Medicaid) of the Social Security Act; the Community Mental Health Centers Act (P.L. 88-164, Title II, October 31, 1963, 77 Stat. 290) appropriating federal funding for staffing and services (Grob, 1994), and the Civil Rights Act (P.L. 88-352, July 2, 1964, 78 Stat. 241) (Axinn & Levin, 1997). All have implications for the identification of elder abuse as a form of domestic violence and a significant social problem today.

In 1992, the Older Americans Act was amended to include Title VII: Allotments for Vulnerable Elder Rights Protection Activities. Chapter III includes a provision for programs for prevention of elder abuse, neglect, and exploitation. State aging agencies were instructed under Section 721 to develop and enhance programs for the prevention of elder abuse, neglect and exploitation, in consultation with Area Aging Agencies.

Involvement in addressing elder abuse is not new to state Aging Agencies. One example is the voluntary elder abuse reporting and intervention implemented by the State of Illinois (Neale, Hwalek, Goodrich, & Quinn, 1996). The amendment to the Older Americans Act reflected recognition within the aging advocacy community that elder abuse was not simply a protective service problem for impaired older adults.

Important studies, like the Boston survey of older adults living in the community by Pillemer and Finkelhor (1988), found that unimpaired older adults, many caring for impaired adult children, were also vulnerable to abuse and exploitation. This category of abuse victim does not demonstrate the level of cognitive or physical impairment required for eligibility for APS programs. It also reflected a growing concern that older Americans require more than in-home services, nutrition and socialization programs, transportation, and caregiver support to remain living independently in the community.

Chapter III of Title VII, amendment to the Older Americans Act, allocated funding for public education and outreach to identify and prevent elder abuse, neglect and exploitation, ensure the coordination of services of the triple As with APS agencies; conduct training of professionals working with the elderly (including law enforcement agents as well as those working within the aging network); promote the development of information and data systems, including elder abuse reporting systems, to quantify the extent of elder abuse, neglect and exploitation in the state; and support the development of model community-based assessment, detection, intervention, and prevention programs.

The primary emphasis of programs and initiatives funded through the Older Americans Act amendment is on the autonomy and self-determination of the older abuse victim. This presumes that identified victims are sufficiently cognitively intact to make an informed judgement about their abusive situation. Linkages with APS agencies enable Triple As to screen out and refer to APS situations that appear to involve a cognitively impaired victim. Only APS is able to intervene in situations where a nonconsenting older adult may be at risk of harm by a family member or significant other.

Domestic Violence Network

Concern about spouse and partner abuse grew out of the grass-roots feminist movement and the victims' rights movement fueled by the civil rights movement of the 1960s (Pleck, 1987; Schechter, 1982). While early domestic violence shelters and crisis intervention programs were initially funded through private donations and staffed by volunteers, political advocacy by feminist legislators and advocates during the 1970s paved the way for funding through Emergency Assistance to Families (Title IV of the Social Security Act), as well as Title XX Amendment to the Social Security Act, for an extensive network of battered women's shelters and programs.

Because of an assumption that the domestic violence network would serve younger women with children, service models developed and operated with public funds were designed with this population in mind. Some studies, notably by Berman and Salamone (1996) and Vinton, (1992), found that domestic violence shelters were excluding older battered women—either by policy, or because of a lack of appropriate programming and staff training.

While some studies were finding that older men were as likely as older women to be victims of abuse or exploitation (NCEA, 1995; Pillemer & Finkelhor, 1988), there was an awakening of interest among domestic violence advocates in the plight of older battered women. The San Francisco-based Older Women's Advocacy Project, the Older Women's League (OWL), and the New York State Office for the Prevention of Domestic Violence are three examples of organizations, two not-for-profit and one government funded, that have begun to focus on the service needs of older women who are victims of domestic violence.

Of particular interest to these groups to date is the victim of "aging-out" spouse or partner abuse. The issue of spouse abuse becomes more complex with the increasing age of victim and perpetrator, however. Frailty and cognitive impairment of one or both partners makes the criminal justice approach favored by many battered women's advocates inappropriate for many older couples. Offering escape and safe refuge to a long-time older abuse victim may precipitate an episode of severe depression. Shelters and other crisis intervention services designed for younger women with children may not feel comfortable to older women, nor offer the needed socialization and peer group support (McDowell & Raymond, 1988).

CRISIS INTERVENTION MODELS

Domestic violence can represent a crisis in the lives of both victim and perpetrator that can represent either deterioration or the possibility for intervention and resolution of relationship difficulties. According to Roberts, a crisis includes five key components: a hazardous event, a vulnerable state, a precipitating factor, an active crisis state, and a resolution (Roberts, 1996). The crisis represents a reaction to a life event that is subjective and destabilizing. It can overwhelm available coping mechanisms and cause impaired ability to function.

Crisis Intervention Strategies for Elder Mistreatment

One model that has been found to be successful in working with people in crisis, including victims of domestic violence, is Roberts' Seven-Stage Crisis Intervention Model (Roberts, 1996). This is a hierarchical model that moves the intervention from assessing life-threatening danger (Stage One); through establishing an emotional connectedness with the person in crisis (Stage Two); identifying major problems in priority order, including the precipitating event (Stage Three); use of verbal and nonverbal counseling skills in addressing emotions (Stage Four); identifying alternative coping strategies (Stage Five); developing and implementing a service plan that the client can act upon (Stage Six); to the final stage, follow-up (Stage Seven). This stage follows the resolution of the immediate crisis, identified prior to Stage One (assessment of life-threatening danger).

This model incorporates many principles of social work practice, such as client self-determination and engagement. Successfully applying it in work with victims of elder mistreatment, however, requires some consideration at each stage of the unique problems and issues an elder abuse victim may present to the practitioner. These can include the client's physical and mental capabilities, cooperativeness and motivation to change, the pathology of the abuser, and the severity of the situation (Quinn & Tomita, 1997).

The Elder Abuse Diagnosis and Intervention (EADI) model is a crisis intervention model that has been developed specifically for practitioners who work with elder abuse victims (Quinn & Tomita, 1997). This model consists of two phases: diagnosis and intervention. The diagnosis phase includes steps in conducting an assessment of whether elder mistreatment is in fact an issue with the older client. It includes protocols and assessment and diagnostic instruments to facilitate making an accurate assessment of whether abuse may be occurring, whether or not the client is capable of disclosing this information directly.

The EADI model parallels Roberts' Seven-Stage Model, beginning with an assessment of the degree of harm faced by the older victim. The intervention phase utilizes information about the victims and abuser gathered during the assessment phase. This includes the client's capabilities, level of cooperativeness, impairment of the abuser, and nature and seriousness of the abuse.

The model provides a guide to practitioners dealing with some of the unique features of elder mistreatment infrequently encountered by professionals working with younger victims of domestic violence. These include crisis intervention strategies to address financial, as well as medical, emergencies. The practitioner may take a more proactive stance with an elder abuse victim, assuming the role of case manager to mobilize other resources and services on the victim's behalf, depending on the assessed level of the victim's functioning (Quinn & Tomita, 1997).

It is at this stage that an assessment of the need for a protective, as opposed to an empowerment, service intervention strategy becomes critical (Dundorf & Brownell, 1995). Ethical practice requires that the least restrictive alternative is selected to ensure that clients are able to remain safely in their community or residence. However, during the assessment phase, information may be obtained that suggests imminent risk of harm for identified victims or abusers, or physical or cognitive impairment on the part of victims that could render them unable to protect themselves or make informed decisions about accepting services.

If imminent danger or possible impairment is identified, practitioners should alert the Adult Protective Services office in the state or county. An alternative for practitioners in states mandating reporting of elder abuse is to follow the guidelines set by state statute and regulation. If the client is willing to accept services and is not cognitively impaired, a local community-based agency funded by the State or Area Aging Agency to provide services to older adults may be a resource. This is particularly appropriate if the abuse does not constitute a criminal act or a matter that should be handled in a court setting or by law enforcement.

If the abuse does constitute a criminal act, a referral to the local police, court, or court-based social service agency can be useful for the motivated older victim. The legal and domestic violence systems often intersect, and victims of aging-out spouse abuse—assuming no major complications that are correlated with age and infirmity—can be served by some domestic violence programs. Studies have shown, however, that this system has developed a limited capacity to date to address the needs of older victims of spouse abuse (Berman & Salamone, 1996; Vinton, 1992).

An assessment may reveal incapacity on the part of the older victim, or severe pathology on the part of the abuser that could cause imminent risk to others—including the victim. In this situation, a referral to Adult Protective Services (APS) is recommended by the EADI model (Quinn & Tomita, 1997). APS is a case management system, and the success of APS interventions—particularly when the client's situation requires long-term treatment to resolve—often depends on collaboration with other service systems, including the community-based aging service network, entitlement programs, and health and mental health service providers. Unlike these service providers, however, APS is empowered by state statute to intervene on an involuntary basis, if necessary, to protect an elder abuse victim who is at risk of further abuse or exploitation.

While APS is unable to impose services on an involuntary elder abuse victim directly, it has access to legal interventions that can range from the least restrictive to the most restrictive. Examples range from arranging for direct deposit of a Social Security check, or obtaining a protective or representative payee, to guardianships that assume full surrogate decision making over a client's possessions or person. APS can also initiate criminal proceedings against an abuser without the cooperation or permission of the victim.

The type of abuse, as well as the profile of the abuser/victim and special needs of the victim, should guide the practitioner as to which service system to engage in order to assist the identified elder abuse victim most effectively. Concrete benefits and services such as food stamps, Supplemental Security Income, home care, Medicaid, and supported housing are often critical to the stabilization of the crisis situation. Medical care for physically abused victims, and orders of protection for those menaced or harassed by abusers, are other services that may be needed immediately upon assessment and detection of abuse.

Longer-range counseling, including the use of support groups, can be useful once the immediate crisis is addressed. Post-traumatic stress disorder (PSDT), a recognized problem with younger victims of family abuse, has only begun to be recognized and treated among older adults (Hankin, Gallagher-Thompson, Abueg, & Laws, 1996) and elder abuse victims (Podnicks, 1993). Victim support groups—another modality used as part of an empowerment strategy with younger victims of partner abuse—have also begun to be used with elder abuse victims who are cognitively intact (McGovern, 1996).

Creative sentencing for abusers has been utilized by some District Attorney's offices, including the Manhattan D.A.'s office, to encourage elder abuse victims to prosecute adult children abusers who are also substance abusers. This includes mandated attendance in Alternative to Incarceration (ATI) programs for substance abusers. The criminal justice intervention has limited application to some forms of elder abuse, such as neglect or abuse by an overwhelmed caregiver or an elderly spouse suffering from dementia. A service plan that considers the needs of the victim's family is often critical to the successful resolution of the abuse situation.

DISCUSSION OF CRISIS INTERVENTION AND SERVICE PLANNING

The case examples presented at the beginning of the chapter can be used to illustrate how professionals working with victims of elder abuse can plan effective crisis intervention strategies and develop appropriate service plans.

The Competent Elder Abuse Victim

The case of Mrs. B. demonstrates that not all crises involving the older victim of family mistreatment are precipitated by growing impairment of the victim. Pillemer and Finkelhor (1988) have pointed out that competent and healthy older adults can become targets of abuse by impaired adult children or grandchildren. Older victims may assume caregiving or protective relationships with children or grandchildren who may be mentally ill or have a substance abuse problem, sometimes taking pride in being the one family member who does not abandon the troubled loved one. This is a case situation that is most appropriately referred to a local area aging agency. In the case of Mrs. B., she did not meet the APS requirement that she be judgment-impaired and lack the capacity to make informed decisions about life choices, such as maintaining a relationship with a substance-abusing and possibly dangerous granddaughter. A community-based agency funded through the local Triple A could have assisted Mrs. B. to consider her options for protecting herself—such as getting an Order of Protection, or reporting the matter to the police in a way that did not put her at risk of harm. She could have also received counseling intended to empower her to set limits on her granddaughter's behavior. The willingness of the District Attorney's office to offer an alternative to incarceration—such as mandatory substance abuse treatment—might also have helped to persuade Mrs. B. to press charges against her granddaughter because it could have provided assistance for her substance-abuse problems.

The Judgment Impaired Elder Abuse Victim

For older victims of mistreatment by family members or significant others, like Mrs. C., the inability to cope with an abusive situation can arise from many causes. These causes can include mental and physical deterioration caused by disease and illness, such as dementia or a debilitating and progressive illness such as Parkinson's Disease. Involuntary confinement and transfer of assets without the consent of the older victim are examples of both physical and financial abuse. However, even when there may be an awareness of being victimized on the part of the victim, impairments induced by complications of illness or abusive treatment, including starvation and other forms of physical abuse and threats, may significantly interfere with an older victim's ability to disclose pertinent information. Abusers may use stereotyped beliefs about older people to manipulate others into thinking that the older victim lacks capacity or should not be believed.

The case of Mrs. C. demonstrates how older victims of family mistreatment may have difficulty seeking or obtaining opportunities for resolution of the crisis precipitated by elder abuse. This may be the case even if they have a compromised physical or emotional status that would not present a similar barrier to a younger victim of domestic violence. This client's lack of capacity, coupled with her deteriorated physical status, makes her a candidate for APS services. Adult Protective Services can also intervene when there is an involuntary element to the case—in this situation, the son consistently refused services on behalf of his mother.

Spouse Abuse that Includes Exploitation of an Impaired Elderly Partner

The example of Mr. M. illustrates how an older victim of mistreatment in a vulnerable state due to a deteriorating physical and mental condition may experience a hazardous event, a precipitating factor (in this case, an impending eviction), and a sense of crisis and fear. In the case of Mr. M., previous coping mechanisms may not be available to him because of his compromised physical and mental status. Resolution of the crisis is hampered, however, because of Mr. M.'s limited perception of his options and his inability to recognize that the person on whom he is relying to protect him and care for him—his wife—may be the cause of the crisis he is experiencing. Although this is a spouse-abuse case, the client's judgment, mental status, and the financial exploitation he is experiencing make him a candidate for APS.

Aging-Out Spouse Abuse

Spouse abuse involving physical abuse, such as in the case of Mrs. S., has been found to be the most common form of abuse among older adults in some studies, most prominently by Pillemer and Finkelhor (1988). This may represent "aging-out" partner abuse, or a longstanding pattern of abuse that continues as the couple grows older. Some studies have suggested that the victim may adapt to this abusive pattern in their relationship, and become depressed if the abusive partner dies or leaves. This may precipitate an emotional crisis. Alternatively, if the victim becomes sufficiently impaired with illnesses correlated with age, the victim may find that the abuse is less easily tolerated, and may choose to leave the abuser. Neither the victim nor the professional social worker may consider traditional domestic violence shelters as an option. These shelters often lack appropriately trained staff or programs for older victims of spouse abuse, and protocols preclude accepting older victims of abuse, especially if they have any physical impairments.

Many of the dynamics of traditional spouse abuse may be present in relationships involving longstanding spouse abuse of one elderly partner by another. However, because this may be a long established pattern, and because both victim and abuser are older adults, there may be factors complicating efforts to apply crisis intervention techniques to the abuse situation. One source of crisis may not be the abuse, but the death or illness of the abuser.

Efforts to implement a safety plan as part of the crisis intervention may be stymied by inability to access services through the domestic violence service system, because of the age of the victim. Publicly funded domestic violence shelters are often prevented from discriminating against clients based on age, however, and in a life-threatening abuse involving two mentally competent spouses, local shelters can be persuaded to accept older women as residents.

COALITIONS ON ELDER ABUSE

In spite of current, as well as historical, differences in funding, etiology, and missions, the interests and concerns of the APS and aging and domestic violence networks are beginning to converge in their concern about elder abuse and exploitation. The recent amendment to the Older Americans Act (Title VII) mandates coordination between the Triple As and APS agencies. It also promotes training about elder abuse by the Triple As for law enforcement agencies and District Attorney's offices.

Coalitions like the National Center for Prevention of Elder Abuse and Neglect, as well as local and state coordinating entities and coalitions, are seeking to bring public, not-for-profit and for-profit organizations (such as banks and managed care organizations) together. Forums to develop coordinated strategies for preventing and intervening in elder abuse and exploitation include monthly steering committee meetings, training, and conferences. Large-scale studies like that undertaken by the APWA's National Center for Elder Abuse—in collaboration with universities, Administration on Aging, and the National Center for Prevention of Elder Abuse—can yield findings that have both program and policy implications.

One example of a successful local coalition is the New York City Elder Abuse Coalition. It has sponsored eight large, well-attended conferences, citywide issues meetings, and borough-wide case conferences. Its steering committee consists of representatives in the fields of aging, academia, social services, police, District Attorneys, and health care agencies. Its formation has led to improved coordination between agencies, and it has had an impact on passage of recent elder abuse and guardian legislation. In addition, the Coalition's efforts have had a positive impact on obtaining funding for specialized gap-filling services for elder abuse victims, including recent approval of funding of a specialized shelter for older adult victims of abuse and exploitation.

PROFILE OF ELDER ABUSE VICTIMS SERVED BY ADULT PROTECTIVE SERVICES

In states like New York, which does not have an elder abuse mandatory reporting system, surveys of APS caseloads can provide a picture of elder abuse that comes to the attention of APS and the extent to which elder abuse is present among incapacitated elders in the community. Descriptive studies of caseload profiles for systems like APS, the local Area Aging Agencies, and domestic violence networks shed important light on the demographic characteristics of elderly abuse victims and their perpetrators, as well as risk factors, types of abuse experienced, and service needs.

One such study examined a random sample of 250 cases authorized for APS in New York State between January 1 and July 15, 1995 (Abelman, 1997). Of these, 158 cases were identified as representing clients 60 years of age and older. A total of 61, or 39%, were found to be abused or neglected by a family member or significant other, as opposed to 97, or 61%, who were victims of self-neglect only (Abelman, 1997).

While self-neglect is considered a form of elder abuse in some states, this is not the case in New York; abuse and self-neglect were differentiated in the study. Abuse was considered to be present if the case record identified evidence of abuse, neglect, or exploitation by another person, while cases were considered to be "self-neglect only" if there was no evidence of abuse, neglect, or exploitation by another person (Abelman, 1997).

The study focused on the following substantive areas:

- *Referral information*: Referral sources and problems APS experienced obtaining access to the client;
- *Recipient demographics*: Age, gender, household composition, income, and resources;
- *Mental and physical limitations*: Cognitive capacity, ability to leave own home, and incapacitating conditions;
- *Risk factors*: Nature of abuse, abuser gender, abuser relationship, and abuser incapacity;
- *Recipient support systems*: Informal and formal supports; and
- *Services provided*: Services objective, services, and legal and emergency interventions.

Selected Findings

Referral Information

- Health care providers were the most frequent referral source (21%). Overall, almost twice as many abuse referrals were received from health care providers than from any other referral source.
- Obtaining access to the recipient was not identified as a problem in a large majority of abuse cases.

Recipient Demographics

- Recipients in the 75-and-older category were the most likely to be identified as abuse victims.

- Abuse victims were more than twice as likely to be female than male (42 female, as compared with 20 male victims).
- Abuse victims were more likely to live with others than live alone.
- Social Security, pensions and homes, or other real estate were the predominant sources of income and resources for abuse victims.

Mental and Physical Limitations

- The majority of abuse victims were sometimes unable to make reasoned decisions (42) as compared with those always unable to make reasoned decisions (9) or always able to make reasoned decisions (11).
- The majority of abuse victims were only able to leave home with assistance (38, as compared with 5 who were unable to leave home at all, and 18 who could leave home without assistance).
- The most frequently cited incapacitating conditions for abuse victims were physical disability and frailty, followed by dementia.

Risk Factors

- The type of abuse most frequently cited for victims of elder abuse on the APS caseload was financial exploitation, followed by neglect by a caregiver and emotional abuse.
- Overall, abusers were most likely to be male (36) than female (25). However, for the 60-to-74-year-old group, abusers were almost equally likely to be male as female. The disparity became greater for the 75-and-older age group.
- Unrelated friends, neighbors and acquaintances were cited as abusers most frequently, followed by adult children and spouses and other relatives.
- Mental incapacity of the abuser was cited in the majority of cases, followed by substance abuse.

Recipient Support Systems

- A relative was the most frequently cited source of informal support for abuse victims in the sample. Health care providers were the most frequently identified formal support, followed by mental health providers.

Services Provided by APS

- The service plan for the majority of identified abuse victims was to remain in the community with voluntary services. The second most frequently cited service plan was to remain in the community with some involuntary services.
- Home care was the most frequently cited service provided, followed by mental health services.
- Orders of support and psychiatric hospitalization were the two most frequently utilized legal and emergency interventions.

NORTH CAROLINA ADULT PROTECTIVE SERVICES

The New York State study described above is in contrast with a study of the State of North Carolina Adult Protective Services caseload. North Carolina has a mandatory reporting system for elder abuse and neglect: APS is responsible for assessing these, as well as other referrals of adults in need of protection (North Carolina Adult Protective Services, 1996).

Disabled adults 60 years of age and over make up 74% of the North Carolina APS cases; disabled adults aged 18 to 59 make up the balance (26%). Of those referred, self-neglect comprised the largest category (42%), followed by caretaker neglect (33%), abuse (17%), and exploitation (8%). Women were most likely to be referred to county departments of social services as needing APS (65%, as contrasted with 35% men). This is proportionally consistent with the gender breakdown of women (61%) as compared with men (39%) 60 years of age residing in North Carolina.

Of the total number of adults receiving services from APS in North Carolina, 59% were White, 39% Black, and 2% were categorized as "other." This latter category includes Native American, Hispanic, and Asian/Pacific Islander. In North Carolina, Native Americans made up 81% of the "other" category.

The data for the North Carolina study was collected between July 1, 1994, and June 30, 1995, based on aggregated statistical information on the state APS program. The collection of this data was made possible through the development of the North Carolina Adult Protective Service Register, which compiles data entered on-line from the county-based APS divisions.

NATIONAL DATA ON ELDER ABUSE AND NEGLECT

National Center on Elder Abuse

The National Center on Elder Abuse (NCEA) was established in September 1993 through a grant awarded to the American Public Welfare Association (APWA) by the Administration on Aging. It is operated by a consortium of four organizations: APWA, the National Association of State Units on Aging, the University of Delaware College of Human Resources, and the National Committee for pre-vention of Elder Abuse (NCEA, 1995). As a central clearinghouse for national elder abuse and neglect data, it reports on incidence and prevalence of elder abuse, including victim and abuser character-istics, reporters and report-receiving agencies for elder abuse and neglect, and types of reported abuse and neglect. Reports are based on data from both APS and Area Aging Agencies (NCEA, 1996).

According to NCEA, there has been an increase in the reporting of domestic elder abuse nationally between 1986, when national statistics began to be compiled, and 1994. The 241,0000 reports made in 1994 represent a 106% increase over the 117,000 reports recorded in 1986. In addition, some experts have estimated that of every one domestic elder abuse incidents reported to APS agencies, 13 others remain unreported. This suggests that the current estimates on incidence and prevalence of elder abuse seriously underrepresent this problem.

Types of Reported Elder Abuse

According to NCEA (1995), neglect (excluding self-neglect) repre-sented the largest category of reported abuse nationally in 1994 (58.5%). This was followed by physical abuse (15.7%), financial/

material exploitation (12.3%), emotional abuse (7.3%), "unknown" (.6%), and sexual abuse (.5%). An "other" category comprised 5.1% of domestic elder abuse reports.

Characteristics of Victims

According to NCEA, data collected in 1994 shows the median age of elder abuse victims as 76.5 years. The majority of elder abuse victims were female (62.1%, as compared to 37.8% male victims). The majority of domestic elder abuse victims were White in 1994 (65.4%), as compared to 21.4% Black, 9.6% Hispanic, and less than 1% each for Native Americans and Asian Americans/Pacific Islanders (NCEA, 1995).

Characteristics of Perpetrators

According to NCEA, in 1994, the gender of perpetrators in a national sample was almost evenly divided (50.6% male and 49.3% female). This is in contrast to collected data from 1990, when males represented the majority of perpetrators (54.7%), as compared with 42.1% females. Adult children of victims are most commonly reported as perpetrators (36.7% in 1994). This is followed by other family members (14.8%) and spouses (13.8%).

Reporters of Elder Abuse

Incidence and prevalence reports of elder abuse collected by NCEA come primarily from states with mandatory reporting systems for elder abuse. Statutes identify certain categories of professionals who are mandated to report elder abuse, although reports may come from nonmandated sources as well.

In 1994, physicians and health care providers reported the greatest percentage of cases (21.9%), followed by family members (14.9%), "other" (13.4%), APS/Aging worker (9.5%), private/voluntary service providers (9.4%), friends and neighbors (9.2%), the victim

(6.4%), anonymous callers (4.5%), and law enforcement (4.2%). A small number (1.8%) are categorized as "unknown" (NCEA, 1995).

Agencies designated to receive reports of elder abuse, according to state statutes, include state or county APS programs law enforcement agencies, including local police departments and sheriff's offices (NCEA, 1995). Area aging agencies and community-based aging service providers may also receive calls about or from victims of elder abuse. Those referrals that suggest the elderly victim is mentally incapacitated and/or refusing services are generally referred on to APS for assessment (Dundorf & Brownell, 1995).

FINDINGS OF OTHER ELDER ABUSE STUDIES

While physical abuse is most often associated with elderly mistreatment, a New York study of the State Protective Services for Adults program found the most common form of elder abuse to be financial (Abelman, 1997). Physical abuse or threats (psychological abuse) may accompany or follow demands for money or material possessions by relatives, but is motivated by material gain and financial exploitation. Other studies, most notably that by Pillemer and Finkelhor (1988), suggest that spouses are more likely to inflict physical abuse than are other relations, including adult children.

CONCLUSION

Abuse and neglect of older adults by family members, significant others, and neighbors has been an issue of increasing concern since the 1980s. The elderly population in the United States is expected to increase by 17%, from 33.5 million in 1995 to 39.4 million in 2010 (U.S. Bureau of the Census, 1996). However, as longevity increases, the growth of the oldest old (age 85 and above)—that cohort found to be most vulnerable to abuse and exploitation by some studies of incidence and prevalence of elder abuse—is of greatest concern.

According to the Bureau of the Census, between 1995 to 2010, this age group is expected to grow by 56%, as compared with 13% for the population between 65 to 84. As the baby-boom cohort ages out, especially between 2030 and 2050, the 85-and-over group will expand sharply, making the cumulative growth in the 85-and-over population between 1995 and 2050 anticipated at more than 400% (U.S. Bureau of the Census, 1996).

Even if the proportion of elders experiencing abuse and exploitation does not increase in the years ahead, the number of victims will increase with the anticipated demographic changes, unless effective ways of addressing the problem of elder abuse and mistreatment continue to be identified. Policy makers must keep in mind the vulnerability and potential for domestic abuse of the aging population in the United States in the coming years, at the same time as they grapple with ways to fund needed health care and other services.

Improved coordination between existing social welfare institutions and programs serving abuse victims and their families is essential. Social workers, with their professional training in the person-in-situation service paradigm, can take a leading role in the identification of gaps in service, new service needs, coordination of service systems, and in developing and testing effective intervention models. These include comprehensive models of assessment, detection, and intervention for elder abuse and mistreatment, like the Elder Abuse Diagnosis and Intervention (EADI) Model developed by Quinn and Tomita (1997). This can be replicated and adapted to many different service systems, from health, to aging, to criminal justice, to adult protective services.

The EADI model, which incorporates knowledge of crisis intervention, cognitive capacity, and mental status of victims and abusers, as well as ethical considerations of autonomy and self-determination, is particularly well-suited to a comprehensive professional approach to elder abuse and exploitation. Roberts' Seven-Stage Model of Crisis Intervention (Roberts, 1996) provides an underlying framework for understanding the importance of sequential steps necessary for crisis stabilization.

While social welfare institutions and service systems, framed by policy decisions, may take a long time to adapt to changing service and demographic imperatives, the service needs of elder abuse victims are immediate and compelling. As Quinn and Tomita (1997) note, prompt action can made the difference between life and death, or financial security or destitution.

Ethical issues in service delivery to elder abuse victims are ever-present (Collopy & Bial, 1994). The National Association of Social Worker (NASW) Code of Ethics requires social workers to respect clients' self-determination and ensure that services are provided on the basis of informed consent (NASW, 1996). However, Section 1 of the Code also instructs social workers that "in instances when clients lack the capacity to provide informed consent, social workers should protect clients' interests" (NASW, 1996, p. 8). A social work professional must weigh factors related to elder abuse victims' cognitive capacity, physical health, and level of risk before making a decision to use a protective or an empowerment service intervention strategy with elder abuse victims.

Professional social workers also have responsibility for addressing both immediate service needs, as well as longer-range policy issues. This includes identifying gaps in existing service systems for elder abuse victims, such as lack of access to emergency shelters, and advocating for resources to address these gaps. As the new NASW Code of Ethics states, "Social workers should act to expand choice and opportunity for all people, with special regard to vulnerable, disadvantaged, oppressed, and exploited people and groups" (NASW, 1996, p. 27). Social workers are ethically bound to value dignity and self-determination along with safety and protection in working with vulnerable elder-abuse victims and survivors.

REFERENCES

Abelman, I. (1997). *A study of the New York State Protective Services Caseload.* Unpublished manuscript.

Axinn, J., & Levin, H. (1997). *Social welfare: A history of the American response to need* (4th ed.). New York: Longman.

Berman, J., & Salamone, A. (1996). *Elder abuse victims and domestic violence shelters.* Unpublished manuscript.

Biggs, S., Phillipson, C., & Kingston, P. (1995). *Elder abuse in perspective.* Buckingham, UK: Open University Press.

Breckman, R., & Adelman, R. (1988). *Strategies for interventions into elder abuse.* Newbury Park, CA: Sage.

Brownell, P. (1996). Social work and criminal justice responses to elder abuse in New York City. In A. R. Roberts (Ed.), *Helping battered women: New perspectives and remedies* (pp. 44–66). New York: Oxford University Press.

Collopy, B., & Bial, M. (1994). Social work and bioethics: Ethical issues in long-term care practice. In I. Gutheil (Ed.), *Work with older people: Challenges and opportunities* (pp. 109–138). New York: Fordham University Press.

Douglass, R. L. (1987). *Domestic mistreatment of the elderly—Towards prevention.* Washington, DC: AARP.

Douglass, R. (1991). Reaching 30 million people to prevent abuse and neglect of the elderly: AARP's strategy for public self-education. In *Journal of Elder Abuse and Neglect, 3,* 73–85.

Dugger, C. (1991, October 31). When love doesn't conquer: Crack and murder. *New York Times,* p. A1.

Dundorf, K., & Brownell, P. (1995). When the victim is elderly. *The Family Advocate, 17*(3), 81–84.

Gelfand, D. (1988). *The aging network: Programs and services* (3rd ed.). New York: Springer Publishing Company.

Grob, G. (1994). *The mad among us: A history of the care of America's mentally ill.* New York: Free Press.

Hankin, C. S., Gallagher-Thompson, D., Abueg, F. R., & Laws, A. (1996). *Complexities in the diagnosis and treatment of post-traumatic stress disorder (PTSD) among older adults.* Poster presented at the 49th Annual Scientific Meeting of the Gerontological Society of America, Washington, DC.

Lam, C. (1996, April 2). Mom-abuse denied. *Newsday,* p. A7.

McDowell, D., & Raymond, J. (1988). Supporting the older battered woman. *The Exchange: National Woman Abuse Project,* pp. 4–9.

McGovern, P. H. (1996). *The impact of elder abuse support groups on the self-esteem of members.* Unpublished paper.

National Association of Social Workers. (1996). *Code of ethics.* Washington, DC: Author.

National Center on Elder Abuse. (1996). *Incidence Report* [On-line]. Available: http://www.interinc.com/NCEA

Neale, A. V., Hwalek, M. A., Goodrich, C. S., & Quinn, K. M. (1996). The Illinois elder abuse system: Program description and administrative findings. *Gerontologist, 16,* 502–511.

Nerenberg, L., & Garbuio, S. (n.d.). Organizing an elder abuse prevention network in your community. *Serving the victim of elder abuse* (pp. 34–41). Washington, DC: PERF.

New York City Department for the Aged. (n.d.). *How to avoid being a victim.* (Pamphlet).

New York Elder Abuse Coalition. (1996). *Elder Abuse Coalition Website* [On-line]. Available: http://www.ianet.org/nyeac/

North Carolina Adult Protective Services. (1996). *Report on Demographics of North Carolina Adult Protective Services Clients.* Available: http://www.state.nc.us/DHR/DSS/aps.htm

Pillemer, K., & Finkelhor, D. (1988). The prevalence of elder abuse: A random sample survey. *Gerontologist, 28,* 51–57.

Pleck, E. (1987). *Domestic tyranny: The making of American social policy against family violence from colonial times to the present.* New York: Oxford University Press.

Podnicks, E. (1992). National survey on abuse of the elderly in Canada. *Journal of Elder Abuse and Neglect, 4,* 5–58.

Quinn, M., & Tomita, S. (1997). *Elder abuse and neglect: Causes, diagnosis and intervention strategies.* New York: Springer Publishing Company.

Roberts, A. R. (1996). Epidemiology and definitions of acute crisis in American society. In A. R. Roberts (Ed.), *Crisis management and brief treatment: Theory, technique and applications* (pp. 16–33). Chicago, IL: Nelson-Hall.

Schechter, S. (1982). *Women and male violence: The visions and struggles of the battered women's movement.* Boston, MA: South End Press.

United States Bureau of the Census. (1996). *Demographic Changes and Growth of the Elderly Population.* Available: http://www.fedstats.gov/key-stats/CENkey.html

U.S. Department of Health and Human Services. (1982). *Protective services for adults* DHHS Publication No. (OHDS) 82-20505. Washington, DC: Author.

U.S. House of Representatives, Select Committee on Aging. (1990). *Elder abuse: Decade of shame and inaction.* Washington, DC: Government Printing Press.

U.S. Senate, Special Committee on Aging. (1997). *Developments in aging: 1996 volume I.* Washington, DC: U.S. Government Printing Office.

Vinton, L. (1992). Battered women's shelters and older women: The Florida experience. *Journal of Family Violence, 7,* 63–72.

Wolf, R. (1988). Elder abuse: Ten years later. *The Journal of the American Geriatrics Society, 36,* 758–762.

CHAPTER 14

Domestic Violence and Substance Abuse: An Integrated Approach

Katherine van Wormer

V ery often, when family members are beaten, alcohol or some other drug is involved. *Cherchez la drogue,* as the French might say. The abuser may be arming himself with 40-proof courage in preparation for an attack; the victim may be drowning her anguish with tranquilizers or alcohol. Moreover, the children may grow up to have problems with substance abuse and/or violence. All of these interconnections we know. What we don't know is the exact nature of the substance abuse/violence configuration: Does drinking cause violence, or does the urge to be violent lead to drinking? How does the victim's drinking come into play? Are such patterns of abuse/ victimization intergenerational?

The absence of clearcut research findings in the substance abuse literature concerning the substance abuse/partner abuse connection is, in part, a reflection of the serious inattention of substance abuse journals (until recently) to this matter. The domestic violence literature, likewise, sheds little light on the near-universal correlation between intoxication and violence. The real world of substance abuse treatment, meanwhile, is strong on ideology and soft on substance. And whether by design or tradition, the particular idealogues concerning substance abuse and domestic violence sharply demarcate the boundaries between them.

Predictably, substance abuse and domestic violence programs view the relationship between substance abuse and partner violence narrowly: the former through the lens of addiction and coaddiction, the latter through the lens of feminism. The absence of a coordination of efforts further impedes the growth of knowledge. As a feminist and member of both a domestic violence women's advocacy board and of a substance abuse treatment center board, and with over 4 years experience as an alcoholism counselor, I am constantly made aware of the potential and necessity for a holistic coordinated approach to fighting the twin evils of substance abuse and domestic violence. Such a concern, or rather, mission, is the impetus for this chapter.

In exploring the links between substance abuse and partner violence, the first task will be to summarize pertinent research findings. In this wealth of information, we will search for themes, filtering out competing explanatory models concerning the role of intoxication in violence. The substance abuse counselor's *addictions* model will be contrasted with the domestic violence program's *feminist* conceptualization. A biopsychosocial consideration of substance abuse and violent behavior reveals the commonalities of these two phenomena, commonalities that provide the basis for an integrated theoretical framework. Before achieving that goal, however, facts will be provided on two related treatment issues—the role of substance abuse in female violence and victimization, and the role of the use of substances in gay/lesbian partner abuse. The final portion of the chapter is devoted to implications for substance abuse counselors and domestic violence workers in working together in problem areas with considerable overlap. A joint enterprise between two agencies in northeastern Iowa is described.

THE CORRELATION BETWEEN SUBSTANCE ABUSE/PARTNER ABUSE

Violence against women is so entrenched that in 1992 the U.S. Surgeon General ranked abuse by husbands and partners as the leading cause of injuries to women aged 15 to 44 (Ingrassia & Beck, 1994). Despite more hot lines and shelters and substance abuse treatment for wife abusers, the number of assaults against women has not declined. A high risk factor reported by virtually all the experts is alcohol and drug abuse. Persons who are assaultive are likely to abuse drugs—especially alcohol—and those who abuse alcohol are prone to assault. Although recognizing that many alcoholics are never violent and many aggressors are sober, research findings reveal the following:

- Approximately one-half of clinical spouse-batterers have significant alcohol problems (Tolman & Bennett, 1990).
- One-half to two-thirds of married male alcoholics are physically aggressive toward their partners during the year before alcoholism treatment (Gondolf & Foster, 1991).
- In men, the combination of blue-collar status, drinking, and approval of violence is significantly associated with a high rate of wife abuse (Associated Press, 1996).
- Binge drinkers, as opposed to daily drinkers, have an inordinately high rate of reported assault (Gondolf & Foster, 1991; Murphy & O'Farrell, 1997).
- The female victims of abuse often also have substance abuse problems (Bennett & Lawson, 1994).
- Sixty percent of female substance abusers were victims of partner assault, according to estimates by treatment providers (Bennett & Lawson, 1994; B. A. Miller, Downs, & Gondoli, 1989).
- Over one-third of substance abuse patients in a V.A. program survey reported assaulting their wives in the previous year (Gondolf & Foster, 1991).

Of the close correlation between substance abuse and partner violence, therefore, there can be no doubt. The only doubt is over the interpretation of this relationship. What all researchers and treatment personnel agree on is the crying need to put a stop to the violence and the high-risk substance abuse. Unfortunately, the relationship between substance abuse and domestic violence programs is problematic (Bennett & Lawson, 1994). At the core of the problem is the tendency to dichotomize problems and to treat various components of antisocial behavior as separate entities. The differences arise not only from differing world views—disease model versus feminist approach—but from a parallel tendency to view reality in terms of linear causation.

THEORETICAL MODEL: INTERACTIONISM

The central guiding social work principle of today is the ecosystems conceptualization. This multidimensional approach views the human organism in its full biopsychosocial context. The ecological framework or metaphor is interactionist; it does not view the person and the environment as separate entities but, rather, looks at the intersection between them. In sharp contrast to linear or simple cause-and-effect thinking, wherein a cause (such as mental illness) precedes an effect (abusive drinking), ecological causality occurs in a circular loop (van Wormer, 1995).

An event or pattern such as violence may be viewed, accordingly, as at once both the cause and effect of substance abuse. Individuals joined in a system are impacted to the degree that they are reciprocally linked to the disturbed group or family member. The stress of substance abuse and/or violence has a synergistic or multiplying effect throughout the family system and related environmental network. From the practitioner's standpoint, what we are talking about is the need to perceive the *total* picture of the client's situation, the need to understand problematic behavior multidimensionally. Narrow specialization by discipline encourages a perception of reality as partial, incomplete, and ideological. Child welfare workers, for example, in their unidimensional focus on abuse of the child, very often overlook the dynamics of family violence in which wife assault as well as, perhaps, substance abuse, plays a vital role in the gestalt of family crisis.

One often finds that seemingly diverse worldviews, which seem to say opposite things, actually provide crucial information and are understandable when seen in terms of an integrative new theory.

OPPOSING MODELS

Persons trained in the highly influential disease model of substance abuse are subject to criticism for their failure to address the multidimensional nature of substance addiction (see van Wormer, 1995). Under this formulation, the substance (usually alcohol) is seen as the primary cause of any and all antisocial behavior. The treatment effort is geared overwhelmingly to acceptance of Step One of the AA (Alcoholics Anonymous) creed of admission that one is powerless over alcohol (or other substance or relationship).

Recently I came across a pamphlet from Al-Anon (the 12-step group for families of alcoholics) entitled "Domestic Violence" (Al-Anon, 1994). The personal story presented marks a positive step by this self-help group to address the dangers facing many of their members who are being abused by alcoholic family members. Some of the wording, however, would raise eyebrows among women's crisis line counselors. For instance:

> It was his violence that brought me to Al-Anon, where I learned I was dealing with a very sick person, and I too was ill . . .

> Arguments are useless against sickness, and in this case, abuse is a symptom of the disease of alcoholism. (p. 2)

Labeling the endangered woman as "sick" and then having her see the abuse as secondary to the alcoholism are examples of forcing the facts to fit the dogma of the disease model. For the sake of clarification (if the reader will forgive a little oversimplification) I will summarize the substance abuse treatment ethos as follows. Generalizations are drawn from my personal experience as an alcoholism counselor and from the literature on addictions work. Substance abuse counselors tend to:

- Work primarily with men in a program developed by white males in the 1930s;
- Perceive violence as a symptom of alcoholism and other substance abuse;
- Blame alcoholic women in their care for their tendency to get involved with violence-prone, alcoholic men;
- Assume that bad behavior (such as battering) will cease with sobriety;
- Subscribe to disinhibition theory, which states that intoxication lowers inhibitions and accounts for any bad behavior that might ensue;

- View the family as a system and the victim as playing a role (as chief enabler, codependent) in perpetuating the disease;
- Focus on abstinence and recovery.

The addictions focus in the substance abuse treatment field is matched by the male culture determinism of the domestic violence field. Let me simplify the basic precepts of the feminist model of wife/partner abuse in order again to clearly enunciate its differences. Workers in domestic violence programs have no less firm and sincere a commitment to their clients than do substance abuse counselors to theirs. And just as their counterparts in addictions work tend to be recovering addicts/alcoholics, many of those who counsel battered women have themselves been abused. Characteristically, however, women's shelter workers tend to:

- Work predominantly with women in a program founded by and for women who have been abused by their spouses/partners, but also by the system;
- Resist the disease model of addictions and to stress individual cultural/responsibility for antisocial behavior;
- Resist even more strongly the victim-blaming notions inherent in the codependency formulation so bandied about in the addictions literature;
- Oppose the primacy given to drug use in dysfunctional behavior;
- View drug usage as an excuse for deliberate acts of aggression, commonly called disavowal theory (Gorney, 1989; Silva & Howard, 1991);
- See partner assault as reflecting perpetrators' underlying need for power and control;
- Subscribe to a feminist model of violence as primary;
- Focus on safety rather than recovery and on social change at the societal level.

With such disparate treatment ideologies, it is no wonder that in my counseling work I often heard animosity expressed by practitioners and recovering alcoholics toward the women's shelter staff. "They just don't understand," it was said. Similarly, today I hear among volunteers working with battered women strong reservations expressed about some of the belief systems of substance abuse treatment providers. Again I hear the complaint "They don't understand."

So how, oh how, will these competing, contradictory models ever be brought together, subsumed under one theory? And how will workers suspicious of each others' creeds and ideologies come to trust and respect each other for their mutual interests, including the protection of victims from further abuse?

As a background for transcending the addictions/feminist split, let us first consider the facts concerning the co-occurrence of substance abuse and violence.

COMMONALITIES BETWEEN SUBSTANCE ABUSE AND VIOLENCE

Basically, we are looking here at facts that emerge from the research and which are not in dispute; facts pertaining to the biological, psychological, and social aspects of drug-related aggression. We can say at the outset that substance abuse and violence are behaviors that are learned, reinforced, cultural, and characterized by denial. And the similarities go far beyond these, spanning the biopsychosocial continuum.

Biological Factors Pertaining to Alcohol

Included in this category are findings from alcohol-violence studies that investigate alcohol-induced aggression, the role of serotonin in substance abuse and aggression, the background of brain injuries among perpetrators, and research on violence in relation to a variety of drugs, both legal and illegal.

Violence, impulsiveness, and early-onset alcoholism in young males are highly correlated (Cloninger et al., 1989). This type of alcoholism, defined by Cloninger and his associates after extensive studies of adopted sons of alcoholics, is highly hereditary, develops in late childhood, and is characterized by high risk-taking and antisocial behavior. Murphy and O'Farrell (1997) speculate that marital aggression among alcoholics may be linked to an underlying predisposition as revealed in the Cloninger team's adoption studies.

"I'm Dr. Jekyll and Mr. Hyde." This is how many of my male clients, in both Washington State and Norway, described their love affair with alcohol. To objectively test alcohol's reputed role in aggression, Taylor (1993) set up an experimental, pseudoshock design. Under highly controlled conditions of the experiment, alcohol was observed to have potent effects on aggression toward others. In other words, intoxicated subjects were more likely to administer shocks to others than were nonintoxicated subjects. A point worth noting in reference to such laboratory studies is that aggression is much more evident when distilled spirits are used as opposed to wine and beer, even at comparable blood alcohol levels (Lang, 1992). In any case, the results of this experiment, according to the author, seem to indicate that one's behavior when drunk is more than a result of social expectations. While subjects receiving placebo manipulations did not respond aggressively to the stimuli, those whose intoxication was real, typically did so. Some verification is found in monkey studies, where intoxication is associated with attacking behavior in high-ranking, male-dominant monkeys although not in nondominant monkeys (Miczek, Weerts, & DeBold, 1992). Other studies, however, do indicate that when human subjects believe they are drinking alcohol—even when they are actually not doing so—they are apt to react with heightened aggressiveness to stimuli (Lang, 1992). One may infer from these results that in cultures where people are expected to get violent when drunk, they will do so. This does not preclude, of course, a biochemical, aggression-inducing response to alcohol as well.

Research into deficiencies in levels of serotonin (the neurotransmitter responsible for a sense of well-being) in the brain reveals that aggression in monkeys is associated with reduced levels of this natural chemical (Pihl & Peterson, 1993). Impaired behavioral control induced by decreased brain serotonin may affect a person's ability to resist drinking alcohol once started. Thus alcohol, serotonin levels, and aggression may be interconnected in predictably destructive ways. Consistent with this finding is the discovery of White, Hansell, and Brick (1993) that alcohol use and aggressive behavior during early adolescence is associated with subsequent alcohol-related violence.

Use of medication, of Prozac-style antidepressants, may be helpful in curbing men's aggressiveness just as it is in curbing obsessive-compulsive behavior, bulimia, etc. (Marano, 1993). Research is currently underway at the University of Washington where the effects of Paxil, first cousin of Prozac, on battering men are being studied.

In summary, alcohol's role in producing violence may be in association with other variables stemming from personality traits, or as an indirect factor in violence in that alcohol impairs the drinker's social judgment. Disruptive effects of the drug on the cognitive processes in the brain presumably limit the intoxicated person's ability to process information rationally. Any bartender can attest to changes in behavior associated with heavy drinking, bellicosity being one pattern especially disturbing in its consequences. As Herman Melville (1856/1943) warned us through his hero in *Moby Dick*, "Better sleep with a sober cannibal than a drunken Christian" (p. 20).

EFFECTS OF OTHER DRUGS ON INTERPERSONAL VIOLENCE

How about the effects of other drugs on aggression? Marijuana, LSD, and heroin do not appear to cause users to become violent (Gelles, 1993). Cocaine, however, like alcohol, is associated with hyperactivity and violence in high doses (Goldberg, 1997). Cocaine acts at the brain's synapses to affect the release of serotonin (see Courtwright, 1995; N. Miller, Gold, & Mahler, 1991). PCP's (the horse tranquilizer) association with dangerous forms of violence is legendary. Its calculated use by gang members in preparation for a fight is reported by Fagan (1989).

Widely used in the 1960s and 1970s in both amateur and professional sports, amphetamines are widely implicated in the occurrence of violent and aggressive outbursts (McNeece & DiNitto, 1994). Because amphetamines (such as speed) increase the adrenaline flow, they may produce impulsive behavior that is violent, although Gelles (1993) argues that underlying personality attributes determine the exact nature of the outcome. Amphetamine psychosis is a condition marked by aggressiveness, paranoia, disordered thinking, and mania, and often accompanied by violent behavior. The psychotic-like behaviors, however, may be caused by sleep deprivation rather than by the chemical effect of the drug itself (Goldberg, 1997). The currently popular drug, methamphetamine (or crank) is especially problematic. Anecdotal reports provided to me by counselors in the field tell of bizarre sexual behavior that is associated with use of this drug.

Psychological Aspects

Due to the interconnectedness of the physiological and psychological aspects of behavior, it is often difficult to separate one from the other. Antisocial personality disorder is a case in point. Studies on jail and prison populations reveal a strong correlation among three elements—a diagnosis of antisocial personality disorder (defined in terms of impulsiveness, high risk-taking, and a tendency to externalize blame), substance abuse, and arrest for violent crimes. For subjects with alcohol problems, according to a tightly controlled empirical investigation by Abram, Teplin, and McClelland (1993), the probability of re-arrest for violent crime was high, but only if an antisocial disorder was also present.

Also related to biological predispositions is a tendency toward obsessiveness, possessiveness, and jealousy stemming from insecurity. Marano (1993) provides a portrait of abusive men in which disturbances at the biological level seem to be linked to disturbances in the cognitive realm and a tendency to overreact. Exposure to violence in childhood is a related pattern. (Interestingly, these same qualities are found among persons with a tendency toward addiction.) Star (1980), similarly, likened violent spouses to alcohol users in such characteristics as extreme jealousy, external blame, sexual dysfunction, and severe mood shifts. Often, offenders, tending to be antisocial and to shirk responsibility for their acts, attribute their destructive behavior to drugs consumed (deviance disavowal). Often, also, persons bent on a violent course including assault and rape will bolster their "courage" through the use of chemicals. This sort of premeditation is characteristic of the antisocial personality.

Social Factors

Subsumed under social factors are cultural variables, such as oppression of women, and situational stressors, such as poverty. We are concerned here with the *context* of partner violence associated with substance abuse.

Sociocultural attitudes concerning the treatment of women and the resolution of conflict are salient dimensions in partner violence. In fact, Kantor and Straus (1989) in an analysis of data from a national family violence survey, found that cultural approval of violence emerged as the strongest correlate of family violence, and was even more significant than the level of drinking itself. Alcohol-linked violent socialization undoubtedly plays a crucial role in intergenerational wife battering. Blue-collar men, argued Kantor and Straus, are especially prone to tolerate male aggression, and consequently to beat their wives more often than white-collar men. Economic stresses at this level, including circumstances of poverty, exacerbate the likelihood of violence. All in all, according to these researchers, husband's drug use, low family income, and a history of violence in the wife's family of origin were consistently associated with violence against the wife. And as Gorney (1989) informs us, once violence is an established norm within the family, it will occur even under conditions of total abstinence. Abusive men with alcohol and other drug problems are apt to be violent both when intoxicated and when sober.

Gondolf (1995) argues effectively that the key to the link between alcohol abuse and wife assault is in man's craving for power and control, a craving fostered by distortions of masculinity rooted in social upbringing. Underscoring this argument is the finding from sex-role studies that wife-assaulters in clinical samples score low on masculinity measures and femininity measures also. Gondolf bolsters this finding with research pointing to verbal deficits and poor communication skills among assaultive men. Drinking to gain a sense of power, therefore, comes naturally to such men, especially when they are under stress. The effect of the drug alcohol, in turn, contributes to a misreading of social cues through cognitive impairment, and violence may provide some sense of immediate gratification. Alcohol use and wife assault, according to this argument, are not causally related, but are both underlying manifestations of a bid for power and control.

A few words should be said about *psychological* abuse. As Chang (1996) makes clear, psychological, like physical abuse, can be explained as an extension of the patriarchal pattern of maintaining dominance and control over a vulnerable partner. Physical abuse does not exist apart from psychological abuse, and it is often the psychological pain that endures long after the physical wounds have healed.

Putting it all together, we can concur with Gondolf in viewing substance abuse and relationship violence as two sides of the same coin. Trying to answer the question whether men are violent because they drink or whether they drink because they are violent may be an exercise in futility. Instead, violence must be viewed interactively within a context of individual, situational, and social factors. This review of contemporary research reinforces the need for a multidimensional understanding of the dynamics of partner violence.

ROLE OF SUBSTANCE ABUSE IN FEMALE VIOLENCE AND VICTIMIZATION

Measures of self-reported partner violence reveal that women readily engage in slapping and hitting their partners, behaviors they often initiate (Morse, 1995). Nevertheless, women are far more likely than men to fear injury and, indeed, to sustain it. Studies of women committing acts of violence while under the influence of alcohol or other drugs, however, are scarce. For example, the extensive government research report, *Alcohol and Interpersonal Violence* (Martin, 1993) focuses almost exclusively on male partner violence. According to Leonard (1993), writing in the same volume, only two studies have specifically examined the possibility that husband-and-wife drinking patterns might interact to predict marital aggression. In Leonard's own research, the wife's excessive drinking was associated with the husband's aggression. The focus is on *victimization*, not victimizing by the wife, however. Kantor (1993) also refers to the lack of attention in the literature to women's alcohol-related aggression. Alcohol-abusing women, she suggests, are more at risk of victimization because they are violating gender-role expectations by the very fact of being intoxicated. B. A. Miller et al. (1989) concur that alcoholic women's stigmatization as being "sexually loose" may set them up for maltreatment. Moreover, if such women become verbally or physically aggressive, the violence in their partners may escalate. Kantor's observation (1993) that it is extremely rare for sober husbands to remain with their addictive wives perhaps best explains the shortage of studies on hard-drinking, battering women.

Studies of alcoholic women in treatment (B. A. Miller et al., 1991), however, reveal that such women are more likely to initiate violence against partners than are battered women in shelters or women without alcohol problems. In any case, such alcoholic women experience more violence from their spouses than do women in a general household sample (Miller et al., 1989). There is a distinct possibility, moreover, that victimization in women leads to the development of alcoholism in women. To test this hypothesis, Downs and Miller (1997) studied women, both alcoholic and nonalcoholic, at 18-month intervals. For women with lifetime alcohol dependence, experiences of partner abuse at the earlier time is associated with more severe alcohol problems at the later time interval. For women without an alcohol-dependence diagnosis, however, the relationship did not exist.

My interpretation of these findings is that highly addictive women are more psychologically vulnerable to experiences of victimization and more apt to use alcohol to escape from the pain of abuse than are nonalcoholic women. Downs and Miller (1997) propose a trauma hypothesis to explain alcoholic women's susceptibility: The cumulative effects of a lifetime of traumatic abuse characteristic of such women, argue Downs and Miller, heighten her ability to be retraumatized by recent partner abuse. These findings have important implications for substance abuse treatment counselors. Recovering women who are involved with abusing men are at primary risk of relapse.

Domestic violence ending in homicide is an area, due to the magnitude of the crime, where hard data are relatively easy to come by. A study of 22,000 Chicago murders since 1965 revealed that among Black couples, women were more likely to kill men than vice versa, but in White relationships, only about 25% of the victims were male (reported in *Newsweek* by Ingrassia and Beck, 1994). Nationwide, about one third of the women in prison for homicide have killed a partner. Whereas men kill partners as the violence escalates, women do so as a means of escape. Nevertheless, the conviction rate—especially among women of color—is higher than that of male murderers (Downs, 1997).

Al Roberts (1996) confirmed, in his in-depth interviews with incarcerated battered women who had killed their partners, that such women had acted following a history of death threats and beatings. In sharp contrast to the community sample of battered women, the battered women in the prison sample frequently had a history of drug abuse. Other relevant factors that emerged in the study were the batterer's extreme jealousy, emotional dependency, and drunkenness.

The role of substance abuse in homicide has been substantiated in a brief report by forensic toxicologists who analyzed results in 20 cases of domestic violence homicides. Alcohol or other drugs was found to be present in the suspect, the victim, or both (Slade, Daniel, & Heisler, 1991).

SAME-SEX PARTNER VIOLENCE

A high consumption rate of alcohol and other drugs is characteristic of gay and lesbian social life (Kus, 1988). A review of the literature on same-sex partner abuse reveals the use of alcohol and/or drugs to be prevalent. Most of the estimates are that over half of the same-sex batterers were under the influence of alcohol or other drugs at the time of the assault (Renzetti, 1997). In one survey of 39 lesbians in abusive relationships, 64% reported use of alcohol or drugs by both partners prior to the incidents of abuse (Schilit, Lie, & Montagne, 1990). Significantly well over a third of the lesbian sample has experienced physically abusive relationships. With such a small sample, however, one cannot draw any definitive conclusions.

In probing the substance abuse/violence link, researchers on gay and lesbian relationships tend to perceive the use of chemicals as an excuse to allow batterers to escape responsibility for their acts (Island & Letellier, 1991; Renzetti, 1997). Extreme emotional dependency is viewed as a likely determinant of the violence (Renzetti, 1997). Island and Letellier argue that the batterers drink as a premeditated strategy before they beat their partners. They view the substance-abuse problems as separate from the "battering disorder." I would again argue for a holistic rather than a monocausal approach. Yet, in the absence of solid research data on same-sex domestic violence, generalizations are hard to make. We can all agree on the need for further research and for greater openness by service providers to meet the needs of battered lesbians and gay men. The group with which I am affiliated, PAVE (People Against Violence) of Waterloo, Iowa, counsels lesbians and gay men as well as battered women. PAVE does not counsel heterosexual battered men, however.

TREATMENT ISSUES

The barriers to cooperation between the addictions providers and feminist crisis intervention workers are formidable. As mentioned earlier, the frameworks are contradictory, ideological, and opportunities for cross-fertilization of research are few. The differences are not irreconcilable, however. The barriers to cooperation could be lifted through the following moves: the adoption of a holistic, biopsychosocial framework for a common understanding of the addictions/violence/victimization configuration; by a repudiation of all victim-blaming terminology and orientations; and participation in joint training workshops in the dynamics of substance and partner abuse.

An illustration of a positive development that may set an example for other communities has taken place in Waterloo, Iowa. Pathways Behavioral Services, a substance abuse agency and PAVE, a grassroots crisis service for battered women, have joined forces in obtaining a grant for mutual training programs. As a starting point, counselors from PAVE will provide workshops on the dynamics of domestic violence.

To what extent incompatible worldviews, however, will impede networking remains to be seen. Counselors at Pathways are steeped in a codependency model which they apply to spouses and partners of substance abusers. Codependency implies shared responsibility in a spouse's problems; women are often faulted or declared to be sick for "enabling" the alcoholic to behave irresponsibly. Where there is partner abuse, the role of male violence in subduing women is apt to be overlooked. Couples counseling, often a part of substance abuse treatment, can be especially dangerous to the battered woman and is contraindicated. PAVE workers, for their part, tend to overlook the significance of substance abuse and addiction in destroying families, destroying lives, and the fact that indeed, for some individuals, involvement in a 12-step program can be a godsend.

FROM BIFURCATION TO INTEGRATION

As long as their worldviews are so vastly different, as long as ideology rather than research shapes practice, domestic violence and substance abuse programs will continue to go their separate ways, and lives will continue to be lost unnecessarily. Substance abuse treatment alone will not address the physical abuse adequately, and supportive counseling and advocacy for battered women will not end addictions problems that may exist.

A biopsychosocial understanding bolstered by empirical research concerning biological (e.g., the link between serotonin depletion and aggression/addiction), psychological (e.g., insecurity/jealousy components), and social (e.g., cultural supports for male drunken aggression) dimensions offers a holistic approach to the violence/ substance abuse link. Such an approach effectively unites what we know about the potency of addiction—and the extensive treatment plan required to help addicts/alcoholics find healthy ways to cope with feelings, pain, and resolving conflict—with an awareness from gender-based research of how violence toward women is related to power-and-control issues in a patriarchal society. Alcoholic battered women need to see how involvement in high-risk situations jeopardizes their sobriety.

In substance abuse treatment agencies, moreover, safety must be given priority. A "sobriety first" approach with women who face ongoing abuse and danger and who may rely on alcohol or tranquilizers as coping devices is almost destined to fail (Zubretsky & Digirolamo, 1996). Alcoholic batterers need work in the areas of empathy, stress management, social skills training, and acceptance of the feminine sides of their personalities. *All* clients need to know how alcohol and other substance abuse contributes to cognitive dysfunction and to a dangerous misreading of cues that may precipitate overreaction and violence.

The move from theory bifurcation to integration is central, as we have seen, to a coming together of treatment forces. Such integration can be enhanced by building on similarities in approaches that already exist. As Gondolf (1995) indicates, both substance abuse treatment and domestic violence programs confront denial and minimization of destructive behaviors. Both address distortions and rationalizations, work on communication skills, and promote personal change. Conjoint substance abuse/violence treatment is only possible, however, when a holistic framework is employed. Under the rubric of integrated theory, substance abuse and aggression would not be viewed in *either/or*—cause-and-effect terms—but as *both/and*—

multidimensional constructs. Thus both disorders—abuse of substance, and abuse of people—are seen as manifestations of the same biopsychosocial forces. Interventions guided by this unifying theory should go far toward addressing the needs of victims and perpetrators alike. Interventions based on myths and narrow ideology, on the other hand, can have a devastating effect on victims and their families and indirectly, on their treatment providers.

CONCLUSIONS

Much remains to be learned about the exact nature of the substance abuse/aggression link. In this chapter, the attempt has been made to get beyond simplistic ideology and to single out from the contemporary, available literature the findings on the incidence of domestic violence (as influenced by gender, intoxicating substances, and cultural norms). To replace the narrow, unidimensional approaches of rival programs, a multidimensional theory has been proposed, a theory that accurately reflects truths as revealed in much of the groundbreaking research currently being done. The current state of the knowledge suggests that the close relationship of substance abuse and violence in men results primarily from (1) a biochemical susceptibility to react to stress through aggression and chemical use; (2) a substance-induced cognitive impairment; (3) cultural definitions conducive to intoxicated aggression in men; and (4) a resented emotional dependency on one's partner. Of substance-abusing, battered women we know (1) a history of past abuse trauma is common; (2) self-esteem is extremely low; (3) psychoactive drugs may be used as a way of coping with the terrors of violence; and (4) that traditional, male-oriented addictions treatment programs may actually compound the problem.

The present situation of dichotomizing problems that are not in reality separable is counterproductive. This discussion has shown, hopefully, how differences in language and assumptions can be reconciled through a basic reconceptualization for a broader, more comprehensive approach. Encouraging developments in networking across disciplinary lines are currently underway. Such collaborations are essential to meet the common good of preventing and curbing the violence.

REFERENCES

Abram, K., Teplin, L., & McClelland, M. (1993). In S. Martin (Ed.), *Alcohol and interpersonal violence: Fostering multidisciplinary perspectives* (pp. 237–252). Rockville, MD: U.S. Department of Health and Human Services.

Al-Anon. (1994). Domestic violence. In *In all our affairs: Making crises work for you* [Brochure, pp. 1–4]. New York: Author.

Associated Press. (1996, September 23). Violence research brings startling results. *Waterloo/Cedar Falls Courier,* p. A6.

Bennett, L., & Lawson, M. (1994). Barriers to cooperation between domestic-violence and substance-abuse programs. *Families in Society, 75,* 277–286.

Chang, V. N. (1996). *I just lost myself: Psychological abuse of women in marriage.* Westport, CT: Praeger.

Cloninger, C. R., Sigvardsson, S., Gilligan, S., van Knorring, A. L., Reich, T., & Bohman, M. (1989). Genetic homogeneity and the classification of alcoholism. *Advances in Alcohol and Substance Abuse, 7,* 3–16.

Courtwright, D. T. (1995). [Review of the book *Alcohol and interpersonal violence*]. *Contemporary Drug Problems, 22,* 569–573.

Downs, D. A. (1997). *More than victims: Battered women, the syndrome society, and the law.* Chicago: Chicago Publishing Co.

Downs, W. R., & Miller, B. A. (1997). *The longitudinal association between experiences of partner-to-woman abuse and alcohol problems for women.* Unpublished manuscript.

Fagan, J. (1989). The social organization of drug use and drug dealing among urban gangs. *Criminology, 27,* 633–667.

Gelles, R. J. (1993). Alcohol and other drugs are associated with violence: They are not its cause. In R. J. Gelles & D. R. Loseke (Eds.), *Current controversies on family violence* (pp. 182–196). Newbury Park, CA: Sage.

Goldberg, R. (1997). *Drugs across the spectrum.* Englewood, CO: Morton.

Gondolf, E. W. (1995). Alcohol abuse, wife assault, and power needs. *Social Service Review, 69,* 274–284.

Gondolf, E. W., & Foster, R. A. (1991). Wife assault among V.A. alcohol rehabilitation patients. *Hospital and community psychiatry, 42,* 74–79.

Gorney, B. (1989). Domestic violence and chemical dependency: Dual problems, dual interventions. *Journal of Psychoactive Drugs, 21,* 229–238.

Island, D., & Letellier, P. (1991). *Men who beat the men who love them.* New York: Harrington Park Press.

Ingrassia, M., & Beck, M. (1994, July 4). Patterns of abuse. *Newsweek,* pp. 26–33.

Kantor, G. (1993). Refining the brushstrokes in portraits of alcohol and wife assaults. In S. Martin (Ed.), *Alcohol and interpersonal violence: Fostering multidisciplinary perspectives* (pp. 281–290). Rockville, MD: U.S. Department of Health and Human Services.

Kantor, G., & Straus, M. A. (1989). Substance abuse as a precipitant of wife abuse victimization. *American Journal of Drug and Alcohol Abuse, 15,* 173–189.

Kus, R. (1988). Alcoholism and non-acceptance of gay self: The critical link. *Journal of Homosexuality, 15,* 25–41.

Lang, A. (1992). Psychological perspectives. In S. Martin (Ed.), *Alcohol and interpersonal violence: Fostering multidisciplinary perspectives* (pp. 121–147). Rockville, MD: U.S. Department of Health and Human Services.

Leonard, K. (1993). Drinking patterns and intoxication in marital violence: Review, critique, and future directives for research. In S. Martin (Ed.), *Alcohol and interpersonal violence: Fostering multidisciplinary perspectives* (pp. 253–280). Rockville, MD: U.S. Department of Health and Human Services.

Marano, H. (1993). Inside the heart of marital violence. *Psychology Today, 26,* 50–53, 76–78, 91.

Martin, S. (Ed.). (1993). *Alcohol and interpersonal violence: Fostering multidisciplinary perspectives.* Rockville, MD: National Institutes of Health.

McNeece, C. A., & DiNitto, D. M. (1994). *Chemical dependency: A systems approach.* Englewood Cliffs, NJ: Prentice Hall.

Melville, H. (1943). *Moby-Dick or the whale.* New York: Heritage Press. (Original work published 1856)

Miczek, K., Weerts, E., & De Bold, J. (1992). Alcohol, aggression, and violence: Biobehavioral determinants. In S. Martin (Ed.), *Alcohol and interpersonal violence: Fostering multidisciplinary perspectives* (pp. 83–120). Rockville, MD: U.S. Department of Health and Human Services.

Miller, B. A., Downs, W. R., & Gondoli, D. M. (1989). Spousal violence among alcoholic women as compared to a random household sample of women. *Journal of Studies on Alcohol, 50,* 533–540.

Miller, B. A., Downs, W. R., Testa, M., & Keil, A. (1991, November). *Thematic analyses of severe spousal violence incidents: Women's perceptions of their victimization.* Paper presented at the annual meeting of the American Society of Criminology, San Francisco, CA.

Miller, N., Gold, M., & Mahler, J. (1991). Violent behaviors associated with cocaine use: Possible pharmacological mechanisms. *International Journal of the Addictions, 26,* 1077–1088.

Morse, B. (1995). Beyond the conflict tactics scale: Assessing gender differences in partner violence. *Violence and Victims, 10,* 251–272.

Murphy, C. M., & O'Farrell, T. J. (1997). Couple communication patterns of maritally aggressive and nonaggressive male alcoholics. *Journal of Studies on Alcohol, 15,* 83–90.

Pihl, R., & Peterson, J. (1993). Alcohol and aggression: Three potential mechanisms of the drug effect. In S. Martin (Ed.), *Alcohol and interpersonal violence: Fostering multidisciplinary perspectives* (pp. 149–159). Rockville, MD: U.S. Department of Health and Human Services.

Renzetti, C. (1997). Violence and abuse among same-sex couples. In A. Cardarelli (Ed.), *Violence between intimate partners: Patterns, causes and effects* (pp. 70–89). Needham Heights, MA: Allyn and Bacon.

Roberts, A. (1996). Battered women who kill: A comparative study of incarcerated participants with community sample of battered women. *Journal of Family Violence, 11,* 291–304.

Schilit, R., Lie, G., & Montagne, M. (1990). Substance use as a correlate of violence in intimate lesbian relationships. *Journal of Homosexuality, 19,* 51–65.

Silva, N., & Howard, M. (1991). Woman battering: The forgotten problem in alcohol abuse treatment. *Family Dynamics Addictions Quarterly, 1,* 8–19.

Slade, M., Daniel, L. J., & Heisler, C. J. (1991). Application of forensic toxicology to the problem of domestic violence. *Journal of Forensic Sciences, 36,* 708–713.

Star, B. (1980). Patterns in family violence. In M. Elbow (Ed.), *Social casework reprint services* (pp. 5–12). Ann Arbor, MI: Books on Demand.

Taylor, S. (1993). Experimental investigation of alcohol-induced aggression in humans. In *Alcohol Health and Research World, 17,* 93–100.

Tolman, R. M., & Bennett, L. W. (1990). A review of quantitative research on men who batter. *Journal of Interpersonal Violence, 5,* 87–118.

van Wormer, K. (1995). *Alcoholism treatment: A social work perspective.* Chicago: Nelson-Hall.

White, H., Hansell, S., & Brick, J. (1993). Alcohol use and aggression among youth. *Alcohol Health and Research World, 17,* 144–150.

Zubretsky, T. M., & Digirolamo, K. (1996). In A. Roberts (Ed.), *Helping battered women: New perspectives and remedies* (pp. 222–228). New York: Oxford University Press.

CHAPTER 15

Developing Services for Lesbians in Abusive Relationships: A Macro and Micro Approach

Christine Heer, Eileen Grogan, Sandra Clark, and Lynda Marie Carson

Until recently domestic violence in lesbian intimate relationships has often been ignored by the systems designed to help battered women. The traditional systems have either resisted responsibility, or denied the problem even existed (Carlson & Maciol, 1997; Pharr, 1987). The police, courts, and social service agencies have been at best ignorant about how to respond, and at worst, discriminatory in making services and entitlements available. Physical violence and sexual assault does occur in same-sex relationships. Further research is sorely needed to measure the extent and severity of abuse among gay and lesbian partners (Carlson & Maciol, 1997).

Until the 1990s the feminist/shelter movement had also resisted acknowledging the problem. Many activists feared that acknowledging woman-to-woman battering would diminish the strength of the feminist paradigm that woman-battering is based in a patriarchal society, and, therefore, that woman-battering is gendered (Hirshorn, 1984; Renzetti, 1992). Some activists in the battered lesbian/gay male movement have made the same assumption (Island & Letellier, 1991). Additionally, many lesbian and domestic violence activists felt personally betrayed when confronted with the knowledge that a woman could hurt her female partner. Finally, acknowledging lesbian concerns of any sort meant that feminists needed to confront their own homophobia (Pharr, 1987; Vardamis, 1983).

Even the lesbian and gay community has been resistant to acknowledging the idea of violence in their intimate relationships (Grover, 1988; Irvine, 1985). In part, this resistance may come from a need to maintain a concept of a lesbian utopia, that is, that women loving women means safety, comfort, and self-actualization. Another explanation is that homophobia impacts the community's acceptance of the problem. Gays and lesbians might fear that recognition of intimate abuse would affirm homophobic stereotypes. To acknowledge the problem of domestic violence may be perceived as giving ammunition to the hostile segments of heterosexual society. Furthermore, some gays and lesbians may not identify certain behaviors as being abusive, or they may believe that a gay man or lesbian who behaves violently has a good reason or excuse. As a result of this systemic denial and resistance, many lesbians and gay men have suffered alone with nowhere to turn.

This chapter addresses these resistances by presenting a chronology and review of the work of the Battered Lesbian Task Force in New Jersey. The chapter begins with an overview of the dynamics of abuse in lesbian and gay relationships and the inadequate response of the shelter system to the unique needs of this population. The chapter then presents what the Battered Lesbian Task Force accomplished in challenging these resistances through education and training, policy change, and direct services for battered lesbians and their abusers.

DYNAMICS OF ABUSE AND CONTROL IN LESBIAN AND GAY RELATIONSHIPS

Research reveals that violence in lesbian and gay relationships is similar to the violence that occurs in heterosexual relationships.

Renzetti (1988) found that 75% of her respondents reported that they were "frequently or sometimes" pushed or shoved. Sixty-five percent reported being "frequently or sometimes" hit with fists or open hands, and 48% were hit or scratched in the face, breasts, or genitals; 35% were forced to have sex with their partners. Renzetti also found that 70% of respondents were "frequently or sometimes" verbally threatened, and at least 64% were verbally demeaned in front of others. Other researchers such as Farley (1992) have found similar rates. Additionally, The New York City Anti-Violence Project has shown that domestic violence accounts for 30% of all cases reported to their program. At this point however, only 34 states have domestic violence laws on the books that apply to homosexual relationships as well as heterosexual relationships (Zorza, 1995).

Battering or abuse in relationships often involves a pattern of behavior where a person uses a variety of tactics including, but not limited to, physical violence or intimidation and isolation, to gain and maintain power and control over her partner (Pence, 1993). A behavior is battering when the batterer achieves enhanced control over the recipient. If the battered partner becomes fearful of the batterer, if she modifies her behavior in response to the abuse, or if the victim maintains a mind-set or behavioral pattern to avoid violence, she is battered (Hart, 1986). Therefore, battering is caused by the abusive partner's belief that she is entitled to control and power in the relationship (Ganley, 1981). Battering and abuse can take the form of a number of tactics: physical violence, sexual violence, emotional abuse, economic abuse, use of children, threats and coercion, intimidation, isolation, minimization, denying and blaming, using privilege (Figure 15.1). An isolated incident of one of these tactics may not be battering (but can still be domestic violence under the law). On the other hand, not all of these tactics, including physical abuse, need to be present for the relationship to be considered abusive or violent.

RESPONSE OF THE SHELTER SYSTEM

Responding to violence in lesbian and gay relationships is not an easy task. In New Jersey, it took the Battered Lesbian Task Force of the New Jersey Coalition for Battered Women nearly 10 years to complete its initial goals, and there is much more work to be done.

FIGURE 15.1   The power and control wheel for lesbians and gays.

Adapted by Roe and Jagodinsky from *Education Groups for Men Who Batter: The Duluth Model,*
by E. Pence and M. Paymar, 1993, New York: Springer Publishing Company. Copyright 1993
by Springer Publishing Company. Reproduced by permission.

The Battered Lesbian Task Force was formed in 1987 to facilitate
the sensitive and effective provision of services to battered lesbians
within domestic violence programs. One of the first activities of the
Task Force was to survey member agency staff to assess the level of
services being offered to battered lesbians, and the level of sensitivity
to lesbian/gay concerns shown by program staff and volunteers. The
survey asked a variety of questions about services for and attitudes
about battered lesbians. The results were enlightening (Table 15.1).

TABLE 15.1   Survey of Services for Battered Lesbians

	Yes		No		Unsure		Other	
Questions	N	%	N	%	N	%	N	%
1a. Have you ever provided services to a battered lesbian?	52	37	62	44	18	13	9	6
1b. Has anyone on your staff ever provided service to a battered lesbian?	90	64	17	12	20	14	14	10
2. If yours is a shelter program, has your program ever sheltered a battered lesbian?	44	31	25	18	44	31	28[**]	20
3a. Are you, or would you be, comfortable providing services to a battered lesbian?	127	90	6	4	3	2	5	3
3b. Are you aware of the special needs of battered lesbians?	45	32	51	36	7	4	38[***]	27
4a. Has your staff ever discussed the issues of homophobia, battered lesbians, or lesbian staff?	48[*]	33	77	55	9	6	7	5
5. Are you, or would you be comfortable with a lesbian staff member?	124	88	6	4	4	3	7[****]	5
6. Are there lesbians currently on your staff?	41	29	34	24	59	42	7	5
7. Do you think your program should specifically advertise services for battered lesbians?	47	33	68	48	18	13	8	6
8. Do you think that it is "safe" for a lesbian staff person to "come out" to other staff in your program?	98	70	17	12	14	10	12[+]	8
9. Would you welcome staff training on homophobia and the special needs of battered lesbians?	122	86	6	4	0	0	13[++]	9

N = 141

*4 respondents answered "Informally."
**22 respondents answered "Not Applicable."
***27 respondents answered "Some."
****2 respondents answered "Maybe."
+5 respondents gave an indirect response, indicating that coming out was a personal choice.
++2 respondents answered "maybe"; 1 answered "Don't care"; and 1 answered "Homophobia only."

369

A surprising number of respondents answered "No" to questions about whether they had ever provided services to or sheltered a battered lesbian, and to questions about whether there were lesbians on staff in their program. The Battered Lesbian Task Force interpreted these responses as naive at best, as well as heterosexist in their assumptions about sexual orientation. Also distressing were the responses to questions about comfort levels with working with openly lesbian staff, and whether it was safe for lesbian staff to come out to their coworkers. In their comments, the majority of the "No" respondents acknowledged that homophobia among staff made it unsafe for a lesbian to reveal her sexual orientation. Others cited that due to lack of training on the issue, it would be unsafe for a coworker to be an out lesbian in their program. Still others responded that sexual preference is a private matter and should not be discussed at work.

At the program level, the majority of respondents felt that their agencies should not specifically advertise services for battered lesbians. Some of the reasons given included: The emphasis in advertising should be on all women; no one special population should be pointed out in advertising. Another common reason was that society is not ready to deal with such advertising due to pervasive homophobia. Advertising could alienate the community, jeopardize funding, and cause some heterosexual women to be reluctant to seek services. Finally, others stated that advertising should not occur until services truly became available and staff had been sensitized to the issues.

Armed with this information, the task force developed the following Plan of Action:

1. Provide education to all 24 domestic violence programs in the state on homophobia and battering in lesbian and gay relationships.
2. Train community educators in every program about how to address the issue of battering in lesbian and gay relationships in public presentations.
3. Develop a referral list of practitioners throughout the state who were experienced in both domestic violence and lesbian and gay issues.
4. Provide a support group for lesbians battered by their female partners.
5. Develop a policy statement on Services for Battered Lesbians.

Education and Training

The New Jersey Coalition for Battered Women is a coordinating organization for member programs. Twenty-three agencies and several individuals are members of the coalition. Because the coalition has no supervisory or monitoring responsibilities, participation in staff education programs are completely voluntary.

The results of the survey precipitated the offer of in-service training for staff of coalition member programs. Battered Lesbian Task Force trainers were available, with the cooperation of their employing agencies. The training program was 3 hours in length. The first half of the training program focused on homophobia, heterosexism, and sensitivity. The program was part lecture and part experiential. The program adapted parts of the training curriculum *Leading Introductory Workshops on Homophobia* by The Campaign to End Homophobia (Thompson, 1990) and "Two Workshops on Homophobia" by Suzanne Pharr (1986). The second part of the training focused on the dynamics of abusive lesbian relationships and recommended intervention strategies. Included in this segment was a discussion on the power-and-control tactics implemented by lesbian abusers, the added weapon of homophobia available to abusers, an analysis of the myth of mutual abuse, and an empowerment approach to assisting lesbian survivors. The training program emphasized the impact of internalized and externalized homophobia and heterosexism on domestic violence victims and workers. The question of mutual abuse, that is, of determining who is the assailant and who is the victim, was addressed in the context of an analysis of an imbalance of power (Heer, 1992; Pence, 1987).

Some programs responded immediately to the offer of training, and training was completed right away. Other programs were more reticent. Some programs initially did not understand why lesbian victimization was being singled out for special training. Others were concerned about being too public about the issue, fearing physical or financial retaliation from the community. Still others identified a concern that if they moved too quickly, programs might not yet be safe for battered lesbians. Task Force members spoke with program representatives in an attempt to resolve concerns. These negotiations were successful, and by the end of the 3-year period, all but two programs in the state had received training.

The response of staff and volunteers to the training program was generally positive. "Eyes and minds were opened, dialogue was begun at a new level, and the agency's commitment to serving all was made clearer," responded one supervisor. Another positive result was that the training created an environment in which some staff/volunteers felt safer coming out to their colleagues.

> I am a lesbian and am not out in my agency. However, after your presentation I am thinking that I might be able to start to come out to some staff.

> I am a lesbian and only partially out at work. I have felt frustrated that I can't be who I am without repercussions . . . when I saw we were going to have this training I was so excited and couldn't wait. There was a part of me that was hopeful that this would open the door. I think I looked at it as a chance to be known and accepted.

While some participants remained adamant about their negative personal views about homosexuality, the training message began to counteract some previous assumptions about lesbian victims. For example, it was now well accepted that lesbian victims should not be discriminated against, and that services must include the context of homophobia, within which the lesbian victim lives.

Training the Trainers

Training was critical not only to the service providers, but also to the program staff who provide community education. The day-long training program provided an overview of the issues, an overview of a recommended training agenda on battering in lesbian and gay relationships, and a "How Do You Answer That One" discussion. Trainers were encouraged to discuss lesbian battering in all of their presentations.

This "Training the Trainers" was offered at the same time that the staff in-service training programs were provided. Thus, some individuals attended the Training-the-Trainer program before they received the sensitivity training. In hindsight, this was a mistaken approach, as some participants' discomfort with the issue of lesbian battering became a barrier to learning how to help community members become comfortable with the issue.

Policy Statement

An important aspect of the Battered Lesbian Task Force Plan of Action was to develop a policy statement on which member programs could agree. The policy statement was to develop a basis and an expectation for member programs' response to battered lesbians seeking services. The Task Force felt it was important to move programs beyond the "We serve all women" position and to encourage them to emphasize the unique isssues that battered lesbians face as a result of heterosexism and homophobia. The following policy statement was developed for battered lesbians receiving services:

> Recognizing that the serious problem of lesbian battering has not been specifically addressed in NJ, the NJ Coalition for Battered Women is committed to ensuring that full services and protection without discrimination are provided to battered lesbians. The Coalition further recognizes that in order to achieve this goal, battered women's programs must be safe places for lesbians, whether they be workers or women seeking assistance.
>
> It is therefore Coalition policy that the following become standard practice in battered women's programs in NJ.
>
> —That training on homophobia and the special needs of battered lesbians be provided to all staff and be incorporated into standard training requirements for new staff and volunteers;
>
> —That programs address homophobia issues among staff not only through training, but also through the conscious development of non-heterosexist shelter environments, intake procedures and outreach efforts;
>
> —That the policies of battered women's programs reflect an acknowledgment of differing sexual orientations, including discrimination statements which prohibit discrimination on the basis of sexual orientation, and benefit policies which are inclusive of the lesbian lifestyle, i.e., bereavement days for the partner's family;
>
> —That programs have clear policies for how homophobic behavior by staff and other women will be handled;
>
> —That programs identify community resources and referrals for battered lesbians and have materials on lesbian battering available;

—That programs clearly communicate the availability of their services to battered lesbians and make every effort to provide special services for battered lesbians, e.g., battered lesbian support groups.

The Coalition further recognizes the serious problem of domestic violence within the gay male community and encourages battered women's programs to provide services to these persons at a level on par with those provided to heterosexual battered men. The Coalition strongly encourages the gay male community to invest resources to address and respond to this problem.

Political Networking and Statutory Changes

The Battered Lesbian Task Force recognized that our efforts to reach out to battered lesbians could not be effective without networking and collaboration with existing systems. The Task Force also realized that intervention efforts could be strengthened if the New Jersey Prevention of Domestic Violence Act §19, 2C:25 (1991) was amended to be inclusive of lesbian and gay relationships.

When the Act was originally written in 1982, the definition of "cohabitants," which identified who was protected under the law included only emancipated minors or persons 18 years of age or older *of the opposite sex* who have resided together or who currently are residing in the same living quarters, persons who together are parents of one or more children, regardless of their marital status or whether they have lived together at any time, or persons 18 years of age or older who are related by blood and who are currently residing in the same living quarters.

This definition clearly excluded lesbian and gay relationships. There was speculation at the time that the definition was written deliberately to exclude homosexuals. One legislator allegedly stated that the committee did not want to give state sanction to homosexual relationships.

In 1989, the legislature was preparing for a significant revamping of the law. Public hearings were held throughout the state, documenting, through both written and oral testimony, ineffective aspects of the Prevention of Domestic Violence Act. The Battered Lesbian Task Force realized that the time was right to pursue policy change. The original strategy was to have lesbian and gay survivors testify at the hearings. This never happened, however, because many survivors were too terrified to speak out, too scared of outing themselves, and too terrified that their abusers would read about their testimony in the newspaper.

The Task Force then took a different tack. Realizing that lesbians and gays were not the only ones excluded by the "cohabitants" definition, committee members reached out to advocates and interest groups representing the abused elderly, who were also being victimized by same-sex caretakers not related to the victim by marriage or by blood. Together, the Battered Lesbian Task Force and groups representing the abused elderly wrote in support of a policy change.

The other strategy taken by the Battered Lesbian Task Force was to break through the collective denial of the lesbian and gay community and engage their political influence in support of the change. It was fortunate that around this same time, gay and lesbian activists successfully completed an 8-year effort to have the state's law against discrimination amended to include "sexual orientation" as one of the protected classes. Members of the Battered Lesbian Task Force were active in this Campaign to End Discrimination,[1] and were able to network with activists from the National Organization for Women, the National Association of Social Workers, and the New Jersey Lesbian and Gay Coalition. When the omission of same-sex partners from the Prevention of Domestic Violence Act was posed as a discrimination issue, community leaders agreed to support the effort to challenge the policy.

Through this networking effort, the goals of the Battered Lesbian Task Force were validated and supported by the other organizations. In fact, the Anti-Violence project of the Personal Liberty Fund, which is the nonprofit program of the New Jersey Lesbian and Gay Coalition, incorporated the fight against lesbian and gay domestic violence in its mission statement. Similarly, the Gay Activist Alliance of Morris County[2] now requires domestic violence intervention training for volunteer Helpline staff.

---

[1]The Campaign to End Discrimination was an organization comprised of representatives of gay, lesbian, bisexual and transgendered groups. Its mission was to campaign to have the state Law Against Discrimination amended to be inclusive of sexual orientation. This goal was achieved in 1990.

[2]Gay Activist Alliance is a social political group located in Morristown, New Jersey.

Ultimately, the New Jersey Prevention of Domestic Violence Act (1991) was amended to include lesbians and gay relationships. The Battered Lesbian Task Force and its supporters were successful in achieving the policy change they had envisioned.

Program Development: Battered Lesbian Helpline

The programs initially developed by the Battered Lesbian Task Force were limited by their connection to mainstream domestic violence shelter programs. Since the resources used most by battered lesbians appeared to be private therapists, family, and friends (Renzetti, 1989) it was determined that outreach should go beyond the shelter program community.

There were concerns that battered lesbians were not using the anonymous hotlines run by domestic violence shelters. The New Jersey Coalition for Battered Women together with the Battered Lesbian Task Force wrote a grant to establish a statewide helpline for battered lesbians. In addition to the request for funds for a special helpline, the Request for Proposal also solicited funds to provide support group services for battered lesbians. The award of grant funds made available from the Victim of Crime Act Grants Program was a tremendous boost to the work of the Task Force. Those programs and staff who were still somewhat reticent about being public about services for battered lesbians were challenged to address these issues directly. Additional grant money was also obtained from another government program, the New Jersey Attorney General's office of Victim-Witness Advocacy.

The Battered Lesbian Helpline was established in 1994. Staff of the Helpline are experienced domestic violence personnel and self-identify as lesbian or bisexual, although this is not required. The goal of the Helpline is to provide support and information to lesbian survivors. The program referral list was developed for the Helpline identifying programs which had received the training program on homophobia and lesbian battering, and who agreed to be so listed. While the programs listed were given out as referrals, the Helpline staff was also charged with encouraging callers and consumers of services to provide feedback on the program's response to them.

In addition to referring within the shelter network, it was also determined that the Task Force needed to compile a list of private practitioners to whom clients should be referred.

Therapist Referral Database. The Task Force began developing a therapist referral database by distributing another questionnaire. Therapists who received the questionnaire were either already included in a gay/lesbian referral list, self-requested the questionnaire, or were recommended by others to receive the questionnaire. Questions on the therapist survey covered three major areas: 1) basic information about the therapist's practice; 2) experience and knowledge about domestic violence; and 3) experience and knowledge about lesbian and gay concerns.

The information gathered about the therapist's practice included formal education and degree; location of the practice; theoretical framework; fee structure and insurance reimbursement eligibility; client populations; and specialty areas. In trying to determine their knowledge of domestic violence and lesbian and gay issues, the questionnaire asked the therapists what their views were on the nature and causes of homosexuality, what their approach would be in working with lesbian/gay clients, what their approach would be to working with battered women, and their views on the use of couples counseling when battering is evident in a relationship.

While some respondents clearly had the knowledge and experience to work with battered lesbian and gay clients, others, it seemed, could benefit from some additional training in the area of domestic violence. A domestic violence training was offered to these practitioners which covered the dynamics and recommended intervention with lesbian victims and batterers. The response to this training was very positive, and the Task Force was able to generate a referral list identifying over 20 therapists who were qualified to work with battered lesbian and gay clients.

In sum, the Battered Lesbian Helpline proved invaluable. As might be expected, battered lesbians have many of the same basic needs of all battered women: Safety, freedom from abuse, and time to think about the next series of steps. A lesbian victim may not be ready to take immediate action. She may utilize a helpline on several occasions to talk about her experience before she even asks for shelter or in-person counseling. This may be the result of her isolation or fear of moving too quickly to action. Calling the helpline may take a lot of courage; she may have been preparing herself for months before actually calling. She may not have any energy left to make an appointment, or to will herself to sit down with a stranger and tell her story. Yet, when she has a quiet moment, she will think about the information offered to her, and how validating it was to talk to someone who didn't blame her, or interrogate her about her decision to stay with her partner, or make her feel like a freak for being a lesbian. She will think about ideas offered to her regarding a safety plan, and when the relationship gets "bad" again, she will have a strategy for getting out before the fear and pain starts again.

One caller identified here as "Caren" stated:

> The people on the Helpline gave me the number of a shelter program that had been trained to be sensitive to lesbians, and there are some lesbians on the staff. They encouraged me to call and talk to the shelter so I could have a connection.

Other Direct Services and an Approach to Working with Battered Lesbians and Their Abusers

The grant received from the office of Victim–Witness Advocacy also provided funding for direct services for victims. Originally, it was planned to offer a support group for victims. However, the group had been poorly attended.

We have learned a lot from this experience about providing direct services to battered lesbians. For example, part of the explanation for poor attendance to the support group may have been the logistics of the group, providing a location which is easily accessible for all potential participants. Another reason may be the fears and concerns brought about by publicly disclosing the abuse in a group. The costs of telling are the same as for heterosexuals; in addition, the victims could lose their already limited support network. Often victims present with a network that includes the controlling abusive partner, and possibly one other lesbian couple; or a wider, looser support system focused on a particular activity, such as a sports team, activist group, etc. Family may not be available, having disowned the victim for coming out as gay. Friends and acquaintances in the community may feel betrayed if the victim accuses a lesbian of being a batterer, due to their own denial.

Victim Counseling and Support.   Counseling of battered lesbians some-times triggers or exposes internalized homophobia, sexism, and shame. For some lesbian victims, the emotional cost of control/abuse adds to considerable stress about their sexual orientation: "I can't do this;" "I never thought I was one of those but now I guess I am;" "I hate it. I'll kill myself if anyone finds out that I let a woman beat me."

The beginning of the support process involves two important foci. First, it is important to create an empowering environment of support and safety. This enables the victim to explore her present and her future. The environment of safety allows the victim to find her voice, to express herself, and to begin to listen to herself. The victim has the opportunity to examine her own values and beliefs about herself, her relationships, and the outside world. The acknowledgment and integration of the victim's experience with homophobia and hetero-sexism validates her multiple levels of oppression (Kanuha, 1990).

The second focus should be to establish a system of healthy connec-tions. A support group helps to reconnect the survivor with other women. Participants are able to share with and learn from each other. They are able to establish ways to be together, to see how interpersonal conflicts can be worked out nonviolently. The empow-ering environment supports the survivor in decision making, in her own way and in her own time. The survivor's ability to see herself in relation to others in a growth-encouraging way is nurtured in these mutually empathetic relationships. The counseling program replicates the self-in-relation process unique in women's develop-ment, often begun in the mother–daughter relationship and contin-ued in adult relationships (Miller, 1976; Turner, 1991).

The experience of abuse and control is about disconnection. The abuser/controller disconnects her victim from her outside support systems and from herself. The abuser becomes the victim's only connection. The abuser tells the victim "I'm all you've got" and reinforces that belief with negative messages, shame, and blaming.

Caren's reconnection with herself and others was an important aspect of her breaking free from her abuser. It was begun with the Helpline, which supported and validated her experience. It was continued by the support group, where she was listened to and valued. Finally, it was reinforced by the social worker, with whom Caren maintained a connection that lasted more than a year.

Batterers' Intervention.   The lesbian community recognizes that intervention on behalf of victims must also involve treatment for the abuser. In this case example, a two-part insight-oriented method is presented. It begins by identifying the control tactics used by an abuser and focuses the treatment on increasing supports as a measure of improving self-esteem.

> *Joan is White, 40 years old, and is a high-school graduate. She has 4 years of military experience. Joan has never been married to a man and has no children. She was referred to counseling by a colleague. Joan has a history of three significant live-in relationships with women, including this most recent one. Joan ended the first two relationships. The current relationship was terminated by Joan's abused partner. The presenting issue was Joan's concern about the end of the relationship. During the assessment process, Joan focused mainly on blaming the end of the relationship on the failures of her partner.*

The intervention goals should include:

1. Defining and identifying control tactics used by Joan in the relationship by:

   - Examining definitions of abuse and control and how she made decisions to increase power to control her partner;
   - Exploring her view of the argument, behavior and/or experience;
   - Identifying her description of feelings about the abuse and the resulting power (Adams, 1988; Pence, 1987);
   - Exploring her belief system that supported her definition as the only acceptable or right one.

2. Increasing her supports in three areas

   - *Health*—Began working with exercise group, joined like group on weekends, began improving diet and eating habits. Decreased use of nicotine with long-term goal of quitting smoking.
   - *Spirituality*—Reconciled with her church and joined a lesbian spirituality group.

- *Creativity*—After 7-year lapse, began to paint again. Started again when asked to do an art therapy exercise in a session.

This last aspect of intervention was based on the hypothesis that a shift in her view of the world and the view of self expands when support systems expand. Developing one or more healthy systems of support can have an impact on all relationships.

An ongoing aspect of the work with Joan will be the examining and re-examining of abuse and power, and her decisions made to be controlling and abusive (Adams, 1988). This aspect must be integrated into all of the areas and issues worked on. For example:

Health

Joan identified past patterns of organizing her partners' health issues. Through the intervention, she was able to focus on taking responsibility for her own health and her own body.

This work brought up issues of self-care and nurturing experiences in her family of origin. Joan was confronted with the recognition of a lack of nurturing experiences in her childhood. This insight was uncovered when Joan was asked to recall what kind of "comfort food" was used in childhood. Joan was dismayed to realize that she was unable to recall any positive experiences related to food. Thus, a grief work process was initiated to mourn past losses and deprivation, as well as current losses, including that of her most recent relationship.

Spirituality

Joan also was able to identify grief over the loss of her church community due to homophobia. By joining a Spirituality group, she was able to recapture a part of her spiritual identity. Joan was able to practice "letting go" of her need for power within her Spirituality group. She relinquished her pattern of "being in charge," by purposefully not speaking until everyone else had spoken; in the process she learned to listen to others.

Creativity

Joan reported that she stopped painting because she believed that she would never be good enough, which she equated with not being powerful enough. The initial art therapy exercise helped her to see that her creativity was about her and her life. She went back and looked at her old paintings, brought them in, and discovered how they reflected her beliefs about abusive power. She was then able to express herself about ending her relationship and how she maintained coercive control over her partner.

FUTURE GOALS

Although some progress has been achieved, there continues to be the need to increase outreach, education, and treatment efforts for battered lesbians and their abusers. For example, the legal system would benefit from special education efforts. Many battered lesbians report that they have not been helped when they have turned to the law. Responding police officers in lesbian domestic violence calls appear to be unable to determine who is victim and who is batterer. Thus, they are more likely to arrest both parties (Leventhal, 1995). Judges are also more likely to impose mutual restraints. Homophobia in the law enforcement and justice systems often has serious consequences for the lesbian victim. One participant reported losing custody of her child because the child was injured in the course of domestic violence; another victim was named as the defendant and her court-appointed attorney's homophobia seemed blatant. The client believes that her conviction was the result of her attorney's incompetence due to his homophobic attitude toward her.

Another area of focus must be to expand intervention programs for lesbian batterers. Batterers must be held responsible for their choice of behaviors. Intervention programs need to be established in which lesbian batterers can address their violence, safe from homophobia.

Finally, the Task Force must expand its work to address the concerns of lesbians of color as well as immigrant and Third World lesbians. The shelter and mental health services are still inadequate in their accessibility to heterosexual women of color, immigrant women, and Third World Women (Crenshaw, 1991). The "triple jeopardy" (Kanuha, 1990) is an enormous barrier to safety for women facing these oppressions.

During the past few years, extensive progress has been made in developing shelter, mental health, and social services for immigrant and Third World battered women. For in-depth discussions of multicultural issues, domestic violence among immigrant families, and social work practice, see *chapters 16–19 of this volume.*

REFERENCES

Adams, D. (1988). Treatment models of men who batter: A pro-feminist analysis. In K. Yllo & M. Bograd (Eds.), *Feminist perspectives on wife abuse* (pp. 176–199). Newbury Park, CA: Sage.

Carlson, B. W., & Maciol, K. (1997). Domestic violence: Gay men and lesbians. In *Encyclopedia of social work supplement* (pp. 101–111). Washington, DC: National Association of Social Workers.

Crenshaw, K. (1991). Mapping the margins: Intersectionality, identity politics, and violence against women of color. *Stamford Law Review, 43,* 1241–1299.

Farley, N. (1992). Same sex domestic violence. In S. H. Dworkin & F. J. Guiterrez (Eds.), *Counseling gay men and lesbians of the rainbow* (pp. 231–242). Alexandria, VA: American Association for Counseling and Development.

Ganley, A. (1981). *Court mandated treatment for men who batter.* Washington, DC: Center for Women's Policy Studies.

Grover, J. (1988). Battered lesbians are battered women. In K. Lobel (Chair), *Fourth National Conference Manual* (pp. 3.11–3.14). Washington, DC: National Coalition Against Domestic Violence.

Hart, B (1986). Lesbian battering: An examination. In K. Lobel (Ed.), *Naming the violence* (pp. 173–189). Seattle, WA: The Seal Press.

Heer, C. (1992). Battering or mutual abuse: How to assess battering in lesbian couples. *The Coalition Reporter.*

Hirshorn, H. (1984, June). The tip of the ice berg: Lesbian battering. *Woman News,* p. 5.

Irvine, J. (1985, January 14). Lesbian battering: The search for shelter. *Gay Community News, 11*(25), 13–17.

Island, D., & Letillier, P. (1991). *Men who beat the men who love them.* New York: Harrington Park.

Kanuha, V. (1990). Compounding the triple jeopardy: Battering in lesbian of color relationships. In Brown & Root (Eds.), *Diversity and complexity in feminist therapy* (pp. 169–189). New York: Harrington Park Press.

Leventhal, B. (1995). *Voices unheard, sisters unseen.* [Video.] Available from Shakti Productions: Maryland.

New Jersey Prevention of Domestic Abuse Act, 2C:25 §19 (1991).

Pence, E. (1987). *In our best interests.* Duluth, MN: Minnesota Program Development.

Pence, E., & Paymar, M. (1993). *Education groups for men who batter: The Duluth model.* New York: Springer Publishing Co.

Pharr, S. (1986). Two workshops on homophobia. In K. Lobel (Ed.), *Naming the violence* (pp. 202–222). Seattle, WA: Seal Press.

Pharr, S. (1987). Lesbian battering: Social change urged. In *NCADV Voice* (pp. 16–17). Washington, DC: National Coalition Against Domestic Violence.

Renzetti, C. (1988). Violence in lesbian relationships. *Journal of Interpersonal Violence, 3,* 381–399.

Renzetti, C. (1989). Building a second closet: Third party responses to victims of lesbian partner abuse. *Family Relations, 38,* 157–163.

Renzetti, C. (1992). *Violent betrayal.* Newbury Park, CA: Sage.

Thompson, C. (1990). *Leading introductory workshops on homophobia.* Cambridge, MA: The Campaign to End Homophobia.

Turner, C. (1991). Feminist practice with women of color. In M. Bricker-Jenkins et al. (Eds.), *Feminist social work practice in clinical settings* (pp. 114–115, SSH Series). Newbury Park, CA: Sage.

Vardamis, S. (1983). Confronting homophobia. *Aegis, 37,* 73–77.

Zorza, J. (1995). *Voices heard, sisters unseen* [Video]. Available from Shakti Productions: Maryland.

Cross-Cultural Issues, Policies, and Practices with Battered Women

Application of the Culturagram to Empower Culturally and Ethnically Diverse Battered Women

Patricia Brownell and Elaine P. Congress

W e are grateful to Dr. Albert Roberts, the editor of this book, for strongly encouraging us to write this chapter. His vision and constructive editorial suggestions inspired us. He, along with our many other social work colleagues throughout the United States, has become increasingly sensitive and responsive to the multicultural issues regarding the delivery of social services and clinical interventions with battered women and their children. Dr. Roberts spent the first 23 years of his life in New York City and grew up alongside other immigrant families, so his identification and understanding of cultural diversity came early to him.

As the twenty-first century approaches, social workers and family service providers in the United States are challenged by the globalization of social issues and the widespread immigration of families from cultures significantly different from the dominant European-American culture.

We came to New York from Wisconsin and Connecticut, respectively, and have worked with immigrant families during most of our professional careers—in public-sector social services (including services for battered women) and community-based clinical services (including crisis intervention with sexual assault victims and other psychiatric emergencies), respectively. Our professional experience is similar to that of the majority of our social worker colleagues who have lived and practiced in states such as New York, Texas, California, and Florida with large immigrant populations. To effectively address problems like domestic violence in work with culturally diverse families, service providers must develop a multicultural understanding of victims in relation to their family members, communities, and cultures of origin. Illustrations of representative family situations include:

- Mr. and Mrs. T. are recent Orthodox Jewish immigrants from Russia. Mr. T. is despondent because he cannot find a job, although his wife was able to do so. He has become verbally and sometimes physically abusive to her.
- Mrs. C. is a first-generation Chinese-American woman who is physically and emotionally abused by her husband when he experiences gambling losses.
- Mrs. S. is a woman from Puerto Rico living in New York City who is abused by her husband when he drinks heavily, particularly during holiday seasons.
- Ms. M. is a nondocumented Mexican woman living in a small town in southern Texas with Mr. G., the father of her children, who is an American citizen; he abuses her and threatens to report her to the immigration authorities.
- Mr. and Mrs. D. are a professional couple who immigrated from India 3 years ago. Mr. D. physically abuses his wife on occasion for being what he defines as too independent and not respecting his role as head of the household.

Each of these families are struggling with the problem of domestic violence, although this may not be given as the presenting problem to a practitioner or service provider. Practitioners used to working with Western families may find that detection of domestic violence and effective intervention remains elusive with families from cultures with which they are unfamiliar.

The purpose of this chapter is to discuss the application of the Culturagram to the assessment, detection, and development of intervention strategies for domestic violence in immigrant families. Case examples presented above are provided to illustrate the use of the Culturagram with immigrant families where domestic violence may be a factor.

OVERVIEW OF THE CULTURAGRAM

There is increasing interest in cross-cultural and multicultural approaches to examining domestic violence as a social and practice issue (Abraham, 1995; Baig-Amin, El Bassel, Krishnan, Gilbert, & Waters, 1996; Brownell, 1997; Levinson, 1989; Levy, 1995). However, to date, there has been little focus on developing a standardized culturally sensitive method for assessing, detecting, and developing service interventions for culturally diverse immigrant families who may be experiencing domestic violence. The Culturagram is one culturally sensitive assessment instrument that can be used by family therapists and practitioners for this purpose.

The Culturagram assists social workers and family practitioners in working more effectively with families from diverse cultures (Congress, 1997). It is an assessment tool that was developed to improve practitioners' understanding and ability to empower culturally diverse families (Congress, 1994), using ten dimensions to assess the impact of cultural values, beliefs, and practices on family functioning and to develop effective interventions.

Although generalizations about ethnic and racial differences among families have proved useful for practitioners (McGoldrick & Giordano, 1996), overgeneralization may lead to misleading or inaccurate stereotyping of families (Congress, 1997). The Culturagram provides a guide for practitioners to elicit culturally sensitive information about families that can also be specific to individual family circumstances within, as well as across, cultures.

Components of the Culturagram that are useful to the practitioner in making culturally sensitive assessments of immigrant families include: reasons for immigration; length of time in the community; legal or nondocumented status; age at time of immigration; language spoken at home; contact with cultural institutions; health beliefs; holidays and special events; impact of crisis events; and values concerning family, education, and work (Congress, 1997).

Domestic violence is defined as a social problem in which the victim's property, health, emotional well-being, or life is threatened or harmed as a result of intentional behavior by a partner, spouse, family member, or significant other (Barker, 1995). Domestic violence was framed both as a social problem and a women's issue in the 1960s and 1970s (Pleck, 1987; Schechter, 1982).

APPLICATION OF THE CULTURAGRAM TO THE ASSESSMENT AND DETECTION OF DOMESTIC VIOLENCE AMONG DIVERSE IMMIGRANT FAMILIES

The Culturagram is intended to be a supplement to a professional assessment of family functioning. The purpose of the Culturagram is to assist the practitioner in incorporating cultural values, beliefs, and experiences into the assessment process; to more accurately detect underlying problems and issues; and to develop a more effective intervention strategy and service plan.

Social problems like domestic violence can be difficult for practitioners to detect even with families from familiar cultures. Family members are often invested in concealing or minimizing domestic violence from those outside the family. Even when the abuse is apparent and explicit, victims and abusers are often resistant to making changes in their relationships and living arrangements.

Domestic violence has been identified as one of the most dangerous and deadly social problems, disproportionately affecting women (Levy, 1995). Incidents of domestic violence can elude practitioners who are working with families from immigrant communities. Even if the abuse of one partner by another is disclosed as the presenting problem, available services may not be seen as viable or appropriate by the victim or abuser. The Culturagram can be useful to the practitioner in detecting domestic violence and developing viable service plans.

The importance and usefulness of understanding the relationship between ethnicity and family functioning has been underscored by

McGoldrick and Giordano (1996). Identifying and understanding risk factors for domestic violence in ethnically and culturally diverse families can result in saving lives and improving the safety and quality of life of family members, as well as reflecting culturally competent practice.

EXAMPLES OF DOMESTIC VIOLENCE AMONG DIVERSE IMMIGRANT GROUPS

Case examples presented above are expanded below to demonstrate the linkage between factors in domestic violence and cross-cultural family values. Some of the ethnic immigrant communities presented here are discussed in greater detail in subsequent chapters of this book.

Domestic Violence Within the Immigrant Russian Jewish Community

Expectations prior to immigrating to the United States can lead to family stress in immigrant families. When the husband expects to be the household provider, his ego may be defined by that role. If he has difficulty finding work and must be supported by his wife, he may act out his disappointment and anger by being abusive to her. The case of Mr. and Mrs. T. illustrates how such role conflicts can arise in Soviet emigré households and can in turn lead to domestic violence (Chazin, 1997).

Mr. and Mrs. T. emigrated to the United States to seek a better life. However, while Mrs. T. has found a job, Mr. T. has been unable to secure one that enables him to utilize his professional education. He has become depressed and resentful, while Mrs. T. is finding the stress of being breadwinner, parent, and homemaker increasingly burdensome. Mr. T. has become abusive to her and their children, increasing her stress.

Domestic Violence in the Chinese-American Community

Social isolation and extreme obedience to one's husband can be a precursor to spouse abuse among first-generation Chinese-Americans. In Chapter 18 of this book, Moo-Yee Lee describes a domestic violence situation in the Chinese-American community. This involves a family she identifies as Mr. and Mrs. Chan.

> *The Chans, both of whom are late middle-aged, have been living in the United States for 30 years. However, Mrs. Chan works for her husband in his Chinatown restaurant, and has always resided with him in the Chinese community. She speaks no English, and her social acquaintances are also Chinese. Mr. Chan believes in traditional values; he considers himself the head of the household and demands unconditional obedience from his wife and children. He enjoys gambling—a traditional Chinese pastime—and when he loses, he abuses Mrs. Chan both verbally and physically.*

Domestic Violence in the Latino Immigrant Community

Working with Latino families can involve different cultural as well as immigration issues (Bonilla-Santiago, 1996). For example, Puerto Rican family issues and dynamics can be different from those of Mexican, Central American, or South American families (Congress, 1997). In addition, government benefits and social services are more accessible for Puerto Ricans than for immigrants from other Spanish-speaking countries. When one spouse is nondocumented, the other is an American citizen, and when domestic violence is a factor in the household, the situation becomes even more complex (National Women's Abuse Prevention Project, 1988).

Machismo and holiday drinking, prevalent in some Latino cultures (Mayo, 1997), are correlated with spouse abuse.

> *Mr. and Mrs. S. are Puerto Rican nationals who both grew up in New York City. Mr. S. views drinking alcohol as an integral part of socializing with his male friends. During holidays, Mr. S.'s drinking intensifies, and he often becomes abusive to Mrs. S., accusing her of flirting with other men.*

Domestic Violence Involving a Nondocumented Spouse

Power and control have been identified as hallmarks of domestic violence (Walker, 1994). When the abused spouse or partner is nondocumented, the power differential between the documented and nondocumented partner is such that it may be almost impossible for the abused nondocumented partner to escape.

Mr. G. and Ms. M. met while Mr. G., an American citizen, was working in Mexico. He brought Ms. M. to the United States, promising to sponsor her for citizenship. Even though they have had two children, he has still not allowed her to obtain a green card. He has become increasingly physically and emotionally abusive, most recently threatening to have her deported and keeping their children in the United States.

Domestic Violence in the Indian/South Asian Immigrant Community

Cultures with strong patriarchal values have been identified with domestic violence (Bonilla-Santiago, 1996; Levinson, 1989). In some developing countries, particularly in rural or provincial areas, gender roles are rigidly defined and all family members accept the role of the male (husband, brother, or father) as dominant. This can begin to change for women who immigrate to the United States and begin to assimilate Western values regarding the role of women in society.

Mr. and Mrs. D. immigrated from a provincial city in India 3 years ago. Mr. D. was a member of a professional class in India, and is employed as an accountant in the United States. Mrs. D. is completing post-graduate studies. Recently, Mr. D. has begun to express concern that Mrs. D. is not meeting his expectations as a traditional wife and is becoming too "Americanized." She in turn challenges his assumptions that he is head of the household and must make all major decisions for the family. With increasing frequency, their arguments have escalated into physical abuse by Mr. D. against his wife. He states it is his right and obligation as her husband to discipline her for misbehaving toward him.

THE TEN DIMENSIONS OF THE CULTURAGRAM

The purpose of this section is to demonstrate how family practitioners can utilize the Culturagram in working with families from diverse cultures to assess whether domestic violence may be a hidden issue. Each example below illustrates the significance of each component or dimension of the Culturagram in the assessment and detection of domestic violence in these families.

Reasons for Immigration

Chazin (1997) points out that the decision to immigrate may impact an immigrant family's functioning once in the united States. The Russian Jewish family situation illustrates how this can result in domestic violence. This family immigrated to seek a better life; however, once in the United States, the husband was unable to find a job, whereas the wife was able to find one and support the family. This challenged the husband's cultural belief that he should be the breadwinner of the family and resulted in depression and anger, which he projected onto his wife through abusive behavior. Mental health services were not considered acceptable in the culture from which this family immigrated, and the religious institution with which they were involved both before and after immigration supported the beliefs of the husband. The presenting problem in this family may be the unemployment of the husband or the children's school difficulties.

Length of Time in the Community

Knowing the length of time family members have lived in the United States may be helpful to practitioners in detecting domestic violence. Families newly arrived from cultures that support husbands' disciplining their wives may not be aware that this is illegal and not socially acceptable in the United States. On the other hand, the example of the Chinese family underscores the importance of a practitioner's exploring the acculturation of a family as a separate issue from the length of time spent in this country. Families who have lived within closely knit immigrant communities, even if they have resided in the United States for a considerable length of time, may still adhere to the cultural values of their country of origin. They may have internalized their community's belief that outsiders should not know their business, and may view American social welfare institutions as alien. However, second-generation adult children who have grown up in the United States are more likely to understand domestic violence as a social and legal problem, and may seek assistance for parents who are victims of family abuse.

Legal or Nondocumented Status

The legal or nondocumented status of one or both partners can alert practitioners to the possibility of a power differential that can exacerbate domestic violence. If nondocumented, the victim may be reluctant to disclose the abuse fearing deportation, separation from children, and losing financial support. If both partners are nondocumented, they may fear the intervention of law enforcement and detection if they seek out available services. Since the passage of the Personal Responsibility and Work Opportunity Reconciliation Act of 1996 (PRA) (PL 104-193, August 22, 1996), even legal immigrants may find many social services inaccessible, depending on the state of residence. However, practitioners as well as many immigrants—both legal and nondocumented—may be unaware of the provisions in the Violence Against Women Act of 1994 (VAWA) (PL 103-322, September 13, 1994) and the PRA that permit provision of emergency and other social services to immigrant women who are victims of domestic violence. However, these options may not available if the victim continues to reside with the abuser.

In addition, while immigrant domestic violence victims may find services to be accessible in large urban areas like Los Angeles or New York City, other victims may not find available services in localities like Southern Texas, regardless of immigration status (Congress, 1997). Health care workers and school social workers may be more likely than mental health practitioners to come in contact with a nondocumented abused spouse or partner.

Age at Time of Immigration

Age of family members at the time of immigration can be another indicator of the degree of acculturation of family members. Those members who immigrated to the country at a relatively young age may be more likely to be aware of domestic violence as a social issue of concern in the United States and of the availability of social services to address it. These young and second-generation family members may be more apt to seek help, if they are the victim of abuse, or advocate seeking help for a victim who is a family member.

Language Spoken at Home and in the Community

Immigrant family members who speak only the language of the country of origin are less likely to have been exposed to American norms and values and more likely to reflect the values and norms of the country origin. Bilingual family members—particularly the husband—may use this as a way of isolating and controlling family members, such as the wife, who cannot speak English.

When only the native language is spoken in the community in which the family resides, there is likely to be a strong reinforcement of values of the country of origin. In some immigrant communities, there is strong pressure not to report undesirable social problems like domestic violence, in order not to discredit the community. Ethnic social service agencies and health care providers who are closely involved with the victim's immigrant community may be most likely to make contact with the victim or her family.

Contact with Cultural Institutions

Cultural and religious institutions may strongly reinforce hierarchical roles within the family, including the right of the husband to exert authority over other family members, even if this involves physical force and verbal threats. Examples include male religiosity (Chazin, 1997), the culturally supported role of the male as head of household and the belief that women are responsible for keeping the household together even in the face of extreme difficulties. Educating religious leaders about the illegality of domestic violence has helped raise awareness of this problem in religious institutions where initial contact with immigrant victims and their families may be made.

Health Beliefs

Some cultures may support the somaticizing of emotional distress, which could lead to victims denying the impact of domestic abuse. Immigrants from rural areas of their country of origin may seek out native healers, who may not view domestic violence from the same cultural and legal perspective as do American-trained health and social service providers. Some immigrant advocacy groups are reaching out to native healers and nontraditional health care providers with information on domestic violence.

Holidays and Special Events

Holidays and special events in the United States are often associated with alcohol consumption. While this may be true of some immigrant groups, such as Latinos—whose festivals often include heavy alcohol consumption (Turner & Cooper, 1997)—it may not be the case for all cultures. Alcohol consumption has been correlated with risk of domestic violence in some studies, especially if the abuser is unemployed and/or the event is sports-related. It should be noted that this link has been questioned even in the dominant Anglo culture (Zubretsky & Digirotama, 1996).

Russian Jewish cultures do not support heavy alcohol consumption as part of celebrations, nor do many Indian/South Asian or Asian cultures. However, holidays and special events that are unique to the country of origin may be times of stress and sadness for immigrants—especially those who have immigrated recently and have lost support systems in the process, predisposing some vulnerable families to domestic violence. Activities such as gambling, which is associated with special occasions and events in the Chinese culture, may be correlated with domestic abuse, as noted by Lee in Chapter 18 of this book. Practitioners working with families from diverse cultures could use the Culturagram as a guide to asking for information about holidays and how they are celebrated, in order to seek information on the possibility of domestic violence as a factor in the family.

Impact of Crisis Events

Values and beliefs of the country of origin may influence family members' reactions to crisis events. As an example, if a wife from a traditional immigrant community is raped, she may be blamed and shunned by her ethnic community as having invited the rape. This may in turn lead to and provide a justification of abuse by the spouse. If she has internalized these beliefs, she may not seek needed counseling or medical care due to feelings of shame and guilt. If medical care is sought, it may be under the pretext of obtaining routine care. The Culturagram can provide an guide for culturally sensitive questioning about examination findings.

Values About Family, Education Disparity, and Unemployment

In cultures that support a hierarchical family structure with a dominant male breadwinner, deviation from cultural norms may lead to family violence (Levinson, 1989). Husbands may become angry if they perceive their wives to be seeking more education than they have themselves or more than they believe is appropriate. If the husband is unemployed (a risk factor for domestic violence in the American culture), he may become abusive, even if the wife is working and supporting the family. She may also seek to protect him by denying or minimizing the abuse, in order to support his dominance within the family. A practitioner may find it useful to seek information on perceived differences in gender roles and status within the family as a way of assessing whether family values could be a barrier to acknowledging spouse abuse.

Women working outside the home may be a source of discomfort to males from some cultures, because they are in contact with male co-workers. Older parents and other community members may also reinforce the notion that the daughter-in-law should be submissive to her husband in order to be a good wife.

If risk factors are present, this does not mean that domestic violence is occurring or will occur in a family. However, they can be viewed as predisposing factors to be noted during an assessment process. If abuse is detected, it may be denied or intervention rejected unless detection and interventions are framed in a culturally sensitive manner. This may be facilitated through referrals to practitioners who are from the same culture and speak the language of the immigrant family. However, a practitioner should explore whether this referral may itself present a barrier because the family is concerned about exposure within their own community. In this event, service providers who are part of the same immigrant community may not be effective.

USE OF THE CULTURAGRAM IN DEVELOPING AND IMPLEMENTING EFFECTIVE INTERVENTION STRATEGIES

A further analysis of the vignettes presented at the beginning of the chapter illustrates how the Culturagram can be used to develop effective intervention strategies for immigrant families where domestic violence is a factor.

Russian-Jewish Immigrant Families

In the case of Mr. and Mrs. T., the services of immigrant advocacy organizations such as the New York Association for New Americans (NYANA) that have experience in working with this immigrant community can be utilized with the permission of the family. These agencies often have employment services, mentoring programs, and culturally sensitive counseling programs that are tailored to the needs, values, and expectations of distinct immigrant groups. However, if the victim decides to leave the household, the lack of Kosher shelters can be a barrier (Cramer, 1990). Planning for culturally sensitive services for victims of domestic violence can ensure greater number of service options for those women who decide to leave an abusive relationship.

Chinese Immigrant Families

Isolation of an immigrant victim of domestic violence by the abuser and other community members keep her from knowing options.

Increasingly, immigrant communities are developing culturally specific domestic violence services for their members (Ching Louie, 1991). However, an older woman like Mrs. C. may be less likely to feel comfortable with service systems designed for younger women with children, and may choose to remain with the batterer while wishing the abuse to stop.

The Chinese culture emphasizes respect and fear of authority (See Chapter 18). Knowing this, the use of law enforcement can be a useful intervention strategy for some victims. According to Lee, the Chinese community does not want involvement with law enforcement agents, and would pressure the abuser to stop the abuse, in the event that the threat of involvement of law enforcement is not sufficient to motivate the husband to stop the abuse of his wife.

Latino Immigrant Families

It is important for practitioners to understand the within-group differences among families from Latino countries of origin. This includes differences in family values and gender roles, as well as ability to access needed services.

Puerto Rican Families. Families like that of Mr. and Mrs. S., whose country of origin is Puerto Rico, have many more service options than those who come from other Latin American countries. This is due to the fact that Puerto Rican nationals have access to all government benefits and services in the United States, assuming that other eligibility criteria are met. However, family pressure on Puerto Rican women to "keep the family together" may create a barrier to their leaving abusive situations (Rios, n.d.). Understanding the concept of "machismo" may help the social worker to understand the origin of the husband's apparently irrational behavior (Mayo, 1997). Bilingual staffing for domestic violence shelter facilities and other services for victims of domestic violence can address this barrier to victims' accepting services.

Nondocumented Latino Family Members. Nondocumented victims of domestic violence, like Ms. M., are especially vulnerable, particularly when they are living with or married to citizens who take advantage of the victim's nondocumented status to threaten her with deportation and separation from children. If there is a language barrier, this exploitation can be further exacerbated. In fact, the Violence Against Women Act of 1994 can protect nondocumented victims of domestic violence from deportation and separation from their children. Education as to options—information that if known by the abuser is likely to be withheld—can provide additional assistance to the victim.

Indian/South Asian Immigrant Families

Most countries are made up of complex subcultures depending on the class, religion, and geographic place of origin of the family. In the case of Mr. and Mrs. D. from India, the fact that they came from a provincial city suggests they may bring with them beliefs that are more traditional than those of immigrants from large urban areas (Gupta, 1992). On the other hand, the educational level of both husband and wife may predispose them to seek a therapeutic intervention such as family counseling (Lipchik, 1994). In a country like India, which has no concept of spouse abuse or laws prohibiting it, it may be considered socially acceptable for husbands to "discipline" their wives.

Providing information to the husband about the illegality of his behavior in this country, and the possible consequences to him and his work if it continues, may serve as a disincentive for him, as well as important information for his wife. This example also illustrates how some immigrant families may choose couple counseling over separation when domestic violence is a problem. While not often supported by the feminist-oriented domestic violence service network in the United States, it may be the only viable service intervention that the immigrant victim will accept (Lipchik, 1994).

CONCLUSIONS

There is growing interest and concern about culturally sensitive practice with families (Congress, 1997). This, coupled with increased knowledge about domestic violence in immigrant communities, points to a need within the domestic violence service community to develop effective ways of working with immigrant families where domestic violence is a factor.

Detecting and developing culturally sensitive interventions with families from diverse cultures remains a challenge, however. The Culturagram is a culturally sensitive assessment instrument that can be utilized by practitioners to improve services to domestic violence victims and their families from immigrant communities.

The Culturagram can also serve as a tool for research on assessment and detection of domestic violence among victims of domestic violence from ethnically diverse immigrant families, as well as on effective intervention strategies. Effective practice models and the incidence and prevalence of domestic violence in immigrant families are increasingly important areas of research for the next millennium. The chapters in this book provide valuable information for family practitioners. They also lay the foundation for this emergent research agenda.

We highly recommend that the reader examine the chapters by Dr. Moo-Yee Lee, on Chinese-American battered women (chapter 18), Dr. Diana Valle Ferrer, on coping strategies of battered women in Puerto Rico (chapter 19), and Dr. Mieko Yoshihama, on emerging legislation and private shelters for battered women and their children in Japan (chapter 17).

REFERENCES

Abraham, M. (1995). Ethnicity, gender and marital violence: South Asian women's organizations in the United States. In *Gender and Society*, 9, 450–468.

Baig-Amin, M., El-Bassel, N., Krishnan, S., Gilbert, L., & Waters, A. (1996). *Toward a model for understanding domestic violence among South Asian immigrant women.* Paper presented at the 1996 Annual Conference of the American Public Welfare Association, New York.

Barker, R. L. (1995). *The social work dictionary.* Silver Springs, MD: NASW Press.

Bonilla-Santiago, G. (1996). Latina battered women: Barriers to service delivery and cultural considerations. In A. R. Roberts (Ed.), *Helping battered women: New perspectives and remedies* (pp. 229–234). New York: Oxford University Press.

Brownell, P. (1997). Multicultural practice and domestic violence. In E. P. Congress (Ed.), *Multicultural perspectives in working with families* (pp. 217–235). New York: Springer Publishing Company.

Chazin, R. (1997). Working with Soviet Jewish immigrants. In E. P. Congress (Ed.), *Multicultural perspectives in working with families* (pp. 142–166). New York: Springer Publishing Company.

Ching Louie, M. (1991, March/April). Hope for battered Asians. *New Directions for Women,* p. 1.

Congress, E. (1994). The use of Culturagrams to assess and empower culturally diverse families. *Families in Society: The Journal of Contemporary Human Services,* 75, 531–540.

Congress, E. (1997). Using the Culturagram to assess and empower culturally diverse families. In E. P. Congress (Ed.), *Multicultural perspectives in working with families* (pp. 3–16). New York: Springer Publishing Company.

Cramer, L. (1990, Fall). Recommendations for working with Jewish battered women. *National Coalition Against Domestic Violence (NCADV),* pp. 4–5.

Gupta, V. M. (1992, June). The weakest link: Domestic violence in our community. *The Indian-American,* pp. 42–44.

Levinson, D. (1989). *Family violence in cross-cultural perspective.* Newbury Park, CA: Sage.

Levy, B. (1995). Violence against women. In N. Van Den Bergh (Ed.), *Feminist practice in the twenty-first century* (pp. 312–329). Washington, DC: NASW Press.

Lipchik, E. (1994). Therapy for couples can reduce domestic violence. In K. Swisher & C. Wekesser (Eds.), *Violence against women* (pp. 154–163). San Diego, CA: Greenhaven.

Mayo, Y. (1997). Machismo, manhood, and men in Latino families. In E. P. Congress (Ed.), *Multicultural perspectives in working with families* (pp. 181–200). New York: Springer Publishing Company.

McGoldrick, M., & Giordano, J. (1996). Ethnicity and family therapy: An overview. In M. McGoldrick, J. Pearce, & J. Giordano (Eds.), *Ethnicity and family therapy* (2nd ed.) (pp. 1–27). New York: Guilford.

National Women's Abuse Prevention Project. (1988). Special issues facing the undocumented woman. *The Exchange,* 2, 10–12.

Personal Responsibility and Work Opportunity Reconciliation Act of 1996, Pub. L. No. 104-193 (August 22, 1996).

Pleck, E. (1987). *Domestic tyranny: The making of American social policy against family violence from colonial times to the present.* New York: Oxford University Press.

Rios, E. A. (n.d.). *Double jeopardy: Cultural and systemic barriers faced by the Latina battered woman.* Unpublished manuscript.

Schechter, S. (1982). *Women and male violence: The visions and struggles of the battered women's movement.* Boston: South End Press.

Turner, S., & Cooper, M. (1997). Working with culturally diverse substance abusers. In E. P. Congress (Ed.), *Multicultural perspectives in working with families* (pp. 236–251). New York: Springer Publishing Company.

Violence Against Women Act of 1994, Pub. L. No. 103-322 (September 13, 1994).

Walker, L. E. (1994). *Abused women and survivor therapy: A practical guide for the psychotherapist.* Washington, DC: American Psychological Association.

Zubretsky, T. M., & Digirotama, K. M. (1996). The false connection between adult domestic violence and alcohol. In A. R. Roberts (Ed.), *Helping battered women: New perspectives and remedies* (pp. 222–228). New York: Oxford University Press.

CHAPTER 17

Domestic Violence in Japan: Research, Program Developments, and Emerging Movements

Mieko Yoshihama

> Every night I lie on my futon with my clothes on so that I can escape quickly if my husband attacks me. I just wish that I could sleep soundly in my pajamas.
>
> —*a Japanese woman who participated in a nationwide survey in Japan*

Violence against women by their intimate partners (domestic violence) knows no racial, ethnic, or cultural boundaries, and women of Japanese descent are not exempt from this type of victimization in Japan, the U.S., or elsewhere. In Japan, despite the relatively slow rise in public awareness, an increasing number of efforts, led predominantly by women's organizations, are emerging to combat this serious, but previously underaddressed, problem.

For the first time, a nationwide study of domestic violence was conducted in 1992 by a grassroots women's group, the Domestic Violence Action & Research Group [DVARG] (DVARG, 1994). The results of this study have been disseminated throughout Japan through news releases, public meetings, and publications. This nationwide study, coupled with consciousness-raising efforts led by the DVARG and several other organizations, have challenged a commonly held notion that domestic violence is not serious or common among the Japanese.

Outside Japan, the DVARG's study results were also presented internationally to publicize the serious nature of, and the lack of governmental responses to, domestic violence in Japan. The release of this study's preliminary findings coincided with the rise of an international movement called the Global Campaign for Women's Human Rights. At the World Conference on Human Rights (WCHR) held in Vienna in 1993, the Global Campaign successfully advocated for an expanded definition of human rights in order to include women's rights. *The Vienna Declaration and Programme of Action* (United Nations, 1993) recognized violence against women as a prevalent and pervasive form of human rights violation and called upon individual member nations to eliminate violence against women in both public and private spheres. The results of the nationwide study by the DVARG were presented both verbally and in writing during the nongovernmental organizations' activities at the World Conferences on Human Rights, Vienna, June, 1993, as well as at two other United Nations Conferences—the ESCAP NGO Symposium on Women in Development (Manila, Philippines, November, 1993) and the World Conference on Women (Beijing, August, 1995) (cf. DVARG, 1993a, 1993b, 1995). In contrast, the Japanese government's reports to the United Nations make cursory, if any, reference to the seriousness of domestic violence in Japan (Japanese Government, 1992; Sorifu Danjo Kyodosankaku Shitsu, 1994).

Following the World Conference on Human Rights was a period of slow, but steady, increase in a number of activities directly addressing the issue of domestic violence in Japan. A grassroots women's organization which had been conducting a semiannual telephone counseling program concerning divorce focused on domestic violence in 1993 (Joseino Tameno Rikon Hotline, 1993). A private women's shelter for battered women opened its doors in

1993 in Tokyo (Mitsui, 1994). The Japan Bar Association conducted a 2-day telephone counseling program on women's rights and domestic violence in 1994 (Nihon Bengoshi Rengokai, 1995). A few municipalities also began addressing the issue of domestic violence by conducting research and organizing symposia and workshops (e.g., Yokohama-shi Josei Kyokai, 1995). In preparation for the World Conferences on Women in Beijing in 1995, interest in violence against women in general and domestic violence in particular grew among women's organizations and local governments; an increasing number of workshops, symposia, and research projects on domestic violence were conducted (e.g., Kanagawa Women's Council, 1995). Following the Beijing Women's Conference, groups concerned about women's rights formed a coalition, the Peking (Beijing)-Japan Accountability Caucus, and have been demanding accountability on the part of the Japanese government in their response to violence against women. These movements appear to have prompted the Japanese government to finally recognize the prevalence of domestic violence and the extent of its consequences in Japan. In July, 1996, the Advisory Committee to the Council for Gender Equality of the Prime Minister's Office issued a plan to enact a law concerning violence against women as part of a blueprint of public policy entitled, "the Vision of Gender Equality" (Sorifu Danjo Kyodosankaku Shingikai, 1996).

This chapter will describe the scope and nature of domestic violence in Japan, based primarily on community-based studies and available official statistics, coupled with the information regarding current program development and research activities undertaken recently to address this problem.

ANTI-VIOLENCE AGAINST WOMEN MOVEMENTS IN JAPAN

Violence against women in general and that by male intimate partners (domestic violence) is by no means a new problem confronting women in Japan. For over a quarter century, women in Japan have organized themselves to address a broad spectrum of issues concerning violence against women, at times in support of specific women who have been victimized, or at other times in demanding institutional changes or lobbying for new or expanded social policies. The issues addressed range from prostitution (e.g., Japanese men using prostitutes) and pornography to rape, child sexual abuse, and sexual harassment in the workplace (for an overview of movements addressing violence against women in Japan, see Yunomae, 1995). For example, the early 1970s saw the rise of women's movements against Japanese "sex tours" to many Asian countries. The popularity of such "sex tours" among Japanese men coincided with the nation's rapid economic growth at the time (*Note*: In 1956, the Prostitution Prevention Law [Baishun Boshiho], a culmination of antiprostitution movements at the time, ended legalized prostitution in Japan). Echoing a protest led by Korean women against Japanese men who visit Korea to use prostitutes, Japanese women began organizing a series of protests in 1973 (Yunomae, 1990, 1995). At the beginning of the movement, activists in Japan coined a new term to describe the social phenomenon in question—men's use of prostitution, which have played a significant role in defining the issue (Yunomae, 1997). The conventional Japanese term for prostitution, *Bai-shun*, consisted of a combination of Chinese characters which denotes "selling spring." Women who protested men's use of prostitution began using a new combination of characters which signifies "buying spring." Because both combinations of characters have identically pronounced as *Bai-shun*, users of the new combination articulated the distinction by prefacing that they are referring to "buying spring" or pronouncing the term differently, such as *Kai-shun*. At times, the term *Bai-bai-shun* is used to refer to both aspects of prostitution. This newly created term has gradually gained acceptance: the new combination of characters representing "buying spring" was first included in a standard Japanese dictionary in the late 1980s, and by most Japanese dictionaries shortly afterwards (Yunomae, 1997).

During the mid-late 1970s, around the same time as women in England and the U.S. began opening battered women's shelters, activists and survivors of domestic violence in Japan saw the need for such a safe haven for Japanese battered women. When women formed an action group in 1975—the International Year of Women—a Task Force on Trials, Mediation, and Divorce was created to address domestic violence (Tawara, 1977). The Task Force demanded that the Japanese Government and the Tokyo Metropolitan Government create a battered women's shelter. The Task Force successfully lobbied for the creation of the first public emergency shelter program for women and their children in 1977 in Tokyo (Tawara, 1977). The new program enabled battered women to escape abusive relationships without requiring that their children be placed in separate institutions, a practice which had been common previously. Nevertheless, to the disappointment of the Task Force members, the emergency shelter program was made a part of the Tokyo Women's Counseling Center, a public social service program predicated upon the Prostitution Prevention Law (problematic aspects of public social service programs for women within this policy framework will be discussed later in this chapter).

During the early 1980s, various women's groups began addressing the issues of rape, pornography, and objectification of women in the media through consciousness-raising activities, public protest, and many other creative and innovative approaches. One of the major results of these activities was the establishment in 1983 of the first—and to date the only—rape crisis center (Tokyo Rape Crisis Center, 1992). Women's movements directed at violence against women became more visible during the latter part of the 1980s, in part in response to specific incidents involving this and related issues. Especially notable were groups of women forming support groups in defense of women accused of killing the men who perpetrated violence upon them (Yunomae, 1990). A public rally held in Osaka was prompted by an incident in which a woman was raped after she publicly confronted a group of men about sexual harassment in a subway in Osaka in 1988. The rally attracted over 450 people, and soon afterward, a women's group in Osaka began telephone counseling for women (Seiboryokuwo Yurusanai Onnatachino Kai, 1990). During the same period, reports of the involvement of several high-ranking politicians in extramarital affairs and prostitution caused a public outcry and resulted in their resignation. This reaction represented a shift in public attitudes, because previously, politicians' extramarital affairs and use of prostitutes had been largely condoned.

In 1988, the Santama Area Group Concerned with Work and Sexual Discrimination, a women's organization in Tokyo, translated a handbook, *Stopping Sexual Harassment* (Hatarakukoto to Seisabetsuwo Kangaeru Santamano Kai, 1988). The following year, this group conducted the first nationwide questionnaire survey of women's experiences with sexual harassment in the workplace (Hatarakukoto to Seisabetsuwo Kangaeru Santamano Kai, 1991). Over 6,500 women participated in this survey. Their accounts collectively articulated the scope of sexual harassment and documented the ways in which it hinders women's full participation in the workforce and undermines their emotional and physical well-being (Hatarakukoto to Seisabe-tsuwo Kangaeru Santamano Kai, 1991). Also in 1989, the nation's first civil lawsuit over sexual harassment was filed (on August 5, 1989), and the term sexual harassment—more precisely, the abbreviated term *seku hara*—became the most popular word of the year.

During the early 1990s, prompted by media reports of several incidents of molestation of students by teachers, women's groups began addressing the issue of child sexual abuse. Other groups of women began speaking out regarding their experiences with incest, and the first self-help group for women incest survivors, Stop Child Sexual Abuse (SCSA), was formed in Tokyo in 1990 (SCSA, 1992).

Another significant development in the Japanese women's movement in the 1990s was the rise of public attention to the issue of "comfort women"—women from Korea, the Philippines, and other Asian countries who had been forced into sexual slavery by the Japanese Army during World War II. Despite the Japanese government's initial denials, an increasing amount of evidence gradually emerged to indicate that the Japanese military was behind the systematic abduction, confinement, and sexual exploitation of tens of thousand women in Asia during World War II. Many Japanese women who had been addressing other forms of violence against women, such as sexual assault, pornography, and prostitution, recognized this action by the military as a systematic means of dominance and violence against women.

Currently emerging movements against domestic violence in Japan have evolved out of these women's grassroots movements, which have addressed a wide spectrum of violence against women.

SCOPE AND NATURE OF THE PROBLEM: RESEARCH FINDINGS

Early Studies

Earlier studies of domestic violence in Japan used methodologies developed in Western society. For example, the Conflict Tactics Scale

(Straus, 1979), a standardized measurement of domestic violence developed and normed based on the experiences of people in the U.S., was used without regard to potentially unique manifestations or definitions of domestic violence among the Japanese (Kumagai, 1979; Kumagai & O'Donoghue, 1978; Kumagai & Straus, 1983). Researchers attributed their finding of a lower rate of domestic violence among Japanese couples compared to those in the U.S. to differences between the two cultures, namely, "a quiet non-expressive Japanese culture as opposed to a verbal expressive American culture" (Kumagai, 1979, p. 91). The validity of the CTS in studying violence among a non-Western population, as well as the use of the couples' children as proxy informants, casts doubt on the validity of their reported rates of domestic violence. In addition to these methodological limitations, attributing a low rate of violence among Japanese couples to a "quiet non-expressive" culture ignores the historical reality of Japanese military aggression in Asia and the frequent practice of corporal punishment by parents and teachers in Japan.

Most other studies are case studies conducted by counselors or other professionals, or quantitative analyses of service-based data, such as studies of women who sought assistance from public social services or family courts (e.g., Hada & Saito, 1992; Kanagawa Josei Senta, 1993; Kumamoto Family Court, 1991; Zenkoku Boshiryo Kyogikai, 1992). The information analyzed in these studies was obtained in the context of providing assistance, and thus, is likely to be skewed towards the type of information necessary for the provision of assistance and documented through the service providers' perspectives. Such information fails to elucidate women's subjective experiences with domestic violence, e.g., the meaning they give to the violence and how they coped with it. Needless to say, the experiences of women who have not sought assistance remain unaddressed in this type of research.

Nationwide Survey of Domestic Violence, 1992

Concerned by the apparent lack of recognition of the seriousness of domestic violence, and the scarcity of empirical research in Japan, a group of Japanese women researchers, practitioners, and activists (including the author) organized the Domestic Violence Action and Research Group (DVARG) in 1992. The DVARG conducted a nationwide questionnaire survey on women's experiences with domestic violence—the first survey of its kind in Japan. The study's multiple purposes included the following: 1) to examine and document Japanese women's experiences with domestic violence; 2) to provide a safe channel through which Japanese women could speak out regarding their experiences with domestic violence if they wished to do so; and 3) to raise public awareness regarding domestic violence in Japan by disseminating the study's findings in community forums and through the Japanese media.

Unlike most previous studies, which focused on physical violence, this nationwide study investigated a wide spectrum of violence perpetrated by male intimate partners against women, including physical, emotional, and sexual violence. Furthermore, since the survey was developed and conducted mutually by researchers, practitioners, and activists in Japan and a US-trained researcher of Japanese descent (the author), the collaboration allowed the development of a methodology which was culturally sensitive, while drawing on theoretical and methodological work on domestic violence accumulated over the two decades in the U.S. For example, the study took into consideration specific sociocultural factors which may affect the manifestation of male violence in Japan, e.g., living arrangements, access to contraceptive methods, and cultural attitudes toward infertility. Behavior-specific questions were constructed by drawing on items frequently used in the U.S. studies, as well as adding potentially unique manifestations of domestic violence (e.g., the partner's overturning a dining table; the partner's refusal to use contraception in the face of a virtual lack of access to oral contraceptives under current drug regulations in Japan) (Yoshihama & Sorenson, 1994).

A total of 796 women participated in the survey; detailed methodologies have been described elsewhere (Yoshihama & Sorenson, 1994). The average age of the respondents was 43.5 years. The majority (63%) were married at the time of the study, and slightly over one fourth (27%) were separated or divorced. The respondents in general had high educational backgrounds, with over 90% having completed high school or its equivalent; one third had graduated from college. The majority of the respondents were working, either full-time (45%) or part-time (27%). Despite the higher proportion of women who were employed and highly educated, the personal incomes of the respondents were rather low. Nearly half of them (45%) had an annual personal income less than ¥1,000,000 (the equivalent of US $8,000).

The findings elucidated the serious nature of domestic violence not only in marital relationships, but also in dating, post-separation, and post-divorce contexts: 613 women (77%) reported having experienced some type of violence with their male partners. The study also dispelled the myth that domestic violence is not serious in frequency and severity in Japan, and that it is largely a problem among the poor and uneducated. Domestic violence reported in this study cut across socioeconomic boundaries. Women who reported experiencing their partners' violence represented a wide range of sociodemographic and socioeconomic backgrounds, such as age, education, employment, and income, and included respondents with graduate educations and/or professional or managerial-level positions. The occupational backgrounds of the abusers in this study ranged from professional (16%), managerial (11%), clerical (41%) and sales positions (15%) to skilled, semiskilled, and unskilled labor (13%), and resembled those of the general male population in the Japanese labor force (Naoi & Moriyama, 1990; Somucho Tokei-kyoku, 1993).

Japanese women reported experiencing a wide range of partners' violence, and of varying degrees of severity. Their partners perpetrated not only physical, but also emotional and sexual violence, within a single episode of violence, as well as over the course of a relationship. In most cases, violence was recurrent: only fewer than one fourth reported experiencing a single episode of physical violence during their lifetime. In some cases, physical violence had subsided but had taken a different form, such as emotional or economic abuse. Physical separation or divorce did not necessarily end the violence.

Physical violence frequently reported by these women included being slapped, slugged with a fist, kicked, thrown around, grabbed, choked, shaken, having an object thrown at them, having their arms twisted, or having their hair pulled. Assault with a deadly weapon was also reported with some frequency. Objects used were often common household items and ranged from bottles, ironing boards, hammers, umbrellas to vacuum-cleaner hoses, baseball bats, golf clubs, and wooden sticks. Nonphysical forms of violence, such as verbal ridicule and other forms of debasement, verbal or behavioral threats of violence, destruction of property (e.g., furniture), and reckless driving were commonly reported. Women also reported various ways in which their partners restricted their activity: for example, restricting or prohibiting contact with family or friends, frequently checking on her whereabouts, following her when she went out, and monitoring her phone calls and correspondence. Abusive acts were not limited to acts committed, but also included those of omission, such as intentionally neglecting to contribute financially and depriving her of emotional support during sickness or pregnancy. These Japanese women also reported a wide range of sexual violence perpetrated by their male intimate partners. Forced intercourse was common, which was sometimes combined with physical violence.

The women's accounts of the incident which they considered as the most physically abusive (hereinafter "the most abusive incident") attest to the extent and severity of violence perpetrated upon them. The partner would cut the telephone line before he beat his partner to prevent her from seeking outside assistance, turned the light off (presumably to prevent from being seen from outside), or undressed her to prevent her from escaping while he battered her. Frequently committed behind closed doors, men's violence against their women partners took place in complete privacy or was witnessed by other family members. Children are frequent witnesses of their fathers' violence towards their mothers. Nearly two thirds of the fathers who physically abused their partners were reported to be abusive to their children. Violence during pregnancy was also reported with some frequency.

About two thirds of the most abusive incidents resulted in injury; slightly more than half of the victims sought medical attention, while a significant minority did not. The average number of days spent in recovery was 23 days (mode, 7 days), excluding permanent injuries. Sites of injury were concentrated in the area above the neck and extremities. Bruises and contusions were the most commonly reported type of injury, followed by lacerations and abrasions. Broken bones were also frequently reported. Other types of injury reported included ruptured eardrums, eye injuries, broken or loose teeth, and bloody noses.

Partners' violence had impacted these women in various ways. A sense of helplessness, hopelessness, or desperation was frequently coupled with a sense of anger and injustice. Many described their experiences as miserable and humiliating. Others described the process by which their partners' violence gradually silenced and isolated them: for example, a fear of further violence kept the respondent from expressing her feelings, thoughts, and opinions in front of her partner, and she often felt forced to curtail outside contacts, such as a job or socializing with friends and family. The abusive partner often instilled in these women negative self-perceptions and self-blame: a number of women described a process by which they had internalized negative images of themselves made by their abusive partners, such as being unattractive or unworthy.

Somatic complaints, such as disturbances in sleeping and/or eating, were commonly reported. A number of women indicated that they would react to the partner's anticipated return or to the sight of the partner with trembling, palpitations, or sometimes, with fever. Other behavioral manifestations of trauma responses, such as jumpiness and being easily startled, were also reported. Frequent suicidal thoughts, as well as homicidal thoughts, were reported: some attempted to take their own lives, and a few others, those of their abusive partners.

The partners' violence resulted in the loss of outside employment for a considerable number of women. It was not uncommon for the male partner to demand, at times with threat of physical violence, that the woman quit her job. Some partners intentionally attacked women's possessions that were critical to their continuation of employment: for example, hiding or destroying her wallet, train commuting pass, car keys, word processor, clothing, and so on. For others, the physical and psychological consequences of the partner's violence made it difficult for them to go to work on a regular basis and/or function productively.

Approximately three fourths of women who had experienced physical violence sought outside help. Nonetheless, only a minority (34%) sought assistance from formal sources, such as the police, family court, and public social services. Many of those who utilized these formal assistance programs reported negative experiences. Often, their cries for help were met with responses deeply rooted in patriarchal ideology. The police were reluctant to respond to what they considered a "domestic, private matter," or even if they did respond, they would reprimand the women for calling the police. Mediators of family court tended to minimize the severity of domestic violence, and often failed to acknowledge the husband's violence as legal grounds for divorce. They instead emphasized the importance of maintaining family harmony and often made remarks such as "Your children need their father," "It is wrong to deprive your children of their father," "Your husband seems to be a gentleman," and "Try harder to be a better wife and mother."

Only one fourth of the respondents knew of assistance programs for battered women, the majority of whom identified public service programs and courts—the very programs with which many previously had negative experiences. Only a minority of respondents knew of women's organizations and other private assistance programs, such as telephone counseling programs, counselors, and therapists.

When asked about their perceptions regarding necessary intervention, the respondents overwhelmingly identified an increased awareness regarding domestic violence at a societal level, followed by the improvement and/or expansion of assistance programs for battered women, as well as reform in the family court systems and legal reform. Only a few preferred no outside intervention.

Sociocultural Context. The Japanese women in this nationwide study reported several forms of domestic violence which appear to reflect sociocultural factors unique to present Japanese society. For example, in Japan, where access to oral contraceptives is limited due to drug regulations, the most frequently used contraceptive method is the condom (Mainichi Shimbun, 1992; Ogawa & Retherford, 1991). Women have relatively less control over condom use than other contraceptive methods, and the male partner's refusal to use condoms puts women in a vulnerable position. A large number of women identified this type of their partners' act as abusive. Many of them reported experiencing unwanted and/or unplanned pregnancies and having had abortions, often more than one during the tenure of the relationship. A high rate of abortions performed on married women in Japan (Mainichi Shimbun, 1992) may be in part attributable to their vulnerability to unwanted, unprotected sexual intercourse.

Reflecting the reality that the living quarters of many Japanese families tend to be small, and often are shared with the husband's parents and siblings (Somucho Tokeikyoku, 1996), a considerable number of women identified as abusive the act of being forced to have sex when they were concerned that other family members might see or hear. In addition, many women reported their partner's overturning the dining table as abusive. In the Japanese home, the dining table represents a locus of family activities and, by extension, a symbol of a woman's legitimate role and place in the family in a society where a rigid sex-role division of labor persists. Moreover, some Japanese women in the study, albeit small in number, reported their partners' throwing liquid at them. This act of throwing liquid is commonly interpreted by the Japanese in religious terms as an act of purifying something which is impure or contaminated. In the context of shared sociocultural meanings, the partner's throwing liquid at Japanese women may inflict humiliation and insult, because the act implies that the object at which liquid is thrown (that is, the woman) is dirty. These forms of violence are not typically included in studies in the U.S. or elsewhere.

Studies of Prevalence

Studies which examined the prevalence of domestic violence are limited in number and scope: prevalence has been estimated only in the context of several population-based studies which primarily examined the attitudes of domestic violence (e.g., Kanagawa-ken, 1995; Sakai-shi, 1995; Yoshihama, 1993). The first of such studies was conducted by the author in Tokyo in 1992 through face-to-face interviews with a representative sample of 83 adult residents of the Ota Ward, Tokyo, who were selected by a multistage cluster sampling method (Yoshihama, 1993). In addition to attitudes towards domestic violence, which was the focus of the study, this study inquired whether the respondents had experienced any type of violence through the following question:

I have been asking you a series of questions concerning violence between married or unmarried couples. In your own relationships with your spouse or boyfriend, have you ever experienced any acts, verbal, emotional, or physical, which you considered as violent? [translated from Japanese by the author]

Twelve percent of women reported having experienced some type of violence during their lifetime, the majority of whom (10%) reported physical violence (Yoshihama, 1993). Similar rates were found in later large-scale studies conducted through anonymous mail questionnaires (e.g., Kanagawa-ken, 1995; Sakai-shi, 1995). The Study of Attitudes Towards Human Rights (Sakai-shi, 1995) examined, through anonymous mail questionnaires, the attitudes towards rights of the oppressed populations, foreigners residing in Japan, the disabled, and men and women among 3,382 citizens of the City of Sakai selected by a cluster sampling method (Sakai-shi, 1995). Approximately 12% of women reported experiencing physical violence, such as hitting and kicking by their marital partners, and 7%, sexual violence, such as forced intercourse by marital partners. The Questionnaire Survey on Society for Gender Equality (Kanagawa-ken, 1995) was conducted by the Office of Women's Affairs, Prefecture of Kanagawa, through anonymous mail questionnaires with a random sample of 2,658 residents. Ten percent of married women reported experiencing husbands' physical violence (Kanagawa-ken, 1995). The observed lifetime prevalence rate in these population-based studies (10–12%) may have been an underestimation. Conducted as a part of attitudinal studies, the investigation of the prevalence of domestic violence has focused primarily on examining individuals' experiences with domestic violence through single or several screening-type questions. An underestimation of the prevalence of domestic violence may result from the fact that people tend to underreport their experiences with victimization when screening questions are used (Koss, 1992; Wyatt & Peters, 1986).

Existing Statistics

Data from existing social and legal programs may augment the findings of community-based studies in suggesting the frequent occurrence of domestic violence in Japan. Statistics on homicides and divorce shed some light on the extent of domestic violence and its consequences in Japan. The data obtained through public service programs, such as public women's shelters, are additional sources of information attesting to the frequent occurrence of domestic violence.

Police Statistics on Homicide and Assault. Similar to the proportion found in the U.S. (U.S. Federal Bureau of Investigation, 1996), approximately one third of female murder victims in Japan are killed by their male intimate partners (Keisatsucho, 1996). Over one third of assault and battery cases between family members are committed by husbands (including common-law husbands) against wives (Keisatsucho, 1996). Although assault and battery committed by husbands' against wives make up less than 1% of the total number of arrests made for assault and battery, given the indifference and refusal of the police to intervene what they consider "domestic disputes," the number of arrests for domestic violence in all likelihood represents only the tiny tip of a very large iceberg.

Divorce. Divorce among middle-aged women is increasing; the divorce rate among women aged 40 years and older has doubled since 1975 (Koseisho Daijin Kanbo Tokei Johobu, 1977, 1996). In Japan, the majority (over 90%) of divorces are filed by mutual consent. In the remaining cases, where one of the party refuses to the other's wish to divorce, the latter is required to file a petition for divorce mediation by a Family Court (Kaji Shinpanho [Domestic Affairs Adjustment Law], 1947, art. 18). Over 37,000 petitions are filed by wives in 1995—representing over 70% of the total petitions filed (Saiko Saibansho Jimusokyoku, 1996). Petitions by women ages 40 years and older are overrepresented. Not only does husbands' physical violence rank as the second most frequently cited reason for wives to file petitions, but husbands' emotional violence ranks fifth. Other frequently cited reasons include excessive drinking, excessive spending, and desertion by husbands. The petitions filed by wives due to their husband's physical violence alone amount to over 11,000 cases annually, representing over 30% of the petitions filed by wives (Saiko Saibansho Jimusokyoku, 1996). A case study of mediation cases involving husbands' violence handled at a family court elucidates the serious nature of husbands' violence, including stabbing with a knife, pouring heating oil on the wife and attempting to set her on fire, and hitting with a wooden stick (Kumamoto Family Court, 1991).

These findings alone suggest the frequent occurrence of domestic violence in Japan. The reasons for petition filing are identified by mediators—one male, one female—who handle the specific cases. It is likely that mediators of the family court, who tend to lack substantive professional training (Saiko Saibansho Jimusokyoku, 1990), may fail to probe and/or to identify husbands' violence experienced by women who file for mediation. Needless to say, it is unknown to what extent a husband has been violent in the marriage of couples who obtained divorce by mutual consent.

Public Women's Centers.   There is one governmentally funded and operated women's center which functions as a emergency shelter in each of the 47 prefectures (equivalent of a state in the U.S.) and other governing bodies. Although these public women's centers are not specifically designed to assist battered women, due to the absence of specialized services elsewhere, women seek refuge from their abusive male intimate partners at these public women's centers. Nationwide, on an average, one third of women who utilized emergency shelters at public women's centers across the nation were those who were fleeing from their partners' violence, according to annual reports compiled by these women's centers (Nihon Bengoshi Rengokai, 1995). In 14 of the 47 prefectures (30%), women who are escaping their partners' violence make up half or more of the women utilizing emergency shelter services.

Women who have been abused by their male intimate partners may turn to emergency shelter services provided by Homes for Mothers and Children, which were established under the Child Welfare Law (Jido Fukushiho, 1947, art. 38). In Homes for Mothers and Children in Tokyo, approximately half of women accompanied by their children, and 28% of those unaccompanied, who utilized emergency temporary shelter had been fleeing from their partners' violence (Tokyo-to Shakaifukushi Kyogigai, Boshifukushi Bukai, 1997).

SOCIETAL RESPONSES TO DOMESTIC VIOLENCE

Attitudes condoning men's use of violence against their partners are prevalent, and domestic violence is not even recognized by many as a problem, let alone as a social problem. Consequently, no specific criminal or civil laws exist which penalize offenders or provide remedies for survivors. Few specialized assistance programs (e.g., battered women's shelters) are available for battered women.

Public's Attitudes

Societal responses to domestic violence in Japan remain severely limited, and incidents of domestic violence in Japan remain largely hidden. Domestic violence in Japan has long been viewed as largely a private matter (Akamatsu, 1992). Studies have documented a high degree of tolerance of domestic violence among the Japanese. In one study, Japanese college students tended to minimize the seriousness of domestic violence compared to their U.S. counterparts (Frieze & Zubritzky, 1987). In another study (Yoshihama, 1993), approximately half of the respondents, regardless of age or gender, justified men's use of violence against their women partners under certain circumstances—a substantially higher proportion than that in similar studies in the U.S. (e.g., 16–31%; Gentemann, 1984; Greenblat, 1983, 1985; Stark & McEvoy, 1970; Straus, Gelles, & Steinmetz, 1980). Moreover, the majority of the Japanese respondents considered domestic violence as a private matter (86%) which occurred infrequently (72%) (Yoshihama, 1993). Many believed that women provoked abuse (61%) or stayed in abusive relationship for reasons related to their personality (72%).

Such attitudes shape the moral environment within which a husband (or boyfriend), his wife (or girlfriend), their families, friends, and community minimize or dismiss the violence. It is in this environment of pervasive normative support for domestic violence that police officers, judges, mediators, prosecutors, attorneys, and medical and social service practitioners respond to incidents of domestic violence. Thus, coupled with the scarcity of specialized assistance programs in the first place, it is extremely difficult for battered women to obtain necessary assistance under current systems in Japan.

Responses of the Criminal Justice System

The Penal Code of 1907 (Keiho) remains the fundamental framework of the criminal law in Japan, in conjunction with the Penal

Code of Criminal Procedure of 1948 (Keiji Soshoho), which was enacted after World War II. Unlike the common-law system in the U.S., the Japanese legal system is based on code law, where precedent plays a relatively small role. Amendments made to the Penal Code over the years resulted in little change in its fundamental structure. The current criminal justice responses to domestic violence, predicated upon the Penal Code which was enacted over 90 years ago, remain limited.

No penal code specifically defines domestic violence as a criminal offense. Despite the Japanese Government's claim that the Penal Code (e.g., Keiho, 1907, art. 204, 208, 220) is sufficient and applicable to assault, battery, and confinement committed by husbands against wives (Sorifu Danjo Kyodosankaku-Shitsu, 1994), in practice, these laws are rarely applied to domestic violence cases. Women's cries for help are often met with indifference on the part of the police, or the police officers may reprimand those women who sought help for calling the police for "domestic matters" or "couples' quarrels." There is a prevailing sentiment that law should not intervene in "family matters."

Although Japanese Penal Code (Keiho, art. 177) provides no spousal exemption for rape, marital rape is hardly recognized as a punishable crime. A district court in Tokyo denied a woman's request for a divorce from her husband, who has forced her to have sex by physical violence. The court attributed blame on the woman for having caused her husband to resort to forced sexual intercourse:

> The marriage presupposes sexual union between both sexes. It is in no way illegal for a husband to demand sexual intercourse from a wife, nor does a wife have any rights to deny such a request. Because of the plaintiff's [wife] complete refusal of a sexual relationship for no reason, the defendant [husband] became sexually frustrated, could not tolerate it, and forced sexual intercourse upon the plaintiff. It is understandable for a healthy man in his 40's to act in this manner when his wife behaved such a way without any reasons. It can not be considered an inhumane (animal-like) violation of human rights. Although it involved a certain degree of violent acts, it is within the range of the degree of force used in fights among ordinary married couples, and thus, it does not warrant a special consideration [by court]. Had the plaintiff [wife] been slightly more considerate for the defendant [husband], discussed the matter with him more, and

made attempts to resolve his sexual frustration to a certain degree, this would not have happened. Thus, it is within the plaintiff [wife] that responsibility lies. (Tokyo Chisai Hachioji Shibu, Judgment of February 14, 1985, English translation by the author)

There has been only once case in which a court found the husband guilty of raping his own wife (Tottori Chisai, Judgment of December 17, 1986). This case, however, involved an estranged couple, and a friend of the husband also perpetrated rape against the wife. An appeal court upheld the lower court's decision and found the husband guilty of marital rape because the marriage had broken down, and the couple was no longer functioning as a marital union (Hiroshima Kosai, Judgment of November 20, 1987). In the same decision, the court contended that married couples have the mutual right to demand sex and the responsibility to respond to such a request. Thus, in principle, this decision represents little change in the prevailing legal opinion denying the possibility of rape in marriage. No precedent exists in which courts have ruled that forced sex in marriage constitutes rape (Kaino, 1995; Kuzuhara, 1990; Tsunoda, 1991).

The legal standard of the degree of coercion in sexual assault poses an additional barrier for women who have been raped by their partners in seeking legal recourse from the criminal justice system. Sexual acts perpetrated by a man without a woman's consent are not sufficient in meeting the legal standard. Coercion used by the perpetrator must be so extreme as to deprive the victim of the ability to resist. A woman's prior sexual relationships in general, and those with the accused perpetrator in particular, are scrutinized and used against her by the defense attorneys, as well as judges (Tsunoda, 1991). Several decisions issued by several judges illustrate biases in their assumptions, based upon which they determined whether the degree of coercion used by the accused was excessive. One judge claimed that a certain degree of physical force, such as "grabbing a woman by the shoulder, pushing her to the ground, ridding her of clothes and pinning her down by getting on top of her, is normative part of consensual sexual intercourse" (Hiroshima Kosai, Judgment of November 20, 1978, English translation by the author). Little legal recourse is available for Japanese women to protect their right to their own bodies under the current male-dominated judicial system.

Women are extremely underrepresented in criminal justice systems. In 1994, less than 3% of prosecutors and police officers were

women, and women made up only 7% of judges (Sorifu Danjo
Kyodosankaku-Shitsu, 1994). Underrepresentation of women is also
evident among practicing attorneys, only 6% of whom are women
(Sorifu Danjo Kyodosankakushitsu, 1994). There are several prefectures in which no female attorney is practicing.

Family Law and Family Courts

As indicated previously, under current Japanese family law, if one
party refuses to divorce, a petition for mediation must be filed (Kaji
Shimpanho, 1947, art. 18). Divorce may be granted by judicial decree
in family court or district court only after mediation efforts have
failed. Over 90% of all divorces in Japan are obtained by mutual
consent of the couple, approximately 8% by mediation, and 1% by
judicial decree (Koseisho Daijin Kanbo Tokei Johobukyoku, 1993a).
Divorce by judicial decree is difficult to obtain, due to the requirement of legal grounds for divorce in district court. Legal bases for
divorce include 1) adultery; 2) malicious, intentional desertion; 3)
the absence of spouse without any contact or knowledge of his/her
whereabouts for over 3 years; 4) incurable severe mental illness; and
5) other grave causes which make the continuation of the marriage
difficult (Minpo, 1947, art. 770). Moreover, even in cases where legal
grounds exist, judges have discretion to dismiss certain cases in
principle (Minpo, art. 770) and in practice (Bryant, 1988), which
makes it difficult for battered women in Japan to obtain a divorce.

Court mediators may use their discretion to deny divorce even
when legal grounds for divorce exist, imposing their belief that
divorce is destructive to family unity and children's welfare (Upham,
1987). A women's group conducted a study of women's experiences
with mediation in the early 1980s and found that many women
had been subjected to mediators' remarks minimizing or denying
husband's violence as legitimate grounds for divorce ("Rikon chotei," 1981). Such remarks included "You should consider one or
two slaps as a whip of love and passion and accept them"; "You
have tolerated your husband's violence for 20 years and had children.
How come you cannot tolerate anymore?"; "Women should endure"; and "You are too stubborn as a woman. That's why your

husband dislikes you" ("Rikon chotei," 1981). Bryant (1988, 1992) contends, based on her direct observation of divorce proceedings in court and survey of court personnel in Japan, that mediators of family court tend to impose their upper-class values, which favor the legal continuation of marriage. The eligibility to become mediators and investigators of family court is based rather on their social status, and not on professional training. Many of them, lacking assessment and counseling skills and/or empathic sensitivity, may fail to address the seriousness of abuse suffered by women and, consequently, dismiss a woman's cry for help for protection and divorce.

When their wish to end abusive marriage is not granted once by their husbands and later by the court system, many women resign themselves to legal continuation of marriage. A considerable number of them choose to continue cohabiting with their abusive husbands due to financial and various other reasons, but make sleeping quarters, and at times financial matters, separate. This living arrangement, a functional—if not legal—divorce between a cohabiting couple is prevalent in Japan and is referred to as a divorce within the home (*kateinai rikon* in Japanese). The official divorce rate in Japan is considerably lower than that of most other industrialized countries (United Nations, 1996) and may superficially appear to reflect the relative stability of the Japanese family structure, a structure which is often characterized by emotional closeness and well-developed kinship among family members. Nevertheless, the official divorce rate does not reflect the relatively prevalent practice of divorce within the home. The plight of those women who are forced to remain in an abusive marriage challenges a commonly held belief about stable, harmonious Japanese families.

Despite numerous criticisms and suggestions for the improvement of mediation services of family court over the last two decades, no incremental, let alone fundamental, reforms have been implemented. A recently published report on family courts points out that many investigators lack substantive professional training and skills (Saiko Saibansho Jimusokokyu, 1990). Training for mediators and investigators of family courts, as well as judges, is urgently needed. A protocol of dealing with cases involving domestic violence during mediation and trial (e.g., establishing use of separate entrances and waiting rooms) must be developed. A fundamental question remains, however, whether requiring mediation for contested divorce cases is reasonable, given the risk of initiation or exacerbation of domestic violence during mediation.

Recent debate over whether divorce should be granted based on the breakdown of the marital relationship, rather than on the determination of fault in the actions of one party, has prompted a closer look at flaws in the current divorce law in Japan (Homusho Minjikyoku Sanjikanshitsu, 1992; also see Kaino, 1996). Whatever reform may emanate from the current debate must address the plight of many battered women who have been trapped in violent marriages.

For many women, divorce results in a significant drop in income. The average per-person income for single-mother headed households is considerably less than that of households headed by a father or two parents. Divorce by mutual consent does not provide any adjudicated mechanism for division of property or child support arrangements. Divorce by mediation or judicial decree, on the other hand, provides such a mechanism. Nevertheless, not all divorces by mediation or judicial decree specify arrangements for child support and/or division of property. The enforcement of child support payment is low. As a consequence, divorced women often raise their children on their own without any child support by their former husbands (Koseisho, 1993b).

Public Social Service Programs

In Japan, the scope of public social service programs for women remains limited, and its guiding principles obsolete. Most public social service programs for women in Japan have been developed and delivered under the Prostitution Prevention Law of 1956 [Baishun Boshiho, art. 34, 35, 36]. Although the Law represents a culmination of women's efforts to end publicly commissioned prostitution, its provision tends to be punitive to women (the prostitutes) and provides little penalty to those men who use prostitutes. Under this Law, each prefecture is required to establish a women's center which provides counseling, medical, psychological, and vocational assessment, and guidance for those women "in need of protection" because they have been, or are at high risk of, engaging in prostitution

(Baishun Boshiho, art. 34), and it may select to establish institutions to rehabilitate these women (art. 36). Nationwide there are 47 women's centers whose functions include emergency shelter (one in each prefecture) and 52 rehabilitative institutions (Koseisho Daijin Kanbo Tokei Johobu, 1995). The number of programs for women is extremely small compared to the programs for the elderly (over 3,500 programs) and children (over 33,000 programs) (Koseisho Daijin Kanbo Tokei Johobu, 1995; Zenkoku Fujinsodanin Renrakukyogikai, 1993). Although 309 of the programs established under the Child Welfare Law are Homes for Mothers and Children that can be utilized by battered women and their children (capacity for 6,057 families) (Koseisho Daijin Kanbo Tokei Johobu, 1995), women without children are not eligible for their services. Thus, with respect to public service programs, few resources are available for battered women in Japan.

The Prostitution Prevention Law mandates each prefecture to employ counselors who are charged to identify "women in need of protection" and to provide counseling and "guidance" (Baishun Boshiho, art. 35). The only eligibility criteria specified in the Law was that these counselors for women be of high social credibility and respect; no reference is made to professional or educational backgrounds (art. 35). The majority of counseling staff (over 70%) are hired on a temporary basis, lacking the stability necessary for the development of professional expertise. Most of them (94%) are women and tend to be older; two thirds of them are age 50 or older (Zenkoku Fujinsodanin Renrakukyogikai, 1993).

Although from the inception, these public women's centers provided emergency shelter for women who had not engaged in prostitution, until the early 1960s, a large proportion of users of shelter were former prostitutes or those women who were at risk of engaging in prostitution. Over the years, however, the proportion of women who were involved in prostitution among the users of these public women's centers has declined to less than 10% during the 1980's (Nishimura, 1986). An increasing proportion of women are seeking assistance from the public women's centers due to difficulties in relationships, such as violence, desertion, and dependence on alcohol or gambling by their partners. Several shelters reports that the length of women's shelter stay has become longer (Kanagawa Women's Council, 1995; Tokyo Josei Sodan Senta, 1996): for example,

TABLE 17.1   The Number of Women and Children Utilizing Emergency Shelter at the Tokyo Women's Counseling Center, FY 1990–1995*

	1990	1991	1992	1993	1994	1995
The number of women sheltered	514	650	624	581	611	615
The number of accompanying children	268	255	309	314	317	341
Total sheltered	782	905	933	895	928	956
The average number of individuals sheltered per day	30.1	29.5	31.3	37.3	39.1	41.0
The average number of shelter stay (day)	14.4	11.9	12.3	15.2	15.4	15.7
Occupancy rate	n/a	n/a	n/a	85.1	89.9	91.1

* Japanese fiscal year is 4/1–3/31.
Note: 1990 data from *Heisei 3 nenban jigyogaiyo* (p. 28), by Tokyo-to Fujin Sodan Senta, 1991.
1991–1992 data from *Heisei 6 nenban jigyogaiyo* (p. 31), by Tokyo-to Josei Sodan Senta, 1994.
1993–1995 data from *Heisei 8 nenban jigyogaiyo* (p. 37), by Tokyo-to Josei Sodan Senta, 1996.

at the Tokyo Women's Counseling Center, the average shelter stay has gradually increased from 14.4 days in 1990 to 15.7 days in 1995 (see Table 17.1). The data on the total number of women and children sheltered and occupancy rates suggest an overall increase in the utilization of the Tokyo Women's Counseling Center (Tokyo Jose Sodan Senta, 1996).

The number of women of foreign nationalities who utilize public women's centers increased during the late 1980s and early 1990s. For example, a women's center in Tokyo sheltered 11 foreign women in 1987; the number jumped up to 66 in 1990 and to 144 in 1991 (Tokyo Josei Sodan Senta, 1996). Since 1992, however, the number of foreign women who used the temporary shelter at the Tokyo Women's Counseling Center has been declining, presumably because of the increase in available private shelters for foreign women during this period. Nevertheless, the number of women of foreign nationalities who seek emergency shelter to escape from their abusive partners (mostly Japanese men) is increasing (Tokyo Josei Senta, 1996).

In response to changing needs, the Ministry of Health and Welfare has broadened the eligibility for receiving services from these public women's programs to include those who have not engaged, or are not at risk of engaging, in prostitution: For example, in cases where no other resources exist, public women's centers are to assist women who face various barriers to their social functioning, such as breakdown of family relationships, poverty, and sexual victimization (cf. Nishimura, 1986; Yoshida, 1994). Yet, there have been no changes in the overall policy—residual in nature, drawing its funding base from the Prostitution Prevention Law. Thus, the original protective and rehabilitative framework remains, which tends to focus on remediation of deficiencies in individuals. The range of services provided by these women's centers remains limited, consisting primarily of emergency shelter assistance, and telephone and outpatient counseling services. Little attention is paid to prevention of difficulties women face or promotion of social justice aimed toward eradicating gender-based structural inequality, which are the root causes of such difficulties (e.g., domestic violence, sexual assault). A broader, more comprehensive approach, as opposed to a remedial, residual one, is needed in order to respond more effectively to the needs of women in general, and those of battered women in particular.

Responses of the Health Care System

The health care system is often one of the first outside agencies to which battered women turn for help. Unlike in the U.S., where domestic violence is recognized as a serious public health issue and professional training and institutional protocols have been developed, the awareness among Japanese health care workers regarding domestic violence is extremely low. Little, if any systematic training exists for health care workers, and consequently, many practitioners do not know how to properly assess whether a female patient has experienced domestic violence. Even with the identification of women who suffer domestic violence, health care workers may lack the knowledge and skills with which to provide effective assistance and to ensure these women's safety and survival. For a comprehensive review of an emerging role of social workers and clinical nurses in hospital and ambulatory care settings, see the chapters in this book by Mary Boes (Ch. 9) and by Leone Murphy and Nancy Razza (Ch. 11).

The Japanese health care system presents additional obstacles to successful intervention in domestic violence: Most health care facilities in Japan do not provide for the privacy of their patients. Examination rooms are typically divided by curtains or partial dividers in order to simultaneously accommodate multiple patients. Without complete privacy and confidentiality, battered women are less likely to disclose their experiences with domestic violence. Furthermore, the highly hierarchical relationship between physicians and patients in Japan tends to discourage patients from discussing personal matters other than those of a strictly medical nature. Several women who participated in the nationwide survey of 1992 described authoritarian attitudes of physicians whom they encountered: e.g., a physician refused to issue a letter documenting the nature of injuries sustained by a woman at the hands of her male partner, despite the woman's request to do so.

The Japanese system of payment for medical care poses additional barriers. Under the current Japanese national health insurance system, one insurance card is issued per household. At the time health care is rendered, a patient is required to show the insurance card in order to have the medical care covered by insurance. In certain instances, battered women may be unable to seek medical attention because they may be separated from their abusive husbands and do not have access to the family's insurance card, or their abusive partners may hide the family's insurance card. Furthermore, Japanese battered women occasionally face a "Catch-22" situation in obtaining medical care. A number of women who participated in the nationwide survey reported that they had been told by health care workers that national health insurance would not cover treatment for injuries caused by domestic violence. The legal grounds for such a denial of services may be found, albeit debatable, in the provisions of the Health Insurance Law (Kenko Hokenho, 1902, art. 60), which denies insurance coverage for injuries resulting from intentional acts of the insured. Because the insured is a husband in many cases, a wife who has been assaulted by her husband may be denied coverage for the treatment of injuries resulting from his intentional acts (e.g., domestic violence). Although the Ministry of Health and Welfare, which administers national medical insurance programs, denies the legal basis for such a practice (Y. Tsunoda, April 10, 1997, personal communication), the practice of local administration offices, which process individual insurance claims, does not appear to be in accordance with the Ministry's policies.

Women may face yet additional barriers to appropriate reimbursement of medical expenses. Japanese law provides that the perpetrator of a crime can be made liable for medical costs incurred by the victim. Although assault and battery is in general considered a criminal act in Japan, *in practice* assault and battery committed by intimate partners is rarely treated as a crime. Therefore, in the absence of pro-arrest and pro-prosecution policies for domestic violence cases, Japanese battered women may not have medical expenses reimbursed for injuries resulting from the "criminal act" of domestic violence because domestic violence is only rarely considered "criminal." Furthermore, civil law provides little recourse for battered women in Japan: Japanese courts have conventionally denied tort claims between married couples (T. Kaino, April 10, 1997, personal communication). Thus, coupled with a lack of legal recourse, the denial of insurance coverage for women who require medical attention due to domestic violence offers these women little assistance and comfort.

NEWLY EMERGING PROGRAMS AND MOVEMENTS

Private Women's Shelters

Private shelters for women have been known to exist as early as feudal times in Japan. For example, a Buddhist temple, referred to as "Kakekomi-dera (a temple to run to)" provided refuge for women who were seeking divorce and assisted them in obtaining divorce in the 12th century—a period when women did not have the right to request divorce. There was a provision that a 3-year stay at this temple allowed a woman to obtain a divorce.

During the mid-1980s, women's groups began establishing shelters for women. At first, shelters were established primarily in response to the needs of foreign women, many of whom were brought to Japan from Asian Pacific countries as part of international trafficking in women. Many were forced into prostitution, exploited, and had their rights and dignity violated. A study conducted by the Yokohama Association of Women's Communication and Network identified a total of seven private shelters for women that were in operation in 1992–3, four of which were primarily and/or regularly assisting foreign women (Yokohama-shi Josei Kyokai, 1995). The first of such shelters, the Women's Home HELP, was established in 1986 in Tokyo by a Christian women's group that has a long history of involvement in antiprostitution efforts. Several other shelters opened their doors to Asian Pacific women during the early 1990s (see Table 17.2 and Figure 17.1).

The latter part of the 1990s has been characterized by the increase in the number of private shelters established specifically or primarily in response to the needs of women who have been abused by their male intimate partners (i.e., battered women's shelters). Five additional battered women's shelters opened recently; shelters in Utsunomiya, Sapporo, and Nagoya were established by grassroots women's organizations. A shelter in Tokyo was opened by a group of therapists, and one in Osaka, by an individual woman. Former staff members of a recently closed public women's center are currently in the process of establishing a private shelter for women in Osaka. In addition, a number of women's groups have developed arrangements to provide emergency shelter through the use of the private homes of their members on an as-needed basis (e.g., Joseino Tameno Rikon Hotline, 1996).

Women who have been abused by their partners frequently turn to shelters which are not designed to serve primarily battered women. For example, at the Micaela Ryo in Yokohama—an emergency shelter for women of all ages and nationalities operated by a Catholic convent—over one fourth of women sought shelter due to their male partners' violence (Yokohama-shi Josei Kyokai, 1995). Moreover, as an increasing number of women from Asian Pacific countries and regions date and/or marry Japanese men, an increasing number of these women have begun seeking shelter to escape violence by their partners. The shelters which were originally established to assist women of Asian Pacific descent exploited in the prostitution industry now assist an increasing number of Asian Pacific women who request shelters due to domestic violence by their partners (Yokohama-shi Josei Kyokai, 1995, 1996). At one such shelter, the Saalaa in Yokohama, 4 out of 11 Filipina women and all of three Chinese women who stayed there between October, 1993 and September, 1994 did so in order to flee from their partners' violence (Yokohama-shi Josei Kyokai, 1995).

The number of women who utilize private shelters is on the rise, and shelters are often full (Yokohama-shi Josei Kyokai, 1995). It is not unusual for shelters to accommodate women and their children beyond their stated capacity limit. Several shelters (e.g., Micaela Ryo,

TABLE 17.2   Private Shelters for Women in Japan

Shelter	Opened	Location	Primary concerns	Type of operating organization
Micaela Ryo	9/1985	Yokohama	Women's issues	Catholic convent; Social welfare foundation
HELP	4/1986	Tokyo	Asian Pacific women; prostitution	Catholic women's organization
DARC	12/1990	Tokyo	Drug addiction	Voluntary women's organization
Friendship Asia House Cosmos	4/1991	Chiba	Asian Pacific women; refugees	Social welfare foundation
Saalaa	9/1992	Yokohama	Asian Pacific women	Voluntary women's organization
Ms. LA	1/1993	Yokohama	Women's issues; Asian Pacific women	Voluntary women's organization
AKK	4/1993	Tokyo	Domestic violence, alcohol addiction	Voluntary women's organization
Women's Net Kobe	12/1994 (currently closed)	Kobe	Women's issues; Domestic violence	Voluntary women's organization
Space Enjo	4/1996	Ibaragi, Osaka	Domestic violence; Women' issues	An individual woman
Women's House	8/1996	Utsunomiya, Tochigi	Women's issues; Domestic violence	Voluntary women's organization
Tokyo Feminist Therapy Center	3/1997	Tokyo	Domestic violence; Women's issues	A group of therapists
Space On	3/1997	Sapporo	Domestic violence; Women's issues	Voluntary women's organization
Kakekomi Josei Center, Aichi	4/1997	Nagoya, Aichi	Domestic violence	Voluntary women's organization
Women's Space Niigata	in operation*	Niigata	Domestic violence; Women's issues	Voluntary women's organization
Ikuno Women's Shelter	P	Osaka	Women's issues; Domestic violence	Former staff of a recently closed public women's center

*Date opened unknown.
P = currently in preparation.

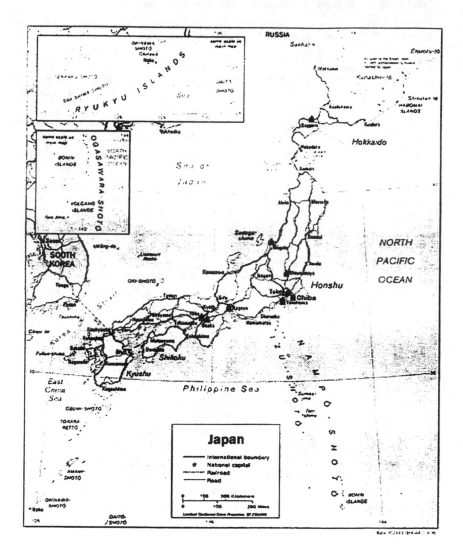

FIGURE 17.1   Sites of private women's shelters.

Cosmos, Saalaa, Ms. LA) indicate that women are staying longer than before (Kanagawa Women's Council, 1995; Yokohama-shi Josei Kyokai, 1995). In addition to the high costs involved in renting an apartment in Japan (typically, move-in costs involve 5 times the amount of the monthly rent), many landlords are reluctant to rent to a woman-headed family or an unattached woman. A lack of transitional housing compounds the difficulty. Homes for Mothers and Children under the Child Welfare Law are the frequent destination of women and children after temporary stays in private women's shelters, but women who do not have children are ineligible.

Private women's shelters vary in size and operating organizational structures. They suffer, almost without exception, from limited, unstable budgets. Many are operated by grassroots women's organizations drawing their financial base from membership dues and individual donations, augmented by sporadic grants from foundations. Similar to grants from foundations in the U.S., foundations' support is typically made for new projects and does not provide ongoing operational expenses. Several shelters have been granted the status of "social welfare foundation," which entitles them to receive governmental reimbursement for services rendered. Only a few others receive governmental funding, which tends to represent a small proportion of the shelter's total operational budget and is subject to sudden budget cuts (R. Shoji, personal communication, March 1, 1997).

A lack of funding is just one obstacle for women's groups in maintaining their shelter programs. After the Women's Net Kobe, a grassroots women's group, rented a small house in 1994 where they organized a range of consciousness-raising activities, they began receiving, to their surprise, calls from women requesting shelter to flee from their partners' violence (Masai, 1997b). The terms of their lease prevented them from providing shelter for these women, and thus, they moved to a larger house in December of the same year, where they made arrangements to accommodate women who are in need of shelter. The very next month, the Hanshin Earthquake destroyed their house. Calls from battered women continued to pour in after the earthquake. The effects of the earthquake were enormous, and appeared to have added to the vulnerability and desperation of battered women. It was not uncommon for a woman to have lost their usual sources of support due to the earthquake, for example, loss of family, friends, or these individuals' homes in which a woman might seek temporary refuge. A public rally was held to challenge the denial by the media and the government of the occurrence of rape in the aftermath of the earthquake. Thirty-seven women reported their experiences of being sexually assaulted; many of the assaults took place immediately after the earthquake (Masai, 1997a). The efforts by the Women's Net Kobe, meant to raise public consciousness, were met with negative response from the mass media, who minimized the extent of violence against women in the areas affected by the earthquake. Too often, women's issues are placed "on a back burner," and such a tendency is likely to be exacerbated during a crisis period such as that following a natural disaster. In spite of the loss of shelter space and the public's denial of the problem, the Women's Net Kobe continues its efforts to address violence against women.

Paralleling the increase in the interests in and efforts of establishing shelters in their local community among women has been the interest in collective actions nationwide. A women's group in Sapporo was instrumental in organizing a 3-day symposium to discuss domestic violence and shelters in October, 1996 (Kakekomi Shelter Kokusai Symposium Jikkoiinkai, 1997). This symposium, for which four practitioners were invited as guest speakers from the U.S., attracted 600 participants. The large number of participants appear to indicate a high degree of interest. The symposium served as an arena for collective information-sharing and skill- and knowledge-building. On February 22, 1997, a meeting was held in Tokyo among organizations and individuals who have been operating or are planning to open a private women's shelter around the nation. This meeting prompted a movement to create a nationwide network of private women's shelters to exchange information and expertise, while drawing mutual support. A planning meeting is scheduled to be held in Tokyo in June, 1997 (K. Kondo, personal communication, April 17, 1997).

Other Assistance Programs

Other private assistance programs available for battered women in Japan include feminist therapy centers (mostly in private group practice) and telephone counseling conducted by grassroots women's groups. The majority of feminist therapists practice in major urban cities, such as Tokyo and Osaka, which, compounded with the relatively high associated fees, makes feminist therapy rather inaccessible for many battered women. The amount of training in the area of domestic violence varies significantly among these therapists. Telephone counseling, on the other hand, is free of charge and can be utilized by battered women. Although telephone counseling programs also tend to operate in large urban cities, they can be accessed by women nationwide. However, because these telephone programs are operated by grassroots women's groups with shoestring budgets, their hours of operation are currently limited to several hours a day for one or two days a week. An expanded range of assistance needs to be developed; services with 24-hour access are critically needed.

Publications and the Media Coverage

Since 1992, an increasing number of articles on domestic violence have been published in both academic journals and popular magazines. Local governments and professional organizations, as well as grassroots women's organizations, have published monographs and research reports during the last several years. These publications tend to focus on research findings, the problematic aspects of current societal responses to domestic violence in Japan, analysis of historical and present responses in other countries, such as the U.S., and/or recommendations for future reforms. Compared to the number of these kinds of publications, relatively little has been written and published which may directly assist battered women and those practitioners who work with them. In 1995, a handbook frequently used in the U.S., *You Can Be Free: A Handbook for Abused Women* (Purple Kobo, 1995), was translated. To date, this handbook is the only one published by an established publisher available through regular bookstores. In the same year, a handbook for battered women was published by a grassroots women's organization (AKK Josei Shelter Unei-iinkai, 1995). In the spring of 1997, a local bar association in Kobe published a handbook of legal rights for women who have been abused by their partners (Kobe Bengoshikai, 1997a), along with a manual for attorneys, which provides practical information in order to effectively use current legal procedures to assist battered women (Kobe Bengoshikai, 1997b). There has been a gradual increase in the coverage of domestic violence in newspapers and by television stations.

Emerging Movements Reshaping Societal Responses

On July 11, 1995, the District Court in Nagoya decided not to impose punishment on a 46-year-old woman convicted for murdering her abusive husband (Nagoya Chisai, Judgment of July 11, 1995). In Japan, prior to this case, there was no precedent in which men's repetitive violence had been considered as cumulative provocation for murder. Supporters of the defendant felt the courts needed to be educated on the serious, life-threatening nature of domestic violence and on the multitudes of difficulties faced by battered women in fleeing from abusive relationships in a male-dominated society. The results of studies of domestic violence, such as the nationwide survey by the DVARG, as well as books and manuscripts by researchers and practitioners, were submitted as evidence for the woman's defense in trial; a researcher who has been involved in the nationwide survey on domestic violence also testified as an expert witness at the trial. Supporters of the defendant had hoped for her acquittal on the grounds of justifiable homicide. Instead, she was found guilty of using excessive force; however, in sparing her from any punishment, the court acknowledged and empathized with the cumulative suffering which had driven her to the crime of which she was found guilty. This decision may symbolize the combined impact of activism and research efforts led by women for women.

The need for the development and expansion of assistance programs for battered women, as well as legal and institutional reform in the criminal justice system, civil and family law, public social services and health care system, is mounting. Together with activism, research may play a critical role in guiding changes in societal responses to domestic violence. Research methodologies need to be further developed. Needless to say, the use of screening questions (e.g., "Have you ever experienced/perpetrated domestic violence?") should be avoided, because general public attitudes, such as the degree of tolerance and justification of domestic violence, differently shape the definitions of domestic violence.

The use of behavior-specific questions per se is not, nonetheless, a panacea. Most previous population-based studies of domestic violence in the U.S. and Canada used behavior-specific questions, such as the widely-used Conflict Tactics Scale (Straus, 1979) and typically measured only the number of times the respondent had experienced specific types of violence by her partner. Such an investigative approach may fail to capture the sense of terror and entrapment instilled in a woman by her partner, which is predicated upon his position of domination and control. Such acts of domination and control may not necessarily take the form of discrete events that are easily observable and measurable. Thus, multiple dimensions of women's experiences with domestic violence need to be explored, such as how the violence occurred, who initiated the violence, antecedents, the function of violence (e.g., expression of anger, coercion, retaliatory), the consequences (e.g., injury sustained, medical care received, psychological and social consequences), the meaning of the violence (e.g., perceived threat to life, perceived abusiveness), and the pattern of coping with violence (Dobash & Dobash, 1988; Rosenbaum, 1988; Weis, 1989). Needless to say, a measurement needs to be inclusive of a range of manifestations of domestic violence experienced by the population of interest and must be culturally relevant (Yoshihama, 1995).

A recent study of women of Japanese descent in Los Angeles (Yoshihama, 1996) has expanded the scope of investigation in several ways: for example, examining a wider range of violence by their intimate partners through a self-constructed measurement covering a wider range of physical, as well as emotional and sexual, violence. Specific types of violence commonly reported by women in Japan, such as the partner's refusing to use contraception, overturning a dining table, and throwing liquid, were also included in the investigation. Respondents were asked to indicate whether they had experienced each type of partners' violence during their lifetime and during the previous year. Furthermore, the severity of domestic violence was assessed based on the respondents' own perceptions in the specific context in which violent acts were committed. The use of women's self-reports regarding their own experiences of violence, supplemented by their subjective perceptions, thus provided the type of multidimensional data which most previous studies overlook. The detrimental effects of domestic violence on women's physical, psychological, and social well-being were elucidated both qualitatively and quantitatively in this study: for example, two standardized measures of mental health were used to assess women's well-being quantitatively. In addition, open-ended questions asked the respondents to describe, in their own words, the impact of their partners' violence on their lives and the ways, if any, in which Japanese culture had influenced their responses to domestic violence. Studies with similar multidimensional assessment employing multiple methodologies, coupled with a culturally relevant measure of domestic violence, are needed in Japan to examine the prevalence of domestic violence and its consequences. There is a need for additional population-based studies of domestic violence to obtain prevalence estimates. Ideally, a nationwide study should be conducted in the near future.

ACKNOWLEDGMENTS

The author's continuous involvement in the Domestic Violence Action and Research Group, Tokyo, Japan and numerous discussions with its members (E. Harada, N. Hattori, T. Kaino, K. Naito, Y. Tsunoda, and T. Yunomae) have inspired the writing of this manuscript. The author would also like to thank Ayako Gumizawa, Eriko Harada, Junko Honma, Tamie Kaino, Sakiko Katayama, Kazumi Naito, Yukiko Tsunoda, Masae Yamasaki, Kyoko Yoshida, and Tomoko Yunomae for their assistance in collecting reference materials. Special thanks to Arno K. Kumagai for his thoughtful review of the manuscript and many valuable discussions.

REFERENCES

Akamatsu, R. (1992). Josei nitaisuru boryoku [Violence against women]. *Kokusai Josei, 6*, 3.
AKK Josei Shelter Unei-iinkai. (1995). *Boryokuno kankeini nayamu anatae* [A handbook for women who are suffering an abusive relationship]. Tokyo: Author.

Bryant, T. L. (1988). Marital dissolution in Japan: Legal obstacles and their impact. In J. O. Haley (Ed.), *Law and society in contemporary Japan* (pp. 221-241). Dubuque, IA: Kendall/Hunt.

Bryant, T. L. (1992). "Responsible" husbands, "recalcitrant" wives, retributive judges: Judicial management of contested divorce in Japan. *Journal of Japanese Studies, 18,* 407–443.

Dobash, R. E., & Dobash, R. P. (1988). Research as social action: The struggle for battered women. In K. Yllo & M. Bograd (Eds.), *Feminist perspectives on wife abuse* (pp. 51–74). Newbury Park, CA: Sage.

Domestic Violence Action & Research Group. (1993a, November). *Husbands' (boyfriends') violence in Japan: Preliminary findings.* Paper presented at the United Nations, Economic and Social Council Asia and Pacific (ESCAP), Asian Pacific Symposium of NGOs on Women in Development, Manila, Philippines.

Domestic Violence Action & Research Group. (1993b, June). *A study on violence by husbands (boyfriends) in Japan.* Paper presented at the NGO Activities during the United Nations World Conference on Human Rights, Vienna, Austria.

Domestic Violence Action & Research Group. (1994). Otto (koibito) karano boryoku [Violence by husbands (boyfriends)]. *Joseigaku Kenkyu, 3,* 122–139.

Domestic Violence Action & Research Group. (1995, August). *A study of husbands' (boyfriends') violence in Japan.* Report submitted to the United Nations 4th World Conference on Women, Beijing, China: Author.

Frieze, I. H., & Zubritzky, M. (1987, July). *College students' beliefs about wife battering and marital rape in the United States and Japan.* Paper presented at the Third National Family Violence Research Conference, Durham, NH.

Gentemann, K. M. (1984). Wife beating: Attitudes of a non-clinical population. *Victimology: An International Journal, 9,* 109–119.

Greenblat, C. S. (1983). A hit is a hit is a hit . . . or is it?: Approval and tolerance of the use of physical force by spouses. In D. Finkelhor, R. J. Gelles, G. T. Hotaling, & M. A. Straus (Eds.), *The dark side of families: Current family violence research* (pp. 235–260). Newbury Park, CA: Sage.

Greenblat, C. S. (1985). "Don't hit your wife . . . unless . . . ": Preliminary findings on normative support for the use of physical force by husbands. *Victimology: An International Journal, 10,* 221–241.

Hada, A., & Saito, S. (1992). Ottono kateinai boryokuto tsumano kaifuku [Husbands' domestic violence and recovery of wives]. *Japanese Journal of Alcohol Dependence & Addiction, 9,* 210–218.

Hatarakukoto to Seisabetsuwo Kangaeru Santamano Kai (Ed.). (1988). *Seiteki iyagarasewo yamesaseru tameno handbook* [translation of *Stopping sexual harassment*]. Tokyo: Author.

Hatarakukoto to Seisabetsuwo Kangaeru Santamano Kai (Ed.). (1991). *Onna 6,500 nin no shogen* [Testimony of 6,500 women]. Tokyo: Gakuyo Shobo.

Homusho Minjikyoku Sanjikanshitsu. (1992). *Konin oyobi rikon seidono minaoshi singi nikansuru chukanhokoku* [An interim report of the procedures concerning marriage and divorce]. Tokyo: Author.

Japanese Government. (1992). *The second report of the Japanese Government to CEDAW* [United Nations Document CEDAW/C/JPN/2].

Joseino Tameno Rikon Hotline [Divorce Hotline for Women]. (1993). DV sodan kekka [Results of consultation regarding domestic violence]. Unpublished internal statistics. Sendai, Miyagi: Author.

Joseino Tameno Rikon Hotline [Divorce Hotline for Women]. (1996). *Jijo group "Shinkokyu Time" no torikumi* [An approach to a self-help group]. Unpublished manuscript. Sendai, Miyagi: Author.

Kaino, T. (1995, Winter). Domestic violence in Japan. *Voice: A newsletter of the National Coalition Against Domestic Violence*, pp. 18–21, 41.

Kaino, T. (1996). Kawaru kazokuho [Changing family law]. In Y. Yamashita, T. Kaino, M. Kamio, & M. Ueno (Eds.), *Hojoseigaku eno shotai* [An invitation to feminist legal studies] (pp. 59–120). Tokyo: Yuhikaku.

Kakekomi Shelter Kokusai Symposium Jikkoiinkai (Ed.). (1997). *Seiboryoku no konzetsuwo* [Toward the elimination of sexual violence]. Sapporo: Author.

Kanagawa Josei Senta. (1993). *Kinkyuhogoshitsu 10-nenno ayumi* [A review of the emergency shelter]. Fujisawa, Kanagawa: Author.

Kanagawa Women's Council. (1995). *NGO Forum Workshop Shiryo: For the elimination of violence against women.* Kanagawa: Author.

Kanagawa-ken. (1995). *Danjokyodoshakai nikansuru anketo chosa hokokusho* [Report of the Questionnaire Survey on Society for Gender Equality]. Kanagawa: Author.

Keisatsucho [National Police Agency]. (1996). *Hanzai tokeisho: Heisei 7 nen no hanzai* [Criminal statistics in 1995]. Tokyo: Author.

Kobe Bengoshikai [Kobe Bar Association] (1997a). *Otto koibitono boryokuni nayamu anatae* [For women who suffer domestic violence]. Unpublished handbook. Kobe: Author.

Kobe Bengoshikai, Ryoseino Byodoni Kansuru Iinkai [Committee on the Equality of Both Sexes, Kobe Bar Association]. (1997b). *"Otto no boryoku" jiken sodan manual* [A manual for responding to domestic violence incidents]. Unpublished manuscript. Kobe: Author.

Koseisho Daijin Kanbo Tokei Johobu [Office of Ministry of Health and Welfare, Statistics and Information Department]. (Ed.). (1977). *Showa 50 nen jinko dotai tokei* [Vital statistics 1975 Japan]. Tokyo: Koseisho Tokeikyokai.

Koseisho Daijin Kanbo Tokei Johobu [Office of Ministry of Health and Welfare, Statistics and Information Department]. (Ed.). (1996). *Heisei 6 nen jinko dotai tokei* [Vital statistics of Japan 1994]. Tokyo: Koseisho Tokeikyokai.

Koseisho Daijin Kanbo Tokei Johobukyoku [Office of Ministry of Health and Welfare, Statistics and Information Bureau]. (Ed.). (1993a). *Heisei 3 nen jinko dotai tokei* [Vital statistics of Japan, 1991]. Tokyo: Koseisho Tokeikyokai.

Koseisho [Ministry of Health and Welfare]. (1993b). *Zenkoku boshisetai tou chosa* [Nationwide study of single mother-headed households]. Tokyo: Author.

Koseisho Daijin Kanbo Tokei Johobu [Office of Ministry of Health and Welfare, Statistics and Information Bureau]. (Ed.). (1995). *Heisei 7 nen shakaifukushi shisetsutou chosa hokoku* [Report of the study of social welfare programs]. Tokyo: Koseisho Tokeikyokai.

Koss, M. P. (1992). The underdetection of rape: Methodological choices influence incidence estimates. *Journal of Social Issues, 48,* 61–75.

Kumagai, F. (1979). Social class, power and husband-wife violence in Japan. *Journal of Comparative Family Studies, 10,* 91–105.

Kumagai, F., & O'Donoghue, G. (1978). Conjugal power and conjugal violence in Japan and the U.S.A. *Journal of Comparative Family Studies, 9,* 211–222.

Kumagai, F., & Straus, M. A. (1983). Conflict resolution tactics in Japan, India, and the USA. *Journal of Comparative Family Studies, 14,* 377–387.

Kumamoto Family Court (1991). Kajichotei nimiru fufukan boryoku [The conjugal violence in family affairs conciliation cases]. *Katei Saiban Geppo, 43,* 81–213.

Kuzuhara, R. (1990). Fufukan deno gokan [Marital rape]. *Hogaku Seminar, 35,* 36–39.

Mainichi Shimbun, the Population Problems Research Council. (1992). *Summary of Twenty-first National Survey on Family Planning.* Tokyo: Author.

Masai, R. (1997a). *Boryokuwo uketeiru joseinotameni shelterwo.* Unpublished manuscript.

Masai, R. (1997b). Symposium de genkiwo moraeta watashi. In Kakekomi Shelter Kokusai Symposium Jikkoiinkai (Ed.), *Seiboryoku no konzetsuwo* (pp. 47–48). Sapporo: Editor.

Mitsui, F. (1994). Boryoku higaijosei notameno kinkyuhinanjo [An emergency shelter for battered women]. *Japanese Journal of Alcohol Dependence & Addiction, 11,* 158–160.

Naoi, A., & Moriyama, K. (Ed.). (1990). *Gendai nihon no Kaisokozo: 1. Shakai kaiso no kozo to katei* [Class structures of contemporary Japan: 1. Structures and processes of social class] (p. 21). Tokyo: Tokyo Daigaku Shuppan.

Nihon Bengoshi Rengokai [Japan Bar Association]. (1995). *Josei nitaisuru boryoku* [Violence against women]. Tokyo: Author.

Nishimura, M. (1986). Fujin fukushi [Women's welfare]. *Jurist, 41*, 212–216.

Ogawa, N., & Retherford, R. D. (1991). Prospects for increased contraceptive pill use in Japan. *Studies in Family Planning, 22*, 378–383.

Purple Kobo (Ueno, K., Kaneko, S., Niwa, M., Harada, E., Matsusato, A., & Yoshihama, M.). (1995). *Otto koitibo no boryoku kara jiyu ni narutameni* [translation of *You can be free: A handbook for abused women*]. Tokyo: Pandora Shuppan.

Rikon chotei wa joseini fukohei [Divorce mediation is discriminatory against women]. (1981, January 9). *Mainichi Simbun*, p. 3.

Rosenbaum, A. (1988). Methodological issues in marital violence research. *Journal of Family Violence, 3*, 91–104.

Saiko Saibansho Jimusokyoku [General Secretariat, Supreme Court]. (Ed.). (1990). *Kateisaibansho 40-nenno gaikan* [An overview of family courts over the past 40 years]. Tokyo: Hosokai.

Saiko Saibansho Jimusokyoku [General Secretariat, Supreme Court]. (1996). *Shiho tokei nenpo: 3. Kaji hen* [Annual report of judicial statistics for 1995, Volume 3 (Family cases)]. Tokyo: Hosokai.

Sakai-shi. (1995). *Dai 3kai Sakai-shi jinken ishiki chosa kekkahokokusho* [The report of the 3rd Study of Attitudes Towards Human Rights]. Sakai, Osaka: Author.

Seiboryokuwo Yurusanai Onnatachino Kai. (1990). *Onnaga mita "Chikatetsu Midosujisen Jiken"* [Women' perspectives on the Midosuji Line Incident]. Osaka: Author.

Somucho Tokeikyoku [Statistical Bureau, Management and Coordination Agency] (1993). *Heisei 4 nen rodoryoku chosa nenpo* [1992 Annual Report on the Labour Force Survey]. Tokyo: Nihon Tokeikyokai.

Somucho Tokeikyoku [Statistical Bureau, Management and Coordination Agency]. (1996). *Heisei 7 nen kokusei chosa hokoku: Dai 2 kan. Jinko no danjo, nenrei, haigusha kankei, setai no kosei, jukyo no jotai. Sono 1. Zenkoku-hen* [1995 Population Census of Japan: Vol. 2-1. Sex, age and marital status of population, structure and housing conditions of households]. Tokyo: Nihon Tokeikyokai.

Sorifu Danjo Kyodosankaku Shingikai [The Prime Minister's Office, the Council for Gender Equality]. (1996). *Danjo kyodosankaku vision* [The vision of gender equality]. Tokyo: Sorifu.

Sorifu Danjo Kyodosankaku Shitsu. (1994). *National report of the Government of Japan for the Fourth World Conference on Women*. Tokyo: Author.

Stop Child Sexual Abuse. (1992). [Activities of the Stop Child Sexual Abuse] Unpublished, untitled handout distributed at the 2nd Asian Women's Conference, Saitama, Japan.

Stark, R., & McEvoy, J., III. (1970). Middle-class violence. *Psychology Today,* *4*, 52–54, 110–112.

Straus, M. A. (1979). Measuring intrafamily conflict and violence: The Conflict Tactics (CT) Scale. *Journal of Marriage and the Family, 41*, 75–88.

Straus, M. A., Gelles, R. J., & Steinmetz, S. K. (1980). *Behind closed doors: Violence in the American family.* New York: Anchor Press/Doubleday.

Tawara, M. (1977, August). Boryoku teishuto tatakau nihonno onnatachi [Japanese women fighting against abusive husbands]. *Watashiwa onna* [Magazine for New Women], pp. 196–199.

Tokyo Rape Crisis Center (1992). [Services of the Tokyo Rape Crisis Center]. Unpublished, untitled handout distributed at the 2nd Asian Women's Conference, Saitama, Japan.

Tokyo-to Fujin Sodan Senta [Tokyo Women's Counseling Center]. (1991). *Heisei 3 nenban jigyo gaiyo* [Summary report of activities]. Tokyo: Author.

Tokyo-to Josei Sodan Senta [Tokyo Women's Counseling Center]. (1994). *Heisei 6 nenban jigyo gaiyo* [Summary report of activities]. Tokyo: Author.

Tokyo-to Josei Sodan Senta [Tokyo Women's Counseling Center]. (1996). *Heisei 8 nenban jigyo gaiyo* [Summary report of activities]. Tokyo: Author.

Tokyo-to Shakaifukushi Kyogigai, Boshifukushi Bukai. (1997). *Kinkyu ichiji hogojigyo ni kansuru chosahokoku to symposium shiryo* [A report of the study of emergency temporary shelter and resource materials for the symposium]. Tokyo: Author.

Tsunoda, Y. (1991). *Seino horitsugaku* [Legal studies on sexuality]. Tokyo: Yuhikaku.

United Nations. (1993). *World Conference on Human Rights: The Vienna Declaration and Programme of Action.*

United Nations, Department of Economic and Social Affairs, Statistical Office. (1996). *Demographic Yearbook, 1994.* New York: Author.

Upham, F. K. (1987). *Law and social change in postwar Japan.* Cambridge, MA: Harvard University Press.

U.S. Federal Bureau of Investigation. (1996). *Uniform crime reports for the United States, 1995.* Washington, DC: U.S. Department of Justice.

Weis, J. G. (1989). Family violence research methodology and design. In L. Ohlin & M. Tonry (Eds.), *Family violence* (pp. 117–162). Chicago: University of Chicago Press.

Wyatt, G. E., & Peters, S. D. (1986). Methodological considerations in research on the prevalence of child sexual abuse. *Child Abuse and Neglect, 10*, 241–251.

Yokohama-shi Josei Kyokai. (1995). *Sheruta chosa hokokusho I: Nihon kokunai chosa hen* [Report of the study of privately-run shelters for women in Japan, I.]. Yokohama: Author.

Yokohama-shi Josei Kyokai. (1996). *Yokohama-shi josei sodan niizu chosa hokokusho I* [Report of the study of women's needs for counseling in Yokohama City]. Yokohama: Author.

Yoshida, K. (1994). Fujinhogo jigyono saikochikuno kanoseiwa arunoka [Can women's protective services be restructured?]. *Hogaku Seminar, 473,* 34–37.

Yoshihama, M. (1993). *Domestic violence: Experience, knowledge, and attitudes among residents of Tokyo, Japan.* Unpublished manuscript, School of Social Welfare, UCLA, Los Angeles, CA.

Yoshihama, M. (1995, July). *Assessment of culture-specific manifestations of male partners' violence.* Paper presented at the 4th International Family Violence Research Conference, Durham, NH.

Yoshihama, M. (1996). *Domestic violence against women of Japanese descent: Understanding the socio-cultural context.* Unpublished doctoral dissertation, University of California, Los Angeles.

Yoshihama, M., & Sorenson, S. B. (1994). Physical, sexual, and emotional abuse by male intimates: Experiences of women in Japan. *Violence and Victims, 9,* 63–77.

Yunomae, T. (1990). Seiboryoku womeguru onnano undo [Women's movements concerning sexual violence]. In T. Kanai & M. Kano (Eds.), *Onnatachi no shisen* (pp. 135–142). Tokyo: Shakai Hyoronsha.

Yunomae, T. (1995, Winter). Movement to stop violence against women in Japan. *Voice: A newsletter of the National Coalition Against Domestic Violence)* (pp. 34–35).

Yunomae, T. (1997). Baibaishun mondai to feminism [Prostitution and feminism]. In Fuji Shuppan (Ed.), *Baibaishun mondai shiryoshusei: senzenhen.* Tokyo: Fuji Shuppan.

Zenkoku Boshiryo Kyogikai [Japanese Association of Homes for Mothers and Children]. (1992). *Oka-san kite yokattane: Boshiryo niokeru seikatsuno tebiki* [A manual for services at Homes for Mothers and Children]. Tokyo: Zenkoku Shakai Fukushi Kyogikai.

Zenkoku Fujinsodanin Renrakukyogikai. (1993). *Ima soshite korekara: Fujinsodanin gyomu jittai chosa hokokushu* [Report of the study of women's counselors]. Tokyo: Author.

JAPANESE STATUTES

Baishun Boshiho [Prostitution Prevention Law]. (1956, c. 118).
Jido Fukushiho [Child Welfare Law]. (1947, c. 164).
Kaji Sinpanho [Domestic Affairs Adjustment Law]. (1947, c. 152).
Keiho [Penal Code]. (1907, c. 45).

Keiji Soshoho [Penal Code of Criminal Procedure]. (1948, c. 131).
Kenko Hokenho [Health Insurance Law]. (1922, c. 70).
Minpo [Civil Code]. (1947, c. 222).

COURT DOCUMENTS

Hiroshima Kosai [Hiroshima High Court]. (1978). Judgment of November 20, 1978.
Hiroshima Kosai [Hiroshima High Court]. (1987). Judgment of June 18, 1987.
Nagoya Chisai [Nogoya District Court]. (1995). Judgment of July 11, 1995.
Tokyo Chisai Hachioji Shibu [Tokyo District Court, Hachioji Branch]. (1985). Judgment of February 14, 1985.
Tokushima Chisai [Tokushima District Court]. (1991). Judgment of November 15, 1991.
Tottori Chisai [Tottori District Court]. (1986). Judgment of December 17, 1986.
A petition filed in the Fukuoka Chisai (the plaintiff remains anonymous) (1989, August 5).

CHAPTER 18

Chinese Battered Women in North America: Their Experiences and Treatment

Mo-Yee Lee and Patrick Au

After more than 25 years of work by feminist activists, scholars, and practitioners who have been the force behind the battered women's movement, the issue of domestic violence has gained enough public prominence that it now can be considered mainstream in North America. In addressing the issue of domestic violence, grassroots activists and concerned professionals have: set up more than 1,200 shelters for battered women in the United States and Canada; established hundreds of programs and services available to victims, offenders, and children; reformed protection order legislation and arrest policies; expanded safeguards for women seeking custody of their children; and offered community education of domestic violence to both laypersons and professionals (Roberts, 1995; Schechter, 1996). The proliferation of our collective knowledge and understanding of violence against women and its treatment in North America has, however, largely neglected the experience of women from diverse ethnoracial backgrounds. The impact of race and ethnicity upon one's experience of battering has been poorly documented or studied. The conceptualization of gender as the primary foundation of battering as a social problem mitigated consideration of race and/or other factors as significant in understanding the phenomenon of domestic violence (Kanuha, 1996). Such a conceptualization, however, may have served a purpose for the early battered women's movement. Instead of portraying a battered woman as "the bad woman" who is poor, or a racial/ethnic minority, or drug-addicted, it is easier to gain public sympathy by portraying her as a victim who does not know how to fight back and is morally deserving of protection (Loseke, 1992; Mahoney, 1994)—an image fitting a collective interpretation of Everywoman that is often equivalent to a white, middle-class, moral, "good" woman (Kanuha, 1996).

The abandonment of women from diverse ethnoracial backgrounds in defining the image of battered women in the battered women's movement, however, shortchanges our understanding of their experiences as well as our provision of culturally competent and culturally sensitive interventions for this population. In addition, such a neglect reproduces the existing racism in society. Our lack of knowledge about woman victims from diverse ethnoracial backgrounds is well matched by our ignorance of the experiences of men who batter. Gondolf (1997), in reviewing existing batterer programs, called for an expanded effort to understand the experience of minority men because they often perceive, interpret, and justify their abuse differently, and their experiences with the criminal justice system and social services are oftentimes different than those of other men. In order to better understand domestic violence and provide effective intervention to stop violence in intimate relationships, it is important to produce additional images of domestic violence that capture the experience of *many* men, women, and children.

The purpose of this chapter is to describe the experience of Chinese battered women in North America and appraise existing services available to them. Because there is a lack of established literature in this area, the discussion is based on interviews with prominent Chinese or Asian professionals and activists working with Chinese battered women, and documents provided by them. The informants come from seven major cities in North America that have a large Chinese population: San Francisco, Santa Clara, Los Angeles, New York, Toronto, Montreal, and Vancouver (see Table 18.1). All informants come from agencies and shelters providing ethno-specific and bilingual services to Chinese battered women.

Apparently, many Chinese in North America are native-born. Their experiences and challenges would be very different from that of the first-generation Chinese, and more likely to resemble the mainstream experiences of battering. The focus of the discussion in this chapter is on Chinese battered women who utilize ethno-specific services. Many of them are foreign-born Chinese who are more likely to be influenced by traditional Chinese values and beliefs. Even so, traditional Chinese values have undergone tremendous challenges in the past several decades as a result of political and socioeconomic changes. It is, therefore, important to notice the process of continuity and the process of change that underlies the evolving value systems affecting the Chinese people.

THE PHENOMENON

Prevalence of Spouse Abuse in the Chinese Community

In the United States, domestic violence is estimated to occur annually in one out of every six households. Nearly one third of all married women report having experienced at least one incident of physical violence during the course of their marriage (Straus & Gelles, 1986). In 1992–1993, 26% of sexual assaults and 28% of aggravated assaults against women were inflicted by the victims' intimates including spouse, ex-spouse, or boyfriend (Bachman & Saltzman, 1995, Table 4). In Canada, it is estimated that 25% of all Canadian women aged 16 years and over have been abused by their current or a previous partner. In the case of married or previously married women, the figure goes up to 29%. Further, 20% of these cases were serious enough to have caused physical injuries (Statistics Canada, 1995, p. 105).

Prevalence studies for the Chinese population in North America regarding domestic violence are unavailable. Official statistics in

TABLE 18.1 Informants of the Study: Personal Communications Conducted in May–June, 1997

Name	Agency	Location	Nature
Au, Patrick Executive Director	Chinese Family Life Services of Metro Toronto	Toronto, Ontario, Canada	Ethno-Specific Chinese Family Service Agency
Cheung, Rhoda Counselor	Support Network for Battered Women	Santa Clara County, California, US	Mainstream Women's Shelter Founded in 1978
Eng, Patricia Executive Director	New York Asian Women's Center	New York, US	Asian Women's Shelter Founded in 1982
Hsieh, Stephanie Program Director/Counselor	Center for the Pacific-Asian Family	Los Angeles, California, US	Asian Women's Shelter Founded in 1981
Lam, Cynthia Executive Director	Chinese Family Life Services of Greater Montreal	Montreal, Quebec, Canada	Ethno-Specific Chinese Family Service Agency
Masaki, Beckie Executive Director	Asian Women's Shelter	San Francisco, California, US	Asian Women's Shelter Founded in 1988
Ng, Kelly Program Director, Family and Youth Counseling	United Chinese Community Enrichment Services Society	Vancouver, British Columbia, Canada	Ethno-Specific Chinese Family Service Agency
Shum, Tina Program Director/Counselor	Department of Social Services of Donaldina Cameron House	San Francisco, California, US	Ethno-Specific Chinese Family Service Agency
Yee, Jo Ann Family Service Manager	Asian Women Home, Asian Americans for Community Involvement	Santa Clara County, California, US	Asian Women's Shelter Founded in 1994
Yung, Vanda Counselor	Chinatown Service Center	Los Angeles, California, US	Ethno-Specific Chinese Family Service Agency

both the US and Canada do not include Chinese (nor Asians) as a separate category in their analyses. One study of spouse aggression in Hong Kong, however, indicated a 14% prevalence rate of physical violence between spouses (Tang, 1994). Professionals and activists working with Chinese battered women in North America, on the other hand, unanimously cited the following observations regarding prevalence of wife assault in the Chinese community.

First, it is an unfounded myth that domestic violence does not occur in the Chinese community, because Chinese women rarely utilize services provided by women's shelters (Chan, 1989). Domestic violence certainly exists in the Chinese community. However, there is a problem of underreporting and low utilization of social services, especially services offered by mainstream women's shelters, as a result of cultural and/or language barriers—reasons that have been repeatedly cited by many other researchers examining the low utilization rate of social services by Chinese in North America (e.g., Sue, Fujino, Hu, & Takeuchi, 1991).

Second, there is a trend of increased reporting, and it is closely linked to the increased criminalization of spouse abuse by the legal system and community education efforts launched by the individual agency. For instance, the number of spouse-abuse cases handled by the Chinese Family Life Services of Metro Toronto has increased from less than 10 cases in 1986 to 118 cases in 1996; 20% of all cases handled by the agency in the same year (P. Au, Personal communication, May 20, 1997). Similarly, the Domestic Violence Assistance Program at the Cameron House in San Francisco has experienced an increase from 80 to 300 cases between 1982 to 1997 (T. Shum, personal communications, May 14, 21, 1997). Both agencies have launched extensive community education programs regarding domestic violence and their services through the media (e.g., television, radio, and public information campaigns).

Finally, spouse abuse in the Chinese community happens across all socioeconomic strata regardless of an individual's immigration status. For instance, R. Cheung (Personal communication, May 9, 1997) noted that the husbands of some Chinese women who contacted the Support Network for Battered Women (a woman shelter in Santa Clara County, California) are accomplished engineers working for big companies in Silicon Valley, California. Likewise, P. Au (Personal communication, May 20, 1997) estimated that 40% of women seeking services from the Chinese Family Life Services of Metro Toronto in 1996 came from middle-class, professional families. A study conducted by the same agency in 1989 on 54 wife assault cases (Chan, 1989) indicated that 26% of the abusers were either entrepreneurs or professionals. Further, 46% of the batterers had attained post-secondary education and 24% were university graduates. Regarding the length of residency, 80% of the abusers and 61% of the victims had been in Canada for more than 6 years. The myth that only poor, uneducated, or new immigrants abuse their spouses is not true in the Chinese community. Those who stay at the women's shelters are, however, predominantly from the lower classes or are new immigrants who do not have alternative, outside resources (New York Asian Women's Center, 1992; J. A. Yee, Personal communication, May 9, 1997).

The Faces of Chinese Battered Women

The Chinese community in North America consists of many peoples from different regions who come to stay in this land for various reasons. Many of them come to North America for a better future, but some arrive here as refugees. They come from different socioeconomic and educational backgrounds. They all speak Chinese, although they may not be able to communicate between themselves because of the different dialects. They share similar traditional Chinese values about family, although they also express unique ways of thinking because of their different sociohistorical contexts. Each group carries its own heritage as well as historical burdens. They are the people from Cambodia, Hong Kong, Malaysia, Mainland China, Lao, Singapore, Taiwan, Vietnam, and other Southeast Asian countries. They are people with many faces.

Case 1

The Chan couple had come to San Francisco from Taishan in Mainland China 30 years ago. Mr. Chan was in his 60s and Mrs. Chan was 8 years younger than he. They were married for almost 30 years and had three children who were all married. Mr. Chan owned a small restaurant in Chinatown and Mrs. Chan helped him. Both of them had their life built around Chinatown and they spoke little English. Mr. Chan was a traditional man who considered himself the head of the household and deserving of absolute respect and obedience from his wife and children. He was hot-tempered and quick to criticize, especially after he lost money in gambling. He would then pick on minor things to degrade and demean Mrs. Chan. Sometimes, he would slap, push, and shove her. Mr. Chan treated her badly for many years and Mrs. Chan just endured his "rough behavior." Given their cultural values, divorce or separation was just unthinkable, because it would bring shame to the family.

Case 2

The Wong couple came to Toronto from Hong Kong 3 years ago. Mr. and Mrs. Wong were in their early 40s and they had a 12-year-old daughter. Both were elementary school teachers in Hong Kong, but because their credentials were not recognized in Canada, Mr. and Mrs. Wong had great difficulty in finding good jobs. Mrs. Wong finally got a receptionist's job at a Chinese dental office. Mr. Wong, however, could not find any jobs other than working in restaurants or factories. Although both suffered a downward shift in their occupation, Mr. Wong found such a change extremely degrading and unacceptable. Further, Mr. Wong resented the fact that Mrs. Wong had a higher salary than he. All along, Mr. Wong believed that a man should be the breadwinner of the family.

Initially, Mr. Wong became easily irritable and agitated after a "bad" day at work. He would become verbally aggressive and would call her names. Mrs. Wong sometimes cried and sobbed quietly. She did not argue with him because she "understood" where his frustration came from. She believed that the situation would improve if she treated him better. Lately, Mr. Wong started accusing Mrs. Wong of flirting with patients at the dental office. The couple got into big fights because Mrs. Wong could not tolerate being degraded as "flirting around with men." Mr. Wong hit her the first time. Mrs. Wong found the situation extremely frustrating and she wrote to her mother who was still in Hong Kong. Her mother wrote back asking her to endure the situation. "You are married to him. Maybe that's fate."

Case 3

*Jimmy came from a wealthy family, and he was an accomplished busi-
nessman in Taiwan; he was in his early 50s. He married Mimi more
than 20 years ago and Mimi was 10 years younger than he. Jimmy
and Mimi had three children. The family moved to Vancouver 5 years
ago. Jimmy still maintained a business, and he flew back and forth
between Taiwan and Vancouver. Both Jimmy and Mimi were educated.
Mimi had never worked after she was married. The abuse started in
Taiwan soon after the birth of the second son. At that time, Mimi
suspected that Jimmy was having affairs. When she confronted Jimmy,
the latter got very agitated and exploded at her. "Even if I have affairs,
so what? Remember, I provide you with everything you need. I'm the
man of the house. If you don't like it that way, you can leave and see
how you can survive." Mimi got very upset, although she did not have
the means to support herself and her children. Further, in Taiwan, she
will lose the custody of her children if she files for divorce [this law was
changed in 1995]. She got so depressed and angry that she refused to
have sex with Jimmy. It was at that point that Jimmy started to hit her
and forced her to have sex with him. The abuse continued after the
family moved to Vancouver. Mimi decided to stay in the marriage
mainly for economic reasons and for fear of "losing face." Her inlaws
and parents also knew about their "conflict." They all "persuaded"
her to stay in the marriage. After all, children need a father, a moral,
"good" woman only marries once in her life, and the family name
should be protected at all cost.*

Case 4

*L. was a construction worker in his late 30s. L. had a schizophrenic
breakdown in his early 20s but currently was in remission. He was the
only son and still lived with his parents in Los Angeles. Three years
ago, his mother was concerned about L. being single since that meant
the family would have no male heir. Through a go-between, the parents
assisted him in going back to China to marry S., who was a young
woman in her early 20s. The couple only met briefly before they were
married in China. The L. family paid good money to S.'s parents for
the marriage. L. then sponsored S. to come to the U.S.*

Under the Marriage Fraud Act, S. was granted a 2-year conditional entry. At the end of the 2-year period, L. will sponsor her to apply for the "Green Card" (Permanent Residency). It will take at least 7 years for her to formally become a U.S. citizen. S. found L. and his parents very controlling. L. did not allow S. to enroll in ESL (English as a Second Language) classes nor to learn how to drive. They found a job for S. in a factory operated by a Chinese owner. However, the L. family took away her salary and gave her a meager weekly allowance. The L. family was afraid that S. would leave L. once she became independent.

The worst experience for S. was that L. would literally wake her up in the middle of the night and demand to have sex with her. Because S. came from rural China and sex education was almost unheard of, she was literally traumatized by the experience. When she did attempt to say no, he beat her. Her inlaws knew about the situation, although they did nothing to help her. S. knew nothing about wife abuse or sexual assault. She thought that L. might have the right to have sex with her; after all, "he is my husband." S. found Los Angeles a totally strange and foreign place. She was totally isolated and could neither speak nor understand English. She felt bad about the situation, although she did not know whom to seek help from. She thought that the situation might improve if she were able to give birth to a son for the L. family. Meanwhile, the only thing that she could do was to endure the situation.

As exemplified by the different cases, the faces of Chinese battered women are as varied as the dynamics of spouse abuse. There is no one Chinese vision of spouse abuse. The dynamics involved are multifaceted and multilayered, influenced by culture-specific, contextual, interactional, as well as individual factors (see Figure 18.1). Despite the fact that Mrs. Chan, Mrs. Wong, Mimi, and S. come from different countries and socioeconomic backgrounds, and have experienced different life circumstances surrounding the abuse, there are two common themes regarding their responses to the abusive situation: (1) they tried to endure the situation, and (2) they did not consider divorce/separation a viable solution (at least at the beginning). Their decisions were also supported and reinforced by their relatives and friends. A closer look at the culture-specific factors may help us better understand their experiences of and responses to the abusive situations.

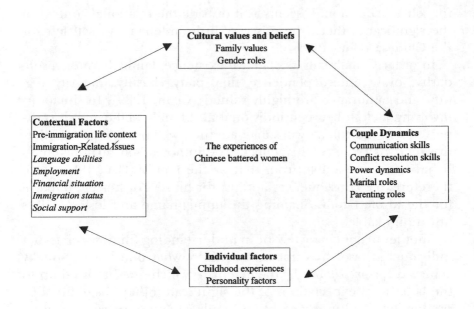

FIGURE 18.1   Factors influencing the experiences of Chinese battered women.

CULTURE-SPECIFIC INFLUENCES OF SPOUSE ABUSE

Feminist social critics focus on how cultural beliefs about sex roles and the resulting institutional arrangements contribute to and maintain gender inequality and the oppression of women by men (Gondolf, 1988; Martin, 1976; Warrior, 1976). For Chinese, such a dynamic is maintained by cultural beliefs and values around family and gender roles that profoundly influence one's definition of self.

As suggested by Chu (1985), the traditional Chinese self as rooted in Confucianism exists primarily in relationship to significant others (Chu, 1985). In the past, the self-other relationships among Chinese were built on the traditional collectivity of extended family/kinship networks. Such a collectivity extends even beyond the living relatives to include their ancestors. Thus, a male Chinese would consider himself a son, a brother, a husband, a father, an heir to the family lineage, but hardly *himself*. Likewise, a Chinese woman is a daughter, a sister, a wife, and a mother, but not an independent woman striving for self-actualization. It seems as if outside the relational context of the significant others, there is very little independent self left for the Chinese (Chu, 1985).

In order to maintain a collective existence, family harmony, solidarity, loyalty, interdependence, filial piety, chastity, integrity, dignity, and endurance are highly valued (Chan, 1989). In situations involving a clash between individual and family well-being, it is expected that individuals will subjugate their well-being for the collective good. As a result of this collective definition of self, an individual's behavior is inseparable from that of the family (Hsu, 1985) and, therefore, has consequences not just for himself or herself, but also for the whole family. Shaming the family name and losing face is just unthinkable.

Another major characteristic in understanding Chinese self is that individual self-worth is not measured by what one has personally achieved for *oneself*, but by the extent to which one has lived up to the behavioral expectations of the significant others, as defined by predominant cultural ideas. In a family situation, these behavioral expectations are circumscribed by the well-defined roles within a hierarchical structure. Power is distributed based on one's age, generation, and gender (Chan, 1989). Based on a patriarchal family structure, Chinese men are legitimate heirs to continue their family lineage and, therefore, are endowed with a strong sense of importance and entitlement. In the past, the social institutions have reinforced such an arrangement by providing men with educational and occupational opportunities, but not women. With a culturally endowed sense of importance and socially viable means to accumulate resources and wealth, men are naturally given permission to exercise authority over women and children.

At the other end of the continuum, women internalize values and beliefs about endurance, perseverance, and submission to men as ultimate virtues for any moral, good woman. The "three obediences" are widely accepted codes of behavior for moral, good women: Before marriage, a woman follows and obeys her father; after marriage, she follows and obeys her husband; after the death of her husband, she follows and obeys her son (Chu, 1985; Lum, 1988). The three obediences establish cultural ideas of unquestionable submission of women to men. If the situation demands the shortchanging of individual well-being to fulfill the ideals, the virtues of endurance and perseverance are used to regulate the discomfort involved. After all, "repeated endurance produces precious gold."

Such a cultural definition of self as influenced by cultural beliefs around family helps us better understand the responses of Chinese battered women to spouse abuse, and the dynamic of abuse.

Responses of Chinese Battered Women to Spouse Abuse and Cultural Influences

Chinese battered women face tremendous pressures in trying to break through the abusive cycle within their cultural milieu. As mentioned by most informants of this study who work closely with Chinese battered women, the first problem is the issue of nonrecognition of abuse as a problem. Because Chinese cultural values support male supremacy and dominance over women, male violence against women in the forms of physical, emotional, and sexual abuse can be justified differently based on culturally acceptable "reasons." For instance, some Chinese (e.g., Vietnamese Chinese) tend to accept hitting as a legitimate way to discipline or educate women (J. A. Yee, Personal communication, May 9, 1997). The Chinese Family Service of Greater Montreal conducted a study on Chinese attitudes and beliefs pertaining to domestic violence (Ming-Jyh, Li, Zhang, & Yao, 1994). Forty-one percent of male respondents in the Montreal study agreed that in a Chinese family, if a man beats his wife or girlfriend, a probable reason is to educate her (Ming-Jyh et al., 1994). Fourteen percent of female respondents were also in agreement with such an assertion. It is, therefore, not surprising that some victims may believe that they deserve the beating because they have indeed done something wrong. The cultural beliefs offer a gracious "excuse" for the abuser, because he is doing it to fulfill his duty as the head of the house.

Emotional abuse in the form of verbal abuse and financial restraint is accepted under the premise that "He is the man, he knows better than I do about *whatever*." Sexual abuse is the most grossly underreported form of abuse. Many Chinese women do not recognize sexual abuse as a form of abuse, especially those with little education. In fact, only 64% of the female respondents who had elementary education agreed that "forcing the other party to have sex" could be considered domestic violence while 91% of the same group agreed that "hitting with fist and kicking" and "verbal intimidation or assault" are domestic violence (Ming-Jyh et al., 1994). Many victims believe that marriage is a license for the man to have sex with them in whatever forms, at whatever time, and under whatever circumstances. In addition, it is considered taboo for woman to talk about sex and, therefore, it is difficult for many Chinese battered women to talk about sexual abuse with their social workers, shelter workers, or doctors. J. A. Yee (Personal communication, May 9, 1997) mentioned a situation whereby a former medical doctor was abused by her husband. She mentioned both physical and emotional abuse, although she never talked about sexual abuse, despite the fact that she had to take medication for pain control after forced sexual relations with her husband. She believed that it was her duty to have sex with her husband.

Because the family name has to be protected at all cost and because individual well-being should be subordinated to family well-being, it is difficult for Chinese women or Chinese families to admit to the occurrence of abuse. First, such an admission will bring shame to the family. Second, such an act may lead to divorce or separation. For many Chinese, marriage is for life. As a result, many women, and even supportive relatives, may go through a massive denial of the abuse. Many women are in fact under pressure from the extended family to either cover up or tolerate the abuse (P. Au, Personal communication, May 20, 1997; R. Cheung, 1997; K. Ng, Personal communication, May 13, 1997). In the study conducted by the Chinese Family Life Services of Metro Toronto on Chinese battered women (Chan, 1989), 50% of the women respondents did not find their relative, family or friends helpful to their situation. Twelve percent of those who had a supportive social network found their supporters to be either too pushy, or too timid in advising them in ways to deal with the abuse.

In many circumstances, some women and their families may give a different label to the problem, such as the man is hot-tempered, or he just lost money gambling (see Case 1 above), or he is just frustrated with his work situation (see Case 2). In fact, over half of the female respondents (53%) of the Montreal study (Ming-Jyh et al., 1994) agreed that a probable reason for a man to beat his wife or girlfriend was "he's in a bad mood." Giving abuse another label, however, is not a helpful solution, because it prevents the man from taking responsibility for his violent behavior and finding solutions to the problem. As a result, the woman still shoulders the responsibility to find a solution *for* the man's problem, which is always an impossible task.

For those women who recognize and admit to the occurrence of abuse, they still have to address the question of "What to do next?" In many cases, these women resort to the traditional virtue of "endurance." In the Toronto study on abused women, the most frequently mentioned coping mechanism was to "endure" (78%). In the Montreal study on Chinese attitudes toward domestic violence (Ming-Jyh et al., 1994), only 27% of those who had elementary education said that they would not tolerate domestic violence. Even for those who attained university education, only 57% would not tolerate domestic violence. Such empirical data is consistent with the observation of all informants of this study—that "endurance" is the first and the most frequently used coping mechanism among their clients in situations of abuse. Many of them may have contemplated leaving their husbands, although they cannot deal with the ultimate dilemma posed by their leaving the abusive relationship.

The dilemma faced by many Chinese women has to be understood within a cultural context. For Chinese women influenced by traditional values, leaving the abuser is not just a demonstration of self-assertiveness or saying no to the abuse. Such an act also means exposing family weakness to outsiders (or at least to the helping professionals involved), shaming the family name, violating the virtues of perseverance and endurance, and causing divorce or separation to the family. So, instead of developing a "victim mentality" (that I am a victim of abuse, it is not my fault and I deserve to be helped) as commonly understood from a feminist perspective, the woman may instead develop an "instigator mentality" (that I am the bad person who brings shame to the family or causes family breakdown because I expose the abuse or leave my husband). The Chinese community clearly reinforces the "instigator mentality" by viewing the woman as the troublemaker. It is not uncommon for the community to shift its sympathy and support from the battered wife to the batterer, once the abuse is made known to the police or any outside agencies (R. Cheung, Personal communication, May 9, 1997; T. Shum, Personal communication, May 14, May 21, 1997). A common scenario is for the inlaws or elders in the family to beg the wife to drop charges on the husband. Individual suffering is no longer important once the family name and losing face is involved.

Not subordinating individual interests to family well being has far-reaching, negative, repercussions on the woman herself. In leaving the abusive relationship, the woman also divorces the network of social support offered by her role as a wife. The more a woman builds her life around the role of mother and wife, the greater is her sacrifice in not giving in to the abuse. Knowing these cultural issues help us better understand the passivity, ambivalence, guilty feelings, and shame characteristics of many Chinese women's responses to spouse abuse.

Dynamics of Spouse Abuse and Cultural Influences

Similar to a feminist understanding of domestic violence, the core dynamic of spouse abuse in the Chinese community in North America is about male dominance and the quest for control and power in intimate relationships. The ways for those power dynamics to be manifested are, however, uniquely influenced by cultural factors. The following characteristics of the dynamics of spouse abuse in Chinese couples elucidate the possible influences of culture on spouse-battering.

In defining who is the abuser, mainstream understanding based on a feminist perspective focuses on male violence against women in intimate relationships. Gender is the fundamental defining concept in woman battering. Because of the patriarchal nature of Chinese families, violence against wives, however, may be instigated by female relatives on the male side, especially from the in-laws (R. Cheung, Personal communication, May 9, 1997; B. Masaki, Personal communication, May 12, 1997; Ming-Jyh et al., 1994). In Chan's study (1989), 20% of the abused wives lived with inlaws. Among those abused women, 64% were also physically and emotionally abused by the parents of their husband. For all battered women, 39% perceived inlaw issues as factors precipitating violence. Even though the data is limited and not representative of all Chinese, such findings did suggest that for Chinese, wife assault may not be confined to male violence against women. Women, especially mothers-in-law, can derive power from their association with the male figures in the family, and induce violent acts against other women. Of course, complex family dynamics such as triangulation (Minuchin & Fishman, 1981) are commonly involved in such a situation. Still, such a phenomenon poses new challenges to the predominant conceptualization of gender as the primary foundation of wife-battering.

Another observation concerns the cycle of violence. Lenore Walker (1984, 1994) described the cycle of violence as involving four stages. A period of tranquility is followed by a stage where tension builds up and finally accumulates in a violent episode. Following the violent episode is often the "honeymoon" period, whereby the abuser becomes remorseful and asks for forgiveness. Rather than having a honeymoon period after the abusive incident in which the abusers seek reparation, the Chinese version of the honeymoon period for many battered women is at best a period of relative calm (P. Au, Personal communication, May 20, 1997; V. Yung, Personal communication, May 22, 1997). The cultural beliefs operate in such a way that the man may not feel guilty about the abuse and, therefore, see no need to seek reparation. Most women will just endure the situation and stay in the relationship. As such, there is no pragmatic need for the man to do anything to keep the woman in the relationship. In this way, cultural factors influence how the abusive cycle is manifested in Chinese intimate relationships.

The final observation is about the involvement of gambling versus alcohol in domestic violence. Alcohol involvement is a widely recognized factor related to spouse abuse, even though not of a causal nature (Zubretsky & Digirotama, 1996). It is part of a routine procedure to assess the influence of alcohol on domestic violence and its treatment (Dziegielewski, Resnick, & Krause, 1996). All informants of the current study, however, raised questions about the role played by alcohol in spouse abuse. T. Shum (Personal communication, May 14, 21, 1997) has provided counseling to Chinese battered women in San Francisco for 15 years. Based on her work experience, only two abuse cases were alcohol-related, and none were drug-related. Instead, one-third of all cases she worked with involved gambling. The detrimental impact of gambling, a favorite pastime for many Chinese, has been well documented (Chinese Family Life Services of Metro Toronto, 1996). Although the relationship between gambling and wife abuse is anecdotal and has yet to be empirically determined, such an observation is supported by many informants of the study.

Apparently, the universal, underlying dynamic of spouse abuse is essentially one of control and dominance. Its manifestation, however, can be influenced by culture-specific and contextual factors. An understanding of those issues will have important implications for assessment and treatment of Chinese battered women.

Pure traditional Chinese values have undergone tremendous challenges in the past several decades. A process of discontinuity in terms of traditional values and beliefs is obvious in both the motherlands of many Chinese (e.g., Mainland China, Hong Kong) and of Chinese who reside in North America. On the other hand, underlying this process of discontinuity is also a thread of continuity that is distinctive of a particular culture (Chu, 1985). It is important to recognize both the patterns of continuity and the pattern of change within a cultural milieu in order to understand any phenomena.

The complex issue of cultural continuity and change is obviously beyond the scope of our discussion. However, the study conducted by the Chinese Family Service of Greater Montreal (Ming-Jyh et al., 1994) on Chinese attitudes and beliefs pertaining to domestic violence is illustrative of some of the issues raised by the present discussion of traditional values and beliefs around family. The findings of the study indicated that the process of change was more obvious regarding the superiority of men. Among the 281 respondents, only 6% of females and 12% of males still believed that "Men are superior to women and a wife belongs to her husband." On the other hand, 35% of male respondents and 19% of female respondents agreed that a woman should accept the "three obediences and four virtues" as the standard for a moral, good woman. Regarding the issue of saving face and protecting the family name, 44% of male respondents and 21% of female respondents still agreed that "No family scandal should be made public." Apparently, despite changes in the society, values around gender roles and the family name are still important for many Chinese in North America. Men seem to be the guardians of traditional values more than women.

CONTEXTUAL FACTORS—IMMIGRATION-RELATED ISSUES

Mary Dutton (1996) warned against a single vision of the experiences of battered women and argued for a contextual analysis of battered women's experience that includes the woman's unique individual and social context. In the same manner, it is dangerous as well as doing a disservice to Chinese battered women if one adopts a single vision of their experiences solely based on an understanding of cultural factors. The experience and strategic responses of Chinese battered women are multifaceted and multilayered influenced by cultural, contextual, and individual factors. While individual factors do not lend themselves to meaningful discussion because of their extreme heterogeneity, one contextual factor that profoundly influences an individual woman's experience is her immigration experience in North America.

Many Chinese batterers have used immigration status as a "weapon" to psychologically threaten the woman and to keep her in an abusive relationship despite physical, psychological, and sexual sufferings (P. Au, Personal communication, May 20, 1997; R. Cheung, Personal communication, May 9, 1997; K. Ng, Personal communication, May 13, 1997). The experience of S. (see Case 4) clearly illustrates this dynamic. These women belong to the more vulnerable group, because they are new immigrants who usually have little social and financial resources, minimal language skills, and little knowledge about North American culture. Many of them are socially isolated and are still struggling to understand and adjust to the new environment.

Immigration-related stress may have a negative impact on couple relationships that triggers off or exacerbates violent behaviors in intimate relationships. Except for those Chinese who immigrate to North America on a refugee status (e.g., Vietnamese Chinese), most immigration is voluntary, planned, and welcomed by the families. Still, leaving the familiar country of origin and venturing into a new culture involves drastic change and disruption in one's life. The degree of cumulative stress experienced by an individual and the discrepancy between his or her expectation and the actual quality of life in North America influences how well an individual adjusts to the life and culture of the receiving country (Drachman, 1992). One common phenomenon affecting some couples is spousal role reversal. Some wives have found employment more easily than their husbands because they tend to accept lower-paying jobs; for instance, garment work. In addition, it is not uncommon for professional men to lose their status because of unrecognized credentials, working experiences, or limited language skills (Ming-Jyh et al., 1994). To most male immigrants, underemployment, downward occupational changes, and redistribution of power in the family are ego-shattering realities that directly threaten their concept of manhood and husbandhood (Chan, 1989). In an attempt to regain a sense of power and to reduce their pain, some men unfortunately resort to spouse and child abuse, gambling, or chemical abuse to deal with the adverse situation (Drachman & Ryan, 1991). Immigration-related stress cannot be an "excuse" for abuse. Further, many abuses in fact happen prior to the immigration (Chan, 1989; T. Shum, Personal communication, May 14, 21, 1997). Immigration-related stress, however, can be perceived as another layer of stress factors that exacerbate the dysfunctional couple dynamics which are, at the core, still an issue of dominance and control.

Immigration-related experiences, on the other hand, significantly influences a woman's help-seeking responses to her battering experiences. Oftentimes, the seemingly passivity of many Chinese battered women is not just a result of cultural values. Their passivity can be a reaction to their immediate life circumstances in North America. One major issue is social isolation. In the Montreal study (Ming-Jyh et al., 1994), when respondents were asked for the reasons for tolerating domestic violence, the two mostly cited reasons, regardless of educational level, were: "Nowhere to seek help because of isolation" and "To tolerate the abuse for the future of the children." Apparently, "Nowhere to seek help because of isolation" is more related to contextual factor than to cultural influences.

Because of social isolation, many women do not have information about available services. Not having the language abilities, many Chinese women cannot utilize mainstream shelters' services. The most often cited reasons by both clients and helping professionals for the low utilization of shelter services by Chinese women are: language barriers, food choices, cultural dissimilarities, fear of fights among children, and stigma of woman shelters (Chan, 1989; R. Cheung, Personal communication, May 9, 1997). In the Toronto study (Chan, 1989), only 6 out of 50 abused women who received counseling services used shelter services, and only 2 women were able to adapt to shelter living without much difficulties.

Not able to utilize the services provided by women's shelters is only part of the issue. Davidson and Jenkins (1989), in discussing the socioeconomic oppression experienced by working-class women, mentioned that "A woman might not find that her partner's violence is her first concern nor her worst oppressor" (p.494). Such a situation is even more true for many Chinese battered women. Equipped with little language skills and no viable means for making a living and supporting their children, many Chinese battered women are "forced" to stay in the abusive relationships for purely economic and survival reasons.

Sometimes, not being able to speak fluent English becomes an insurmountable barrier, even when the woman actively seeks outside help such as calling the police or going to the emergency room at the hospital. R. Cheung (Personal communication, May 9, 1997) mentioned situations whereby the police used various members of the household as translators, or even only talked to the batterer to gather information because "he is the only one who speaks English." Language is clearly a formidable barrier to the help-seeking efforts of many immigrant women.

In understanding and assessing the experience of Chinese battered women and their strategic responses to their plight, one needs to consider cultural and contextual as well as individual factors, including couple dynamics. Each battering situation constitutes a unique configuration of the interaction of those factors. Each factor may take on varying importance in an individual's experience. Neglecting any one dimension, however, is likely to result in a biased understanding of the situations of Chinese battered women.

RESPONSES OF THE CRIMINAL JUSTICE SYSTEM

The criminalization of spouse abuse can be considered a significant victory for those working diligently to end violence against women in intimate relationships. Currently, all states and provinces in the United States and Canada have passed civil and/or criminal statutes to protect battered women (Roberts, 1996b). Many police departments have also responded with a proarrest policy and provide immediate protection to battered women (Roberts, 1996b). The five cities surveyed in this study all have pro-arrest polices or even mandatory arrest laws/zero-tolerance policies to prevent batterers from intimidating and pressuring victims to drop charges or restraining. In those situations, the police will prosecute the abuser regardless of the victim's decision, if there are visible injuries (K. Ng, Personal communication, May 13, 1997; Roberts, 1996a).

The responses of criminal justice systems to spouse abuse have positively affected the Chinese community. A Chinese battered woman has expressed the advantages of being in North America as follows:

> Wife beating is really common in China. No laws deal with this prob-
> lem. . . . [In North America] domestic violence is illegal and the social
> welfare system protects women victims, which, in turn, encourages
> women to seek help. (Ming-Jyh et al., 1994, p. 12)

The implementation of mandatory arrest laws further assists victims to receive the needed help who might otherwise choose to "endure" the situation. Before the advent of such a policy, many Chinese battered women would not prosecute their abusers for both cultural and contextual reasons. They are also under tremendous pressure from their extended families and communities to "give a second chance" to the abuser. In fact, many abuse cases are being reported by neighbors and friends, and not by the victim herself (R. Cheung, Personal communication, May 9, 1997; J. A. Yee, Personal communication, May 9, 1997). Many Chinese offenders, further, are ignorant of the legal consequences of wife-battering in North America (V. Yung, Personal communication, May 22, 1997).

The responses of the criminal justice systems to spouse abuse have forced the Chinese community to face the issue that will otherwise remain hidden. Informants from the Chinatown Service Center at Los Angeles, Chinese Family Life Services of Metro Toronto, and United Chinese Community Enrichment Services Society in Vancouver mentioned the pressure of increased referral of male batterers from the courts to receive group or individual treatment after the advent of pro-arrest or mandatory arrest policies. The involvement of the court system is a strong deterrence against men's violence toward women in the Chinese community. In traditional Chinese society, government is perceived as an oppressive authoritarian apparatus with which anybody in their right mind should avoid having any contact. The old saying: "Never go to court when alive and never go to hell after death" clearly illustrates the fear of government in many Chinese. Further, many Chinese men feel degraded and shamed by the procedure of being body-searched when arrested (T. Shum, Personal communication, May 14, 21, 1997). K. Ng (Personal communication, May 13, 1997) mentioned that there is no one reoffense in all the male offenders whom he has treated in the past 5 years. All of them are afraid of the legal penalty.

As a result, court involvement by itself can be a very effective deterrence in stopping visible abuse in the Chinese community. The question is whether such intervention can alter the power dynamics in couple relationships. The man may learn how not to abuse his wife in a way that will cause him trouble with the court system. It does not mean, however, the cessation of violence in intimate relationships. Edleson and Syers (1991) found that many men who received group treatment still used threats despite a decrease in violent behavior. The impact of court involvement on the dynamics of spouse abuse in Chinese couples needs to be further investigated.

Despite the overall positive impact of the criminal justice system in preventing and stopping spouse abuse in the Chinese community, language and cultural barriers still exist. When victims and the police or judge do not share a similar language, the latter have to rely on translators. The problems of using translators and cultural biases of an individual police officer or judge are considerable. In situations where translators are unavailable, police may rely on information provided by the husband or other family members who may, intentionally or not, distort the situation.

Lacking any coordinated or planned efforts to deal with the issue of cultural and language barriers in the criminal justice system, many agencies serving the Chinese community take the initiative to develop a beneficial and positive working relationships with their respective police departments and courts. Oftentimes, such individual outreach efforts involve doing consultation and training related to cultural issues. The success of these efforts, however, depends very much on the openness and flexibility of individual police departments and courts that vary from place to place.

TREATMENT PROGRAMS FOR CHINESE BATTERED WOMEN

Chinese battered women in North America face tremendous pressure and many obstacles in confronting and escaping abuse. The criminalization of spouse abuse and the corresponding responses of the court system serve important and irreplaceable social control functions. On the other hand, individual men and women still need to find solutions to attain a life that does not contain violence in intimate relationships. Because cultural values influence a person's problem perception, perceived problem resolution, and help-seeking behaviors (Lee, 1996), treatment for Chinese battered women needs to be sensitive to those culturally based dynamics. Grassroot efforts initiated by the Chinese community have established various culturally and linguistically sensitive services to assist Chinese men and women. These organizations provide invaluable and irreplaceable services for those who cannot effectively utilize mainstream services because of cultural and language barriers.

Women's shelters for Asians and family services agencies for Chinese are the two major types of organizations that provide services for Chinese battered women and their families in North America. Their inception mostly involves the efforts of concerned Chinese/Asian grassroot activists and professionals who recognize the insurmountable barriers faced by Chinese women in seeking help from mainstream agencies.

Women's Shelters

The Center for the Pacific-Asian Family at Los Angeles, founded in 1981, was the first Asian women's shelter established in the United States (Hsieh, 1997). In 1982, the New York Asian Women's Center was opened on the East Coast by formerly battered women, sexual assault survivors, and other concerned women to combat the problem of battering and sexual assault in the Asian communities (New York Asian Women's Center, 1992). In San Francisco, the Asian Women's Shelter was opened in 1988 as the third shelter in North America to serve the Asian population. Likewise, in 1994, Asian Americans for Community Involvement opened the Asian Women Home in Santa Clara, California. Similar to other shelters, these Asian women's shelters provide crisis intervention, hotline services, residential services, legal services, referral services, counseling, support groups and activities, advocacy, accompaniment services (the staff/volunteers accompany the battered woman in accomplishing various tasks), and community education. The distinctive aspect of these shelters, however, is their attempts to provide culturally and linguistically sensitive services to their clients. These shelters have developed innovative programs specifically for Asian women.

Language Access. To overcome language barriers faced by Asian women seeking help from mainstream shelters, many Asian women's shelters provide 24-hour Asian multilingual hotline services (e.g., New York Asian Women's Center, Asian Women's Shelter in San Francisco, Center for the Pacific-Asian Family). All shelters, further, provide a language match between the shelter staff and battered women as best they can. Still, Asia encompasses many different groups. Even Chinese have many diverse dialects. Some shelters have developed innovative programs to deal with such an issue. A good example is the Multi-Lingual Access Model developed by the Asian Women's Shelter in San Francisco since 1988 (B. Masaki, Personal communication, May 12, 1997). In this model, the shelter provides 58 hours of training for bilingual domestic violence advocates who also function as translators. These people are language advocates who are also equipped with knowledge about domestic violence. Their names are placed in an on-call "language bank" that can be accessed at all times to provide language services for all Asian battered women. Masaki mentioned that this model has been such a success that it will be expanded on a citywide base in 1998, with six additional agencies in San Francisco offering such services to their clients. As expressed by many Chinese battered women, being able to speak in their own language makes it easier for them to seek outside, professional help. They feel understood and acknowledged by the shelter staff and are more comfortable at expressing themselves (R. Cheung, Personal communication, May 9, 1997).

Culturally Sensitive Shelter Environment. Besides providing a language match, most Asian women's shelters strive to provide a culturally sensitive shelter environment (New York Asian Women's Center, 1992). Food has been mentioned by several informants as a major concern for their clients. Some Asian women's shelters (e.g., Asian Women Home) allow women to prepare food for themselves and their children. Such a minor modification, however, assists many Chinese women and their children to better adjust to their life at shelters (J. A. Yee, Personal communication, May 9, 1997). Because isolation is a widely used strategy by Chinese male batterers in controlling their spouse, and many Chinese women also lack language skills to access useful information, educating women about their rights and service available to them becomes an important part of the empowering process (S. Hsieh, Personal communication, June 11, 1997). Sharing similar cultural values, many shelter staff members recognize the cultural dilemma for a Chinese woman in leaving the abusive relationship. While not replicating the dynamics of abuse, in which the women were told what to do or what was best for them, the shelter staff members fully respect the women's decision while at the same time providing the required assistance.

Similar to mainstream philosophy, the ultimate goal of shelter services is to empower Asian/Chinese women. Through the empowering process that fosters an internal locus of control and a positive sense of self in Chinese battered women, they will become more aware of their needs and resources. Consequently, there is a greater likelihood for them to develop solutions that are appropriate to their needs and viable in their unique cultural milieu. From this perspective, services at the shelters are provided in a way that respects the client's culture and supports self-determination. These empowering efforts have been successful in helping many battered women to leave the abusive relationships. For instance, only 30% of Asian women who stayed at the New York Asian Women's Center between 1982–1992 returned to the batterers (New York Asian Women's Center, 1992).

Besides Asian women's shelters that specifically serve Asian women, including Chinese, some mainstream shelters attempt to provide culturally sensitive services by including Chinese-speaking staff. Such a situation is more prevalent in Canada because there are no ethno-specific women's shelters. Culturally and linguistically sensitive services are provided mainly through the Chinese-speaking staff in shelters and the use of translators.

Ethno-Specific Family Services

Because of the cultural dilemma created by leaving one's marriage and the pragmatic, economic concerns of many Chinese battered women, many of them prefer to seek help from a family service agency. Although some Chinese women know that a shelter provides a safe place for them, many of them still choose not to use the service because they attach a feeling of homelessness to a shelter, and/or perceive that their marriages will dissolve once they leave home (Chan, 1989). Counseling services provided by ethno-specific family agencies allow them to talk to someone about their problems without having to leave their homes.

The development of ethno-specific agencies in the different parts of North America is neither coordinated nor planned. Each agency has their own distinctive history, although all represent grassroot efforts to provide needed services for ethnic Chinese. Many agencies, not by coincidence, have made domestic violence a priority of their services to the Chinese community. Such a phenomenon probably reflects the need of the Chinese community for services to assist both battered women and their husbands. For instance, over 20% of all family cases served by the Chinese Family Life Services of Metro Toronto in 1996 were spouse abuse cases (P. Au, Personal communication, May 20, 1997). The United Chinese Community Enrichment Services Society in Vancouver recently launched a 3-year Family Violence Prevention and Intervention Project to deal with the increasing reports of spouse abuse cases (K. Ng, Personal communication, May 13, 1997). Similar services are provided by ethno-specific agencies in the United States. For instance, Donaldina Cameron House in San Francisco started domestic violence assistance services 15 years ago. The Chinatown Service Center at Los Angeles has provided services for domestic violence victims and offenders since 1991.

Services for Battered Women. An array of services is provided for battered women, including counseling services, legal assistance, referral services, and support groups. The actual services provided by each agency vary depending on the resources available. All agencies, however, provide counseling services. Besides being linguistically sensitive, the helping professionals also provide therapy in a manner that takes into consideration culture-specific issues.

Because Chinese tend to be more reserved, and disclosing family problems is almost equivalent to shaming the family name or losing face, talking about family abuse to an outsider is very difficult for most women. In addition, many of them do not have prior experience with therapy. As such, it is necessary for the staff to carefully explain to them about the therapy process and respect their reserved attitude. The pacing of therapy becomes a very important part in enjoining and engaging the clients. Clients are given time and space to slowly open up at their own pace and in a way that they feel comfortable. Lack of direct eye contact will not be misinterpreted as a symptom of avoidance or anxiety, because it may be a sign of respect in the more traditional Chinese. Being silent or reserved does not necessarily mean resistance or unwillingness to seek help; it may be just a matter of the client's needing more time to open up herself.

Because "no family scandal should be made public" and because of the strong fear of shaming the family name and losing face, issues of confidentiality should be communicated clearly and unambiguously to Chinese clients. Case management services, including escort services, may be prominent because of the usual lack of resources and language skills of many Chinese battered women.

Some agencies also provide "telephone therapy" because of the relative privacy, flexibility, and feeling of anonymity afforded by such a mode (Shepard, 1987). Such a form of therapy can be more readily accepted by those women who otherwise will not seek help because of the strong fear of losing face, both for herself and the family. Further, many Chinese battered women may not have the means of transportation to attend sessions. Telephone therapy makes it easier, at least at the beginning stages, for the helping professionals to reach out to those battered women who might otherwise not be able to utilize the much needed services.

Services for Offenders. The vast majority of mainstream treatment programs for offenders are characterized as group-based, psychoeducational approaches (Rosenfeld, 1992). Because of the lack of resources and training, very few treatment groups are offered to Chinese-speaking offenders. The Chinatown Service Center at Los Angeles has run batterer groups since 1991. In 1997, Chinese Family Life Association of Metro Toronto also began offering group treatment to offenders. The first one is a 52-week, 2-hour, open group using the Duluth Model as the basic guide. The second one is a 16-week treatment group focusing on anger management, marital relationships, and relational skills. The difference in the length of the two groups is a reflection of the different policies adopted by the state/province regarding the ideal length of treatment for batterers. Both groups, however, focus on culture-specific issues, including traditional values and beliefs around gender roles, family relationships, and communication; in-law relationships; conflict resolution; parenting issues; immigration and its impact on couple relationships; and cultural aspects of adjustment to life in North America.

The dynamics exemplified by these Chinese batterers' groups resemble the mainstream experiences, but are not limited to them. The beginning stage is characterized by group members' immense anger, resistance, and blaming. It may be the first time that their manhood as a Chinese man is being openly challenged in a way that they cannot neglect or avoid. Speaking from her several years of experience running Chinese batterers' groups, V. Yung (Personal communication, May 22, 1997) mentions the very difficult group dynamics at the beginning stage because all members reinforce and fuel each other's anger and blaming. Currently, a model of open group is adopted instead because members at different stages of their development can assist each other to understand the problem of dominance and control. These men progress slowly to be less blaming and more able to be confronted about power-and-control issues, and recognize their contribution to the marital problems. The group process is oftentimes slow and frustrating for the leaders. However, it yields useful outcomes at the end, when the member requests additional counseling services or mentions his new but difficult learning through participating in the group (P. Au, Personal communication, May 20, 1997; V. Yung, Personal communication, May 22, 1997).

Individual counseling for male batterers is also offered by some agencies. For instance, the United Chinese Community Enrichment Services Society in Vancouver provides an 8-session individual counseling service using a cognitive-behavioral approach and focusing on stress and anger management. Culturally relevant metaphors have been found to be useful in assisting Chinese men to learn new, adaptive behaviors in relating to their spouses (K. Ng, Personal communication, May 13, 1997).

Culturally sensitive treatment is readily received by Chinese offenders, despite their initial suspicion and resistance (P. Au, Personal communication, May 20, 1997; K. Ng, Personal communication, May

13, 1997). T. Shum (Personal communication, May 14, 21, 1997) mentioned that she would sometimes receive complaints from the husbands of their clients: that Cameron House is unfair in the sense that the agency only provides services for battered women but not for the men. However, due to the absence of federal or state financial support and the inability or unwillingness of many Chinese batterers to pay for services, services for men have been developed on a sporadic and fragmented manner, despite great demand from the community.

Couple Therapy.   Couple therapy, despite being practiced and supported by some professionals (Lipchik & Kubicki, 1996), has been cautioned against by most feminist therapists because of the issue of power imbalance in relationships. On the other hand, informants from these family service agencies suggest that couple therapy is, oftentimes, being requested by both Chinese men and women, and is an appropriate form of treatment in the Chinese community. Strongly influenced by the ideals of "marriage for life" and family togetherness despite adversities, it is estimated that between 80% to 90% of those women who seek help from a Chinese family services agency choose to stay in the marriage (P. Au, Personal communication, May 20, 1997; K. Ng, Personal communication, May 13, 1997; V. Yung, Personal communication, May 22, 1997). In such a situation, the best thing for a therapist to do is to advocate for a violence-free relationship. Couple therapy becomes a viable choice of treatment under the following conditions: the woman requests couple treatment; there is a cessation of violence in the relationship; and the man is willing to take responsibility for the abuse (P. Au, Personal communication, May 20, 1997; K. Ng, Personal communication, May 13, 1997).

Community Education.   Both Asian women's shelters and ethno-specific agencies perceive community education as serving significant preventive and remedial purposes with respect to ending spousal violence in the Chinese community. Consistent with their beliefs, all agencies launch extensive efforts regarding community education of domestic violence. The targets include victims, offenders, and the general public and involve mainstream helping professionals.

Oftentimes, Chinese battered women do not seek help because they are ignorant of available services. Many of them do not even label their suffering as abuse as a result of ignorance or denial. Thus, effective dissemination of information about spouse abuse and services available to Chinese battered women is the necessary first step in reaching out to this population. Effective ways that have been used by various agencies include: pamphlets printed in Chinese about domestic violence and services offered by an individual organization; informational brochures (e.g., "A Resource Manual and Divorce Information for Battered Women and Abused Children in the Bay Area," prepared by the Cameron House); advertisements or educational programs in Chinese newspapers; radio-broadcasting services; and multicultural television channels of the respective cities.

Community education, to Chinese men, serves a very important preventive function. As mentioned before, some Chinese men believe it is their right and duty to educate and discipline their spouse through corporal punishment. The mere knowledge of spouse abuse as a criminal act with legal consequences can be an important first step in deterring them from using violence toward their spouses. Educating the Chinese community about detrimental consequences of abuse for an individual and his/her children will, in the long run, reduce the community pressure being put on battered women to yield to the abuse. Such a change in attitude will reduce the negative social consequences for the woman when she decides to leave the abusive relationship. Such education is even more important for the younger generation. The best way to stop a man's violence against a woman is to educate children early on about gender equality and mutual respect. To this end, some agencies have launched large-scale, citywide campaigns to raise the community awareness of the issue (e.g., Domestic Violence Campaign for Chinese in San Francisco, 1996; British Columbia Family Violence Day in Vancouver).

Another target for community education is the various professionals involved in providing services to Chinese battered women. Some effective ways that have been used are: providing consultations or training/seminars around cultural issues to mainstream organizations; conducting studies on Chinese battered women (e.g., Toronto, Montreal); and organizing conferences around issues of Asian/Chinese battered women (e.g., Voices Heard: Taking Steps Past Domestic

Violence in Asian Communities in Ohio, May 30, 1997; Gathering
Strengths: Coming Together to End Domestic Violence in our Asian
and Pacific Islander Communities, June 20–21, 1997, San Francisco).

Lacking state or provincial financial support for community education, many ethno-specific organizations rely on private fundraising
to launch educational campaigns for various target populations.
According to Shum (T. Shum, Personal communication, May 14,
21, 1997), "patch-up" work is inadequate to stop violence in intimate
relationships. The Chinese community needs to be educated about
domestic violence and available services for dealing with it.

THE FUTURE

The services available to Chinese battered women can best be described as innovative efforts initiated and provided by the local
Asian/Chinese community to best serve their people. The roles of
ethno-specific social services in a multicultural society are always
controversial because of the fear of fragmentation of social services
as a result of the existence of so many diverse groups in society
(Lee, 1993). In addition, there is the pragmatic concern of financial
consequences for the government. Nevertheless, being culturally
and linguistically similar, these ethno-specific agencies successfully
provide culturally sensitive, direct services to many Chinese battered
women and their families. In other situations, they serve as mediators
or "brokers" between their clients and mainstream organizations
(Lee, 1993). Despite inadequate financial support and the lack of
trained professionals in many situations, these organizations maintain a safety net for many Chinese in North America, who otherwise
have immense difficulties utilizing mainstream services as a result
of cultural and language barriers.

In appraising the services provided by these ethnic organizations,
many informants mentioned the need for more extensive community
education, improved networking and coordination with the mainstream organizations, and more treatment groups for Chinese male
batterers. There is also a lack of treatment programs for children
who are often the forgotten victims of domestic violence. Currently,
New York Asian Women's Center is one of the few organizations
that provide regular programs and services for children who witness

parental violence. In addition, there are virtually no services for gay and lesbian Chinese couples—another silent group in the Chinese community. Expanded effort to provide services for these neglected groups is necessary.

The most critical issue, however, is how supportive is society in assisting those battered women and their children to lead an independent life in situations when they decide to leave the abusive relationship. The problems of housing, employment, and childcare are common to all battered women, even though Chinese battered women face additional barriers because of language and cultural factors that may be further compounded by racism in society. The continuing advocacy work by activists and helping professionals to ensure the exemption of battered women from the recent welfare reforms (which aims to eliminate welfare benefits for immigrants) and to allow battered women to self-petition for their immigration status is certainly hopeful signs that they are not a totally neglected group.

CONCLUSION

Chinese battered women are both similar to and different from other battered women in North America. They are similar to all other abused women in the sense that they are victims of male dominance and control. Their battering experience can also be different, however, as a result of the additional burdens imposed by traditional Chinese cultural beliefs and values, their immigration experience, and/or racism in the society. Oftentimes, they are locked in a vicious cycle that makes it extremely hard for them to escape violence in intimate relationships. Besides embattling the traditional values, they have to choose between "being exploited by their husbands if they stay in the abusive relationship, or being exploited by the socioeconomic system if they leave the abusive relationship" (B. Masaki, Personal communication, May 12, 1997).

Being in North America renders Chinese women legal protection from spouse abuse, although many Chinese battered women have not been able to benefit from such protection because of cultural and language barriers. The ethno-specific organizations, including both shelters and family services agencies, have provided a safety net for many first generation Chinese-Americans or Chinese-Canadians. These community-initiated programs work diligently to serve their local Chinese communities, despite inadequate financial support in many situations. The effectiveness of their work, however, depends on how well the legal, criminal, and mainstream social service systems coordinate with each other to serve in the best interest of battered women of all colors.

REFERENCES

Bachman, R., & Saltzman, L. E. (1995, August). *Violence against women: Estimates from the redesigned survey, Special Report NCJ-154348, National Crime Victimization Survey.* Washington, DC: U.S. Department of Justice, Bureau of Justice Statistics.

Bureau of Justice Statistics. (August, 1995). Violence against women: Estimates from the redesigned survey (Special report NCJ-154348, National Crime Victimization Survey).

Chan, S. L. L. (1989). *Wife assault: The Chinese Family Life Services experience.* Toronto: Chinese Family Life Services of Metro Toronto.

Chinese Family Life Services of Metro Toronto. (1996). *Working with gambling problems in the Chinese community, development of an intervention model.* Toronto: Author.

Chu, G. (1985). The changing concept of self in contemporary China. In A. J. Marsella, G. DeVos, & F. L. K. Hsu (Eds.), *Culture and self: Asian and Western perspectives.* New York: Tavistock Publications.

Davidson, B. P., & Jenkins, P. J. (1989). Class diversity in shelter life. *Social Work, 34,* 491–495.

Drachman, D. (1992). A stage-of-migration framework for service to immigrant populations. *Social Work, 37,* 68–72.

Drachman, D., & Ryan, A. S. (1991). Immigrants and refugees. In A. Gitterman (Ed.), *Handbook of social work practice with vulnerable populations* (pp. 618–646). New York: Columbia University Press.

Dutton, M. A. (1996). Battered women's strategic response to violence: The role of context. In J. L. Edleson & Z. C. Eisikovits (Eds.), *Future interventions with battered women and their families.* (pp. 105–124). Thousand Oaks, CA: Sage.

Dziegielewski, S. F., Resnick, C., & Krause, N. B. (1996). Shelter-based crisis intervention with battered women. In A. R. Roberts (Ed.), *Helping battered women: New perspectives and remedies* (pp. 159–171). New York: Oxford University Press.

Edleson, J., & Syers, M. (1991). The effects of group treatment for men who batter: An 18-month follow-up study. *Research on Social Work Practice, 1,* 227–243.

Gondolf, E. (1988). *Battered women as survivors.* Lexington, MA: Lexington Books.

Gondolf, E. W. (1997). Batterer programs: What we know and need to know. *Journal of Interpersonal Violence, 12,* 83–98.

Hsu, J. (1985). The Chinese family: Relations, problems and therapy. In W. S. Tseng & D. Y. H. Wu (Eds.), *Chinese culture and mental health* (pp. 95–112). Orlando: Academic Press.

Kanuha, V. (1996). Domestic violence, racism, and the battered women's movement in the United States. In J. L. Edleson & Z. C. Eisikovits (Eds.), *Future interventions with battered women and their families* (pp. 34–50). Thousand Oaks, CA: Sage.

Lee, M. Y. (1996). A constructivist approach to the help-seeking process of clients: A response to cultural diversity. *Clinical Social Work Journal, 24,* 187–202.

Lee, M. Y. (1993, June). *Canadian multiculturalism policy and the development of ethnic specific mental health services: The case of Hong Fook Community Mental Health.* Paper presented at the Sixth Biennial Conference on Social Welfare Policy, St. John's, Newfoundland.

Lipchik, E., & Kubicki, A. D. (1996). Solution-focused domestic violence views: Bridges toward a new reality in couples therapy. In S. D. Miller, M. A. Hubble, & B. L. Duncan (Eds.), *Handbook of solution-focused brief therapy* (pp. 65–98). San Francisco: Jossey-Bass.

Loseke, D. R. (1992). *The battered women and shelters: The social construction of wife abuse.* Albany: State University of New York Press.

Lum, J. (1988). Battered Asian women. *Rice, 2,* 50–52.

Mahoney, M. R. (1994). Victimization or oppression? Women's lives, violence and agency. In M. A. Fineman & B. Mykitiuk (Eds.), *The public nature of private violence* (pp. 59–92). New York: Routledge.

Martin, D. (1976). *Battered wives.* San Francisco: Glide.

Ming-Jyh, S., Li, N., Zhang, W. M., & Yao, K. (1994). *Research on conjugal violence in Chinese families of Montreal.* Montreal: Chinese Family Service of Greater Montreal.

Minuchin, S., & Fishman, H. C. (1981). *Family therapy techniques.* Cambridge, MA: Harvard University Press.

New York Asian Women's Center. (1992). *New York Asian Women's Center: Tenth anniversary report 1982–1992.* New York: Author.

Roberts, A. R. (1995). *Crisis intervention and time-limited cognitive treatment.* Thousand Oaks, CA: Sage.

Roberts, A. R. (1996a). Court responses to battered women. In A. R. Roberts (Ed.), *Helping battered women: New perspectives and remedies* (pp. 96–101). New York: Oxford University Press.

Roberts, A. R. (1996b). Police responses to battered women: Past, present, and future. In A. R. Roberts (Ed.), *Helping battered women: New perspectives and remedies* (pp. 85–95). New York: Oxford University Press.

Rosenfeld, B. (1992). Court-ordered treatment of spouse abuse. *Clinical Psychology Review, 12,* 205–226.

Schechter, S. (1996). The battered women's movement in the United States: New directions for institutional reform. In J. L. Edleson & Z. C. Eisikovits (Eds.), *Future interventions with battered women and their families* (pp. 53–66). Thousand Oaks, CA: Sage.

Shepard, P. (1987). Telephone therapy: An alternative to isolation. *Clinical Social Work Journal, 15,* 56–65.

Statistics Canada. (1995). *Women in Canada: A statistical report* (3rd ed.). Ottawa: Ministry of Industry.

Straus, M. A., & Gelles, R. J. (1986). Societal change and change in family violence from 1975–1985 as revealed by two national surveys. *Journal of Marriage and the Family, 48,* 465–479.

Sue, S., Fujino, D. C., Hu, L. T., & Takeuchi, D. T. (1991). Community mental health services for ethnic minority groups: A test of the cultural responsiveness hypothesis. *Journal of Consulting and Clinical Psychology, 59,* 533–540.

Tang, C. S. K. (1994). Prevalence of spouse aggression in Hong Kong. *Journal of Family Violence, 9,* 347–356.

Walker, L. (1984). *The battered woman syndrome.* New York: Springer Publishing Company.

Walker, L. (1994). *Abused women and survivor therapy: A practical guide for the psychotherapist.* Washington, DC: American Psychological Association.

Warrior, B. (1976). *Wifebeating.* Somerville, MA: New England Free Press.

Zubretsky, T. M., & Digirotama, K. M. (1996). The false connection between adult domestic violence and alcohol. In A. R. Roberts (Ed.), *Helping battered women: New perspectives and remedies* (pp. 96–101). New York: Oxford University Press.

CHAPTER 19

Validating Coping Strategies and Empowering Latino Battered Women in Puerto Rico

Diana Valle Ferrer

Violence in the family has been a part of family life throughout recorded history. The actual extent of family violence is not known; estimates of child abuse, wife abuse, and elder abuse vary depending on the source. Estimates of the incidence of wife abuse also vary considerably. For example, on the basis of a nationally representative study of 2,143 U.S. families, researchers estimated that violence (behavior legally considered assault if it were to occur between two unrelated adults) occurs each year in at least one out of six couples who live together, married or unmarried (Straus & Gelles, 1995). Puerto Rico Police Department (1995) statistics reveal that 19,411 cases of spouse abuse were reported in 1995. In 92% of these cases, the victim was a woman; the most frequent type of wife abuse reported was aggravated assault (e.g., use of weapons, committed in front of children) which was perpetrated in 56% of the cases. Forty percent of the 625 women murdered in Puerto Rico between 1987 and 1994 were victims of domestic violence.

Domestic violence statistics, argues Abbott (1996), may well be underestimates. We agree with Abbott when she asserts that "only the most severe cases are reported in the crime statistics, and shame and fear tend to restrict the victims' reports of abuse" (Abbott, 1996, p. 236). However, although the figures vary, and wife assault is likely to be underreported behavior, it may be that between 33% (Rivera Ramos, 1991) and 60% (Preamble Law 54 for the Prevention of and Intervention with Domestic Violence, 1989) of all adult women in relationships have been or will be abused by their partners in Puerto Rico.

Historically, in Puerto Rico, and as has been evidenced in many other countries, Silva Bonilla, Rodríguez, Cáceres, Martínez, and Torres (1990) assert that violence against women in the family has been supported by two main ideas: first, that women are the property of men, and second, that the home is a private or domestic sphere where strangers should not interfere. Socioeconomic constraints, derived from the sexual hierarchy through which women are made economically dependent on men, place women in a subordinate position within society (Silva Bonilla, 1985). She explains that social and economic factors are mediated in each person by their personal history (e.g., their socioeconomic class), the ideology which they support or question, and their accumulation of concrete social experiences. In a more recent publication on wife abuse, Silva Bonilla and others (1990) elaborate on the notion that women have been ideologically conditioned to feel and think of themselves as the property of men (father, husband, boyfriend, lover) and "responsible" by their "nature" to produce and maintain "good," loving marital and family relationships. Women assume the responsibility of maintaining the integrity of the family and the marriage. When the marriage "fails" the woman feels guilty for its "failure." She feels that she might be responsible for the abuse. Furthermore, Silva Bonilla argues that even though many women subscribe to these ideological premises, they actually participate in a historical questioning of them. Women in their praxis, in their daily lives, actively question and resist the ideas that many times are kept intact in their affective and emotional sphere.

COPING WITH ABUSE

How does a woman cope with battering in an intimate relationship? How does she appraise the situation? What cognitive, emotional, and behavioral efforts does she make to manage the battering situation? How does previous exposure to violence and current battering influence her coping strategies? How does she cope, survive, and resist in a hierarchical structure where she has unequal power?

Ramona, a 37-year-old Puerto Rican woman, the mother of three children, is a victim/survivor of 18 years of physical and psychological abuse in her marriage. She is also a victim/survivor of child abuse perpetrated by her father and a witness of abuse perpetrated by her father against her mother. Ramona described the variety of coping strategies that she used to deal with a battering incident, explaining:

> Our daughter went to our next door neighbor's house and found my husband kissing our neighbor on the mouth. At that point I would have liked to be dead. . . . When he came back home I told him "your daughter saw you kissing that woman." He said that it was not true, that our daughter was inventing things. When I insisted that our daughter was not a liar, he shouted and insulted me and locked himself in our bedroom. That night I slept in my daughter's bedroom. Next day, I called a lawyer friend of ours to ask for his advice and he told me that after so many years of marriage I should not get a divorce nor ask for a protective order under Law 54. He said that I should talk to my husband and appeal to his feelings, because he knows that he loves me and men are "like that." So I tried to talk to him, I cooked breakfast for him and took it to our bedroom, I told him "We have to talk." He answered that he didn't have anything to talk to me about. I told him that I couldn't continue like this, that the situation was intolerable, that I needed time to think about it and I asked him to leave our home. He said that I was crazy and that they would have to kill him before he would leave the house. I said O.K., but I'm going to put a chain and lock on the door so the neighbor cannot come in, "She has to respect me, this is my home." Then he said, "If you do that I'll kill you" and he took a knife from the kitchen and tried to stab me. I pleaded with him not to hurt me and I promised

that I would not do it, "I won't put a chain and lock on the door."
He went back to the bedroom, I don't know what for, and then I ran
like crazy, I took my children and left. I went to my sister's home, I
was away for a week and I requested a Protective Order. . . . I felt so
hurt, so humiliated . . . , it was not the first time that he had cheated
on me or beaten me . . . , she was my friend . . . I never thought he
would go so far, that's why I decided that he had to leave before he
destroyed me and my children.

Although the literature on the incidence, dynamics, and psychological impact of wife abuse is extensive, researchers, practitioners,
and policy analysts have paid less systematic attention to the range
of ways women cope with, resist, and survive wife abuse. Battered
women have been viewed as either masochistic, frigid, provocative,
or nagging (Gayford, 1977; Gelles & Straus, 1988; Roberts, 1996) or
passive, helpless, and apathetic (Bowker, 1993; Walker, 1979, 1984).
These profiles emerge from different psychological and sociological
theoretical perspectives; however, by concentrating on the characteristics of the female "victim," they contribute to blaming the woman
and perpetuating the violence directed at her. Even discussing family,
social structural, and sociocultural levels, many researchers fail to
recognize the woman as an active social agent, the unequal distribution of power in the family and in the society, and the socially
structured and culturally maintained patterns of male/female
relations.

Moreover, the work of feminist theoreticians and researchers like
Gordon (1988), Davis (1987), Hoff (1990), Kelly (1988), Bowker
(1993), and Emerson and Russell Dobash (1988) challenge definitions of battered women as victims or provocateurs, arguing instead
that these women might be better understood as survivors. In their
historical, social, and psychological research these theoreticians have
clearly demonstrated that women who are battered are not passive
in confronting the violent situations in which they live. However,
only few studies have integrated the psychological literature on coping with the research on wife abuse. Mitchell and Hodson (1986)
have studied women's coping responses to wife abuse; nonetheless,
they have not integrated feminist perspectives and ideas. On the
other hand, feminist researchers Hoff (1990) and Kelly (1988) have
carried out important qualitative studies focusing on women's cop-

ing, resistance, and survival strategies in battering situations. Nevertheless, in their groundbreaking studies, they have not integrated the accumulated theoretical and empirical knowledge on stress, appraisal, and coping.

By "coping," we refer to the effort that people exert to manage specific external and/or internal demands that are appraised as taxing or exceeding the resources of the person (Lazarus & Folkman, 1984). At the very heart of this concept is the fundamental assumption that people are actually responsive to forces that impinge upon them (Pearlin & Schooler, 1978). Since many of these forces are social and relational, the understanding of coping is necessary for understanding the impact exerted on people by institutions like the patriarchal family and society in general, and how people respond to them. Yet, we know relatively little of the coping strategies that women use in response to such a prevalent and taxing experience as wife abuse, which we define as the use of physical and nonphysical force by a man against his intimate cohabiting partner. Wife abuse is conceptualized as part of a continuum of violence against women in patriarchal social and familial structures.

The purpose of my study is to examine the ways Puerto Rican women cope with wife-abuse situations and to ascertain what aspects of women's lives, personal and contextual, influence their coping responses to battering. More specifically, I sought answers to the following questions:

1. How do women's coping responses to battering vary as a function of the frequency and severity of the battering?
2. How does previous exposure to violence relate to the coping strategies used by women in response to battering?
3. How do the primary and secondary appraisals of the battering situation influence the coping strategies used by women?

For the purpose of this study, the term "wife abuse" is used to define a broad category of abuse against women in intimate relationships, even though the intimate partners may not be legally married. Battering is theoretically defined as the use of coercive behavior (physical, sexual, and/or psychological) by a man against his intimate cohabiting partner, to force her to do what he wants her to do, regardless of her own needs, desires, rights, or best interests.

THEORETICAL FRAMEWORK

In this study, multiple theoretical and research perspectives from the psychological literature on stress, appraisal, and coping (Lazarus & Folkman, 1984) and feminist theories and research on violence in the family, specifically wife abuse, are used. Wife abuse is understood as part of a continuum of violence against women in patriarchal social and familial structures. The research is guided by feminist theory supplemented by Gramsci's (1971) concept of ideological hegemony and Foucault's (1981) concepts of power and resistance.

It is argued that violence against women does not happen in a vacuum: it occurs in the sociohistorical context of the patriarchal society. Violence against women in intimate relationships takes place in the context of the patriarchal family, which is one of the basic units of the patriarchal organization. In a similar fashion, coping and resisting violence in intimate relationships exists in the patriarchal context, and women use the coping strategies that they perceive as available to them at that moment. Women think, feel, and act to manage the internal and external demands that they appraise as taxing.

In the patriarchal family and social institutions of male dominance over women and children, women's interests are subordinated to the interests of men (Frye, 1983; hooks, 1984; Lerner, 1986; Weedon, 1989). In the relations of power existing within the family, specifically in intimate relationships, battering is used as a tool for social control to maintain and perpetuate the interests of men over those of women (Martin, 1983; Pagelow, 1981; Roberts, 1996; Schecter, 1982). The childhood exposure to violence (emotional abuse, sexual abuse, physical abuse, neglect) that women experience in their families of origin is another tool in the continuum of violence against women that men use to control and "teach" women who has the power (Kelly, 1988).

Many women, because of the ideological hegemony of domesticity (Barrett, 1988; Gramsci, 1971) enforced in patriarchal societies, might feel and think that the interests of their partners (husband, cohabiting partner) or men in general are their interests. However, hegemony is not total, and power is not absolute, and wherever there is power there is resistance to that power (Foucault, 1981).

The family, the home, the "homeplace" is the site of oppression and also the site of resistance (hooks, 1990).

COPING THEORIES

The application of coping theory to understand and explain how women deal with abusive episodes is a way to explicate and clarify their efforts to manage these encounters. As mentioned earlier, the concept of coping has been applied to wife abuse in an unsystematic, informal way, or by implication (Hoff, 1990; Kelly, 1988; Silva Bonilla, Rodríguez, Cáceres, Martínez, & Torres, 1990). In addition, those researchers who have applied coping theory to battering situations have not used a feminist perspective. Richard Lazarus and Susan Folkman's theory of stress, appraisal and coping (1984) was selected as the conceptual framework to guide the analysis of women's coping responses to wife abuse.

Lazarus and Folkman's theory is transactional; the person and the environment are viewed as being in a dynamic, mutually reciprocal, bidirectional relationship. Stress is conceptualized as a "relationship between the person and the environment that is appraised by the person as taxing or exceeding his or her resources and endangering his or her well-being" (Lazarus & Folkman, 1984, p. 19). The theory identifies cognitive appraisal and coping as two processes which mediate between the stressful person-environment encounter and the immediate and long-term outcome.

Cognitive appraisal is a "process through which the person evaluates whether a particular encounter with the environment is relevant to his or her well-being and, if so, in what way" (Lazarus & Folkman, 1984, p. 31). There are two kinds of cognitive appraisal: primary and secondary. In primary appraisal, the person evaluates whether he or she has anything at stake in this encounter. In secondary appraisal, the person evaluates what, if anything, can be done to overcome or prevent harm or improve the prospects for benefit.

In this theory, coping is defined as "constantly changing cognitive and behavioral efforts to manage specific external and/or internal demands that are appraised as taxing or exceeding the resources of the person" (Lazarus & Folkman, 1984, p. 141). According to Lazarus and Folkman, this definition addresses limitations of traditional approaches to coping. First, it views coping as process-oriented, rather than trait-oriented. Second, it views coping as contextual, that is, influenced by the person's appraisal of the actual demands in the encounter and the resources for managing them. Finally, the authors make no a priori assumptions about what constitutes good or bad coping, since their definition recognizes the efforts the person makes to manage the environment without taking into account if the efforts are successful or not.

In this theory, coping has two major functions: First, problem-focused coping deals with the problem that is causing the distress by altering the troubled person-environment situation. Emotion-focused coping regulates the stressful emotions. Lazarus and Folkman (1984) have identified several forms of problem-focused and emotion-focused coping. For example, problem-focused forms of coping include aggressive interpersonal efforts to alter the situation, as well as cool, rational, deliberate efforts at problem solving. Emotion-focused forms of coping include distancing, self-controlling, seeking social support, escape/avoidance, accepting responsibility or blame, and positive reappraisal.

Lazarus and Folkman's (1984) Stress, Appraisal and Coping Transactional Model views coping as process-oriented rather than trait-oriented and does not judge coping strategies as "good" or "bad." Wife-abuse literature points to contextual factors, such as frequency and severity, influencing the ways women cope with battering. Guided by these and by a feminist perspective which proposes that there is a continuum of violence against women in patriarchal societies, the following relationships were hypothesized:

H1.1 The number of women's coping responses to battering will vary as a function of the frequency of the current battering.

H1.2 The number of women's coping responses to battering will vary as a function of the severity of the current battering.

H2.1 There is a difference in the use of coping strategies between the women who experienced or witnessed abuse in their families of origin and the ones who did not experience or witness abuse.

H2.2 The women who experienced or witnessed abuse in their families of origin will use more emotion-focused coping strategies than the ones who did not experience or witness abuse in childhood.

H2.3 The women who experienced or witnessed abuse in their families of origin will use less problem-focused strategies than the ones who did not experience or witness abuse in childhood.

H3   The greater the stakes in the intimate relationship, the higher the rate of emotion-focused coping responses.

H4.1 The women who appraise that they are in control of the battering situation will use more problem-focused coping strategies than the ones who perceive they are not in control.

H4.2 The women who perceive that they are in control of the battering situation will use less emotion-focused coping strategies than the ones who perceive they are not in control.

The diagram in Figure 19.1 outlines the hypothesized relationships between previous exposure to violence, severity and frequency of battering, and primary and secondary appraisal and coping strategies, both emotion and problem-focused. The diagram suggests pathways through which battering, child abuse, and appraisal may influence coping. This model draws upon previous work that has examined similar factors influencing women's reactions and responses to wife abuse (Blackman, 1989; Browne, 1987; Kelly, 1988; Mitchell & Hodson, 1983, 1986; Walker, 1984) and adjustment and coping with stressful events (Folkman, 1984; Folkman, Lazarus, Gruen, & DeLongis, 1986; Folkman & Lazarus, 1988; Lazarus & Folkman, 1984; Pearlin & Schooler, 1978).

METHODOLOGY

The research sample in my study consisted of 76 women who had sought assistance from one of three agencies in San Juan, Puerto Rico, which offered counseling, legal services, or shelter to women victims/survivors of battering. To be included in the study, a woman must have been battered (physically, sexually, or psychologically) at least twice in the last year by a man with whom she has or had an intimate relationship.

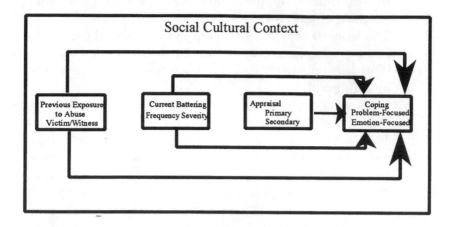

FIGURE 19.1   Conceptual framework: A model of women's ways of coping with battering in intimate relationships.

Adapted from Mitchell & Hodson's conceptual framework (1983).

The 76 participants were screened by agency workers when they telephoned or attended the agency's offices to request or continue psychosocial counseling or legal orientation. They were interviewed by the researcher in the offices, the shelter, or in their homes between the months of January and July of 1994. The data were gathered with a structured interview schedule used on the entire sample and a semistructured in-depth interview, with open-ended questions on a subsample of participants. Embedded in the interview schedule were several scales, such as a modified version of the Conflict Tactic Scales (CTS) (Straus, 1979) and the 66 Ways of Coping Questionnaire (Folkman & Lazarus, 1988).

The computer program Statistical Analysis System (S.A.S.) was used to conduct data analysis. Frequency and descriptive statistics were used to describe the data. T tests, analysis of variance and measures of association were used to test for differences and associations between the variables.

The mean age of the women was 34.4 years; 93.4% identified themselves as Puerto Rican, 20% were married or living with the batterer, and 80% were separated or divorced, 62% of them for less than a year. The majority (68%) of the women had been in a relationship with their partner for less than 10 years, and in 62% of the cases the battering had begun before the first year of marriage was over (in 12%, before getting married). In terms of education, 30% had completed high school, 36% had some college education, and 14% were college graduates and postgraduates. The majority of women had few independent financial resources (only 38% were employed, and of these 52% earned less than $10,000 a year); however, their family income (when living with or separated from the husband) was more substantial, with only 46% making less than $10,000 a year and 29% earning $20,000 or more a year. The mean number of children was 2.5. At the time of the interview, a mean of 2.0 children lived in the homes of the women. Five women had no children living with them at that point.

All the women participants manifested having been victims/survivors of psychological abuse in their current intimate relationship. Sixty-six percent were victims/survivors of physical abuse, 43% of sexual abuse, and 42% of economic abuse. Forty-three percent of the women had been victims of child abuse in their families of origin, and 61% had witnessed abuse in their families of origin. In 65% of these cases, the father was the aggressor, and in 11% the perpetrator was the stepfather. In 76% of the cases, the participant's mother was the victim of abuse.

LIMITATIONS OF THE STUDY

The major limitations of the present study are shared by research using nonexperimental, cross-sectional, retrospective designs. First, the cross-sectional design allows for alternative explanations of the findings. For example, severity of the current psychological abuse or previous exposure to childhood abuse may influence coping, and coping may influence the woman's appraisal or reappraisal of the current or previous abuse.

Similarly, it is possible that in addition to primary and secondary appraisal influencing coping, coping may influence the women's appraisal of what is at stake and what control they have over their situation. Thus, while the pathways in the model presented earlier are unidirectional, we recognize that these processes are likely to be bidirectional and reciprocal.

Second, the self-selected nature and small size of the sample make it difficult to assess the generalizability of the findings. For example, are women who seek assistance from agencies which serve women victims/survivors of abuse more likely to have identified abuse as a social or common problem for women, thus using more problem-solving coping strategies to try to change or alter the abusive situation? Are the coping strategies used by women who have made a decision to seek help different from those used by women who have not? Nevertheless, these women can provide useful and vital information, especially if the study is considered exploratory in nature and followed by larger, more representative samples of women in Puerto Rico.

FINDINGS

This study's findings are placed in the context of the conceptual framework that we proposed to help us understand how personal, social-cultural, and contextual factors are related to the ways women cope with battering in intimate relationships. The model (see Figure 19.1) suggests potential paths through which previous exposure to violence, frequency and severity of current battering, and the primary and secondary appraisals of the worst battering incident in the year of the study influenced women's coping strategies in a social context of structural oppression and discrimination and a situational context of abuse.

In general, the results of the study suggest that women victims/survivors of battering used both emotion-focused (e.g., seeking social support, escape avoidance) and problem-focused (problem solving, confrontive) forms of coping to deal with the worst battering incident during the study year. Furthermore, the relative proportions of each form of coping vary according to how the battering encounter is appraised (e.g., amenable or not amenable to control; the magnitude of the stakes) and if the woman was or was not a victim/or witness of child abuse in her family of origin. The quantity or number of coping strategies used during the encounter vary according to the severity of the current psychological abuse (verbal aggression) and if the woman was or was not a victim/survivor of child abuse. Previous exposure to abuse in the family of origin influenced the proportion of emotion-focused and problem-focused forms of coping, as well as the total number of coping strategies women use.

The findings in the present study suggest that the women participants who were victims of abuse in childhood, who appraised that the stakes (e.g., risk to the integrity of the marriage and the family, women's health security and physical welfare) in the battering situation were high, and who perceived that they were in control during the battering incident used more problem-focused coping strategies as a response to the worst battering incident during the year of the study. In addition, the women who were abused in their families of origin used significantly more coping strategies, both problem-focused and emotion-focused, to deal with the battering situation than did nonvictims. Moreover, in the current study, only the severity of psychological abuse (verbal aggression) in the marriage, rather than physical or sexual abuse, was positively related to the use of more coping strategies in the worst battering situation.

Women's appraisal of the battering situation psychologically mediates the women with the environment. Their appraisal of the immediate battering situation is individual and contextual at the same time that it is influenced by social-cultural variables, such as the hegemonic ideology of family and marriage and the social structure that oppresses and discriminates against women.

It can be observed how the "macro" level of cultural and social structural variables influences the "micro" level of the individual woman's actual life context and her response to it. The view of women as both influenced and influencing the social structure and culture is imperative, and recognizes that coping involves changing the environment as well as one's self (Lazarus & Folkman, 1984). Women appraise and cope in the battering relationship responding to personal history, cultural, and social structural variables (both "concrete" and "perceived") and in the process they change the immediate situation, themselves, and their environment.

The important message that we can draw from these findings is that we have to view the women victims/survivors of battering as actively coping in the battering situation; appraising harm, threat, and control of the immediate situation; drawing strength from their past history and their present resources; and evaluating the constraints in the environment. Women as individual, active agents are firmly embedded within the social-cultural, political, and economic context in which they live. However, cultural and social structural variables interact with women's commitments and beliefs that shape cognitive appraisals in every situation, as well as with the demands, constraints, and resources of the immediate battering situation. The women's personal history of abuse, the demands of the current psychological abuse, and their appraisal of the battering situation help us understand women's ways of coping with battering in intimate relationships.

IMPLICATIONS FOR SOCIAL WORK

Implication for Social Policy

In the United States and in Puerto Rico, social policy has long been dominated by the medical or psychological treatment model that view any problem as existing entirely within the individual. Only unidirectional, static, antecedent-consequent causality is addressed. The individual or psychological focus adopted from the medical model is also evident in public policy development around the issue of violence against women. Romany (1994) argues that "The Puerto Rican experience shows how deeply ingrained dysfunctional characterizations of woman battering are, and the significant role the helping professions have played in maintaining them" (p. 289). Even though the feminist and battered women's movements in Puerto Rico were at the forefront in bringing violence against women into public discussion, and were fundamental in the establishment of the first shelter for battered women in 1979 and the approval of Law 54 for the Prevention of and Intervention in Domestic Violence in 1989, the helping professions' discourse dominates in the implementation of the law and the provision of services to women victims/survivors of domestic violence.

Law 54 clearly recognizes the political nature of violence against women and its patriarchal foundations; conservative and liberal ideologies of familialism and domesticity, which are at the core of the idea of preserving the violent family and the status quo, however, permeate social policy and social work in Puerto Rico. Social work and the other helping professions operate within a sociocultural, political context that takes as "natural" the nuclear heterosexual family. On the other hand, social policy focuses on individual "victims" (women and children) and on "why are families so violent?" which obliterates the gender perspective of violence against women. So called "liberal" policies place the violent family at the top of the ladder of social institutions to be preserved (Romany, 1994). The social organization of the family that makes it "violent prone" (Gelles & Cornell, 1990) and the dysfunctional, helpless woman with her helpless, depressed, anxious, and aggressive children (Gibson & Gutiérrez, 1991) are at the center of the issue and in need of being "rehabilitated" and "treated." Institutional, social work and other helping professions' discourse privilege the dysfunctional and pathological over the sociocultural, political, and gender dimensions of violence against women in intimate relationships.

For example, women survivors of violence are seen as suffering from learned helplessness and the "battered woman syndrome" (Walker, 1979, 1984), which is meant to explain why women do not leave their violent partners; though many of its adherents also think it explains why women become victims of violence (Dobash & Dobash, 1992). Like most psychologically or individually oriented approaches, it identifies the primary roots of victimization in the background of the victim, and not in the aggressor or the social structure. Dobash and Dobash (1992) argue that "it is not clear from these accounts whether a majority or small proportion of women who are abused by their male partners suffer from learned helplessness" (p. 225). Most of this literature implies or explicitly states that "all battered women, possibly all women, suffer from learned helplessness." However, as stated before, the results of the study, as well as other research on the reactions and responses of women who endure, resist, cope, and survive abuse, reveal that they do not remain helpless or passive, but rather seek help from a wide variety of formal and informal sources, while they make the decision to "save," change, or end the intimate relationship.

"Women's lives-in-violence, their stories of survival and resistance" asserts Romany (1994, p. 296) "are filtered through the lens of expert categorizations—a logical consequence in a society compartmentalized by expert knowledge, giving preeminence to the scientific, objective and primarily male ways of knowing (Harding, 1986; Smith, 1990; Keller, 1985)." Moreover, social policy, programs, and services regarding violence against women continue to try to solve social, structural problems by using individual counseling and therapeutically oriented solutions.

In recent years, social policy and social work dealing with violence against women has moved from the gender perspective of the earlier battered women's movement to the "professionally" and therapeutically oriented perspective that focuses on the family as a unit and on the children of battered women, and not on women's needs and rights in the context of the structural oppression where they live. As the shelters for battered women, originally developed through the efforts of grassroots feminist organizations, have been institutionalized and managed by the helping professions, the focus has shifted to family- and children's-oriented work, once again making women's voices and experiences silent and invisible. As pointed out by Gibson and Gutiérrez (1991), programs focused originally on providing services to battered women "quickly understood" the necessity of developing programs for children. Since many of these programs are run with a protective services focus on children and the family as a unit, it is not surprising that researchers (Gibson & Gutiérrez, 1991) have identified as limitations of these programs the fact that women "focused most of their attention on support and counseling for themselves and arrangements for independent living" (p. 561). Recognizing that women's focus is on "realistic concrete needs," they recommended that workers use this focus to develop supportive and trusting relationships with women. Gibson and Gutiérrez (1991) go on to advise workers that "willingness to provide concrete services and be an advocate with community agencies can be an effective *entry work* on emotional issues" (p. 561).

Clearly, in Puerto Rico as well as in the U.S., the focus has changed from women to children and from advocacy and community work to psychologically oriented work. Women's experiences of gender-based violence and its consequences are again made invisible or hidden beneath the violence that plagues the family unit (Romany, 1994). Restructuring the family system, building new ways of interacting, and looking into the emotional and psychological "deficits" of women and children seem to have taken the place of using a gender perspective with a vision of transforming the position of women in society. The need to confront structural violence, poverty, sexism, racism, and other persistent inequalities has once again been erased as a central issue for social policy, programs, and services.

Without oversimplifying the complexities of women's ways of coping with abuse, the present study provides a view of women actively coping in the battering context; appraising harm, threat, and control over their immediate situation and drawing strength from their past history, their present resources, and evaluating the constraints of their environment. This snapshot view of women confronting abuse makes imperative a social policy that takes into account women's experiences, appraisals, and concrete needs and rights in their path of transforming themselves, their families, and their social-cultural context.

Social policy should validate and facilitate women's coping and resistance to abuse, instead of silencing and erasing their contextual experiences. Can social policy, programs, and services for women survivors of abuse in Puerto Rico move away from a victim-blaming, deficit-focused agenda to a more complex vision of women's coping, resisting, and surviving in a gendered, violent, unequal society? Social work and social workers face a challenge to collaborate with feminist scholars, researchers, and activists to develop, examine, and provide critiques of legislation and social policy affecting women such as equal pay and opportunities, housing, child care, marriage, divorce, custody, welfare benefits, and job and training opportunities.

IMPLICATIONS FOR DIRECT SERVICES

The importance of knowledge of women's ways of coping with abuse in intimate relationships must not be overlooked in the provision of direct services to women. While helping practitioners are not likely to be surprised by the fact that personal history, the severity of verbal aggression, and the appraisal of the abusive situation influence how women cope with abuse, such findings help to remind us of their importance. In working with women survivors of domestic violence, one may overlook the complexity of the association and relationship of individual, contextual, and sociocultural variables in the response to abuse. The determination of what efforts a particular woman victim/survivor of abuse has made to protect, avoid, confront, or escape the abuse, in addition to the variables that influence her ways of coping, are important components of a comprehensive assessment of her situation.

Assessing women's situations and facilitating women's decision-making, problem-solving, and healing processes is more effective if the helping professional analyzes battering within the context of the dynamics of oppression, based on gender, race, ethnicity, class, and age among other factors, and in a framework of male power and dominance over women. In this way, women's ways of coping with abuse are viewed as a process, and contextualized in the battering situation and the patriarchal society in which it occurs.

The findings of the present study illustrate the complexity of women participants' experience: the types, frequencies, and severities of the abuse they experienced in childhood and in intimate relationships, the resources (or lack of resources) in the community, and the constraints of the battering situation; the way they thought, felt, and acted during incidents of severe battering; how their appraisal of the battering situation was circumscribed by an ideology of domesticity that encourages women to try to save their marriages at all costs and feel responsible for its "success" or "failure," and the enormous strength and determination it takes to cope with abuse. This section explores the ways that social workers might use to understand, assess, and facilitate women's processes of protection, self-defense, decision making, problem solving, healing, and social action. In order to support, women social and psychological intervention should involve:

1. Validating Women's Experiences

When battered women seek help, social workers need to listen and believe what they say. The reported abuse must always be taken seriously. The woman needs to tell her history in her own way, without being interrupted or pressured to make immediate decisions. This involves a genuine sense that the social worker has truly heard what she is saying and can validate her experience by an appropriate response. Questions, comments, and interpretations from the social worker that may seem "appropriate" may feel distancing, judgmental, or even damaging if they serve as barriers between the social worker and the women's own experience (Dutton, 1992).

A woman participant in our study expressed pain, anger, and disbelief when she remembered the night she arrived at a women's shelter. After going through an ordeal of abuse where, among other violent actions, her husband had threatened to kill her with a gun while playing Russian Roulette, she was asked during the intake interview if she was on drugs. She had escaped from her husband's aggression, leaving her children in her sister's home, where they had been visiting. When she arrived at the shelter she was scared, disheveled, and feeling guilty for having left her children behind. Apparently, the social worker misunderstood her reaction to the abusive incident as evidence of drug use. The participant felt hurt, damaged, and revictimized by the social worker who was supposed to help her. The participant stayed overnight in the shelter and left early next day. She went back to get her children at her sister's home. Her husband found out about it and went to pick her up to take her back "home" to continue the abuse.

Nonjudgmental acceptance and understanding was mentioned by many of the women participants as helpful in their process of identifying the abuse, asking for help, and decision making.

2.   Understanding Women's Feelings Toward the Abuse and the Abuser

Women participants in the study expressed feelings of humiliation, anger, grief, sadness, fear, impotence, guilt, insecurity, and loneliness among others, during the abusive incidents. It is important that the social worker identify, accept, and validate women's sometimes contradictory feelings toward the abuse and the abuser. Anger, for example, was one of the most common reactions to the experience of abuse of the women in the study. Facilitating the acknowledgment and safe expression of anger is the essential task of rage expression (Dutton, 1992). Overt expressions of anger are generally considered to be unacceptable for women (Jaggar, 1988; Lorde, 1984) and thus are distrusted and experienced negatively by both battered women and helping professionals. Women who are viewed as passive and helpless are not expected to feel or demonstrate anger and rage; therefore, one of the first tasks in working with women's anger is for the woman herself to identify, name, and accept the feeling, and for the professional to accept it. Anger and rage can be used positively, and turned into positive, active, powerful action. Free-floating anger has to be channeled in a manner that is not destructive or converted into anxiety and depression. Lorde (1984) argues that women should learn to "cherish, respect our feelings, respect the hidden sources of power" (p. 133).

Learning to trust our perceptions and using our emotions positively can have a surprisingly powerful effect. However, the social worker needs to be careful not to condone violent acts, and yet support the women's right to feel angry and use that anger creatively (Dutton, 1992; Lorde, 1984). The emotional and physical energy accompanying feelings of anger can be directed toward expression in a variety of ways, including journal-keeping, creative writing, and other expressions of art; self-protection, empowerment, and social and political activism (Dutton, 1992).

Feelings of anger and humiliation led a woman participant in the study into action:

> I told myself, wait, I have the enemy in my home and I have to kick him out, completely, because he is destroying me, destroying the values I have taught my daughters and I don't want them to learn that they have to allow any man to act with them the way their father has acted with me.

The importance of expressing our feelings was manifested by another participant:

> I think one should not be silent, should not take it. You can't, because that's like dying, you are killing yourself slowly, you are killing who you are. . . . It does not matter how evil . . . you have to express it because that is the only way you can be free.

Other feelings, like loneliness and grief, have to be explored, named, and accepted. Many women in our study talked about their feelings of loneliness, both while still living with the abuser and afterwards, if they had left him. Some of them remarked:

> My greatest worry is my loneliness. . . . I told my daughter that I was looking for help, that if something happened to me she should know that it was him who did it, I asked her not to forget me, please come visit once in a while because I feel very lonely . . . he even criticizes me because no one visits . . .

> I decided that this is the moment for me to leave, get a divorce, because I have a man at my side but he doesn't support me, I don't have anything, what am I doing here?

I don't have any one, I have someone, and I don't have any one . . .
I don't want to forget about myself . . .

People can't see both parts of me, that I'm not that strong, that I
have my moments of vulnerability, that I need support sometimes,
someone to hold me and tell me that everything is going to be all right.

Sometimes it is hard for helping professionals to accept, and even
to listen to battered women express their feelings of love for their
abusers. Sometimes women are reluctant to disclose these feelings
because they might feel embarrassed or ashamed and fear judgmental reactions from the social worker. A social worker reluctant
to hear contradictory feelings fails to provide the context where
healing is possible. The emotions surrounding the loss of a relationship and loss of love can be shattering. Dutton (1992) argues that
"it is not the loss of the abusive aspect of a relationship that battered
women grieve, but the loss of the real or hoped for loving, caring
relationship" (p. 138). If helping professionals are reluctant to listen
nonjudgmentally to battered women's feelings of anger, rage, sadness, grief, love, humiliation, and shame, the message is that their
experiences and their feelings must remain invisible and silent.

3. Supporting and Advocating for Self-Protection and Safety Planning

All the women participants in the study used coping strategies directed at protecting themselves and their children. They sought
psychological and medical treatment; they called the police; sought
support from family, friends, social workers, and counselors; and
went to hospitals or to shelters. During the most severe battering
incident occurring in the year of the interview, the participants (in
descending order of frequency) cried, shouted back and insulted the
batterer; they left the house; responded to the aggression physically;
called the police; listened; locked themselves in their rooms; and
pretended to be asleep. All of these strategies were carried out to
protect themselves psychologically, physically, and sexually. As social
workers, we have to support women's ways of coping to protect
themselves, which may include a wide range of emotion- and prob-

lem-focused strategies. The social worker must recognize the woman's strategies and her ability to defend herself.

Safety planning should also be discussed with the women, whether or not their immediate decision is to separate from or to remain with the abuser. Informing about and building options toward safety acknowledges the battered woman's central role of choice (Browne, 1988; Dutton, 1992). Many of the women interviewed in the present study shared stories of using plans and information they had discussed previously with family, friends, neighbors, and social workers/ counselors. One of the participants narrated that she had the local battered women's shelter telephone number hidden inside a Bible she had next to her bed. She had it hidden there for months, and immediately after the most severe incident of battering had ended, she called the shelter and made arrangements to go there. It is of the utmost importance that we trust the women's appraisal of danger, risks, and control over the battering situation, as well as share with her the options available to her and be available when she needs us.

4.   Sharing Educational Material About Violence and Abuse

It is useful to share, in conversation and/or in writing, articles, books, movies, and statistics about violence against women in your country and other countries around the world. Talking and reading about the roots of violence and oppression against women, as well as women's ways of coping, resisting, and survival can be a very powerful experience. Many women participants in the study talked about how magazine articles, T.V. programs, movies, and educational material given to them by counselors or friends had helped them to understand abuse and identify themselves as victims/survivors of abuse; other radio and television shows had offered them information about service programs and shelters in their community. Universalizing as well as contexualizing their experiences was very helpful in their process of consciousness-raising and realization that the root of battering was not in themselves, but in the sociocultural context where they live.

5.   Recognizing and Building on Women's History, Experiences, Coping Strategies and Strengths

Women's experiences with abuse, and sharing those experiences with understanding family members, friends, and professionals made

them aware of inner strengths that many were unaware they pos-
sessed. Many women participants expressed that they felt stronger
after having been through the battering experiences. Some of them
used positive reappraisal coping strategies to find strength in their
history of abuse. After the worst battering incident of abuse in the
year they were interviewed and in response to the *66 Ways of Coping
Questionnaire,* 84% of the women expressed that they had rediscov-
ered what was important in life, and 76% said that they came out
of the experience better than when they went in. Some of their
comments were:

> I feel valor and strength to confront the situation.

> I did not value myself, now I learned to love myself . . . I learned by
> myself as a consequence of the abuse.

> I did not value myself . . . now I know my body is important, I am
> important.

One woman narrated how she had stopped using crack—she
started using it after being coerced by the abuser—by looking at
herself in the mirror. She would stand in front of the mirror and
tell herself, "I'm not filth, I'm a worthy person."
This acknowledgment of personal strength and determination
was reflected in many of the women's responses to the structured
interview. While most women stressed the support they received
from others, especially mothers, parents, and sisters, it was their
own strength and determination that was the crucial factor in their
reappraisal of the battering situation and how it had helped them
survive and become stronger. Many of the women recognized their
own strengths in retrospect, demonstrating how important it is for
social workers and helping professionals to support and build on
women's strengths, instead of pathologizing, underestimating, or
disbelieving their recollection of their past.
The use of other coping strategies, such as distancing, self-controlling, and escape-avoidance is often necessary to resist and survive
the abuse. Viewed as a process, not as a trait, and as valid efforts to
cope with the abuse or its after-effects, these coping strategies are
recognized for their survival and resistance value. Viewed in the
context of the abusive situation and the structural oppression of

women, all coping strategies are recognized as valid efforts to deal with the environment and to exercise power and resistance.

6. Understanding that Violence Against Women Is Rooted in the Hierarchical Structure of Power Relations in the Family and in Society

Viewing violence against women and women's responses within the cultural, racial, ethnic, political, and economic contexts within which the woman and her family live is essential in working with women who are battered. Understanding women's appraisal of and coping with abuse in a context of women's oppression and paying attention to the interplay of sexism, racism, and economic inequality is crucial in working with battered women.

Women's choices of coping strategies are influenced by their appraisal of the stakes and control over the abusive situation, as well as of their personal and family histories. Appraisal of the abusive situation and a personal history of child abuse is at the same time influenced by a patriarchal culture and a hegemonic ideology of familialism, domesticity, and maternity where women are adjudicated responsibility for the "success" or "failure" of family life and simultaneously seen as a "property" of the man who is seen as the head of the household/family. Contradictory demands are made upon women to be "strong," "passive," "vulnerable," "weak," and "responsible." Listening to, understanding, and analyzing these contradictory demands upon women can be empowering and revealing. When asked about the influence of culture and family ideology on their ways of coping with abuse, some of the women participants in the study answered as follows.

> You hear that when people get married, the husband works, that his obligation is to be a good provider. That you have to do what he says, he is the one who gives the orders . . . it's like a rule, and it has to be that way . . .

> The man is the one that thinks, he knows how to do it.

> It's like I want to be good, I want to please everybody, I want to support everybody, I want to help everybody, but when I get home I

feel depressed and I ask myself, who is going to give to me? Whom could I rely on? Who is going to provide a shoulder for me to cry on?

You have to be submissive, have patience, tolerance . . . give in. What he says is the way it has to be. One gets used to that type of upbringing, and you accept it.

Another woman spoke about the crevices of the dominant ideology.

Because I was told that women have to endure, tolerate, suffer and the man? well, happy all the time and I always say no to this.

One woman explained the process of internalizing the hegemonic family ideology as well as the questioning of it:

It's like when you have a pair of shoes that hurt you, and you grow a callus and after some time they don't hurt you anymore. When you find options . . . you study them . . .

Listening to women, recognizing their ways of resistance, accepting their questioning of the dominant ideology, and sharing options is an empowering experience. To recognize and share the experiences of women, social workers must recognize and contest the dominant ideology of familialism, domesticity, and maternity, and ensure space for women to get away from caring and obligations to men. Moreover, we must recognize and discuss with women the power imbalances and unequal treatment that women receive in our society.

CONCLUSIONS

In summary, my study found first that the women participants in the present study who had been victims or witnesses of abuse in childhood used significantly more coping strategies, both problem-solving-focused and emotion-focused, to deal with the worst battering incident of the last year, than the women who were not victims or witnesses of childhood abuse. Second, the women who were more frequently abused in childhood were more likely to use emotion- and problem solving-focused strategies to deal with the worst battering incident during the year of the study. Third, the severity of psychological abuse (verbal aggression) during the marriage is associated with the use of more coping strategies to deal with the worst incident of abuse during the year of the study. Fourth, the higher the stakes during the worst battering incident, the more likely were the women participants to use problem-focused strategies to deal with the incident. Fifth, the women participants who felt in control of the situation during the worst battering incident used more problem-focused strategies than the women who felt they had no control during the worst battering incident of the past year.

These findings suggest, first, that women participants in the study were behaviorally and emotionally engaged in managing efforts to protect, defend, avoid, escape, confront, plan, and problem solve to deal with the worst incident of battering in the past year. Second, the experience of abuse in their families of origin did not render the women passive or helpless in coping with current abuse. Third, when appraising high stakes and feeling in control over the situation during battering incidents, women are more likely to use problem-solving strategies to deal with abuse. Finally, psychological more than physical abuse is related to the use of more coping strategies to deal with it.

These findings exhort us to change the way we think about women victims/survivors of abuse in intimate relationships. Rather than viewing them as helpless, deficient, passive women, we must comprehend the complexity and multidimensionality of abuse in intimate relationships and all the factors—personal, familial, social, cultural— that impinge on women's feelings, thoughts, and actions in coping with, resisting, and surviving abuse. When women face abuse, they are confronting their inner thoughts and feelings about womanhood, mothering, about who they are and what they stand for, in a society where women are seen as subordinate and inferior to men. Women confront not only the abusive actions of "the man she loves and who loves her" but society's ideas about how he and she should feel, think, and behave. When women confront abuse they confront economic hardships, loss of a home, loss of love, loss of friends, loss of their children, loss of self-esteem and self-respect, and loss of their lives. They confront their society, their community, their family, their children, and most of all they confront themselves. Coping under extreme circumstances of duress, women victims/survivors of abuse face up to the formidable task of appraising their circumstances and making decisions about their lives and the lives of their children. We must not underestimate, simplicize, or trivialize their situation with reductionist explanations or interpretations that they are "masochists," or suffer from "problem-solving deficits," or from "learned helplessness." The women participants in this study demonstrated high-level emotional and cognitive coping under the most difficult circumstances of abuse from their spouse, in a context of economic, political, and social oppression.

REFERENCES

Abbott, A. (1996). Epilogue: Helping battered women. In A. R. Roberts (Ed.), *Helping battered women: New perspectives and remedies* (pp. 235–237). New York: Oxford University Press.

Barrett, M. (1988). *Women's oppression today: The Marxist/feminist encounter.* London: Verso.

Blackman, J. (1989). *Intimate violence: A study of injustice.* New York: Columbia University Press.

Bowker, L. H. (1993). A battered woman's problems are social, not psychological. In R. J. Gelles & D. R. Loseke (Eds.), *Current controversies on family violence* (pp. 154–165). Newbury Park, CA: Sage.

Browne, A. (1987). *When battered women kill.* New York: Free Press.

Davis, L. V. (1987). Battered women and the transformation of a social problem. *Social Work, 32,* 306–311.

Dobash, E., & Dobash, R. (1992). *Women, violence, and social change.* London: Routledge.

Dobash, R. E., & Dobash, R. (1988). Research as social action: The struggle for battered women. In K. Yllo & M. Bograd (Eds.), *Feminist perspectives on wife abuse* (pp. 51–74). Beverly Hills: Sage.

Dutton, M. A. (1992). *Empowering and healing the battered woman: A model for assessment and intervention.* New York: Springer Publishing.

Folkman, S., & Lazarus, R. E. (1988). The relationship between coping and emotion: Implications for theory and research. *Social Science Medicine, 26,* 309–317.

Folkman, S., Lazarus, R., Gruen, R. J., & DeLongis, A. (1986). Appraisal, coping, health status, and psychological symptom. *Journal of Personality and Social Psychology, 50,* 517–549.

Foucault, M. (1981). *The history of sexuality: Vol. I: An Introduction.* Harmonds-worth, England: Pelican.

Frye, M. (1993). *The politics of reality: Essays in feminist theory.* Freedom, CA: Crossing Press.

Gayford, J. J. (1975). Wife battering: A preliminary survey of 100 cases. *British Medical Journal, 25,* 194–197.

Gelles, R., & Cornell, C. P. (1990). *Intimate violence in families.* Newbury Park, CA: Sage.

Gelles, R. J., & Straus, M. A. (1988). *Intimate violence.* New York: Simon and Schuster.

Gibson, J. W., & Gutierrez, L. (1991). A service program for safe-home children. *Journal of Contemporary Human Services, 72,* 554–561.

Gordon, L. (1988). *Heroes of their own lives: The politics and history of family violence.* New York: Penguin.

Gramsci, A. (1971). *Selections from the prison notebooks.* London: Lawrence and Wishart.

Harding, S. (1986). *The science question in feminism.* Ithaca, NY: Cornell University Press.

Hoff, L. A. (1990). *Battered women as survivors.* London: Routledge.

hooks, B. (1984). *Feminist theory: From margin into center.* Boston: South End Press.

hooks, B. (1990). *Yearning: Race, gender and cultural politics.* Boston: South End Press.

Jaggar, A. M. (1988). *Feminist politics and human nature.* Totowa, NJ: Ronman and Litlefield.

Keller, E. (1985). *Reflections on gender and science.* New Haven, CT: Yale University Press.

Kelly, L. (1988). How women define their experiences of violence. In K. Yllo & M. Bograd (Eds.), *Feminist perspective on abuse.* Newbury Park, CA: Sage.

Komter, A. (1989). Hidden power in marriage. *Gender and Society, 3,* 187–216.

Lazarus, R. S., & Folkman, S. (1984). *Stress appraisal and coping.* New York: Springer Publishing Company.

Lerner, G. (1986). *The creation of patriarchy.* New York: Oxford University Press.

Lorde, A. (1984). *Sister outsider.* Trumansburg, NY: Crossing Press.

Martin, D. (1983). *Battered wives.* New York: Pocket Books.

Mitchell, R. E., & Hodson, C. A. (1983). Coping with domestic violence: Social support and psychological health among battered women. *American Journal of Community Psychology, 11,* 629–654.

Mitchell, R. E., & Hodson, C. A. (1986). Coping and social support among battered women. In S. E. Hobfall (Ed.), *Stress, social support and women.* Washington, DC: Hemisphere.

Pearlin, L. I., & Schooler, C. (1978). The structure of coping. *Journal of Health and Social Behavior, 19*, 2–21.

Preamble Law 54 for the Prevention of and Intervention with Domestic Violence. (1989, August 15). Pio Piedras: Women's Affairs Commission, Office of the Governor of Puerto Rico.

Rivera Ramos, A. N. (1991). *The Puerto Rican woman: Psychosocial research.* Río Piedras: Editorial Edil.

Roberts, A. (1996). Myths and realities regarding battered women. In A. Roberts (Ed.), *Helping battered women: New perspectives and remedies* (pp. 3–12). New York: Oxford University Press.

Romany, C. (1994). Killing the angel in the house: Digging for the political vortex of male violence against women. In M. Albertson Fineman & R. Mykitiuk (Eds.), *The public nature of private violence* (pp. 285–302). New York: Routledge.

Schecter, S. (1982). *Women and male violence: The visions and struggles of the battered women's movement.* Boston: South End.

Silva Bonilla, R. M., Rodríguez, J., Cáceres, V., Martínez, L., & Torres, N. (1990). *Hay amores que matan: La violencia contra las mujeres en la vida conyugal.* Río Piedras: Ediciones Huracán.

Silva Bonilla, R. (1985). *El marco social de la violencia contra las mujeres en la vida conyugal.* Río Piedras: Publicaciones Centro de Investigaciones Sociales, Universidad de P.R.

Smith, D. E. (1990). The conceptual practices of power, public wrongs, and the responsibility of states. *Fordham International Law Journal, 13*(1).

Straus, M. A. (1979). Measuring intra-family conflict and violence: The conflict tactics (CT) scales. *Journal of Marriage and the Family, 41*, 75–88.

Straus, M. A., & Gelles, R. J. (1995). *Physical violence in American families: Risk factors and adaptations to violence in 8,145 families.* New Brunswick: Transaction Books.

Walker, L. E. A. (1979). *The battered woman.* New York: Harper & Row.

Walker, L. E. A. (1984). *The battered woman syndrome.* New York: Springer Publishing Company.

Walker, L. E. A. (1993). The battered woman syndrome is a psychological consequence of abuse. In R. J. Gelles & D. R. Loseke (Eds.), *Current controversies in family violence* (pp. 133–153). Newbury Park, CA: Sage.

Weedon, C. (1991). *Feminist practice and poststructuralist theory.* Oxford: Basil Blackwell.

Indices

Author Index

Subject Index

Springer Publishing Company

Family Violence and Men of Color
Healing the Wounded Male Spirit

Ricardo Carrillo, PhD and **Jerry Tello,** PhD, Editors

"Family Violence and Men of Color is the best book on cross-cultural issues and domestic violence that I have ever read. It is a good combination of literature review, clinical interventions, and cultural imagery that will not only inform the reader but help them develop a true appreciation for the essence of different cultures."
— Daniel Sonkin, PhD, Marriage, Family, and Child Counselor

"This innovative book examines an important, timely topic...and makes an original contribution to existing literature in the area of domestic violence. The content will greatly enhance practitioners and students' understanding and skills in working with men of color, especially in situations involving domestic violence."
— Elaine P. Congress, DSW, Director of the Doctoral Program
Associate Professor, Fordham University Graduate School of
Social Service

Providing a culturally integrated perspective of this controversial subject, this volume reviews research on the prevalence of homicide, child abuse, and domestic violence in special populations, including African American, Latino/Chicano, Asian American, and Native American.

Contents:
- Violence in Communities of Color
- The Noble Man Searching for Balance
- Clinical Treatment of Latino Domestic Violence Offenders
- A Post-colonial Perspective on Domestic Violence in Indian Country
- Healing and Confronting the African American Batterer
- Asian American Domestic Violence: A Critical Psychohistorical Perspective
- Asian Men and Violence
- Epilogue

1998   192pp   0-8261-1173-4   hardcover

536 Broadway, New York, NY 10012-3955 • (212) 431-4370 • Fax (212) 941-7842

Springer Publishing Company

Crisis Intervention and Trauma Response
Theory and Practice

Barbara Rubin Wainrib, EdD
Ellin L. Bloch, PhD

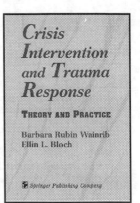

"The doctor said that the surgery on my wife's cancer was a failure and that there was nothing more that they could do. I felt as if I was in a bad movie, and everything around me had come to a halt."
—James G., husband of a cancer victim

Crisis Intervention and Trauma Response offers short-term, problem-oriented, therapeutic interventions formulated to produce constructive change for the client as quickly and directly as possible. Presenting their successful General Crisis Response model for intervention, the authors use actual case examples like James G. to encourage therapists to focus on clients' inner strengths and cope with the immediate crisis. The book is filled with exercises to develop techniques for building verbal and non-verbal skills, and awareness of individual and cultural differences. A Crisis and Trauma Assessment checklist is included for effective therapeutic interventions, whether in your office or at a trauma site.

Contents: • About this Book
• Crisis, Trauma, and You:
Theories of Crisis and Trauma
• How We Respond to Crisis and Trauma
• Principles and Models of Intervention
• Assessment for Crisis and Trauma
• Suicide and Violence:
Assessment and Intervention
• Putting it All Together: The Pragmatics

1998   176pp (est.)   0-8261-1175-0   softcover

536 Broadway, New York, NY 10012-3955 • (212) 431-4370 • Fax (212) 941-7842